CW01497289

1 MONTH OF
FREE
READING

at
www.ForgottenBooks.com

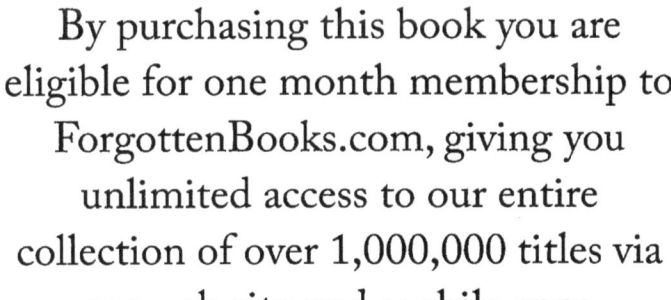

By purchasing this book you are eligible for one month membership to ForgottenBooks.com, giving you unlimited access to our entire collection of over 1,000,000 titles via our web site and mobile apps.

To claim your free month visit:
www.forgottenbooks.com/free1117361

ISBN 978-0-331-39352-1
PIBN 11117361

LEADING INSURANCE MEN

OF

THE BRITISH EMPIRE.

COMPILED BY

R. B. CAVERLY AND G. N. BANKES.

1892.

LONDON :

THE INDEX PUBLISHING COMPANY, LIMITED,

6, KING STREET, CHEAPSIDE, E.C.

ESTABLISHED 1870.

THE INDEX

An International Review of Insurance.

PUBLISHED MONTHLY AT 7 . PER ANNUM, POST FREE.

The Index is one of the largest Insurance Journals published in Great Britain, and contains more illustration in the way of Portraits, Office Buildings, Cartoons, &c., than any other Insurance Publication in the World.

The Index, in addition to giving the Insurance News of the Month in an attractive form, publishes a *resumé* of the contents of the other leading Insurance Journals in the shape of an *Insurance Review of Reviews.*

EXTRACTS FROM COMMENTS BY OUR CONTEMPORARIES.

" One of the largest and best Insurance Journals in the world."—*The Insurance Agent*, New Orleans.

" Of our foreign exchanges THE INDEX, of London, pleases us most."—*Views*, Washington, D.C.

"The leading organ of the Insurance business in the British Isles."—*Commercial List and Price Current*, Philadelphia.

" Until yesterday we had thought that Insurance journalistic enterprise was solely to be found in the New World. We are agreeably undeceived. The best Insurance number ever produced bears London impress ; and can be asked for as No. 1, Vol. 7, of THE INDEX. . . . . Our enterprising contemporary is to be congratulated on having placed England in the van, so far as Insurance journalism is concerned."—*Money.*

" A striking Insurance publication is the January number of THE INDEX, which deals with the London Insurance world. The issue comprises sixty-eight pages, and a large number of portraits. . . . . We very readily congratulate our contemporary upon its energy and enterprise."—*The Policyholder.*

"The first number of THE INDEX, Volume 7, dated January 31, continues the splendid series of ' Insurance Centres of Great Britain.' . . . . As a souvenir of the profession, A.D. 1891, the number is a gem which will certainly be held in high esteem throughout the ranks."—*The Capitalist.*

"The present number of our contemporary, THE INDEX, far excels even the high standard attained by recent numbers of that high-class Insurance periodical. The number before us is a double number for February and March, of 100 pages, and contains, besides pictures of several chief offices, between 80 and 90 portraits of leading Life Assurance officials in London."—*The Agent's Journal and Official Gazette.*

" A periodical with over a hundred illustrations is a decided ' new departure ' in Insurance journalism, and THE INDEX is to be congratulated on its enterprise."—*The Insurance Agent.*

"The March number of my excellent contemporary, THE INDEX, ought to be in the possession of every Insurance man in the English-speaking world. . . . . It is a marvellous and particularly valuable storehouse of Insurance information touching most of the persons and offices of most importance in the business."—*Assurance Agents' Review.*

" THE INDEX aims to conduct its paper along American lines, and, if we may credit reports, it s distancing competitors who stick to the old styles."—*The Insurance Monitor*, New York.

PUBLISHED BY

THE INDEX PUBLISHING CO., Ltd., 6, King Street, Cheapside, London, E.C.

PREFACE.

IT is with much pleasure that the compilers are now able to present this volume to the public The work of compilation has been arduous, and attended with far greater difficulties and delay than they anticipated when they first undertook it, and though they feel that the results of their labours will amply justify them for the delay in the eyes of their readers, yet they feel it will not be altogether out of place to a certain extent to account for it.

Not only have they had to carefully note the various changes in the status of some of the subjects of the sketches contained in this volume, which naturally have amounted to a very large number in so vast and ever increasing a profession as that of Insurance, in order to bring their book up to date, but they have been more than once checked in their progress by the natural modesty of many of the gentlemen, whom not to include would have been to have produced a work very far short of the excellence which it has been their object to attain ; a result which the compilers feel sure would have been regretted by all, and not least by the gentlemen alluded to themselves, when a deference to it would have caused such lamentable gaps in the work.

It may be as well to state that the term LEADING INSURANCE MAN as used in connection with this volume is intended to designate any official holding a leading position at a Head Office, Branch Office, or in a District.

The compilers think that they may also add a few words as to the arrangement of the book, which has not been one of the least items of their undertaking. The arrangement under the several headings has as far as possible been alphabetical, but it will be noticed that in places the exact order has had to be sacrificed. If the alphabetical order had been strictly followed, however, as the work progressed it would have been found necessary to separate some portraits from the biographical sketches appertaining to them. The compilers therefore decided that such a course would be undesirable, and hence the departure from the hard and fast rule.

In several cases it has been found impossible to obtain the portraits of certain members of the Insurance fraternity, in most instances for the reason that no photographs of these gentlemen are in existence.

In conclusion it is hoped that LEADING INSURANCE MEN will be received with the same satisfaction as that with which it is put before the public. Some errors there must be in a work such as this ; changes in the Insurance ranks occur almost daily, and some are taking place while the book is in the press, yet the compilers feel that they have spared themselves nothing that would tend to make their work of interest and value to the Insurance fraternity at large.

INDEX.

―

INDUSTRIAL BRANCH OFFICIALS.

HEAD OFFICE OFFICIALS.

Ackland, Thomas Gans, F.I.A., F.S.S., is the Actuary and the Manager of the Gresham Life Assurance Society, and was born on the 27th of June, 1851. In his seventeenth year (March, 1868), he entered the service of the Gresham as a Junior Clerk, and in the following year he joined the Institution of Actuaries as an Associate. He passed the three Examinations qualifying him for a Fellowship in 1871, 1872, and 1875 respectively, and in 1876 he received the Certificate of Competency. In 1881 he was appointed Examiner for the Preliminary Examination of the Institute, and for the Intermediate Examination in 1882, and again in 1887. During the sessions of the Institute, 1883-4, 1884-5, 1885-6, he held the appointment of Official Lecturer to the students of the Institute of Actuaries in the subjects of the Part II. Examination, and in 1886 he was elected a Member of the Council of the Institute, and again in 1888 and 1889. In July, 1883, he was appointed Actuary to the Gresham Life

T. G. ACKLAND, F.I.A., F.S.S.

Assurance Society, and in November, 1888, to be Actuary and Manager (as Principal Officer). The year previous (1887) he was appointed one of the Actuaries selected by the Treasury for certifying the Annuity Tables of Friendly Societies.

Mr. Ackland is the Author of a Paper in the Journal of the Institute of Actuaries (vol. xxiii., p. 354), on "The Graduation of Mortality Tables," and is the joint Author with Mr. A. H. Smee, M.R.C.S., of a treatise "On the Risks Incidental to Continental Warfare, and the Rates of Extra Premium Required to cover such Risks," which was published by Messrs. C. and E. Layton in May, 1888. He is also joint Author with Mr. Hardy, F.I.A., F.S.S., of "Exercises and Examples (with solutions) for the use of Students of the Institute of Actuaries," which was also published by Messrs. C. and E. Layton, in September, 1889.

Adler, Marcus Nathan, M.A., F.I.A., the Actuary of the Alliance Assurance Company, of London, was born at Hanover in the year 1837. His father was the Chief Rabbi of Great Britain, and his brother now holds that distinguished position.

Mr. Adler was educated at University College, London, and studied Mathematics under Professor De Morgan. In 1857 he took the B.A. degree, with Honours in Mathematics, at the London University, and two years later he obtained his M.A. degree. In the same year that he graduated (1857) he commenced his Insurance career, and entered the service of the office of which he is now the scientific head. His upward progress was very rapid, as ten years later (1867), at the early age of thirty, he was appointed to his present position.

In Actuarial work he has always taken a very prominent part. He has been for a series of years one of the Vice-Presidents of the Institute of Actuaries. He has always taken an active interest in Friendly Societies, and acted as one of their Public Valuers for a number

MARCUS NATHAN ADLER, M.A., F.I.A.

of years, till the engrossing duties of his office obliged him to relinquish the post. He has also another and unique honour to add to his laurels. Working in conjunction with Mr. A. H. Bailey, F.I.A., he was the first Actuary to successfully reconstruct an insolvent Assurance Company, this being the Great Britain Insurance Office. He was also the originator of the "B" Annuity Schemes for the East Indian Railway Companies, which have been adopted to such a very large extent, and for which he has received much honour in Financial as well as Insurance circles.

In Actuarial and General Insurance Literature, Mr. Adler has made a wide reputation. Though not exactly what might be described as a voluminous writer, he has contributed widely to the Insurance press, and has also made a mark in other branches of authorship, notably in statistical and oriental branches of Literature. In 1869 his University recognised his ability and work by electing him a Fellow of University College.

Perhaps the work with which Mr. Adler's name will, after all, be longest and most popularly associated, will be his efforts to relieve the overcrowded and unhealthy condition of certain parts of the Metropolis. This he proposed to do by inducing the working class population to live more largely in the suburbs, and in order that they might be able to do this, he submitted to the County Council a comprehensive scheme, under which Railway and Tramway Companies would have to carry working men at certain hours of the day at a uniform fare of one penny for any distance ; in fact, to introduce a similar plan to that known as the "Zone system," which has proved so enormously successful on the Austrian and Hungarian Railways.

The North Metropolitan Tramways Company, Limited, without waiting for any action on the part of the County Council, at once adopted Mr. Adler's suggestion on their lines in the East of London. Other companies are beginning to make similar concessions ; and the innovation has proved an enormous success and, beyond doubt, a very great boon to thousands of the working classes.

JAMES ALLAN.

JOHN ANTONIO

Allan, James, is the Assistant Secretary at the Head Office of The London and Lancashire Fire Insurance Company, Liverpool. His Insurance experience was gained at the Glasgow branch of The Guardian, and the Edinburgh and Dublin branches of The Commercial Union; subsequent to which he was appointed Resident Secretary in Dublin of the London and Lancashire Fire Insurance Company. In that position he met with such success that in September, 1890, he was promoted to his present post at the Head Office. Mr. Allan is a gentleman of much ability and sound judgment.

———

Adlard, A. B., is the Actuary to the Law Life Assurance Society, to which position he was appointed in 1889, after having served the Society as Assistant Actuary for several years. Previous to joining the staff of the Law Life, Mr. Adlard was engaged for some time in the Life Department of the Alliance Assurance Company at their Head Office.

Antonio, John, Sub-Manager of the Patriotic Assurance Company, at its headquarters at Dublin is a native of Scotland. He commenced his Insurance career in the Scottish Branch of the Alliance Insurance Company in Edinburgh, where he remained for seven years, after which he received an appointment in the Scottish Branch of the Imperial Insurance Company. In 1880 he was appointed Chief of the Fire Department of the Irish Branch of the West of England Insurance Company, which position he held till July, 1887, when he was selected out of a considerable number of applicants for the post which he now holds, in the office of the Patriotic Assurance Company, then created for the first time. Mr. Antonio is an efficient and hard-working official, and very popular amongst his colleagues in the Insurance profession.

E. G. LAUGHTON ANDERSON.

Anderson, Edward George Laughton, the Secretary of the London Guarantee and Accident Company, was born on the 16th of October, 1837, and educated at the City of London School, then situated in Milk Street, Cheapside. After a brief experience in commercial life, Mr. Anderson in 1854 entered the Insurance profession under the auspices of Mr. Arthur Scratchley, M.A., one of the first actuaries of his day. In 1869 he founded the London Guarantee and Accident Company, of which he has been the Secretary ever since. In establishing the Company, he entered a field till then looked upon as almost a private preserve, but in spite of persistent opposition, ingeniously directed, he steadily pushed his Company into the front rank, and the result of his continued labours has been to acquire for it a reputation of the highest character for liberality and fair dealing, while its financial position is one of exceptional strength.

ROBERT ANDERSON.

Anderson, Robert, is the Secretary of the Essex and Suffolk Equitable Fire Insurance Society, Colchester, established 1802. He was called to the Bar at the Middle Temple, in 1851, and for about five years practised his profession, after which he entered the head office of The Yorkshire Insurance Company, at York, where he remained until 1868, when he was appointed Secretary of the Essex and Suffolk Equitable, which position he still fills.

———

Akers, Alfred, the Secretary of the Securities Insurance Company, Limited, was born at Whitney, Oton, in 1854, and was educated at the City of London School. His first commercial experience was gained in the offices of Messrs. Broom, Hays and Akers, Chartered Accountants, and with them he remained until early in the year 1882. Then, on the formation of the London and Provincial Fire Insurance Company, Limited, he left them to take up the position of Accountant to that Company. In 1887 the Board of Directors appointed him Assistant Secretary. His next appointment in the Insurance world was the position he at present holds.

H. W. ANDRAS, F.I.A., F.S.S.

Andras, Henry Walsingham, F.I.A., F.S.S., the Secretary of the University Life Assurance Society, was born at Lee, Kent, in 1851, and is the son of the Rev. J. A. Andras, M.A. After passing the Matriculation Examination of the University of London in the First Class, and the first B.A. at the same University, which he did with Classical Honours, he commenced his Insurance career in December, 1873, in the Life Department of the Head Office of the Commercial Union Assurance Company, and after remaining in the service of this Office for seven years, he was appointed Managing Clerk in the Life Department of the Norwich Union Life Assurance Society at its London Office, where he also performed the duties of Assistant Actuary. Six years later (in 1886) he accepted the appointment of London Secretary of the Provincial Life Insurance Company. This position he occupied for over a year, resigning it in June, 1888, to take an important appointment in the University Life Office. Mr. Andras was specially appointed Assistant Secretary with the view of shortly succeeding to the Secretaryship of the Society, held for so many years by Mr. McCabe, and in August, 1890, he was formally appointed Secretary of the Society upon the retirement of that gentleman after 52 years' service. Mr. Andras passed the Final Examination for the Fellowship of the Institute of Actuaries in 1885, and has had considerable experience as a Consulting Actuary in the practical actuarial work of his profession with regard to Life Assurance Societies, Friendly Societies, Pension Funds, etc.

HARRY ARMOUR

Armour, Harry, the Secretary of the Scottish Accident Insurance Company, under Mr. Martin L. Martin, has passed the whole of his Insurance career in the service of that Company, having originally entered it in the capacity of Agency Superintendent in 1878. The duties of that post necessitated his travelling to nearly every part of the United Kingdom, appointing Agents and otherwise assisting in the promotion of the general welfare of the Company, and so successfully did he fulfil his arduous duties that in 1885 the Directors, as a recognition of his services, promoted him to the post of Assistant Secretary. This post he held until the beginning of 1889, when he was further promoted to the office of Secretary to the Company, Mr. Martin generously resigning the post in his favour, and continuing as General Manager alone.

THE HON. EVELYN ASHLEY.

Ashley, The Honourable Evelyn, the Chairman of the Railway Passengers' Assurance Company (Limited), of London, is a son of the late Right Honourable the Earl of Shaftesbury, the very distinguished philanthropist and statesman. Mr. Ashley has seen a good deal of political life, having sat in the House of Commons for some years as Member for Maidstone and afterwards for Lancaster. In a later Administration, while Lord Derby was Foreign Minister, he filled the position of Under Secretary of State for the Colonies. He has left politics for a time, though there is no doubt he will, at an early date, return to his early love ; if he does not the Insurance world will be the gainer, though perhaps at the expense of the Administration Departments of the Government, for Mr. Ashley is by no means an "ornamental" Chairman of the Company. His work in the office is hard, practical, and far-searching ; and he has done much to bring the Railway Passengers' to the position it at present holds.

J. A. ASHTON.

GEORGE W. BAIN.

Ashton, J. A., the Manager and Founder of the Band of Hope Friendly Society, was born in London, in 1833. He was for some time Agent to the Wesleyan and General Assurance Society, and during his engagement in that capacity in Lancashire he was so much struck by the evil effects of the public house sick clubs on the colliers and cotton workers, that he conceived the idea of a similar club or Friendly Society, the basis of which should be the temperance movement. This resulted in the establishment of the Band of Hope Friendly Society in 1877, and though the new Society had many difficulties to cope with at the outset, owing to strikes, depression in trade, etc., yet through the energy of Mr. Ashton, backed on by the material co-operation of Mr. Crompton (who was also one of the founders of the Society), it survived, and now stands high amongst similar societies.

Bain, George Washington, is the General Manager of the Commercial Plate Glass Insurance Company, Limited, of Sunderland. Mr. Bain began business in the Sun Fire and Life Office, at Belfast, under the old-established Agency of that Company, in the year 1870. He went to Sunderland in the year 1876, as District Manager of the Belfast Fire Insurance Company, Limited, and Provincial Life Office. At the same time he began the Insurance Brokerage business, and has built up one of the largest and best connections in the North Country. In the year 1880 Mr. Bain launched the Commercial Plate Glass Insurance Company, Limited, and having established ramifications through the United Kingdom, has succeeded in building up a large and safe business. Mr. Bain is well known in every Insurance centre, and belongs to a family who are intimately associated with every branch of the Insurance business.

HENRY MELLEISH BAKER.

Bailey, Arthur Hutcheson, F.I.A., F.S.S., the Actuary of the London Assurance Corporation, was born at St. John's Wood, London, in 1823, and was educated at King's College, London. In the year 1841 he entered the profession of Life Insurance, joining the staff of the Protector Life Association, which office was amalgamated in 1847 with the Eagle Insurance Company. In 1855 Mr. Bailey was appointed Secretary of the Equity and Law Life Assurance Society, and the following year was made Actuary in addition. In these posts he continued until 1861, when he received his present appointment.

Baker, Henry Melleish, the Secretary of the Church of England Insurance Institution, of King Street, London, was born in the year 1833.

When just fifteen he entered the Insurance world, also commencing his life's career in the service of his present Office. He spent twenty years in working through various grades and departments till, in 1868, he was given the position of Accountant to the Institution.

Two years later, on the death of the late Mr. Andrew Francis (1880), he was selected by the Board of Directors to succeed him in the appointment as Secretary, which position he still occupies.

J. HOWARD BARNES, F.I.A., F.S.S.

Barnes, J. Howard, F.I.A., F.S.S., Assistant Actuary and Assistant Secretary to the Pelican Life Office, entered the Insurance profession in 1878, in which year he received an appointment to a clerkship in the Life Department of the Head Office of the Northern Assurance Company, at Moorgate Street, London. Mr. James Valentine, now the General Manager of the Northern, was then only Assistant Actuary, and so Mr. Barnes thus had the advantage of receiving his early training in the details of the business directly under such efficient supervision. In 1880, he passed his first examination at the Institute of Actuaries, which success he followed up by passing the second examination, in which he was placed first on the list in order of merit in 1883, and in 1885 the third examination, thus becoming a Fellow of the Institutes. In that latter year, too, he was appointed Chief Clerk in the Life Department of the Northern Assurance Company. He had now sufficiently distinguished himself to be marked as a fitting person to assist in the work of compiling the necessary tables for the second part of the Text Book which the Institute was bringing out, and he was accordingly deputed to do so, his name being specially mentioned in the preface to the completed work. Mr. Barnes received his present appointment as Second Officer to the Pelican Life Office in 1889, since which time he has busied himself actively in its interests, with resulting good effects to the Office and credit to himself.

EDWARD BAUMER.

Baumer, Edward, who holds the position of Assistant Secretary to the Sun Fire Office of London, has passed the whole of his commercial and Insurance career in the service of that Corporation, having first joined its staff so long ago as the year 1854. The various positions he filled in turn on the staff gave him opportunities of acquiring a wide and very varied experience of all the intricacies of Fire Underwriting, of which he fully availed himself, and so earned the confidence of the Board of Directors and the Management of the Company, that in the year 1881 they rewarded his energies and abili-ties by offering him his present appointment.

Mr. Edward Baumer is a son of Mr. C. H. Baumer (who, by-the-way, is still living), another old and trusted servant of the Sun Fire. This gentleman entered the service of the old Corpora-tion nearly three-quarters of a century since, namely, in the year 1820. Three years ago a grand-son of that gentleman (and the son of the subject of this article), received an appointment on the staff of the Office, and thus three generations of this family have been in its active service, and the connection has been a long and close one, and one likely to be continued.

GEORGE WILLIAM BELL.

Bell, George William, the Manager and Secretary of the Law Fire Insurance Society, of 114, Chancery Lane, London (which office dates its establishment from 1845) was born on the 26th of November, 1822. He was called to the Bar by the Honourable Society of the Middle Temple in 1846. He was appointed by the Directors of the Law Fire to his present post of Secretary in 1868, and it is under his management that that office has attained the eminent position of third the list of Metropolitan Fire Insurance Companies. During the last forty years Mr. Bell has been actively engaged in many philanthropic works. About thirty years since he founded The Boys' Home. This was started in the Euston Road, with two boys. It grew very rapidly as its sphere for usefulness increased, and eventually it had to be moved to buildings which were specially erected for it in the Regent's Park Road, where now one hundred and fifty poor boys receive the advantages of food, clothing, and technical education. Of this admirable institution he still retains the management, and is the Treasurer. Mr. Bell's early Insurance training was received in the Atlas Office, the service of which he entered in the year 1842, so that in the present year he will celebrate his Jubilee of Insurance work.

In the literary and scientific worlds Mr. Bell holds a high reputation. He has contributed largely to the Press, and he is a member of the Councils of King's College, London, of King's College Hospital, of the Royal Botanical Society and of the Royal Humane Society.

THOMAS B. BELL.

Batten, John Maxwell, M.A. (Cambridge), is the Secretary of the Chief Office for Great Britain and Ireland of the Equitable Life Assurance Society of the United States. He is a son of the late Mr. J. Hallet Batten (of the Bengal Civil Service), formerly Commissioner of Agra, and was born in India in the year 1853. Mr. Batten, whose school life was spent at Haileybury College, of which school he was head boy for two years, has also the pleasure of placing to his record that he was a foundation scholar of St. John's College, Cambridge, where he graduated in First Class Honours in 1875. Following this he was an Assistant Master at Haileybury College, Herts, after which he acted in the same responsible capacity at Kelly College, Tavistock, and Newton College, South Devon, which position he resigned to take up the higher appointment of Head Master of Plymouth College, which he held for some time. Throughout the whole of his educational career, Mr. Batten was a staunch believer in the combination of hard work with athletic sports, and carried his principles into practice from the beginning. At Cambridge he was the Captain of the Rugby Football Club, playing in the International Match England r. Scotland in 1874, and represented his University in Racquets. There, as in other fields, he distinguished himself by earnestness in the pursuit nearest his hand or immediately in view. Early in the year 1886 he accepted an appointment on the London staff of the Equitable Assurance Society of the United States. His first duties were in the responsible position of Superintendent of Agencies ; and, after gaining much valuable experience in this and other departments, he was, in the month of April, 1891, appointed to the position of Secretary of the British Branch of that very important Society.

Bell, Thomas B., General Manager and Secretary of The Lion Fire Insurance Company, Limited, was born in 1847, and is a native of London. He has had a large experience in Insurance matters, in connection with several Offices, and since he received his present appointment the affairs of his Company have steadily prospered.

FREDERICK BELL, F.I.A

Bell, Frederick, F.I.A., the Actuary of the Church of England Insurance Institution, was born in London of Scotch parentage. After receiving an ordinary commercial education, he commenced his business career in a merchant's office in the City of London. Commerce, however, was not his bent, and after two years he abandoned it, to begin his Insurance experience in the London Office of the Liverpool and London and Globe Insurance Company, where he remained for just over four years.

He resigned his position in this office to take up an appointment on the staff of the Head Office of the Sun Life Insurance Company, and in the service of this important Office he remained for very nearly seven years. In the month of January, 1870, he was appointed to the position of Assistant-Secretary to the Life Offices Association, and in March of the same year to a similar position on the staff of the Church of England Assurance Institution.

When subsequently the Consulting Actuary of the Institution, Mr. W. M. Makeham, F.I.A., retired, Mr. Bell was appointed by the Directors to take up the additional duties of the post thus rendered vacant.

WILLIAM BENTHAM, J.P.

Bentham. William, J.P., the General Secretary for England of the Standard Life Assurance Company, has had very considerable experience of commercial and financial business as well as of Insurance. Mr. Bentham commenced his business life in the service of the London and County Banking Company, in 1844, at their Croydon branch.

Rapidly passing through the junior grades of the service in that great institution, in London and branches, he became Branch Sub-Manager at a very early age, and afterwards Branch Manager. In 1853, he was appointed sole Inspector for the Standard Life Assurance Company in England at a time when systematic inspection of Life Agents in the country was practically a thing unknown.

This appointment he filled with profit to the Company and credit to himself for ten years, at the expiration of which time he was selected by the Board of Directors for the position of Resident Secretary for their Corporation in Ireland. This was in the year 1863, and he remained in that post for twenty-five years.

In 1888, the late Mr. Williams retired from the position of General Secretary to the Company in England, and Mr. Bentham was offered the vacant office by the Board. He accepted it, and has ably fulfilled the duties since.

During his long residence in Dublin, Mr. Bentham made very many friends, and they, to show their esteem of him personally and their appreciation of his abilities, invited him to a complimentary banquet given in his honour before he left. This was very largely attended ; and, in addition to this compliment, Mr. Bentham was also the recipient of numerous valuable testimonials from friends and institutions.

G. W. BERRIDGE, F.I.A.

Berridge, George William, F.I.A., the Actuary and Secretary of the Equity and Law Life Assurance Society of London, has now held that position for nineteen years. Previous to receiving this appointment he had gained a long and varied experience in all that pertains to the science and theory of Life Insurance, while holding different important appointments on the staffs of the Guardian, the London and Provincial Law, and other important Life Offices.

In the position he holds he followed a distinguished group of predecessors, among them being Professor Sylvester, F.R.S., A. H. Bailey, F.I.A. (the present Actuary and Chief Officer of the London Assurance Corporation), and T. B. Sprague, M.A., F.I.A., F.F.A. (now the Actuary of the Scottish Equitable Life Assurance Society).

Besides his immediate business, Mr. Berridge has rendered very valuable assistance to the Actuarial world. In addition to the post of Honorary Secretary to the Institute of Actuaries, which he held for some time, he has also acted as one of the Vice-Presidents of the Institute.

To Actuarial literature he has also contributed largely, having written various papers, which have been read before the Institute, and also published in its Transactions. Many of these have een of great value to the Students and professors of Actuarial and Insurance Science.

Bird, Neilson, Secretary of the Clyde Steamship Owners' Association, was born in Glasgow, the son of a solicitor, where he received his early education, and having been destined by his father for the legal profession, was articled to a Solicitor, at the same time going through the usual College course to enable him to pass the examination for Membership of the Faculty of Procurators. He then went into partnership with his father, and worked for some years with moderate success, until, on the union of the Clyde shipowners against the irregular and oppressive manner of dealing with the loading of vessels by the Board of Trade, by which the cargo carrying trade was becoming heavily handicapped, Mr. Bird was called in to assist them, the result being the formation of the Clyde Steamship Owners' Association, he being the Secretary. This brought the Board of Trade to more reasonable terms, and finally, in 1883, they appointed a Committee to deal with and report on the whole subject of the load line, which practically settled the dispute. Mr. Bird also at this time became Manager of two Steamship Clubs, the first for the Insurance of Steamers, and the second a Freight and Demurrage Club, the only ones of the kind in Scotland, and both with a large and increasing roll of members.

The Clyde Sailing Ship Owners next started an Association, encouraged by the success of the

NEILSON BIRD.

Steamship Owners, for mutual protection and assistance of their peculiar interests, of which Mr. Bird's former achievements pointed him out as the most fitting man to be Manager. This Association was then the only one of its kind in the United Kingdom, and it was not long before it had made itself felt in the attacking and abolition of many of the abuses under which the Sailing Ship Trade had been labouring, notably, amongst others, the "Custom of the Port" by which vessels had been detained unreasonable times in port when it suited the capricious convenience of certain merchants. A Collision Club was subsequently added to this Association, which is now one of the largest in the Kingdom: also a Club for dealing with disputed questions of Freight and Demurrage. Meanwhile, the Clyde Associations did good service to the Shipping Trade in successfully opposing the Merchant Shipping Bill, brought into Parliament in 1884 by Mr. Chamberlain, the then President of the Board of Trade, and which, in the opinion of qualified and impartial judges who listened to both sides of the question, was unnecessary and totally without foundation as to many of the charges brought against Shipowners. Mr. Bird took a leading part in this opposition, and when, out of deference to Mr. Chamberlain's feelings on the withdrawal of his Bill, a Royal Commission was appointed to inquire into the loss of life at sea, Mr.

GEORGE WILLIAM BLANCHETT.

Bird was selected to form a Committee to watch the case on behalf of the Shipowners. To this work he devoted himself for three years, and it is greatly to his credit that though the composition of the Royal Commission was such that an adverse report to the Shipowners' interests might have been well expected, through his exertions it was eventually toned down to such a degree that it was rendered practically harmless. Mr. Bird deservedly enjoys the esteem and confidence of the Shipowners, not only of Glasgow but of the other ports of the United Kingdom.

Blanchett, G. W., is Assistant Secretary in London of the Standard Life Assurance Company. Mr. Blanchett has had a very long experience in the Insurance world, and has been in the service of The Standard since 1854.

BENJAMIN BLENKINSOP, A.I.A.

Blenkinsop, Benjamin, A.I.A., the Secretary and Principal Officer of the Hand-in-Hand Insurance Society of London, was born at Penryn, in Cornwall, in 1831, and entered the Insurance profession in 1852, when he was attached to the staff of the Globe Insurance Company. Here he remained till 1861, when he entered the service of the Hand-in-Hand in the capacity of Chief Clerk in the Fire Department. With this Office he has remained ever since, receiving his present appointment in the year 1873.

Beaumont, S. A., Managing Director of the County Fire and Provident Life Offices, comes of a family with whose existence that of the two Offices is closely bound up, both his father and his grandfather, who, indeed, was their original founder and promoter, having preceded him in the position which he now occupies. Mr. Beaumont has passed his whole Insurance career, extending over a period of more than a quarter of a century, in the service of the two Offices, having worked his way steadily upwards through all departments of the business, and eventually being promoted to his present post in 1878, on the death of his late father.

ROBERT BLYTH.

Blyth, Robert, the Manager of The Scottish Amicable Life Assurance Society, is a native of Glasgow. After his school education in that city, and a year spent in London at college, he, in 1861, entered the office of Messrs. McClelland, Son, and Smith, Chartered Accountants. Ten years later, Mr. Blyth was made a partner, Mr. Adam Gillies Smith, now the Manager of The North British and Mercantile Insurance Company, having retired, and the firm being changed to McClelland, Mackinnon, and Blyth. During the twenty years of Mr. Blyth's partnership his practice as an Accountant steadily increased, and for some years he has held the position of one of the leading men in the profession. He was a member of the Council of the Institute of Accountants and Actuaries of Glasgow. In 1889 the Debating Society of the Institute selected him as one of its lecturers. He was selected for his present post in charge of the Scottish Amicable, in 1891, on the death of the late Mr. Marr. Mr. Blyth has not allowed his professional business to monopolise his time, but takes an interest in the Philosophical, Geographical and Archæological Societies of Glasgow, and his face is a familiar one at the Boards of some of the City Charities.

WILLIAM GIBSON BLOXSOM.

Bloxsom, William Gibson, the Manager of the Scottish Metropolitan Life Assurance Company of Edinburgh, is a native of that town, and was educated at Merchiston Castle School and the Edinburgh Institution. At the age of seventeen he entered the office of the Standard Life Assurance Company, where he remained for six years, leaving it to become Inspector of Agents to the Reliance Assurance Society in Manchester, in which capacity he proved highly successful. He was subsequently appointed Inspector of Agents to the Scottish National Insurance Company. now the Scottish Union and National, and during the time he held this appointment the business in the district under his charge largely increased. While there the idea of forming a new Company suggested itself to him, and a number of friends joining him in the enterprise, on 6,000 shares having been subscribed for it, Mr. Bloxsom resigned his position with the Scottish National to take over the management of the new Company, and in a short time, without the intervention of brokers, no less than 16,000 shares had been taken up. The Articles of Association of the new Company, which was happily named the Scottish Metropolitan, were that time in a great measure of an entirely novel character, and were all drafted by Mr. Bloxsom. The Scottish Metropolitan has been the foremost to adopt improvements of various kinds in Life Assurance contracts, many of which have been since imitated by other and older Companies. Mr Bloxsom has been a great athlete in his time, especially in the football field, and now that he has abandoned that form of pastime has taken up golf with great success. He is a member of one of the leading Amateur Choral Societies of Edinburgh, and altogether, with his many genial qualities, is a most popular member of Edinburgh society. He is an adept at organization, a skilful mathematician, and thorough in office details

WILFRED A. BOWSER, F.S.S.

Bowser, Wilfred Arthur, the Manager and Actuary of the London, Edinburgh, and Glasgow Life Assurance Company, Limited, of London, was born in the year 1846.

He is the son of Mr. Alfred T. Bowser, who for so many years held the position of Chief Officer of the Whittington Life Insurance Office. In the service of this Company Mr. W. A. Bowser made his first connection with, and gained his first experience of, Life Insurance business, practically as well as scientifically. After hard work for several years here, he resigned his appointment to accept one on the London Staff of the Queen Insurance Company, and in various departments, still gaining valuable knowledge, he served this Office for five or six years, and then had gained a reputation and experience sufficient to justify the management of the English Life Insurance Company, in appointing him to the position of Chief Life Clerk. This was in the year 1867, and he held that appointment until 1870, when the business of the office was transferred to another company.

In the year following (1871), Mr. Bowser founded the London and County Provident Institution, a Friendly Society doing monthly business only, and he acted as its Manager for some years, and with success and still increasing reputation.

In 1878, the Directors of the Colonial Assurance Company made him a direct offer of the appointment of the Managership of their office. This Mr. Bowser accepted, intending to take over with him the whole of the business of the London and County Provident Institution, and amalgamate the business of the two offices, under the title of the London and County Life Insurance Society. This consolidation, which would have been good for both, was rendered practically impossible by the restrictions of the Board of Trade, and to get over the difficulty Mr. Bowser formed the London, Edinburgh, and Glasgow Life Insurance Company, to take over the capital and business of both offices. This was done, and the new Company commenced business in 1883,

W. SINCLAIR BOYD.

HENRY BOYD.

with Mr. Bowser holding the same position that he does at the present time.

To Insurance literature Mr. Bowser has been a frequent and valuable contributor. Among his articles on Actuarial subjects are—" Observations on the Rate of Mortality in Infancy and Childhood "; "Notes on the observations of the Rev. John Hodgson, M.A., on the Mortality of the Clergy of England and Wales, with remarks on the tables deduced therefrom "; " A paper on the Table of Mortality deduced from the New Experience Observations," etc., etc.

Boyd, W. Sinclair, is one of the Managers and Underwriters of The Ulster Marine Insurance Company, and a partner in the firm of Sinclair and Boyd, Marine Insurance Brokers, Belfast. He has been engaged in Marine Insurance and Shipping affairs for many years, and is highly respected and esteemed in the North of Ireland.

Boyd, Henry, is a partner in the firm of Sinclair and Boyd, Managers and Underwriters of the Ulster Marine Insurance Company, Limited, Lloyd's Agents and Marine Insurance Brokers, Belfast. He is a Director of the Ulster Marine Insurance Company, Limited, etc., and a very prominent citizen of Belfast.

Brain, Herbert Burgess, the Secretary of the Provident Clerks' Guarantee and Accident Associations, was for seventeen years Chief Clerk in the Office. During this time he assisted largely in the extension and development of the Associations under the late Mr. W. T. Linford, the then Secretary. When this gentleman died, in 1886, Mr. Brain was appointed to the vacancy.

W. A. BOWIE.

HENRY BROWN.

Bowie, William A., the Assistant Secretary of the Scottish Temperance Life Assurance Company, received his early Insurance training in the Life Department of the Scottish Imperial Insurance Company, where he did a considerable amount of valuation work, which has since proved a most profitable experience to him. When the Scottish Temperance Life Office was first inaugurated, Mr. Bowie transferred his fortunes to it, and as Chief Clerk for the greater portion of its existence has had the pleasure of helping in the development of the Company from year to year. He has also a very good record to show of business done in an out-door capacity. In June, 1891, he was appointed to his present post, the Directors conferring the promotion on him in consideration of his past services, and with a view to his being thereby enabled to lend still greater assistance in developing the business of the Company.

Brown, Henry, Manager of The Sickness and Accident Assurance Association, Limited, Edinburgh, commenced his actual Insurance career as Resident Secretary, in Manchester, of his present Company, in 1887, prior to which time he had been engaged in the Insurance department of Messrs. Rylands and Sons, Limited, Manchester. Mr. Brown was so successful as Resident Secretary, as to secure for himself the appointment of General Superintendent of Branches of The Sickness and Accident Assurance Association towards the end of 1888, and, on the resignation of the original Manager in April, 1889, he was selected by the Directors for his present appointment. During his tenure of office he has done much to improve and strengthen the position of his Company.

CHARLES ROUSE BROWNE.

Browne, Charles Rouse, is the Secretary of the Old Westminster Fire Office, and he represents the fourth generation of his family that have held the management of this most successful Company, his great grandfather having been appointed its Secretary in 1768. The present holder of that office entered the service of the Company in the year 1850, and after passing through the various departments and gaining a thorough insight into the practical and theoretical working of each, was in 1869 appointed to be Assistant Secretary. This position he held until ten years later, when his father retired, and he was then (in 1869) promoted to the Secretaryship. Mr. C. R. Browne has always taken an active and important part in the organisation and development of the London Salvage Corps, and in 1872 he was appointed Honorary Secretary to that valuable Institution.

T. G. C. BROWNE, F.I.A., F.F.A., F.S.S.

Browne, T. G. C., F.I.A., F.F.A., F.S.S., Actuary and Secretary of the Guardian Assurance Company, of London, commenced a career in the Insurance World that has won him universal respect and esteem in the office of the Standard Life Insurance Company in Edinburgh, in the year 1862. While in the service of this Company, he passed the several examinations of the Faculty of Actuaries of Edinburgh, gaining the Fellowship of that body. In 1874 he came to the Metropolis, and his services as Chief Clerk were secured by the London and Provincial Law Assurance Society. In London he found a wider scope for his abilities and energies, and applied these to such purpose in increasing his knowledge and reputation, that in 1874 he was appointed Life Manager of the Guardian Office. Here he continued to work with the same zeal, and the practical advantage of his experience and theoretical skill were recognised by the Board of Directors of the Company, who offered him the position of Actuary, which he accepted, and to which subsequently was added the Secretaryship of the Company.

S. STANLEY BROWN.

Brown, S. Stanley, the General Manager and Secretary of the Employers' Liability Assurance Corporation, Limited, of London, received the first portion of his education at the City of London School, from whence he went up to Corpus Christi College, Cambridge. At the conclusion of his University career he entered a Solicitor's office, with a view of adopting the Law as a profession, but in 1871 the Governors of Dulwich College selected him for the position of Clerk (practically Secretary), and as such he remained until 1874, when the Board of Directors of the Commercial Union Assurance Company appointed him to the office of Secretary to that Corporation. This was his entrance to the Insurance world, and he utilised the materials to his hand in gaining a thorough knowledge of the intricacies of Insurance work to the fullest extent, as is plainly shown in the masterly way in which he reorganised the New York Branch of the Company. By this and other work he so established his reputation as an Insurance man that on the founding of the Employers' Liability Assurance Corporation in 1881, he was selected as being the best man to fill the position of General Manager and Secretary, which post he still holds.

EDWARD W. BROWNE.

Browne, Edward William, is the Manager and Secretary of the Colonial Mutual Life Assurance Society, Limited, in London. He was born in the ancient historical city of Edinburgh, and was educated at the Circus Place School, and the Edinburgh Academy. His first entry into the Insurance World was in the Head Office of the Life Association of Scotland, in his native city, in the year 1862, and he completed his training as clerk, with seven years' employment in the Head Office of the Queen Insurance Company, in Liverpool. For some years he held the position of Manager for Scotland to the Briton Medical and General Life, and the Britannia Fire Association. His next appointment was as Manager of the Belfast Fire Office, at Belfast, which he resigned to return to Scotland as the Manager there for the London and Lancashire Life Assurance Company, and the Fire Insurance Association. He was next the Agency Superintendent of the Imperial Life Insurance Company, for the Liverpool and Manchester districts. While here he received the offer of the position of Agency Manager from the Marine and General Life Assurance Society, at its Head Office in London, and while holding this post he successfully created that Society's now large Agency connection and general business throughout the United Kingdom. His name was brought very prominently before the Insurance World in 1888, during the exposure of the notorious Insurance Frauds in Belfast, which he was largely instrumental in bringing to light.

JOHNSON BROOKS.

Brooks, Johnson, the Assistant Secretary of the United Kingdom Temperance and General Provident Institution, has been for nearly thirty-five years in the service of that Institution, during which time he has passed through various departments, fulfilling his duties faithfully and efficiently, and earning the respect and esteem of all connected with him. In the October of 1888, on the promotion of Mr. Cash to the post of Managing Director, in addition to that of Secretary, which he already held, Mr. Brooks was promoted to his present post, the results since having shown that his selection by the Directors was both judicious and wise.

———

Burne, James, has been the Secretary of The Lancashire and Yorkshire Accident Insurance Company, Limited, of Manchester, since the month of May, 1889.

He commenced his early business life in an Insurance Office, where he remained for upwards of two years, gaining some practical experience in the business. He then received the offer of an appointment on the staff of the Lancashire and Yorkshire Railway Company, and in the service of that corporation he remained for very nearly twenty years. During that time he passed through various departments and positions, gaining a wide experience of commercial life, and also a knowledge of organisation that has doubtless been very useful to him since. He resigned the position with this Railway Company to take up the appointment he at present holds, and in which position he has been very successful.

ARTHUR C. BROWNLOW.

Brownlow, Arthur C., is the Manager of the Sub-office of The Sun Life Assurance Society, High Holborn, W.C. He was born in November, 1853, and educated at Clifton and Caius College, Cambridge. He entered the service of The Sun Life Assurance Society in 1880, and in July, 1890, was promoted to his present position.

— — —

Burnett, George Henry, the Manager of the Fire Department of the North British and Mercantile Insurance Company in London, was born in London in the year 1836. He comes of a sound commercial stock, his father having been the chief partner in the firm of Messrs. Burnett and Company, the well-known Navy Agents After receiving a good education, he entered the service of the Northern Assurance Company (London Office), where for seven years he had the advantage of serving under Mr. E. H. Mannering, the present Secretary of the Sun Fire Office. At this time the Mercantile Insurance Company was but recently established, and its Directors were getting together a staff of high excellence. They offered the position of Foreign Clerk to young Mr. Burnett, and he accepted it, thus first forming the connection he has retained to the present day. From the position in which he entered the office he was soon promoted to that of Foreign Superintendent. After the Amalgamation of the Mercantile with the North British Insurance Company, Mr. Burnett rapidly rose in the estimation of his Board, and has frequently to take long journeys to look after the interests of the Company abroad. One of these was to Chicago, in 1870, after the great fire, when the North British and Mercantile paid out very close upon half a million sterling in settlement of its losses in that terrible disaster. In 1872, on the death of Mr. Whyting, the Manager of the Company, Mr. Burnett was promoted to his present position, in which he has still further enhanced his already high reputation as one of the first Fire Managers of the day.

WILLIAM BROWN.

J. M. BUCHANAN.

Brown, William, is the Secretary of the Free Church of Scotland Fire Insurance Trust Limited, the Head Office of which is in Edinburgh. Mr. Brown is a native of Edinburgh, where he originally gained his Insurance experience while in the service of the Scottish Union and National Insurance Company, for which he acted in the capacity of Inspector of Agents. In 1888, on the Free Church of Scotland Fire Insurance Trust being established for the purpose of insuring Churches, Colleges, Schools, Manses, and other buildings belonging to the Free Church denomination, he was selected for the post which he at present holds, and has since brought the Company to a high state of prosperity. Mr. Brown also carries on business in Edinburgh as an Accountant and General Insurance Agent and Broker, and enjoys the esteem of all the principal business men in that city.

Buchanan, J. M., is the General Manager of the Goldsmiths' and General Burglary Insurance Association, a recently established office, which, unlike other Companies catering for this class of business, devotes itself entirely to Burglary Insurance. Mr. Buchanan who promoted this Association, has been actively and closely connected with this new Branch of Insurance business since it was first introduced to the public by the Mercantile Accident and Guarantee Insurance Company, of Glasgow, he having acted in the capacity of Chief Superintendent for that office till its amalgamation with another Company. The Goldsmiths' have in Mr. Buchanan a practical Manager, who has had exceptional opportunities of gaining a thorough knowledge of the requirements and working of the business, and who is personally acquainted with the exact means and methods by which these can be best supplied.

THOMAS CASH.

Cash, Thomas, the Managing Director and Secretary of the United Kingdom Temperance and General Provident Institution, is a native of Peckham Rye, where he was born in 1827, his father being Mr. William Cash, an eminent member of the Society of Friends, and an active worker in the Temperance cause, in both of which respects Mr. Thomas Cash follows his example. In 1856 he sat as a member of the Joint Committee of the National Temperance Society and the London Temperance League, which had just then been amalgamated ; and twelve years later he was also one of the Committee of the Association for Promoting the Amendment of the Licensing System. He was elected a Director of the Temperance Provident Life Institution in 1862, becoming its Secretary in 1862, the additional dignity of Managing Director being conferred on him by a grateful Directorate in 1888. Mr. Cash is a strong advocate of the non-alcoholic treatment in medical cases, and has from the beginning been a warm supporter of the London Temperance Hospital. He was a member of the Provisional Committee in 1871, and on the opening of the Hospital, originally in Gower Street, he was elected Chairman of the Board of Directors, which post he still holds.

Among the most prominent converts to the cause of Temperance that Mr. William Cash made during his distinguished career, the name of the late George Cruikshank will always stand foremost. While Mr. Cash was Chairman of the National Temperance Society, this celebrated artist interviewed him with the object of securing his influence in circulating his famous series of pictures, entitled, "The Bottle." Mr. Cash asked the artist how he could conscientiously continue to use the drink, the evil effects of which he so powerfully depicted. This pointed question led Mr. Cruikshank to think seriously of the matter, and eventually to become a total abstainer.

There can be no question but that a very great measure of the financial success of the Temperance Hospital in the Hampstead Road, London, must be ascribed to the personal influence of Mr. Cash, and he has further proved his business capabilities by the manner in which he has conducted the affairs of the "United Kingdom" Company.

WM. D. CAIRNEY.

JOHN HENRY CHATTERTON.

Cairney, William D., the Secretary of the Scottish Alliance Insurance Co., Limited, Glasgow, is a native of that city, and belongs to a well-known and highly respectable family, his father being Mr. William Cairney, of the firm of Messrs. Thomas Skinner and Co., shipowners, Glasgow and London. He received his business training in the office of Messrs. McClelland, Mackinnon and Blyth, the well-known Chartered Accountants, of Glasgow, with which firm he remained some years, afterwards going into business on his own account as a Chartered Accountant, which business he still carries on.

In 1888 he formed the Scottish Alliance Insurance Co., of which he was appointed Secretary. Mr. Cairney is highly respected in Scotland as a gentleman of strict integrity and high business qualifications.

Chatterton, John Henry, is the Secretary of the Millers' Mutual Fire Insurance Company, and an Insurance Broker of Mark Lane, London. This gentleman has had a varied experience of business. At a very early age he commenced in the wine trade, in London, as shipping clerk. At the breaking out of the gold fever, he went to Australia in 1852, and spent some time in Adelaide, Melbourne, and the gold fields, and in Tasmania. After a brief return to England, he again emigrated, about the time of the opening of the Grand Trunk Railway, to Canada. Too late to join the first expedition to the Red River which was then just added to the Canadian dominions, he nevertheless during the next two years visited all parts of that extensive country in search of fortune, but that still eluding him, he returned, and, at the somewhat advanced age of 27, obtained the post of junior clerk in the Western Gas Company.

Here at last his experience of the world began to tell, and he very soon was at the head of the office. In 1872, on the amalgamation of that company with the Gas Light and Coke Company, he retired with a pension, and was immediately appointed Accountant to the Barnet District Gas Water Company ; this appointment he held for one year, and then migrated north to Sunderland, where he was engaged for two years re-organizing the staff, and revaluing and rating the Sunderland and South Shields district of the Water Company. In 1876, the Millers feeling dissatisfied with the new rates imposed upon them, started two companies, the Millers' and General of Birmingham, and the Millers' Mutual of London. The former company speedily ran its course, and demonstrated the want of judgment of its promoters, by eventually winding up with a series of calls to the tune of something like £60,000. The latter Company (the Millers' Mutual), was entrusted to Mr. Chatterton's care, and for seven years he piloted it through many storms, learning his business as a fire insurance man as he went along. After serving the customary apprenticeship to the business, he learnt that it then cost more to insure in the Mutual than in the regular offices and he at once transferred the whole of the business to the Equitable Fire Office, and set up as a Broker. In 1878 the Millers of the United Kingdom formed to themselves a National Association of British and Irish Millers, and appointed Mr. Chatterton secretary, and for 12 years everything connected with Flour Milling had its head quarters in Mark Lane. Latterly, however, the Council of the Association thought that their Secretary stood in the way of "cheap" insurance, and they parted. Mr. Chatterton is considered an authority on the Fire Insurance aspects of Milling.

JAMES CHATHAM, F.I.A., F.F.A.

Chatham, James. F.I.A., F.F.A., of the Scottish Equitable Life Assurance Society, St. Andrew Square, Edinburgh, was born in that city in 1857. He has been the Secretary of the Actuarial Society of Edinburgh, and also of the Faculty of Actuaries. Of the latter body he is in addition one of the Examiners. Mr. Chatham's business career commenced as an apprentice in a merchant's office at Leith. At that time the science of shorthand, which has now become so indispensable an adjunct to commercial business, was almost an unknown quantity; but Mr. Chatham applied himself so assiduously to its study and practice that in an open competition in the year 1876, he succeeded in gaining a medal. Appointed in 1879 shorthand clerk to Mr. T. B. Sprague, F.I.A., F.F.A., he has since remained in the office of the Society, where he now fills an important position. Once launched in the Insurance world, Mr. Chatham turned his attention and studies more particularly to Actuarial Science, and passed in succession the examinations of the Faculty of Actuaries of Edinburgh and the Institute of Actuaries of London, and holds the diplomas of both bodies. As an Actuary his career has been a very distinguished one. We have already mentioned above several of the appointments he has held, but this by no means completes the list of honours he has won. Two years ago Mr. T. B. Sprague offered £70 to the Institute of Actuaries as a prize to be competed for in an open contest, the subject chosen being, "The Rate of Mortality and Discontinuance among Insured Lives." In this, as in similar competitions, all papers were sent in under *noms de plume* ; and it is not too much to say that when the decision of the judges was announced, a great many people shared the astonishment of Mr. Sprague to find that the coveted post of winner had been secured by Mr. Chatham, and that, adding to the honours won thereby, the second place was gained by one of the most distinguished Actuaries of the United States. No one had previously doubted Mr. Chatham's abilities, but this achievement certainly placed the seal on his reputation. In the winter session of 1891-92 the Faculty of Actuaries inaugurated a new and what will probably prove a most valuable innovation. This took the form of a course of special lectures to the Students of that body. When this course was decided on, the Council of that learned body unanimously offered Mr. Chatham the position of Lecturer. It is hardly necessary to say that he acknowledged the honour and compliment by accepting it, and his lectures have been among the most successful on record, the lecture hall being crowded. As a coach for the actuarial examinations of various bodies, Mr. Chatham enjoys a very high reputation, and is also in the gratifying position of a rapidly-growing consulting practice. He has contributed various papers to the "Journal of the Institute of Actuaries," and the "Transactions of the Actuarial Society of Edinburgh."

JAMES WILLIAM CHESSHYRE.

R. G. COCHRANE.

Chesshyre, James William, Founder and Managing Director of the County Hail Storm Insurance Company, is a well-known Hertford man, having been for a period of thirty-eight years Manager of the London and County Bank in that town. He was interested in the origin of the Royal Farmers' Insurance Company and other Offices in 1840, and in 1848 established the County Hail Storm Insurance Company, of which he has been the Manging Director for forty-four years. Under his management the Company has put by a Reserve Fund out of profits of three times the amount of its paid-up capital, and has paid dividends to its shareholders averaging 30 per cent. per annum since its establishment. Mr. Chesshyre was also associated with the late Lord Salisbury, Lord Granville, Lord Beaconsfield (then Mr. Disraeli), Lord Cowper, and many other noblemen and gentlemen in the county of Hertford, in establishing a scheme of Insurance against the Cattle Plague, which proved a great success, not only in preventing the spread of the plague, but in giving a fair compensation for all losses incurred by the insurers, and was eventually wound up with considerable profit to its shareholders.

In 1862 Mr. Chesshyre took an active part in the establishment of Haileybury College, and was appointed Treasurer, which post he has held ever since.

In 1869 he was presented with a handsome service of plate of the value of £300, by 250 subscribers, in testimony of the appreciation of his services in the promotion of many valuable institutions in the county of Hertford.

Cochrane, R. G., is the Sub-Manager of the Fire Department of the Guardian Assurance Company at its Head Office in London, and has the management of the home Fire business of that company.

Mr. Cochrane received his first insurance training in the office of the Northern Assurance Company at Glasgow, and subsequently he had an extensive experience as a Surveyor for the Royal. In 1874, he was appointed Secretary in Edinburgh to the Scottish Provincial Insurance Company, which appointment he held until 1886, when he became Secretary to the Manchester Branch of the Guardian, where his success was so great that the Directors invited him to accept the position he now occupies at the Head Office. Mr. Cochrane is a good organiser, and has a happy faculty of winning the co-operation of those acting under his direction.

JAMES CHISHOLM, F.F.A., F.I.A.

Chisholm, James, F.I.A., the Manager and Actuary of the Imperial Life Insurance Company, is the son of David Chisholm, for many years the Actuary of the North British and Mercantile Insurance Company, and in December, 1861, he entered the office of that Company in Edinburgh, receiving his early Insurance training under the auspices of his father. In February, 1869, he transferred his services to the head office of the Imperial Life Assurance Company in the capacity of Actuarial Assistant, and rose steadily in his profession until, in the year 1882, his talents pointed him out for promotion to his present post as Manager and Actuary of that office. In the same year he was elected a Fellow of the Faculty, and in the following year of the Institute of Actuaries. He is the author of various able papers which have been from time to time read before the Institute of Actuaries, and also of a work entitled "Tables of the Value of Policies of all Durations," which was published in 1885, and joint author with G. James E. Pollock, of "The Medical Handbook of Life Assurance," published in 1889. Mr. Chisholm is most highly esteemed both in Actuarial and Insurance Circles.

JOHN G. CLENSY.

Clensy, John Gornall, Secretary of the Liverpool Victoria Legal Friendly Society, was born in Liverpool in the year 1852. He became connected with the Society in the year 1870, and steadily worked himself up through every department of its business until in the September of 1885,—the same year in which the Society removed its Head Offices from Liverpool to London—he was, in recognition of his sterling and undoubled abilities, promoted to his present position. Since then he has, by his untiring energy and perseverance, won the confidence and esteem of the Agents and Members of the Society, and it is in no small degree owing to his efforts that the Liverpool Victoria now occupies its present prosperous position among its contemporaries.

WILLIAM PALIN CLIREHUGH, F.I.A., F.S.S.

Clirehugh, William Palin, F.I.A., F.S.S., is the Actuary and Manager of the London and Lancashire Life Assurance Co. He was practically the founder of this office, and has been connected with it since its establishment in 1862.

With so many other successful Insurance men, Mr. Clirehugh received his early training in Actuarial and Life Insurance science and practice in Scotland, and he had the advantage of serving for some time under Mr. Jenkin Jones, during which period he had exceptional advantages for gaining considerable experience in the theoretical, as well as the practical, work of an Actuary.

Leaving Scotland, Mr. Clirehugh was appointed to the important position of Accountant in the London office of the National Mercantile Life Assurance Company. This appointment he held for some time. It will be remembered that this office was eventually amalgamated with the Eagle Life Assurance Company of Pall Mall, S.W. His life work, however, has been devoted to the service of the London and Lancashire Life, of which he has always been the chief official, and may be said to be responsible for the great success that office has achieved, and is, therefore, entitled to all the credit attaching to the same.

Mr. Clirehugh is a Fellow of the Institute of Actuaries, and also of the Statistical Society. He has taken an active interest in the Life Offices Association, and has for some time been a member of the Committee of that body. He believes this body will be able to exert an influence for much effective good in the sphere which its work concerns, and it certainly will not be his fault, or due to any lack of energy on his part, if it does not.

Mr. Clirehugh was born in Dundee, in the year 1830, and is very popular among his colleagues and with his staff. In the Life Insurance world he has done much good work, and is very highly respected for his abilities, as well as for his personal character.

JAMES CLUNES.

Clunes, James, the Manager of the Fire Department of the London Assurance Corporation was born in Edinburgh in 1847. His Insurance experience has been very extensive. For nearly twenty years he served on the Staff of the Alliance Assurance Company, and in that valuable school he availed himself of all the opportunities there afforded him for gaining wide and varied practice in the science of Fire Underwriting. His position with this office he resigned in 1881 to take up the important position of Sub-Manager of the Fire Department of the Commercial Union Assurance Company, the responsible duties of which post he continued to discharge until the year 1882. In that year he received the offer of his present appointment, and accepted the honour.

HENRY COCKBURN, F.I.A., F.F.A.

Cockburn, Henry, F.I.A., F.F.A., the Manager of the Life Department and the Actuary in London of the North British and Mercantile Insurance Company, was born in Edinburgh in the year 1848, and was educated at the Edinburgh Academy. In 1864 he entered the Insurance world, joining the Head Office Staff of the Standard Life Assurance Company in his native city, and he remained in the service of this Office for eight years, the last six months of which were spent in its London West End Office. From 1872 to 1875, he filled the position of Chief Clerk in the London Office of the Norwich Union Life Insurance Society, leaving it in the last-named year to take over the duties of his present position. Mr. Cockburn is an executive officer of great capacity with the North British and Mercantile, and occupies a high position in the Insurance world. He is a Fellow of the Faculty of Actuaries, and of the Institute of Actuaries, on the Council of which he has sat successively for a number of times. He is also one of the two honorary librarians of that Institute, an original member of the Council of the Life Offices' Association; and a member of the Actuaries' Club. He has much to be proud of in the success of his Company, towards the attainment of which he has so materially contributed.

FRANCIS ERNEST COLENSO, F.I.A.

Colenso, Francis Ernest, F.I.A., the Actuary . and Secretary of the English and Scottish Law Life Assurance Association of London, is a son of the late Bishop Colenso, of Natal, and was born in London.

He might fairly be taken as an example of hereditary genius, for not only is he the son of one who will most probably rank as the greatest mathematician of the present day, but is the nephew of the late eminent Actuary, C. J. Bunyon. It was in the office of the latter (then the Actuary to the Norwich Union Life Assurance Society) that he made his first connection with the business of Life Insurance.

While studying the theory and practice of his Life profession here, he entered as a student of the Law in the Middle Temple, and was called to the Bar by that Honourable Society in the year 1877.

At this time it was his intention to follow the Law as a profession, and he proceeded to Natal, where his name was, of course, as a "household word," and for three years practised in that Colony as an Attorney of the Supreme Court for upwards of three years.

The law not proving so fascinating a pursuit as he had anticipated, he returned to England, and renewed his connection with the Norwich Union Life Office, receiving the joint appointments of Assistant-Secretary and Assistant-Actuary, both of which positions he filled until November, 1886.

At that time he was selected by the Board of Directors of the English and Scottish Law Life to fill the position he now holds, and in which he has so well and ably acquitted himself, fully justifying the high opinions formed of the promise his abilities gave for his future career.

ARTHUR J. COOK, A.I.A., M.J.I.

Cook, Arthur J., A.I.A., M.J.I., is the Secretary of the Victoria Mutual Assurance, and indeed is the man to whom the Society entirely owes its present prosperous condition. Mr. Cook originally gained his experience as Chief of the Agency Department and confidential shorthand amanuensis in two large Life and Fire Companies, subsequently entering the service of the Victoria Mutual. The Society was then in a very small way, but Mr. Cook set himself energetically to the task put before him, and succeeded not only in saving the Society from lapsing altogether into nonexistence, as it undoubtedly would have done had it not been for his efforts, but in raising it up to the substantial position which it now occupies, actually increasing its funds to tenfold those which he found on taking up his duties, and the income accruing from interest to nearly a hundred-and-fifty-fold. Mr. Cook is a well-known man in the literary world, having contributed many important articles to the various Insurance Journals, as well as having written some very interesting and instructive papers on many of the vexed Insurance questions of the day. His pamphlets "Surcharged and Declined Lives," "Surrender Values," "Hints as to Moderate and Low Premiums," "Large and Small Life Assurance Companies,' and "Lecture on Lifeand Old Age Assurance," as well as on less technical matters—"A Trip to Paris," and "Shorthand Clerks,' have all had a very wide circulation ; and, being a linguist in addition, he is at the present time an occasional contributor to the *Moniteur des Assurances* of Paris and *Los Seguros* of Barcelona. He is an Associate of the Institute of Actuaries, a member and Auditor of the Institute of Journalists, a Freeman and Liveryman of the City of London (Worshipful Company of Fanmakers), a member of the Société de Statistique of Paris, and a Fellow of the Shorthand Society. He is married to a sister of the late Mr. Cornelius Walford, of Insurance Guide and Handbook and Cyclopædia, &c., fame.

THOMAS H. COOKE, F.I.A.

Cooke, Thomas H., F.I.A., is the Actuary of the Northern Assurance Company, the service of which Corporation he entered in the year 1867. After passing through different departments, in each of which he gained much valuable and practical experience in the science and also the theory of the Life Insurance business, Mr. Cooke was, after fifteen years' service, appointed to the position he now occupies. His first connection with the Actuarial world was made in 1869, when he joined the Institute of Actuaries as a student, receiving the honour of a Fellowship of that body in 1873. He is also a member of the Actuaries' Club, to which he was elected in 1880.

Colquhoun, E., F.I.A., the Manager and Actuary of the Legal and General Life Assurance Office, began his Insurance career in 1868 in the office of the Equity and Law Life Assurance Society, in whose service he remained for eighteen years, at the end of which period in 1886 he received his present appointment. Though he has not had such a varied experience in different Insurance Companies as many of his contemporaries, Mr. Colquhoun is a very well-known man in the Insurance and Actuarial world, being a Fellow of the Institute of Actuaries by virtue of examinations successfully passed, and a member of the Council of that body, as well as of the Committee of the Life Offices Association.

JAMES COOPER.

JAMES COWAN.

Cooper, James, Secretary of the Mutual l late Glass Insurance Company, Limited, at Darlington commenced as an Agent to the United Kingdom Temperance and General Provident Institution at Northallerton, Yorkshire, in 1860, where he did a very fair business in the first year of his work, being an enthusiastic total abstainer and having the advantage of a sympathetic Superintendent, always ready to help and advise him in any difficulty. He remained at Northallerton until 1871, combining his agency with his private business of a photographer, and at the latter date removed to Darlington, where he continued in both the same lines for another thirteen years. In 1884, on some of the leading tradesmen determining to form a Local Plate Glass Insurance Company at Darlington, Mr. Cooper applied for, and obtained, the Secretaryship of the Company, first known as the Darlington Mutual Plate Glass Insurance Society, but the success of the Company was so much beyond the expectations of its promoters, that in 1887 Mr. Cooper was empowered to extend the business beyond Darlington ; the name of the Company being changed accordingly to the Mutual Plate Glass Insurance Company. In 1886 the South Durham and North Yorkshire Durham District Superintendency of the United Kingdom Temperance and General Provident Institution falling vacant, Mr. Cooper was appointed to fill it, and has since done a most successful business for the Institution. He also holds a District Agency for the Palatine Insurance Company, to which he was appointed in 1890.

Cowan, James, holds the position of Fire Superintendent to the Caledonian Insurance Company, at their Head Office in Edinburgh. Mr. James Cowan is a Scotchman by birth, having been born in Glasgow in the year 1841, and is therefore at the present date forty-nine years of age. He has passed the whole period of his Insurance career, and indeed of his business career altogether,—for he has never from the very beginning of it been anything else than an Insurance man,—in the service of the Caledonian Insurance Company, having first been apprenticed to it as junior clerk in the Surveyor's office at the Glasgow Branch, at the early age of fifteen, in the year 1856. Here he served his time, and subsequently remained, devoting himself with great assiduity to the thorough acquirement of the details of the work of the special department in which he was employed, for nine years, at the expiration of which time, in the year 1865, his unceasing diligence was fittingly rewarded by his appointment to the post of Fire Surveyor to the same branch office at Glasgow. He continued at this post for another period of eight years until 1873, at the end of which he received the only promotion that he could receive in his particular line of Insurance work from the Directors of the Company which he had served so well,—that is, his transference to the corresponding position at the Head Office at Edinburgh, as Superintendent of the Fire Branch of the Company's business, where he still remains, one of the most trusted officials of one of the most important companies in, or indeed, it may with safety be asserted, as well as out of, Scotland.

LYMAN BEECHER COWIN.

Cowin, Lyman Beecher, was, until the re-insurance of their English and Continental business, the General Manager for Europe of the Fire Department of the South British and National Insurance Companies. Mr. Cowin was born in 1853, in the Isle of Man, and was educated at the High School, Carlisle, and Allesley Park College, Coventry, at which latter place he received a sound practical and commercial training. He has been in the Insurance business almost ever since leaving school, but his practical training commenced with his entry into the Surveying department of the Mutual, Manchester, in 1872, where he acquired much experience in the kind of business to which that Company then chiefly restricted itself, namely, that of the insurance of cotton and cloth manufactories, a business involving some of the most difficult technical points of Fire Insurance. Two years afterwards he joined the Equitable Fire, in which he successively occupied the positions of General Agency Inspector and Surveyor, Local Manager for the Midlands, West of England and South Wales Districts, and finally of London Secretary, which latter post he held for over nine years.

When the South British and National were looking about for a General Manager for Europe, with plenty of experience and yet capable of carrying on their business abreast of the times, they were recommended to Mr. Cowin, who, on being offered the appointment at a handsome salary, accepted it. This was in 1886. Mr. Cowin applied all his energies to the service of his new Companies, and with good effect, for in spite of the somewhat poor condition in which he found the business, he worked it up to such a degree that the Companies were in a fair way to rank amongst the best British Fire Offices. The good condition to which he had brought it may be estimated by the fact that when, owing to some unaccountable panic, the Head office officials in New Zealand resolved to re-insure their European business, that business was considered in Insurance circles to be so good that Mr. Cowin had no difficulty in disposing of

GEORGE S. CRISFORD, F.I.A.

the whole of the business of the United Kingdom to his former Company, the Equitable, of Manchester, while the bulk of the Continental business was taken up by the Alliance, Commercial Union, the Royal Exchange, and other leading English Offices. A better testimony to Mr. Cowin's work could not be required.

Crisford, George Stephen, F.I.A., Actuary and Manager of the Rock Life Assurance Company of London, Honorary Secretary of the Institute of Actuaries, and Joint Editor of the Journal of the Institute, was born in London on the 13th of August, 1841. His first insight into the world of Insurance was obtained in the office of the National Provident Institution, the service of which Society he entered in 1863, and in the same year he joined the Institute of Actuaries. During the year 1875 he was appointed by the Board of Management of the National Provident to superintend and re-organise the Agency department of the Institution, and the result of his work in this respect is felt in that Office in the present day.

Four years after this (in 1879) he was appointed the Actuary and Manager of the West of England Insurance Company at Exeter, where he remained for five years, resigning that position in 1884 to take up the post he occupies at the present time. Mr. Crisford holds a Certificate of Competency from the Institute of Actuaries, and is also one of the Public Valuers appointed by the Lords of the Treasury under the Friendly Societies' Act of 1875. In authorship Mr. Crisford has done much valuable work for his profession. Among the papers he has contributed to the Journal of the Institute may be mentioned an "Essay on Surrender Values," —to this was awarded the Messenger Prize offered by the Institute of Actuaries in 1878, and two other papers, entitled "Office Premium Loadings, and how they are dealt with under the various Methods of Valuation and modes of Distribution of Profit." Among the pressure of all his other work Mr. Crisford has invented a "Perpetual Calendar" which, for its ingenuity and perfection, has received much attention and praise.

CHARLES ILDERTON CROFT.

Croft, Charles Ilderton, the Manager of the Agency Department of the National Provident Institution, of Gracechurch Street, London, E.C., commenced his Insurance career in the year 1861, in the London Office of the Standard Life Assurance Company. His position on the staff of that office he resigned to take the appointment which had been offered him of Agency Superintendent of the Norwich and London Accident Insurance Company, which position he retained for nearly four years, resigning it to return to the staff of the Standard Life as an Inspector, and this appointment he held until the year 1883.

In that year he was offered by the Directors of the National Provident Institution the appointment he holds to-day and which he accepted, and has filled with great ability and to the satisfaction of all concerned.

Mr. C. I. Croft was born in London in 1843, and was educated at Christ's Hospital and King's Coll., London.

JOHN H. CROFT.

Croft, John H., Secretary in London of the Royal Insurance Company of Liverpool, was born in 1843, and entered the Insurance world about thirty-two years ago in the office of the Globe Insurance Company, Cornhill. When the amalgamation of the Globe with the Liverpool and London took place, Mr Croft was offered and accepted a position in the Liverpool Office of the Royal. Before long his abilities were recognised by his appointment as Chief of the Agency Department in the London Office of the Company under Mr. J. B. Johnston, the then Secretary. Here he spent ten years, doing much to the building up and extension of the Agency Department. He then transferred his services to the Scottish Commercial, being appointed Resident Secretary in London for that office. In 1880, Mr. Bongard, the Assistant-Secretary of the Royal in London, died, and Mr. Croft was offered the position, which he accepted, and when, in 1885, Mr. Johnston retired after forty years' service, he was appointed by the Directors to succeed to the important office he holds at present.

J. F. L. CROSLAND, M.Inst M.E.

Crosland, J. F. L., M.Inst.M.E., is the Chief Engineer of the Boiler Insurance and Steam Power Company, with headquarters at Manchester. After passing through an apprenticeship as a locomotive engineer, during which time he acquired a thorough mastery of the details of his craft, he worked for some years on his own account as a consulting engineer in Manchester, and amongst other things, in conjunction with Mr. J. S. Crosland, introduced the Crosland Patent Compound Engine and other inventions and improvements in the steam engine to the public. In 1863 he joined the Boiler Assurance Company as Assistant Engineer, and by his knowledge of, and assiduous attention to his business, materially assisted in the development of an undertaking which was at that time the only one of its kind in existence. Since his appointment to the Chief Engineership of the Company, its business, already large before that event, has rapidly spread, and no less than 30,000 engines and boilers are now insured with and under the careful inspection of the Company. In the course of Mr. Crosland's long experience he has himself had no fewer than from 80,000 to 85,000 boilers under his supervision—an experience probably unique. Besides his high attainments as an engineer, Mr. Crosland is gifted with very pronounced literary and artistic tastes. He has for more than twelve years been a prominent member of the Manchester Arts' Club, of which he acted for some time as Honorary Secretary, and still is a member of the Committee. He is also a popular and familiar attendant at the meetings of the Manchester Literary Club, with which he has been connected for upwards of fourteen years, having also been for some years a member of the Council.

JOHN A. CUNNINGHAME.

Cunninghame, John A., the General Manager and Secretary of the Yorkshire Fire and Life Insurance Company, received his early training in the practice and principles of the Insurance business in the Glasgow Offices of the North British and Mercantile and the Scottish Widows' Fund Assurance Companies. He next entered the office in that city of the Lancashire, from which, while still a young man, he was transferred to the Head Office of the Company in Manchester, receiving the responsible appointment of Fire Superintendent and Chief Clerk. From this position he was promoted by the Directors to be the Resident Secretary of the Company at the Birmingham Branch Office on the occasion of their purchase of the business of the Birmingham Fire Office. After some years here he was transferred to the management of the more important Branch Office at Liverpool, where he distinguished himself by the marked ability and success with which he conducted the business. In 1877 the position of Secretary in London to the Caledonian Insurance Company was vacant, and it was offered to Mr. Cunninghame, who accepted it. Here he remained until 1884, when he was elected to his present position, and the progress of the Company under his management has amply justified the choice of the Board of Directors in selecting him for such an important charge.

THOMAS CROMPTON.

THOMAS COLLINS.

Crompton, Thomas, the Treasurer of the Band of Hope Friendly Society, is a native of Farnworth, where he owns a considerable business. He has been connected from the beginning with the Band of Hope Friendly Society. From the commencement of his business career he had always taken the deepest interest in the condition of the working class and the bettering of it, an end which his resources fortunately enabled him in a great measure to effect. On the founding of the Band of Hope Friendly Society by Mr. Ashton, he immediately perceived what a beneficial effect it would have on these classes, and, addressing all his care towards its promotion, succeeded, by the material help that he was fortunately in a position to afford, in carrying it through the preliminary difficulties of its existence, and setting it on the firm basis on which it now stands.

Collins, Thomas, is the Corresponding Secretary of the Manchester Unity of Oddfellows. Mr. Collins is a Staffordshire man, his ancestors having for many generations held property at Bradley, where several of them were Vicars, and he himself having been born at Stafford in 1830. After receiving his education at the Grammar School at Brewood, he entered a solicitor's office at Wellington for two years, afterwards removing, in 1848, to Wolverhampton, where he worked his way up to be managing clerk to one of the leading firms of solicitors in that town, which post he held for no less than thirty years.

Mr. Collins' first connection with the Oddfellows was in the same year as that in which he moved to Wolverhampton, he being in that year initiated in the Terra Firma Lodge in that town, to which two of his brothers already belonged. Since that time he has never ceased to

display an unremitting devotion to his Order. Elected Secretary in 1851, he held that post for five years, eventually resigning it to take charge of the Widows' and Orphans' fund. He acted as District Auditor for two years ; subsequently being elected Provincial Deputy-Grand Master in 1853, and Provincial Grand Master in 1854 ; and having again served as District Auditor he became for the second time Provincial Grand Master in 1856, the only instance in the whole history of the Wolverhampton Lodge. He suggested and carried out the idea of a Past Grand Masters' Lodge for the purpose of discussion, and also drew up the rules for a Juvenile Branch to be established in the district ; but both these projects flagged at the time, and it was reserved for his later years to see them placed on a substantial basis.

Mr. Collins was one of the originators of the rules as to the appointment of District Auditors, and was the first elected to that post in Wolverhampton. Between 1859 and 1864 he was actively occupied in opening new lodges, of one of which he acted for some time as Secretary.

He enjoys the honour of having attended no less than thirty-seven A.M.C's the largest number but one ever attained by any living member of the Unity ; having been elected to represent Wolverhampton in 1853, and continuing to do so until his election as Corresponding Secretary, excepting Durham, in 1855.

Mr. Collins was elected to his present post in 1878 at Exeter, at a period when the Order was in a violent transition stage from a number of isolated lodges to a single United Body.

Mr. Collins has throughout his career been the recipient of numerous testimonials to the vast services which he has rendered to the Unity.

CHARLES DARRELL

Darrell, Charles, the Secretary of the Union Assurance Society, of Lombard Street, London, is a Yorkshireman, being the third surviving son of the late Mr. John Darrell, of West Ayton, in the county of York. He received the first portion of his education at Mr. Potter's Academy in Scarborough, whence he proceeded to St. Peter's School at York—an educational establishment that has succeeded in turning out several men who have risen to eminence in science, art, and letters. After leaving school, he entered the service of the Union Assurance Society in the capacity of a Junior Clerk, in January, 1857, being then little more than sixteen years of age. He had opportunities given him of learning much concerning general Insurance business and the details pertaining thereto by being employed at various times in different departments, in each of which, by utilising the facilities afforded him, he gained much experience that has been of great value to him in later years. Eventually, the ability he had shown warranted the management of the Society in their giving him a position in the Secretary's office. In this department he remained, and in the year 1874, when a vacancy in the Secretaryship, occurred consequent on the resignation of Mr. Clement J. Oldham, Mr. Darrell was selected by the Board of Directors to receive the honour of an offer of the appointment. This he accepted, and in fulfilling the duties thereof has won golden opinions from all with whom he has been brought in contact, not only from his colleagues but from those working under and with him.

GRIFFITH DAVIES.

Davies, Griffith, of the Head Office of the Alliance Assurance Company, in London, was the Managing Director of the Shropshire and North Wales Assurance Company. He is nearly related to several well-known and eminent Insurance men, being a nephew of Mr. Griffith Davies, F.R.S., the late Actuary of the Guardian Life Office of London (author of the standard text book "Davies on Annuities"), and is also a cousin of his namesake, the late Actuary of the Law Life Assurance Society, nd Consulting Actuary to the Provincial Life Office, amalgamated with the Alliance.

After a London Grammar School education, Mr. Davies entered upon his Insurance career, in the year 1855, on the staff of the Westminster Fire Office, under the guidance of Mr. Charles E. Fothergill, and in 1861 was appointed to a position in the Head Office of the Royal Insurance Company in Liverpool. Four years later (in 1865) he entered the service of the London and Lancashire Fire Office in London, and when the Head Office of that Company was, in 1867, transferred from London to Liverpool, he was ordered to that centre.

In September, 1868, Mr. Davies was appointed by the Alliance Assurance Company to the position of Chief Clerk at their Birmingham Branch Office. In the year 1878, on the death of Mr. Elsmere, he was selected by the Directors of the Shropshire and North Wales Fire Assurance Company, Shrewsbury, to fill the position of Managing Director thereby rendered vacant, and the appointment was held until the amalgamation of that Office with the Alliance, in January, 1890.

Dames, B. H., Assistant-Secretary of the Colonial Mutual Life Assurance Society Limited, in London, commenced his Insurance career in 1879 in the London Office of the Staffordshire Fire Insurance Company, afterwards the London and Staffordshire. In 1881 he entered the service of the Standard Fire Office, and at the end of the following year obtained an appointment in the London Office of the Standard Life Assurance Company, leaving that Office in 1886 to take up the duties of Chief Clerk in the Colonial Mutual. He was promoted to his present position of Assistant-Secretary upon the retirement of the late Secretary in 1889.

CHARLES DAVEY.

S. KENNARD DAVIES.

Davey, Charles, the Secretary of the Crown Accident Insurance Company, Limited (Bristol), began his commercial career with ten years' service in a Mercantile Counting House. This was followed by a four years' service in the office of a firm of chartered accountants in London. In March, 1885, he became more particularly associated with Insurance by taking the post of Chief Clerk in the West of England and South Wales Branch of the Scottish Accident Insurance Company at Bristol. Here he remained until June, 1887, when, on the formation of the Crown Accident Insurance Company, he resigned that position to take up that which he at present holds.

De Paiva, Ernest Augustus, Sub-Manager of the Foreign Department of the North British and Mercantile Insurance Company in London, was born at Heckmondwike in Yorkshire. He entered the service of the Mercantile Insurance Company in 1862, within the first year of its foundation; and in 1874 was made Chief Clerk of the Foreign Department of the North British and Mercantile. In that capacity he acted until 1878, when the Directors appointed him Foreign Agency Inspector. He visited and reported upon the salient features of a large number of the European, Colonial, Transatlantic and other fields of Fire Insurance to which the vast business of this Company extends, and was also engaged in the practical work of selecting and appointing representatives and opening up many new agencies and sundry branches. In the year 1886 he was promoted to the appointment he at present holds.

Davies, Shelly Kennard, is the Deputy-Underwriter of the London Assurance Corporation. He commenced his career in the London Office of the Thames and Mersey Marine Insurance Association in 1863, and resigned his appointment there in 1870, to take one in the Thetis Marine Insurance Company, which was then started. The disastrous character of underwriting business in 1872 brought this among other young companies into liquidation, and Mr. Davies in 1875 went into the employment of the late Mr. Henry Burnand, of Lloyds, who had formerly been Underwriter to the Thames and Mersey. A year later he was admitted a subscriber to Lloyds, and commenced business on his own account as an Insurance Broker, a business he continued to conduct until he was elected to his present position in 1886.

JAMES DAVIDSON.

GORDON DOUGLAS, F.F.A., F.I.A.

Davidson, James, the General Manager of the Scottish Employers' Liability and Accident Assurance Company, is a native of Methlick, Aberdeenshire, where he was born in 1846, and where he also received his education in the Parish School up to the time of his entering the Aberdeen University. While at the latter place of learning he pursued his studies with credit, obtaining honourable mention as an English and Classical Scholar. On leaving the University he entered upon a commercial life in Aberdeen, where he has had a highly successful career for over a quarter of a century. Immediately on the passing of the Employers' Liability Act in 1880, the leading Employers in the North of Scotland were amongst the first to combine in their own self-defence, the outcome of which combination was the formation of the Scottish Employers' Liability and Accident Insurance Company, of which Mr. Davidson was appointed General Manager.

Mr. Davidson is one of the very few men who, without previous training, have made a mark in the Insurance profession as Managers. And, remarkably enough, the conspicuous success that has attended his career is associated with a class of Insurance which has proved the most difficult branch of Accident business. Mr. Davidson gave up his profession of accountant ten years ago to organise the Scottish Employers' immediately the Employers' Liability Act was passed, and his Company claims to have been the first to offer Employers an assurance against their liabilities under that Act and the Common Law of Great Britain. The success of his management may be estimated from the fact that both as regards Premium, Income and Reserve Funds, the Scottish Employers' Liability and Accident Assurance Company holds a position which no other Accident Company has ever yet been able to attain to in so

short a period of existence. In social circles, Mr. Davidson is held in high esteem, and has been the recipient on more than one occasion of valuable testimonials from the members of his staff, not the least among them being his own portrait in oil, by Mr. A. D. Reid, as an evidence of "their appreciation of the brilliant services which Mr. Davidson has rendered the Company, and to mark the high respect in which he is held by them."

Douglas, Gordon, F.F.A., F.I.A., Actuary of the Life Association of Scotland, is the son of the late Dr. James Douglas, of Edinburgh, and has spent the whole of his business career in the service of the Association, having entered it in 1873; and, after gradually and steadily working his way up through the various stages, being appointed Assistant-Actuary in 1885, and further promoted in 1891 to his present important position as Actuary to one of our largest Life Offices. Mr. Douglas is well known in the Actuarial world, and early in his career filled successively the offices of Treasurer and Vice-President of the Actuarial Society of Edinburgh. He was elected a Fellow of the Faculty of Actuaries in 1884, and in 1885 we find him appointed Secretary to the Faculty, an office which he held for about two years. In 1890 he was elected to a seat at the Council Board of the Faculty of Actuaries, which position he still holds. He was elected a Fellow of the Institute of Actuaries in 1887. In 1888 he read a paper before the Actuarial Society of Edinburgh, entitled "Statistics as to the Mortality Experience among Assured Lives engaged in the Liquor Trade," since printed as one of the Transactions of the Society, and in which the author entered very fully into his subject, and proved that the customary extra premiums on such lives are not only justified but absolutely necessary.

T. C. DEWEY, F.I.A.

Dewey, Thomas C., F.I.A., has been one of the Managers of the Prudential Assurance Company Limited of London since 1873. He was born in the year 1840, and in his seventeenth year (1857) entered the service of the Company who still retain his services. He has made the last four Quinquennial Valuations of the Industrial Branch of the Prudential, a work each time of colossal magnitude ; and in 1889 he gave voluminous evidence before the Select Committee of the House of Commons on Friendly Societies, his examination extending over three days. In the following year, 1890, he also was called before the House of Lords' Committee on Children's Assurance, when he gave much valuable evidence. Mr. Dewey is a Member of the Council of the Institute of Actuaries.

Dove, John Matthew, the Secretary of the Liverpool and London and Globe Insurance Company, is the son of the late Mr. Percy M. Dove,

for many years the well-known Manager of the Royal Insurance Company at Liverpool, and received his early training under his father in that Company's Head Office until the year 1863, when, on the death of his father, and the consequent promotion of Mr. McLaren, the former Sub-Manager, to the Managership, Mr. Dove in his turn took Mr. McLaren's place. Here he remained for five years. In 1873, on the retirement of Mr Swinton Boult from the active management of the Liverpool and London and Globe Insurance Company, and the appointment of Mr. Henry Thompson, the former Sub-Manager, in his stead, the Directors of the Company were forced to look round for a new Sub-Manager, and their choice fell on Mr. Dove. In this capacity he acted for three years, when at the end of that period, in 1876, he was called upon, on the sudden death of Mr. Thompson, to take the whole weight of the management upon himself, which he has since done with great credit to himself.

DAVID DEUCHAR, F.I.A., F.F.A.

Deuchar, David, F.I.A., F.F.A., the Manager and Actuary of the Caledonian Insurance Company of Edinburgh, was born in that old city on the 11th of September, 1843. His first training in the Insurance profession was received in the Head Office of the Standard Assurance Company under the late Mr. W. T. Thomson. In 1866, after passing the necessary qualifying examinations of the Faculty of Actuaries he was appointed Assistant Actuary to the Office of which he is at present the Chief Officer. Three years afterwards (1869) he went to the Edinburgh Insurance Company to fill the position of Joint Actuary, and to this post he was afterwards apponted, in addition, Joint Secretary. In the year 1875, Mr. Deuchar returned to his old office—the Caledonian—to take his present position, and since that date the Company has made rapid, and at the same time solid progress. His Actuarial honours have been very high. He has been a Member of the Council of the Institute and Honorary President of the Actuarial Society; he has been employed as Actuary to the City of Glasgow Bank Relief Fund, the East [Coast Disaster Fund, the Royal Bank of Scotland Officers' Widows Fund, and various other Funds. In the year 1889 he had the honour of being selected, with Mr. A. H. Bailey and Mr. R. P. Hardy, to recommend terms for the fusion of the Bonus scheme of the Scottish Provincial Insurance Company with that of the North British and Mercantile. The literary work of Mr. Deuchar has been mainly devoted to that branch peculiarly belonging to his profession and has always been of a high standard. Among his writings may be mentioned the paper he contributed in 1874 to the Journal of the Institute of Actuaries on the "Interpretation of the Statements required by the Life Insurance Companies' Act, with Reference to Expenses," and also an elaborate examination of the expenses of Life Offices, which appeared anonymously in *The Review* at the latter part of 1881, and which was afterwards re-printed in an abridged form in the Journal of the Institute of Actuaries in 1882. As mentioned, he was the Honorary President of the Actuarial Society, and in volume I. of the new

J. J. W. DEUCHAR, F.I.A., F.F.A.

Series of the Transactions of that Society is a paper which he contributed on "The 5th and 6th Schedules of the Life Assurance Companies' Act," and when in 1887 he was again elected to the Presidency of the Society he gave an Inaugural Address on "The Progress of Life Assurance Business in the United Kingdom during the last fifty years." This is printed in the second volume of the before-mentioned same Series of Transactions.

Deuchar, J. J. W., F.I.A., F.F.A., the Actuary and Secretary of the Norwich Union Life Insurance Society of Norwich, was born in Edinburgh. In the year 1868 he made his first connection with the Actuarial and Insurance profession by becoming a member of the staff of the Standard Life Office in his native city. For nine years Mr. Deuchar remained in that Office, gaining much valuable experience both by practice and observation, and at the same time by studying deeply the theories and practice of Actuarial Science. He passed the final examination of the Faculty of Actuaries, and in the year 1877 he was appointed to the onerous and responsible post of Assistant-

Actuary to the City of Glasgow Life Insurance Company. While holding this position he continued his studies, reading law in the ancient University of Glasgow, and passing well in that subject. It was while he was holding this position that the Insurance and Actuarial Society of Glasgow commenced its work, and of this Society it may be said that Mr. Deuchar was practically the originator and the founder. This was followed by the honour of election to a Fellowship by both the Faculty and the Institute of Actuaries.

For a number of years Mr. Deuchar has been one of the Public Valuers appointed by the Lords of the Treasury under the Friendly Societies' Act of 1875, and since the year 1883 he has been Examiner in Actuarial Science to the Institute of Accountants and Actuaries of Glasgow. To Insurance literature, Mr. Deuchar has been a wide and valuable contributor. He has written numerous papers on Actuarial subjects, several of which have afterwards appeared in the columns of the Journal of the Institute of Actuaries, and others have been published in the transactions of the Glasgow Society.

Douglas, Robert R., is the Manager of the United Kingdom Marine Mutual Insurance Association, Limited; the United Kingdom Small Damage Indemnity Association, Limited; the Running-Down Indemnity Association, Limited; and Joint Manager of the Steamship Owners' Underwriting Association, Limited.

Mr. Douglas is a native of Hartlepool, and the son of Rev. James Douglas, who was for over fifty years Presbyterian Minister of that town, and who is known as the "Father" of the Presbytery of Darlington. At fifteen years of age he was articled to the late well-known firm of Messrs. E. S. Jobson and Co., the business of which is now carried on by Messrs. George Horsley and Co, West Hartlepool. Messrs. Jobson and Co. were at that time the Hartlepool agents of the Neptune Marine Insurance Company, Limited, of West Hartlepool, and the work of the agency, including the preparation of policies, was always carried on by the apprentices. Mr. Douglas was, therefore, identified with underwriting at the commencement of his business career. After oversix years with this firm, in 1873, he left the Hartlepools, and was for about a year and a half in the office of Monsieur A. Farouet, shipbroker, Rouen, France, where he acquired the French language. In 1875 he commenced business in Liverpool as a Ship and Insurance Broker, where his French connection brought him considerable business. In 1879 he formed the United Kingdom Marine Mutual Insurance Association, Limited, at Liverpool, for the insurance of sailing vessels, and undertook its management, the chief objections to Mutual Marine Insurance at that time being the length and intricacy of the rules. To overcome this, he adopted—or, rather, inaugurated—a system of issuing a policy on Lloyds' form without rules

ROBERT R. DOUGLAS.

voiding the insurance in certain trades, substituting warranties, easy of reference, for such rules. The United Kingdom was a success, and it is still one of the largest Mutual Associations for the Insurance of sailing vessels in Great Britain. In 1882 he formed and undertook the management of the United Kingdom Small Damage Indemnity Association, Limited, for indemnifying owners of first-class iron and steel sailing vessels against the risk of particular average under 3 per cent. of vessels' value. This Association, which was the pioneer of Small Damage Associations for iron sailing, still continues to be the largest such Association. It was, however, in the winter of 1883 and 1884 that he brought before the public that form of Mutual Insurance with which his name is most closely identified, for it was then that he originated the "premium basis" of Mutual Marine Insurance, now so well known to shipowners. Associating himself with Mr. B. M. Bannatyne, Mr. Douglas, in 1884, undertook the joint management, in conjunction with that gentleman, of the Steamship Owners' Underwriting Association, Limited, of Liverpool, and in February, 1887, Messrs. Douglas and Bannatyne opened offices at 9, Crosby Square, London, E.C., and established and undertook the management of the Steamship Owners' (London) Underwriting Association, Limited.

In 1885 Mr. Douglas formed and undertook the management of the Running-Down Indemnity Association, Limited, to cover vessels valued at less than £8 per ton against the oftentimes very serious risk of damage done in collision.

Mr. Douglas is the author of a very useful work, entitled "Index to Maritime Law Decisions," published by Messrs. Stevens and Sons, Chancery Lane.

J. L. BROWNE.

Browne, J. L., is Secretary of the Cardiff Mutual Iron Steam-Ship Insurance Association. He is a native of Newcastle-on-Tyne, and commenced his business life in the office of Messrs. Tyzack, Whitely and Company, North Shields, after which he was for two years employed in the Bank of England, in London. Mr. Browne next went into the ship brokering business, and was shortly afterwards appointed to his present position.

Dunn, Michael. Secretary to the Cardiff Mutual Iron Steam-Ship Insurance Association and Joint-Secretary to the West Coast Steam Ship Assurance, was born at Wreckenton, in the county of Durham, in 1859, and commenced his Insurance career in 1874, in the office of the Tyne and Wear Iron Steam Ship Insurance Association, remaining in the employ of that Company at their offices in Newcastle until 1883, when he was appointed to a higher position in the North of England Iron Steam-Ship Insurance Association. He relinquished the last-named appointment in January, 1884, to take up his present important position with the Cardiff Mutual Iron Steam-Ship Insurance Association. Mr. Dunn is also Joint-Secretary of the West Coast Steam-Ship Insurance Association having their offices in the Exchange, Cardiff.

Duncan, Alexander, is the General Manager of the Scottish Union and National Insurance Company at its Head office at Edinburgh. Mr. Duncan, who is a Scotchman by birth, was formerly engaged in Edinburgh for a number of years in the capacity of Manager in that city for the Alliance, or, as it is called in Scotland, the Insurance Company of Scotland; the latter Company's business having been bodily taken over by the Alliance. Mr. Duncan resigned his post with the Alliance to remove to Liverpool, in order that he might take up the duties of Sub-Manager to the Liverpool and London and Globe, under Mr. Dove. He was recalled to Edinburgh, in 1889, to become General Manager of the Scottish Union and National on the retirement of Mr. McCandlish from that post.

Duncan, J. H., F.I.A., is the Fire Manager of the Royal Exchange Assurance Corporation. Mr. Duncan previously served as Assistant-Secretary at the London Office of the Royal Insurance Company, which post he resigned in 1890, on receiving his present appointment.

J. J. DYMOND, F.I.A.

Dymond, Joseph John, the Principal Officer and Consulting Actuary of the Friends' Provident Institution, was born in 1825, and after leaving school at the age of fifteen, entered the service of the Devon and Cornwall Banking Company, where he remained for seventeen years, passing through all the stages of office, from Junior Clerk to Branch Manager. In the year 1857, he was selected by the Directors of the Friends' Provident Institution to succeed their deceased Secretary, Mr. Benjamin Ecroyd, who had filled that post since the foundation of the Institution, twenty-five years before. Since that time, Mr. Dymond's business history has been simply that of the Institution of which he was the Chief Officer, a quiet almost uneventful history, marked by a steady progress, year by year, as great, perhaps, as was possible for an office with so limited a constituency. Mr. Dymond's efforts as Secretary and Manager to the Friends' Provident Institution have long been directed to the liberation of the Life Assurance contract from troublesome and unnecessary conditions and restrictions, in some of which changes his Office led the way; and he has eventually had the satisfaction of witnessing the practical removal of every condition but the payment of the Premiums from the Life Policies of the Institution. Mr. Dymond is a Fellow of the Institute of Actuaries, to which honour he was elected, not by examination—for his practical work gave him no time for such tests—but as the reward of merit. Since 1880, he has been compelled by failing health to gradually lessen his attention to business, and in 1889, he finally ceased to be an executive officer of the Institution, retaining, however, a certain amount of connection with it as Consulting Actuary, and for the purpose of the Statutory returns to the Board of Trade, Principal Officer.

Engelbach, Harold, F.I.A., is the Actuary and Secretary, and, indeed, the principal official of the National Assurance Company of Ireland. Mr. Engelbach is, perhaps, and deservedly, one of the best-known and most highly-respected Insurance Managers in the United Kingdom. He was born on November 4th, 1838, and having been educated with a view to his father's profession of an actuary, he commenced his business career in the Colonial Office, where he continued till his change to the Alliance Assurance Company, in which office the industry that he had displayed in his first post, and which was still continued with never-flagging perseverance, was rewarded by his advancement to the position of Chief Clerk in the Life Department; and on the retirement of his father, who had hitherto occupied the post of Actuary to the Alliance, he became jointly responsible with Mr. M. Adler, who at present remains in the same post alone, for the actuarial duties. In 1870, he was appointed to his present post in the National of Ireland, in succession to Mr. Todhunter, the former Secretary. Mr. Engelbach's career as Secretary has been most successful, the Company, under his management, having since his connection with it taken over the business of the Liberal Annuity Company, of Dublin,

HAROLD ENGELBACH, F.I.A.

in 1876, of the Dublin Widows' Fund in 1878, and of the Great Britain Mutual Life Assurance Society in 1882; from all of which accretions to its own well-patronised established business it received others of considerable value. As an instance of the progress which it has made since Mr. Engelbach's accession to the management, we may state that the first account published under the Life Assurance Act of 1870, the year—it will be remembered, in which he joined — disclosed the Life Income from all sources —premium and interest — to have been £18,900, while in 1888 the Life Income from all sources was £39,400, or more than double the former sum. The Fire Income as shown by the first account in 1870 under the above-mentioned Act, was £13,012, while in 1889 it was £192,600, or nearly fifteen times the former amount. The National Assurance Company of Ireland has earned prosperity by the quality of the Insurance granted by it, which is of the very best, and which is in a great measure due to Mr. Engelbach's influence. Mr. Engelbach holds a very enviable position among Insurance Managers. He is recognised as a man of broad views, excellent judgment, and endowed with the qualities which mark him out as a leader amongst his fellows.

JOHN WILKINSON FAIREY.

Fairey, John Wilkinson, the Sub-Manager of the British Equitable Life Assurance Society of London, was born in 1837, and was appointed to his present position in 1868.

Dawson, Alfred, the Secretary of the Merchants' Marine Insurance Company Limited, of London, was born in May, 1841, and received his education first at Mill Hill Grammar School and afterwards at the Mansion School, Leatherhead, Surrey. In June, 1858, he made his *début* in the Insurance world with a firm of underwriters and insurance brokers, with whom he remained five years. This was followed by four years' experience with a large firm of ship brokers, whom he left to take up the appointment of cashier and accountant of the Merchants' Marine, when that Office started in

June, 1871. In 1875 he was appointed to be Assistant-Secretary to the Company, receiving the further promotion to his present appointment in 1880.

Ells, Charles G., is the Deputy Underwriter to the British and Foreign Marine Insurance Company, at their London Office. Mr. Ells received his early training in the office of the Universal Marine Insurance Company, which he entered immediately on leaving school, and gradually worked his way up through the various departments of the office until, on the retirement, owing to failing health, of the late Mr. W. T. Putchett, he was appointed Deputy Underwriter of that Company, subsequently transferring his services in the same capacity to the British and Foreign.

CHARLES G. ELLA.

J. T. FATHERLY.

Fedden, Alfred Player, Assistant-Manager of the Hong Kong and Fine Art Insurance Companies, is the son of the late Olcher Fedden, Secretary of the Bristol Branch of the Liverpool and London and Globe Insurance Company, and commenced his Insurance business in the London Office of the Yorkshire Insurance Company. In 1886 he removed to the London Office of the Northern Assurance Company, whence he was in 1887 transferred to the Bristol Branch of the same Company. In 1888 he resigned his post with the Northern to take up that of Chief Clerk to the Hong Kong Fire Insurance Company, and in 1890 he was promoted to be Assistant-Manager to the two Companies.

———

Ferguson, James, is the well-known underwriter of the Northern Maritime Insurance Company, Limited, of Newcastle-on-Tyne. He is a native of Newcastle, and served his apprenticeship with Messrs. Nelson, Donkin and Co., steamship owners of that city, and at the beginning of 1875 he entered the offices of the Northern Maritime Insurance Company, Limited, of which the late Mr. Nelson was chairman, and of which Mr. Stanley Mitcalfe (the present chairman) was Secretary and Underwriter, and in January, 1881, he was appointed underwriter, which position he has since held with great credit to himself and to the Company's advantage.

Fatherly, J. T., Manager of the North-Eastern Plate Glass Insurance Company at Newcastle-on-Tyne, entered upon his Insurance career in 1886 with the Northern Accident Insurance Company in that town. After having remained in their service for three years, he severed his connection with them to accept the post of District Superintendent of the Accident Department of the London, Edinburgh, and Glasgow Assurance Company, which position he held till March, 1890, when he resigned it to take up his present post with the North Eastern Plate Glass Insurance Company, having acquired a good deal of experience in this class of Insurance when in the service of the Northern Accident. About six months later he was again offered the post of District Superintendent to the London, Edinburgh and Glasgow (Accident Department), which he accepted, so that he now occupies the two posts.

———

Fisher, Frederick, Sub-Manager of the Prudential Assurance Company, Limited, of London, was born in the year 1845. After receiving a sound commercial education, he entered the service of the Prudential in 1858, and has remained with them ever since, passing through various grades and departments until 1879, when he was appointed to his present position.

Foley, P. J., M.P., the Managing Director of the Pearl Life Assurance Company Limited, of Adelaide Place, London Bridge, E.C., was born in the year 1836, and is therefore now in the fifty-third year of his age.

In the year 1864 Mr. Foley founded the Office with which his name has since been so prominently connected. From very small beginnings it has grown till now it has an income exceeding a quarter of a million sterling, and with invested funds amounting to over two hundred and ten

Mr. Foley has proved himself to be possessed of all the qualifications necessary for the conduct of such a gigantic and complicated institution as a large Industrial Life Assurance Company. The skill of a military commander, the ability of an actuary, and the power of institution in the highest degree, are all in such a case necessary for success, and here in this case have met the coveted reward.

Fisher, Richard Charles, F.I.A., was the Actuary of the Economic Life Assurance Company

P. J. FOLEY, M.P.

thousand pounds. From the date of its commencement of business to the end of last year, the amount this one office has paid out in claims approaches three-quarters of a million sterling.

Nor does this work, gigantic as it is, approach the completion of Mr. Foley's life's labour. He was, in the year 1886, selected by the late Mr. Parnell, M.P., to be one of his most prominent lieutenants; and as Member of the House of Commons for Galway his reputation as a politician has grown as high as that which he holds in the Insurance world.

for about twenty years (from 1869 to 1889). He received his early Insurance training under Mr. Rainbow, the late Actuary of the Crown Life Office, the service of which Company he entered in the year 1840 as special assistant to the Actuary. In this office he remained upwards of twenty-nine years, eventually becoming its Assistant-Actuary. On retiring, Mr. Fisher was presented by the Directors of the "Crown" Life Assurance Company with a very handsome testimonial of plate. Mr. Fisher is a member of the Actuaries' Club.

A. FORROW.

Forrow, Alexander, is Secretary of the British Branch of the Mutual Life Insurance Company of New York. His introduction to Insurance commenced nearly twenty years ago, when, as Secretary to the Associated Docks Committee of London, he acted as Minute Secretary at the important and protracted conferences in relation to the warehousing of produce, which took place between the Directors of the Fire Offices and Dock Companies of London. In this capacity, and during subsequent years, he acquired a valuable knowledge of the principles which govern the classification of goods and fire risks. On the amalgamation of the Dock Companies of London, in the latter part of the year 1888, Mr. Forrow, with a number of other leading Dock officials, retired. But his extensive commercial experience and powers of control, having for many years had charge of the staff organization of the East and West India Dock Company, were well known in the city, and having thus made many powerful friends, he found himself in the fortunate position of being able to make choice of several advantageous appointments, which immediately offered. On the advice, however, of his friend Colonel Birt, of the Millwall Dock Company, he turned his attention to Life Insurance. The Mutual Life Insurance Company of New York had but recently commenced operations in Great Britain. A careful examination of the claims of that Company satisfied Mr. Forrow that a prosperous career awaited it in this country,

a forecast since abundantly justified. An interview with Mr. Haldeman, the able General Manager, followed. It did not take long for each man to recognize in the other what both were seeking. In a few straight words, Mr. Haldeman told Mr. Forrow there was a valuable post for the man who could be found to fill it. Mr. Forrow replied that he would not wait to be told to go if he failed to prove himself to be that man. With this understanding he joined the Company as Agency Superintendent, and applied himself with such success to the duties of his new position that, at the end of the year, he was appointed Secretary. Mr. Haldeman's action in making this appointment was freely criticised at the time. But events have proved the soundness of his judgment in the estimate he formed of Mr. Forrow, who, though well enough known in commercial circles, was comparatively new to Life Insurance work, and personally, a total stranger to him. We may add that Mr. Forrow is a man of considerable literary attainments, he is a well-known lecturer on historical and biographical subjects, and his book on "The Thames and its Docks" is a standard work of reference to all desiring information on the origin and history of the Docks of London. Although he has done so much work, Mr. Forrow is still in the prime of life, and looks forward to many years of service with the great Company with which he has identified his fortunes.

Fortune, David, the Secretary of the Scottish Legal Life Assurance Society of Glasgow, has been for very many years connected and prominently identified with the leading Friendly Orders in Scotland, and other movements which tend to the amelioration of the industrial classes.

Like most of our large Industrial Corporations, the Scottish Legal has had a severe crisis to pass through; there were serious dissensions within its ranks, and serious attacks from the outside; and at the same time the whole question of Industrial Assurance was being freely, and in some cases somewhat unjustly, criticised. At this juncture Mr. Fortune threw in all his influence and experience with the "reform party" of the Society. For some considerable time this agitation had been going on, but Mr. Fortune's influence and energy turned the scale in the right direction, and the Society was saved. Its affairs were brought (through his work) prominently before the House of Commons, with a result that the Chief Registrar called a special meeting of the Members in the City Hall, Glasgow, which was presided over by Mr. James Wallace, Advocate, of Edinburgh. At this meeting a new

DAVID FORTUNE.

code of rules was adopted, and Mr. Fortune received the reward of his labours by being elected the President, and the confidence the members had in his ability, and the appreciation they had of the able manner in which he carried out the re-organization of the Society and conducted its affairs, was shown by their twice re-electing him to fill that important office.

While he held this position the funds of the Society were increased from £170,131, to £264,899, while the management expenses were very considerably reduced.

Eighteen months after he took office, a Quinquennial valuation of the affairs of the Society was made by Mr. Charles Prentice, F.R.S.E., and through the efforts of Mr. Fortune, backed as they were by his colleagues, £20,000 of the large surplus then declared was laid aside as a bonus to be distributed among the members. At the last valuation made in 1889 by Mr. James Meikle, F.I.A., F.F.A., and Mr. Campbell K. Duff, C.A., F.F.A., a further surplus of £22,237 was shown.

On Friday, 18th of July, 1890, Mr. Fortune was examined before the Select Committee of the House of Lords on Infantile Insurance, and was complimented by the President of the Commission (the late Archbishop of York—then the Bishop of Peterborough) on some of the regulations of the Scottish Legal he (Mr. Fortune) had been instrumental in introducing.

In June, 1891, owing to the resignation of Mr. W. W. Bain, who had for nearly eight years held the post of Secretary of the Society, and had received an important appointment in Australia, at the Annual Meeting of the delegates, a successor had to be appointed to this important office. At the request of Representatives of the Staff and other sections of the Society, Mr. Fortune accepted nomination for the post, and he was unanimously elected Secretary of the Society.

In addition to his duties as President of the Scottish Legal, Mr. Fortune was Chairman of the Congress of Friendly Societies, by whose efforts the Bill introduced in the year 1887 by Sir John Lubbock, M.P., for the Amendment and Consolidation of the Friendly Societies' Acts was drafted.

G. H. FORSTER.

ERNEST C. FOWKE.

Forster, George Henry, the Managing Director and Founder of the Leeds and North of England Boiler and Accident Insurance Company, Limited, of South Parade, Leeds, was born in the West End of London, in the year 1844.

His business career began with an apprenticeship to the woollen trade, but this branch of commerce was evidently not congenial to his taste, for he abandoned it very shortly after completing his indentures to accept an appointment as traveller and collector on the staff of the Boiler Insurance and Steam Power Insurance Company, Limited, of Manchester. In this position he was very successful, so much so that, after a very few years' service, the Board of Directors of that Company promoted him to take charge of their business in the Yorkshire District. This appointment necessitated his residing in Leeds, where the business and his abilities soon enabled him to build up a very valuable connection for the Office whose interests he then represented. While doing his best in this sphere he gained the confidence and esteem of many of the leading firms in the City of Leeds and the surrounding districts, and in other parts of the County of Yorkshire, during the first two years of his residence among them.

He soon instinctively recognised the desire existing among the firms and gentlemen with whom he was doing business for the establishment of a local office for undertaking the insurance (with regular inspection) of boilers, and also against accidents of every kind. He therefore devoted his abilities and energies to the establishment of an office that should cover this ground on the "Mutual" principle. In this he was so far successful that in 1883 the Company was "floated," and operations were forthwith commenced. The word "mutual," however, among

the hard-headed Yorkshiremen, seemed to have a prejudicial effect, and the directors decided to re-register the Corporation as a proprietary Company. This was done, and no difficulty was found in allotting the shares, as the Company started with an influential Directorate.

Mr. Forster, in addition to the credit attaching to him as the promoter and founder of a successful and prosperous Insurance Company, enjoys a high reputation in social life.

In the year 1870 the members of the staff of the Company, of which he is the official head, presented him with an artistically-illuminated address, together with a handsome and costly case of dessert knives and forks as a mark of the high esteem in which they held him and their appreciation of the efforts he had made in their best interests.

Fowke, Ernest C., the Secretary of the British Workman's Assurance Company, was born in 1860, and received his education at the Grammar School, Atherstone, Warwickshire, where he distinguished himself both as a scholar and an athlete. He was then articled to his father, the Chairman of the British Workman's Assurance Company, and a Solicitor, and, after finishing his articles with a London firm, was appointed Solicitor to the Company. In this capacity he remained for five years till 1890, when he was requested to undertake the duties of Secretary to the Company, in addition to those which he had already been carrying on. Mr. Fowke's two appointments entail a considerable amount of work, but by hard work and perseverance he has overcome all difficulties and settled down to an already very successful career.

Fothergill, Charles George, is the Manager and Secretary of the London and Lancashire Fire Insurance Company. He entered the Insurance profession in 1849, commencing his business life, in fact, in the Westminster Fire Office. After twelve years' service with that Company, he received the appointment of Assistant Secretary at the Head Office of the Royal Insurance Company, being subsequently, in the latter part of the same year, transferred to a similar post in the London Office of the Company. There he remained till 1868, when he returned to Liverpool as the Sub-Manager, which post he occupied for six years, eventually, in 1874, accepting the offer made to him of the Managership of his present Company. The London and Lancashire, at the time of Mr. Fothergill's accession to office, was not in a very flourishing condition; the business requiring a thorough reorganization and reform. Mr. Fothergill was the very man to carry these out; and by his powers of resolution and capacity for business, together with the large experience which he had gained in his previous career, for all of which, indeed, he had been selected by the Directors, he not only succeeded in removing all former causes of dissatisfaction with the conduct of the Company, but started it on a career of prosperity which it has maintained ever since, and still continues to maintain. Amongst other evidences of the vast increase in the reputation of the Company may be instanced the fact that its name is now as prominent and as powerful on the American Continent, in the Colonies, and all over the world, as it is at home.

Mr. Fothergill's strict maintenance of discipline in his business is no doubt one great reason of his success in raising his Company to its present pitch of prosperity; but he is, nevertheless, of a genial kind-hearted nature, well-informed, and most generous in his allowance for the failings or idiosyncrasies of others. He has not contributed very largely towards Insurance literature, but a paper read by him before the Institute of Actuaries as long ago as 1857, "On the causes of fires in London during the twenty-four years from 1833 to 1856 inclusive; with some remarks on the deduction of correct rates of premium," deserves notice from its treatment of the risk-classification system and the impulse it gave to the re-adjustment and amendment of many of the faulty systems of the various companies then in existence.

CHARLES G. FOTHERGILL.

Frankland, Frederick William, F.I.A., is the Assistant-Actuary of the Atlas Assurance Company of London.

He is a son of Professor Frankland, of London, and was born in the year 1854. After receiving a sound education at University College, London, he chose for a profession that in which he has done so much good and able work.

His first connection with the Insurance World was made in 1876, when he received an appointment on the staff of the New Zealand Government Life Insurance Department. Here he remained until 1878, when he was appointed Actuary for Friendly Societies in the Registrar-General's Department of the same Colony.

His abilities and skill as an Actuary had become so widely known that in 1884 he was offered the high appointment of Actuary (afterwards Commissioner and Actuary), of the New Zealand Government Life Insurance Department. This position he accepted, and took up his duties in February, 1884.

While holding this post he did much good work in reorganising portions of the working of the department, in popularising its system and Life Insurance generally in the Colony, and also in Insurance Literature. Several of the more important of the articles that came from his pen, were re-published by the Government of the Colony in the Registrar-General's reports, and also in the Journal of the Institute of Actuaries. It may also be said that the policy-holders in the Government Life Insurance Department (N.Z.) are largely indebted to Mr. Frankland for many of the privileges they enjoy, they being the result of recommendations made by him while he was in the service of the State.

In March, 1890, Mr. Frankland received an offer of an appointment as Assistant-Actuary of the Atlas Assurance Company, and as it was at the time urgently necessary, for family reasons, that he should return to England, he resigned the management of the Life Insurance Office with which he had become so strongly identified, and entered on his new duties on the 1st of July, 1890.

Mr. Frankland is also the author of a scheme of Diseased Life Insurance, which has been pronounced to be safe by the Consulting Actuaries of the New Zealand Govt. Life Ins. Dept.

Mr. Frankland is a Fellow of the Institute of Actuaries. He first joined that body in 1878, and was elected to the full Fellowship in 1884.

F. W. FRANKLAND, F.I.A.

Gilman, Charles Rackham, J.P., is the Secretary and Founder of the Norwich and London Accident Insurance Association, established in 1856, and also the Secretary of the General Hailstorm Insurance Society. He is the son of the late Mr. Charles Suckling Gilman, who established the latter Society in 1843, and its business is carried on in the same office as the Norwich and London Accident

CHARLES RACKHAM GILMAN, J.P.

Mr. Gilman has done much to benefit his native city Norwich and the neighbourhood. When the Cattle Plague broke out in 1865, he was selected, by reason of his connection with agricultural matters, to become the Secretary of the Norfolk Cattle Plague Association, founded by the leading agriculturists of the county, with a view to mutual assistance and compensation for loss during the continuance of the visitation, and the valuable services which he afforded to the Association during the period of its existence, were specially recognized by the members. In 1882 Mr. Gilman was requested to enter the Town Council in which his father formerly sat in the Conservative interest, with which request he complied, and had no sooner taken his seat than he was elected by the unanimous vote of the Council, Mayor and Chief Magistrate of the City. In this latter capacity Mr. Gilman's well-tried business qualities stood him in good stead, coupled as were with the tact and public spirit necessary for such an office. Among the chief events, of his Mayoralty may be noted the confirmation of the Corporation's rights over Mousehold Heath, of which he was appointed one of the Conservators, and is still Chairman of that body; also the opening of the new buildings of the Norfolk and Norwich Hospital by Their Royal Highnesses, the Duke and Duchess of Connaught. Mr. Gilman has been a Justice of the Peace of Norwich for many years, and a great supporter of the local charities and benevolent institutions of all descriptions. He is much interested in music, and is Chairman of the Committee of Management of the Norfolk and Norwich Musical Festival, with which he has been connected for more than twenty years.

Mr. Gilman, though noted for his adherence to the principles which he has laid down for himself in all matters, whether of business or otherwise, is always most courteous and considerate to his opponents, which has won him the respect of all who have had to do with him, whether as friends or adversaries.

C. STOREY GILMAN.

Gilman, C. Storey, is the Assistant-Secretary of the Norwich and London Accident Insurance Association, of Norwich, and is the son of Mr. Charles Rackman Gilman, its founder. He was educated at Westminster School, on leaving which he travelled abroad for a period of twelve months. On his return to England and his native city, in 1883, Mr. C. S. Gilman entered the service of the Norwich and London Accident Insurance Association, and, after three years' service, and having been called to the Bar by the Honourable Society of the Inner Temple, was promoted to his present post of Assistant-Secretary to his father in November, 1886. Mr. C. S. Gilman is the worthy son of a worthy father, and inherits all that father's gifts; and, though he is still a young man, has already given ample evidence of a distinguished professional and public career lying before him.

Gamble, Alfred Francis Morgan, F.I.A., the Assistant-Actuary of the Equity and Law Life Assurance Society, was born in the year 1859, and was educated at Westminster School. After leaving school he served for a short time on the staff of the Life Department of the Commercial Union Assurance Company. His position with this Corporation he resigned in 1881, to join the staff of the office in whose service he has since remained. In Actuarial circles Mr. Gamble is looked upon as a rising member of his profession.

Freeman, John Robert, the Assistant-Secretary of the General Life and Fire Assurance Company, of London, is a member of Downing College, Cambridge, and is a Barrister-at-Law, having been called to the Bar by the Honourable Society of Lincoln's Inn. He is the only surviving son of the late George Scott Freeman, who was long a Director of the General, and was for twenty years its Secretary. Mr. J. R. Freeman was for some years Counsel to the Company, and on the death of the late William Swain Champness he was selected to succeed him in the position he holds at present. Mr. Freeman is the author of the "Life Assurance Agents' Legal Handy Book," and is a Member of the Reform Club.

WILLIAM SUTTON GOVER, F.I.A., F.S.S., D L.

Gover, William Sutton, F.I.A., F.S.S., D.L., was the Founder of the British Equitable Life Assurance Company, and has been its Actuary, Secretary, and Managing Director from its foundation until to-day. This is not the only Insurance Society that owes its start to the work and influence of Mr. Gover, for he was one of the founders of the British Empire Mutual Life Assurance Society, and at its formation was its Actuary and Secretary, and these positions he held for some seven or eight years afterwards. He was also the Founder and Chairman of the House Property and Investment Company Limited, one of the most prosperous and best of all the numerous land and house investment societies of London. Many others have been founded on its principles or similar ones, but it has always maintained its place at the head of them with ease. Mr. Gover was besides all these one of the original members of the Institute of Actuaries. He has been a member of the Common Council of the City of London since 1867, and in the year 1870 he was elected Member of the School Board for London, for the City of London. He has served numerous Corporation offices, among them being the Chief Commissioner of the Court of Sewers (London), the Chairman of the Bridge House Committee, the Markets Committee, and several other of the Committees of the Corporation. He was also the Deputy-Governor of the Honourable Irish Society; and it must also be noted as not the least among the children of Mr. Gover's fertile brain, is the Perpetual Investment Building Society, which he founded.

In Masonry, Mr. Gover stands as high as he does in Financial and Insurance circles—he is a member of the Grand Lodge, and has filled the offices of President of the Board of Grand Stewards, P.M. Grand Masters' Lodge, No. 1, P.Z., St. James' Chapter, etc.

FREDERIC FIELD GOVER, F.S.S.

Gover, Frederic Field, F.S.S., the Assistant-Actuary of the British Equitable Life Assurance Company, of Queen Street Place, London, E.C., is a son of Mr. William Sutton Gover, F.I.A., F.S.S., the Founder and Managing Director and Actuary of that Society. He was born in London in 1861, and was educated at various private schools up to the age of fifteen, and afterwards for three years under a private tutor.

He received his Insurance training under the effective instruction of his father, and also studied for some time under another leading Actuary. At an early age he entered the service of the British Equitable Society. Here he has since remained, gaining experience in the practical working of each department, and also of the thorough theory of Life Insurance.

Mr. F. F. Gover has a growing reputation in the Actuarial world, in the best circles of which he is looked upon as a young man of much promise and ability.

Gunn, N. B., the Colonial and Foreign Secretary of the Standard Life Assurance Company, gained his first insurance experience in the service of the Scottish Widows' Fund Life Assurance Society, which he entered in 1865, remaining there nine years, at the end of which period he removed to the office of the Scottish Provident Institution. He continued in this office for ten years, from 1874 to 1884, in which latter year he was appointed Assistant-Actuary to his present Company, being subsequently promoted to his present post in 1890. Mr. Gunn is a well-known man in the Actuarial world, having been elected Associate of the Faculty of Actuaries in Scotland after examination in 1869, and Fellow of the same in 1871. In 1886 he was elected Fellow of the Institute of Actuaries, and in 1889 he was appointed Valuer under the Friendly Societies' Acts.

RICHARD GRAYLING.

Grayling, Richard, the Joint Managing Director of the London and Manchester Industrial Assurance Company, was born in London in 1823, and has lived an active life. His earlier years were spent in commercial pursuits, which eventually took him to Manchester, where he soon afterwards determined to turn his attention to Life Assurance business. He was appointed Agent at Manchester for the Friend-in-Need Assurance Society, and, throwing himself into his new vocation with undaunted energy, rapidly acquired a large collection. The formation of the London and Manchester followed, and Mr. Grayling was elected to fill the post of a Director of it. That he possessed the necessary qualifications to occupy the position is amply demonstrated by the unanimous manner in which time after time he has been re-elected to a seat on the Board of the prosperous Company to which he belongs, and of which he has latterly been Joint Managing Director with Mr. William Woodward.

COLONEL J. T. GRIFFIN.

Griffin, Colonel James Theodore, the Chairman of the Executive Council and Treasurer of the English Department of the Mutual Reserve Fund Life Association, is well known in many walks of life, having occupied, and still occupying, many posts of honour and distinction. He has long interested himself with Insurance matters, and has been familiar with the Mutual Reserve Fund from its inception, carefully noting its growth and progress. When it was decided to establish a branch for Great Britain and Ireland he accepted the Chairmanship of the Executive Council, and later on was appointed Treasurer as well. In both these offices he commands the respect of his associates, and adds strength to the Association. He has full faith in the principles on which the Association is founded; and the fact that he occupies so prominent a position gives confidence to all who know him. Colonel Griffin is thoroughly conversant with the theory and practice of Life Assurance. He is a Fellow of various learned Societies, and at present fills the exceptional and honourable post of President of the Baptist Union of Great Britain and Ireland.

W. F. GREENING.

MATTHEW GREGORY.

Greening, W. Francis, Joint Secretary of the Employers' Liability and Workpeople's Provident and Accident Insurance Company, at their headquarters at Birmingham, is a native of that city, and after receiving his education at King Edward's Grammar School, commenced work there for a short time in an accountant's office. On the formation of the Employers' Liability and Workpeople's Provident and Accident Insurance Company, of which Mr. Greening's father was made Managing Director, he left his first employers and entered the service of the Company, with whom he has remained ever since. For some years he worked in the office, but afterwards took up the Inspectorship of Agencies all over the United Kingdom, which post he held till 1889, when, on the death of his father, he was appointed to his present post of Joint Secretary.

Gregory, Matthew, the Agency Manager of the Provident Association of London, is now thirty-one years of age, and commenced his connection with the Association in which he now holds so high a position as an Agent in the year 1881.

In this capacity he displayed such marked abilities that the Directors very soon promoted him to the position of District Manager. Here again his record was so good that he was offered by them the appointment he now occupies, but as he was occupying an important position in a commercial house in the Provinces, in deference to the wishes of his Principal he respectfully declined the offer. Subsequently, the offer was renewed, and this time was accepted, thus enabling Mr. Gregory to identify himself still more closely with the interests of the Association.

Occupying the highest position in the Association under the Managing Director, Mr. Gregory has succeeded in winning the confidence of the thousands of representatives of the Association scattered throughout the United Kingdom. He is also responsible for the Agency Organization of the Provident Free Home Assurance Company, Limited, a separate Company formed to conduct the Life Assurance Department of the Provident Association of London.

GEORGE GRAY.

JOHN H. HAIG.

Gray, George, the Secretary of the City of Glasgow Life Assurance Company, at the Head Office in Glasgow, was educated at the High School of Edinburgh, and afterwards served for some time in the office of an eminent firm of Writers to the Signet in that city, while at the same time he attended the law classes in the University there. In 1845 he entered the service of the City of Glasgow Life Assurance Company, in which he earned and gained promotion from time to time, till in 1860 he was appointed to the responsible post of Secretary, which he still holds, and which was then instituted in that Office for the first time. He has been offered appointments outside of his profession in China and Canada as well as at home, but he preferred remaining in the office where he has now spent so many years of his life.

Haig, John H., is the Secretary of the Goldsmiths' and General Burglary Insurance Association, Ltd. He commenced his Insurance career in the office of the Mercantile Accident and Guarantee Insurance Company of Glasgow, with which office he was associated from its commencement until its amalgamation with the Scottish Alliance, when he entered the service of the latter Company, but left shortly afterwards to accept his present position.

During the period of his association with the "Mercantile," Mr. Haig had ample opportunity, in his capacity as Chief Clerk, of grasping the details of Burglary Insurance, which, as is now generally known, was first introduced to the public by that Company, and the experience gained there should be of much service to him in his new position.

Haldeman, Donald Carmichael, General Manager for the United Kingdom of the Mutual Life Insurance Company of New York, may fairly be regarded as one of the most successful Insurance men in England. To have attained the position of General Manager in these islands for the great Mutual of New York is in itself a *primâ facie* fact of no ordinary significance, but for a man of considerably less than two score—indeed, we believe Mr. Haldeman has not so very long since passed his thirty-second year—not only to have attained, but occupied, that position for nearly five years, may be regarded as unque. Mr. Haldeman was born in Pennsylvania, but he comes from an old and well-known English family, memorials of which are to be seen in more than one of our Metropolitan churches, Westminster Abbey included. Beginning his Insurance life in 1880, as private secretary to the late Mr. N. G. Goodrich, the British Representative of the Equitable Life Assurance Society of the United States, Mr. Haldeman was early initiated into the principles which lie at the root of effective management. The latter years of his service with the Equitable were passed in the active duties of a General Agent. In this department he was so successful that when in the year 1886 he visited America he was offered the British management of the Mutual Life Insurance Company of New York, the Trustees of which had determined to open a Branch in this country, and were, in fact, on the lock-out for a good man. Mr. Haldeman accepted this offer, and in 1887 he commenced operations for the Company by opening the London Office at 17/18, Cornhill. Under his able and skilful management the career of the Company has been

D. C. HALDEMAN.

scarcely less successful here than in the United States, notwithstanding the opposition it has had to encounter. But the Mutual Life started well. It came with a great reputation, and it was fortunate in its selection of a General Manager. The management in New York wisely left Mr. Haldeman, a free hand, with the result that when he came across a good man whom he could thoroughly trust he made it well worth his while to take service with the Company. His selection of the Secretary, Mr. A. Forrow, is an illustration of this. While several of the leading British Offices were what the Yankees would say "fooling around" with this gentleman, Mr. Haldeman went straight for him and secured him, with the result that there is no Company in London represented by two stronger men than the Mutual of New York. Avoiding any kind of competition likely to irritate the British Offices, Mr. Haldeman has run the Mutual Life for all it is worth, and, carefully guarding against ruffling John Bull's prejudices, he has Anglicised the Company to such an extent that so far as its policies are concerned, it is, to all intents and purposes, a British Company. While doing this, he has cleverly kept in the forefront all the undoubted advantages of the American system, with the result that, although less than five years have elapsed since the London Office was opened, and in face of a tremendous competition, its British business to-day will compare favourably with that of the two or three British Offices which stand at the top of the tree. Mr. Haldeman may well be congratulated on his record, and, if we are not mistaken, it will not be his fault if, before he is many years older, the Mutual Life of New York is not as well known in Great Britian as in the United States.

Hamilton, The Right Honourable Lord Claud J., the Chairman of the Employers' Liability Assurance Corporation, Limited, of London, was born at Stanmore Priory, Middlesex, in February, 1843, so that he is still in the prime of life. His father, who died a few years since, was the first Duke of Abercorn, and his mother was Lady Louisa, the daughter of the sixth Duke of Bedford. His aristocratic connections are, therefore, of the most extended kind.

He received his primary education at Bayford, Herts, going from there to the celebrated old school on the Hill at Harrow. He did not go to a University, but entered the army, joining the Grenadier Guards in 1862. He remained with the regiment till the year 1867, when he resigned his commission. In the same year he was appointed Lieutenant Colonel Commanding of the 5th Battalion of the Royal Inniskilling Fusiliers, which command he relinquished for the HonoraryColonelcy in 1891. In 1887 he was appointed Aide-de-Camp to the Queen.

Before leaving the army, he turned his attention to politics, and first entered the House of Commons as Member for Londonderry City, 1865, being then only twenty-two years of age. He was appointed a Lord of the Treasury in Mr. Disraeli's Government. This seat he held until the General Election, in November, 1868, sitting on the Conservative side, but at that election, which returned Mr. Gladstone's government to power, he was unseated. During the two years previous to that he had acted as Aide de Camp to his father, who, for that period had been Lord-Lieutenant of Ireland.

LORD CLAUD J. HAMILTON

In 1869, Lord Claud unsuccessfully contested the borough of Brecon, but in the same year he was returned triumphantly for Kings Lynn, on the seat becoming vacant through Lord Stanley's succession to the peerage, and he sat for that borough until 1880, when he was defeated at the General Election, but was invited a few months subsequently to stand for the important constituency of Liverpool, and accepting the offer he was again successful, polling 21,019 votes. At the two next General Elections he was again returned, but now has for a time retired from active politics, the other demands on his time and work being so enormous, that by the doctor's orders he had to take a rest in this direction, as in some others.

In the year 1871, when the Marquis of Salisbury retired from the Board of the Great Eastern Railway, Lord Claud J. Hamilton was elected a Director in his place, and he so far gained the confidence of his colleagues and shareholders that, four years later, on the Vice-Chairman of the Company retiring he was elected to the vacant position which he holds. This is not his only connection with railways, for he is a Director of the Grand Trunk Railway of Canada, and is also a member of the Superintending Committee of the Railway Clearing House, which is one of the most gigantic and complicated organisations in the world and without which it would be impossible to carry on the intricate railway system of this country.

He has travelled very extensively, and has been round the world.

EDWARD HADFIELD.

JAMES DALBY HOBSON.

Hadfield, Edward, the Secretary of the Boiler Insurance and Steam Power Company Limited of Manchester, was born in Salford in 1847. His father, of whom he is the second son, was the late Henry Henshaw Hadfield, who was for so many years the Honorary Secretary of the Manchester Academy of Arts. The greater part of his education was received at a private school in his native city, and subsequently he attended a Public School where he remained until his commercial life was commenced by his entering the offices of Sam Mendel, one of the most noted merchant princes of Manchester. In the year 1866 he began his Insurance career as a Clerk and Collector in the office in which to-day he holds so high a position. Four years later (1870) he was promoted to the post of Chief Clerk, and this was followed shortly afterwards by the appointment of Chief Superintendent of Agents. The able manner in which he fulfilled the duties of this position led the Board of Directors to give him the still further promotion of the appointment of Assistant-Secretary. In October, 1889, the Secretary of the Company (Mr. Hartley) died, and the Directors then gave Mr. Hadfield his present appointment.

Mr. Hadfield is a member of the Manchester Literary Club, of the Lancashire and Cheshire Antiquarian Society, and of the Arts' Club of Manchester.

Mr. Hadfield's father was a well-known artist in the North of England, and was also a direct descendant of Thomas Henshaw, the founder of the Blue Coat School of Oldham, Lancashire, and of the Blind Asylum, Manchester. An obituary notice appeared of him in all the Manchester papers on the 29th of October, 1887. Mr. Hadfield, senior, was also a cousin of the late Thomas Oldham Barlow, R.A., the celebrated engraver.

Hobson, James Dalby, the Assistant-Secretary of the Queen Insurance Company of Liverpool, at its London Office, was born in Leeds in the year 1849.

After receiving a thorough commercial education he commenced his Insurance career in the service of the Queen Insurance Company. In those days it was the custom to "apprentice" juniors and give them a thorough training in every branch of the business. This admirable idea was originated in Liverpool, and its results, judging by the after careers of the men so trained, has more than proved its efficacy and usefulness. It was in this manner that Mr. Hobson entered the office in which his career has been so marked.

In turn he passed the various departments, gaining experience and practical knowledge in the science of Underwriting in each, and using the information thus gained so well that he gained the thorough confidence of the Management and the Board of the Office. This is proved by the fact that he was appointed Chief of the Life Department.

After this Mr. Hobson was appointed to the position of Chief Clerk in the London Office of the Company, in which he served four years, leaving it on being appointed to the post he occupies at the present time.

W. H. HAMBRIDGE.

Hambridge, William Henry, is the Secretary of the Royal London Friendly Society, of which Institution he was one of the founders.

For over thirty years he has been what may be described as the leading spirit of the most equitably-managed Friendly Society, and one which has done much to popularise Industrial Insurance among the working classes and masses of the community of this country. During the first fourteen years of the existence of the Society, he sat as a member of its Executive Committee, and then took up the more active appointment of Secretary, the duties of which office he has continued to discharge to the present time.

He has been chiefly responsible for the admirable organization of this Institution, and can congratulate himself on the fact that the Institution he has done so much to foster and bring to its present position has paid away in death claims very nearly a million sterling.

Hardy, Ralph Price, F.I.A., was born on the 29th of August, 1838. His Insurance career was commenced in May, 1854, when he entered the service of the Eagle Life Insurance Company, and in the same year he joined the Institute of Actuaries. In February, 1868, he was appointed to the position of Chief Clerk of the Mutual Life Society, and less than two years later (in December, 1869), he was offered and accepted the appointment of Actuary and Secretary to the London and Provincial Law Life Assurance Society. Upon the merging of this Office into the Guardian Fire and Life Assurance Company, he was appointed the Manager of the Courts Branch of the latter Company. In February, 1887, he retired from this position, and, in the following July, was appointed Actuary and Secretary of the British Medical and General Life Assurance Company, Limited, having been (in conjunction with Mr. A. H. Bailey) appointed by the Court of Chancery, one of the Actuaries to report upon the affairs of the Office and to prepare the reconstruction scheme. In 1875, Mr. Hardy was selected and appointed to be the Consulting Actuary to the United Kingdom Temperance and General Provident Institution. To Actuarial Literature, Mr. Hardy contributed "Valuation Tables," in 1873; "Old Age Pensioning: with reference to certain pro-

to work to re-organise the whole of the working and staff of the Corporation. The thoroughness with which he set about his task may be understood by the fact that he succeeded in obtaining the appointment of a new Actuary and Underwriter, and he has been remarkably fortunate in the new colleagues selected to work with him, as each in their own particular departments have

E. R. HANDCOCK.

posed schemes, and to the existing Poor Law provision ;" and "On the formulæ for determining the value of benefits, according to the principle of collective assurance," and he has a large consulting practice. He has also been recently appointed Consulting Actuary to the Securities Insurance Company, Limited, of Old Broad Street, E.C.

Handcock, E. Robison, the Secretary of the Royal Exchange Assurance Corporation of London, is a native of Queen's County, Ireland, and comes of a family that has written its name boldly on the history of the world in the Army and elsewhere.

He was appointed to his present position in 1874, and with characteristic energy at once set

been able to show results that have been more than gratifying to all and each interested.

That he had many difficulties to meet and overcome while carrying out this work will go without the saying, but he did surmount them all, and also succeeded in establishing Branch Offices, with all the necessary organisation to each in Manchester, Birmingham and Liverpool, and other chief cities of the United Kingdom.

The first report of the Corporation that it issued. was given to the public in 1889, and it fully proved the beneficial result of Mr. Handcock's energy. He has also earned the gratitude of the staff in perpetuity by the founding and carrying so far to a successful issue of a Pension Fund for the Clerks of the office.

HENRY HARBEN, F.I.A.

Harben, Henry, F.I.A., L.C.C., the Vice-Chairman of the Prudential Assurance Company, Limited, of London, was born in Bloomsbury in 1825.

On completing his education he commenced business life as a surveyor and soon gained a valuable and important connection, but the attractions of the Insurance profession were too strong to resist, and he consequently entered upon what has proved to be his life's vocation.

This was in the year 1851, when he received the appointment to the important position of Accountant to the Prudential Insurance Company, the office with which he has ever since been connected, and in the remarkable rise and progress of which he has taken so very prominent and active a part.

Four years later (in 1855), Mr. Harben was promoted to the Secretaryship of the Company, and from that day its rise from comparative insignificance to its present proud position, may be fairly said to date. It is not too much to say, and it is a fact generally admitted by the Insurance fraternity, that what the Prudential is, it owes almost entirely to the genius, the ability, the energy, the enterprise, and the power of organisation of Mr. Harben.

In the year 1874, when by its position the Prudential had become the leviathan of the Insurance world, with its many hundred *employés*, and its complicated but perfectly organised machinery was in thorough working order, Mr. Harben considered his active life's work done, and he consequently resigned the Secretaryship and became a Director and Deputy-Chairman, in which position he continues to aid the Company by his advice and experience.

Mr. Harben is a Fellow of the Institute of Actuaries, and has contributed to the transactions of that body, having read before them papers on Vital Statistics, etc.

He was a member of the Old Metropolitan Board of Works, and on that Institution being displaced by the London County Council, he was returned by a handsome majority of votes to that important body.

COLONEL CHARLES HARDING, F.S.S.

Harding, Charles, F.S.S., F.R.G.S., the Manager of the Accident Insurance Company of London, is a scion of an old Devonshire family, and was born in London in 1834. He was introduced to the Insurance World by Mr. Arthur Scratchley, M.A., the eminent Actuary, and under him he received his early training. For some time he held the position of Assistant-Secretary of the Western Life Assurance Society, which office was established in 1842, and on the formation of the Western Fire Insurance Company, Limited, of London and Manchester, in 1864, he was appointed its Secretary. The business of this Company was subsequently taken over by the Alliance Assurance Corporation, and Mr. Harding shortly afterwards (in 1869) succeeded the late Cornelius Walford as Manager and *ex-officio* Director of the Accident Insurance Company, Limited. He has for many years taken an active interest in the Auxiliary Forces, and originally was a member of the Honourable Artillery Company. He is a Corresponding Member of the Council of the Royal United Service Institution, and, in 1885, he was gazetted as the Honorary Colonel of the Fourth Volunteer Battalion of the Queen's Royal West Surrey Regiment. He was elected to the Fellowship of the Royal Statistical Society as long ago as 1857, and to that of the Royal Geographical Society in 1864. He is besides a member of several other learned and scientific societies, and of several well-known clubs. He has been a voluminous contributor to current literature both in prose and verse, and has acted as Dramatic Critic for journals of repute; he is further a Grand Officer of the Ancient Order of Free and Accepted Masons.

W. H. HAYWARD.

Hayward, William Henry, the Founder, Organiser, and General Manager of the British Natural Premium Provident Association, Limited, of London, has had a long and extensive Insurance experience.

After some years of a very successful commercial career he entered the Insurance world early in 1873. The connections and experience he had gained in his business life, and which he availed himself of to the fullest extent, soon enabled him to gain a prominent position as an Underwriter in the field of Life Insurance.

In the year 1875, he became connected with the New York Life Insurance Company, in the service of which Office he was very successful, and was soon promoted to a responsible position, being appointed District Manager for that Office in the important district of Yorkshire and Durham with headquarters at Bradford. This position he held from 1878 to January, 1887, when he resigned it to return to London.

It was in the latter year that the Mutual Reserve Fund Life Association decided to extend its operations to Great Britain, and Mr. Hayward was selected by its Management to open the field, organise its agency staff here, and supervise its business with the position of General Manager. In this he was so successful that he was eventually made a Council Officer of the Association. For three years he held this appointment, opening and starting several branches and numerous agencies. In September, 1890, on the Head Office deciding on a reorganisation of its European staff, Mr. Hayward resigned this appointment, and shortly afterwards commenced the organisation of the Association of which he is the present Official Chief, and which began business in the Autumn of 1891.

Hendriks, Frederick, F.I.A., the Actuary and Secretary of the Universal Life Assurance Society of London, was born in 1827, and holds the unique position of being the senior practising Actuary in London, his first appointment as Actuary being dated as far back as 1847.

In that year, before he had reached his twentieth birthday, he was selected to succeed the late Mr. Hulley as Actuary to the Globe Insurance Company, and this position he held for over twenty-two years.

In 1864, when that Company was amalgamated with the Liverpool and London, Mr. Frederick Hendriks, though entitled by the Act of Parliament regulating the amalgamation, to become the Actuary to the joint Companies, voluntarily resigned the appointment he had held for so many years with such great credit to himself, and in the same year (1864) he was offered and accepted the position he fills at present, holding at the same time also the offices of Consulting Actu-

FREDERICK HENDRIKS, F.I.A.

ary to the Clergy Mutual Assurance Company, to the Equitable Reversionary Interest Society, and also to several Railway and other Superannuation Funds.

Mr. Hendriks is very nearly the Senior Member of the Council of the Royal Statistical Society and also of the Actuaries' Club. He is a Fellow —under its Charter—of the Institute of Actuaries. In addition, he is an Honorary Member of the Economic Society of Madrid, and also of the International Statistical Institute.

To the Transactions of all these learned Societies, as well as to the press, Mr. Frederick Hendriks has been a frequent, valuable, and voluminous contributor on subjects connected with the Science and Practice of Insurance, General Statistics, International Coinage, and also Political Economy.

He has also given evidence before several Royal Commissions both at home and abroad. It was as some recognition of this that the late King of Sweden voluntarily conferred on him the Honour of Knighthood of the Order of Vasa ; and in France he took the second place among the candidates nominated for the Corresponding Membership of the Institute of France. His life may, therefore, be justly said to be full of honours.

It may be noted that he is an elder brother of Mr. Augustus Hendriks, F.I.A., of the London Office of the Liverpool and London and Globe Insurance Company.

A career so distinguished marks him as one of the most prominent Insurance men of the world. He has the esteem of all his colleagues, as well as of all who have had the honour as well as pleasure of serving under or with him.

AUGUSTUS HENDRIKS, F.I.A.

Hendriks, Augustus, [F.I.A., F.S.S., Vice-President of the Institute of Actuaries and the Actuary and Resident Secretary in London of the Liverpool and London and Globe Assurance Company, was born on the 12th of March, 1834. In 1852, he entered the service of the old Globe Insurance Company, with whom he remained until the completion of the amalgamation of that Office with the Liverpool and London in 1864, when he was appointed to the position of Actuary to the combined Companies, which appointment (to which had been added that of Resident Secretary in London) he continues to hold. The value of the services he has rendered were acknowledged by the Chairman of the Company at the last annual general meeting of the share-holders, by his saying that Mr. Hendriks' work had been given throughout with "good judgment and steady quiet persevering industry." Mr. Hendriks' reputation as an Actuary stands very high, as is evidenced by the fact of the position of Vice-President he holds in the Council of the Institute.

Henshaw, E. S., the Secretary of the Builders' Accident Insurance Company, Limited, is also the Secretary of the Central Association of Master Builders in London. The latter body founded the Accident Company in 1881, and appointed Mr. Henshaw to the position he has held to the present day.

Hewat, Archibald, F.F.A., F.I.A., Secretary of the Edinburgh Life Assurance Office, having served his apprenticeship and clerkship in the Head Offices of the Scottish Equitable, and of the Standard respectively, has passed the rest of his Insurance career in the service of that Company, having become its Resident Secretary in Glasgow at an unusually early age, his success there resulting in his promotion to the post which he now holds. Mr. Hewat is looked upon as one of the leading Insurance authorities of the day, has contributed largely to Insurance literature, and is frequently being called upon to deliver lectures on Insurance subjects to the various Insurance Institutes of the United Kingdom. He has passed the President's chair of the Edinburgh Institution Club formed, in 1865, for the purpose of keeping up old friendships and promoting the welfare of the scholars. He takes an active interest in other institutions of more or less local importance, such as the Actuarial Societies of Edinburgh, and of Glasgow, of which he is a member; the Chartered Accountants' Students Society, of which he is an Extraordinary Member; the Institute of Bankers in Scotland; and of Accountants in Glasgow, of which latter he is an Honorary Member; and the Philosophical Society of Glasgow, of which he

ARCHIBALD HEWAT, F.F.A., F.I.A.

was an Auditor and Member of Council (Social Economy Section), to all of which he has delivered lectures. Also the Scottish Women's Benefit and several other Friendly Societies, all of which he has aided in every way in his power, and not least by his agreeable presence and kindly advice at their meetings. He has held the post of Public Valuer, by appointment, of the Lords of H.M.'s Treasury. He is a Fellow, by Examination, and has been a Member of Council, of the Faculty of Actuaries in Scotland; he is also a Fellow of the Institute of Actuaries, London; and of the Royal Statistical Society. Mr. Hewat's father was a J.P., a Director of the Chamber of Commerce, of the Merchant Company, and of the Philosophical Institution. He was the originator of the one o'clock time gun on Edinburgh Castle, so well-known to all inhabitants of that city. His partner was Sir James Spittal, once Lord Provost of Edinburgh. Mr. Hewat is Vice-President of the Edinburgh Peeblesshire Society of which his grandfather, the Rev. William Marshall, of Manor, was the founder, and which is the oldest but one of the Edinburgh clubs. Mr. Hewat is married to the only daughter of the late Andrew Fergus, M.D., M.R.C.S., Eng., a distinguished member of the medical profession.

Hobson, Henry Gamble, the present Manager and Official Actuary of the Star Life Assurance Society, of Moorgate Street, London, was born in the County of Suffolk, in the year 1845. He received the first part of his education at King's College, London, whence after a successful record he passed the Matriculation Examination of the London University, from which in due course of time he graduated, and obtained a first-class certificate in Mathematics from New College.

He entered the service of the Star Life Office in 1864, being appointed to the position of Assistant-Secretary under his father, the late Mr. Jesse Hobson, who at that time was fulfilling the duties of Secretary of the Institution. Mr. Jesse Hobson, it may be noted, was the second gentleman to fill the post of Secretary in the history of the Star Life Office.

Mr. W. W. Baynes, F.I.A., F.S.S., succeeded Mr. Jesse Hobson in the position of Secretary, and held that post for almost nineteen years. During all this period Mr. Henry Gamble Hobson was pushing his way and gaining very valuable experience. His original appointment of Assistant-Secretary he retained, and in addition was, in successive order, given the responsible duties of Chief Clerk, and further of Official Actuary, and while acting in the latter capacity, gave very valuable assistance in every way to the Actuarial organisation of the Office. For the last four quinquennial valuations he has been practically responsible, and each

HENRY GAMBLE HOBSON.

one of these has received the commendations not only of the Insurance Press but also of Mr. Hobson's Actuarial *confrères.* Mr. Hobson has thus attained many years' actual experience, involving the highest degree of practical knowledge, practice, and work, and the effect that work has had is placed plainly in evidence by the figures of his office since.

In the year 1890, Mr. W. W. Baynes, F.I.A., F.S.S., was compelled, through ill-health, to resign his position, and Mr. Henry G. Hobson was by a unanimous vote of the Board of Directors, chosen to succeed him, and he then took up the duties of the position he holds to-day.

When Mr. Hobson took charge of the Actuarial business of the Society, the affairs of the Office were at a fairly steady ratio. What he has done to improve on this is shown by the figures of the last two valuations:—in 1883, the number of policies in force for valuation purposes was 25,014, and at December 31st, 1888, the corresponding number of policies was 30,918, a great increase, and an increase that is likely to tell largely in the future growth of the Society in funds, etc.; whilst the new business has leaped up from £863,415 in 1889, to £1,706,000 in 1891. The last valuation as well as the previous one was made on the basis of $3\frac{1}{4}$ per cent., assumed (Institute of Actuaries H.M.). Mr. Hobson was formerly a Fellow of the Institute of Actuaries.

EDGAR HORNE.

Horne, Edgar, the Chairman of the Prudential Assurance Company Limited, was born in Clapham, near London, in the year 1820, and was unanimously elected to his present position in 1875.

From its formation he had been a member of the Board of Directors of this Institution which has now grown to such enormous proportions, and he may be fairly said to have watched over and assisted to guide its best interests from the start and its early years of struggles. He is thus able to fully realise how very often small beginnings rightly managed lead to great endings.

Mr. Horne is the senior partner in the well-known firm of Horne, Son, and Eversfield, of Parliament Street, Westminster, the Government Auctioneers and Surveyors.

In municipal life Mr. Horne has for many years held a very prominent position. He has held many civil offices, and is a member of the West-minster Court of Burgesses, and in addition to this he holds several parochial appointments both in St. Margaret's and in Bloomsbury.

He has proved himself to be a most able man of business, and beyond question has been a very great and powerful factor in the rise and progress of the gigantic Corporation of which he is the Official Chief, and, therefore, has exercised and continues to do so, a unique and great influence on the Industrial progress and thrift of the nation itself.

Hodgson, Matthew, the Secretary and Principal Officer of the Clergy Mutual Assurance Society, was born in 1841, and in 1860 joined the staff of the Office of which he is now the Official Head. He is the grandson of the Reverend John Hodgson who was the founder and first Secretary of the Society, on whose death, in 1871, he was appointed to his present position.

WILLIAM HUGHES, F.I.A.

Hughes, William, F.I.A., one of the Managers of the Prudential Assurance Company, Limited, was born in London, on the 12th of December, 1839. His Insurance career commenced in the year 1858, when he entered the service of the Consolidated Insurance Company as Clerk, and in the employ of that Corporation he remained until 1865, when it was absorbed by the Prudential Office, and Mr. Hughes was one of the officials taken over with the business, so that practically it may be said that the whole of his Insurance Life has been spent in one office. In 1871, he passed the final examination of the Institute of Actuaries, and in the same year he was admitted to a Fellowship. Two years later he received his present appointment, in which his powers of organisation and his thoroughly practical as well as theoretical knowledge of Insurance matters have had full scope. Mr. Hughes is the author of a paper on "The Insurance Clauses of the Married Women's Property Act," which he read before the Institute of Actuaries, in December, 1887, and which was afterwards printed in the Journal of the Institute.

Humphreys George, M.A., F.I.A., F.S.S. etc., the Actuary and Secretary of the Eagle Insurance Company, of London, and the Honorary Treasurer of the Institute of Actuaries, made his first connection with the Actuarial world by becoming an Associate of the Institute of Actuaries shortly after he left Cambridge in 1853. He subsequently resigned his membership of the Institute on entering the service of the Government. In 1870, he retired from this on the abolition of the office he had held. He was appointed to the Eagle Assurance Company in succession to the late Mr. Charles Jellicoe, and in the same year he rejoined the Institution of Actuaries, of which he has since filled the offices of Honorary Secretary and a Vice-President.

EDWARD PATTEN HUGGETT.

Huggett, Edward Patten, is Assistant-Secretary of the Gresham Life Assurance Society. He entered the Gresham in November, 1864, as the Head of a Department, was subsequently appointed Under-Secretary, and, in 1883, Assistant-Secretary. Mr. Huggett devotes his attention mainly to the Foreign branches of this large Institution, and is held in high esteem by all the Continental representatives of the Society, and his long and faithful services are fully appreciated by the Board and by his colleagues at the Head Office. Mr. Huggett takes an active interest in public work in the district in which he resides. He has been for some years a Member of the Local Board of Health, and was recently elected to a seat on the School Board.

Hill, Gray, is the Secretary of the Liverpool and London Steamship Protection Association Limited, and of the Liverpool Shipowners' Mutual Protection and Indemnity Association Limited, which offices he has filled since the foundation of both Associations, the second in 1873 and the first in 1881. He has also been the Secretary of the Liverpool Steamship Owners' Association and of the American Chamber of Commerce at Liverpool since 1867, and was for seventeen years Secretary of the North Atlantic Steam Traffic Conference. Mr. Hill is Senior Partner in the firm Hill, Dickinson, Dickinson and Hill, of Liverpool, Solicitors, having a large shipping and mercantile practice; he is Past President of the Liverpool Law Society, a Vice-President of the Association for the Reform and Codification of the Law of Nations, and a Member of the Council of the Incorporated Law Society of the United Kingdom. He is also a Director of the Law Debenture Corporation Limited, Law Guarantee and Trust Society Limited, and the Liverpool Reversionary Company Limited. Mr. Hill has taken an active part in discussions and arrangements as to the proper form of Contracts of Affreightment in regard to the several interests of Shipowners, Merchants, and Underwriters, and all kinds of legislation affecting Merchant Shipping. He is also the author of an interesting book of travels, called "With the Bedouins."

THOMAS HARRIS.

SAMUEL HUNTER, A.I.A.

Harris, Thomas, Secretary of the Guardian Plate-Glass Insurance Company at the Head Office of that Company at Manchester, commenced his business life in a mercantile house in that same city, which he entered in 1872. In 1874, he obtained an appointment in a public institution in Manchester, which has since been taken under the control of the Civil Service, and where he remained till 1878, when he became Shorthand Clerk and Correspondent to a firm of Land, Estate and Insurance Agents. In 1881, he was appointed to a similar position with his present Company, which he held till 1886, in which year, on the Secretaryship becoming vacant, Mr. Harris was selected to fill that position. Mr. Harris' business is an important one, extending not only over Great Britain but including also a large Continental business.

Hunter, Samuel, A.I.A., Actuary and Superintendent of the Life Department of the Patriotic Assurance Company, has occupied that post since 1879, previously to which he was for fifteen years connected with the Scottish Widows' Fund. He is an Associate of the Institute of Actuaries by Examination. Mr. Hunter has a high reputation in the scientific world as an astronomer, having, previous to his connection with the Insurance profession, been Assistant to the late Earl of Rosse. He was afterwards selected by the late Astronomer Royal, Sir G. B. Airy, to take charge of the Suez Station for the observation of the Transit of Venus, in 1874. Several of his drawings of Nebulæ are published in the Transactions of the Royal Society, amongst others the "Great Nebula of Orion." A series of his drawings of portions of the moon's surface were photographed by the late Countess of Rosse, and copies privately circulated with a descriptive pamphlet. In the Memoirs of the Royal Dublin Society appears a paper by him describing the "Machines used for Polishing Specula,"

R. ALDINGTON HUNT, F.S.S., A.I.A.

Hunt, R. Aldington, F.I.A., F.S.S., the General Manager of the Wesleyan and General Assurance Society, of Birmingham, was born in the year 1842, and is consequently now in his forty-ninth year.

His first connection with the Insurance world was made through the Office of which he is now, and has been for several years, the official head and guiding spirit. This was in the year 1857, when he was but fifteen years of age. He worked his way assiduously through every department, and acquired a thorough practical acquaintance with the intricate details of the working and the organisation of a large Industrial Assurance Office. In the practical work he proved his ability very early, and his power of knowledge of the theoretical side of the science of Life Insurance, is shown by his gaining the Associateship of the Institute of Actuaries, and a Fellowship of the Statistical Society of London.

In the year 1871, he was appointed to be the Secretary of the Society, for which his knowledge of the affairs of the Office peculiarly fitted him, and the duties of this post he discharged with much credit to himself, and advantage to the Society for nearly twelve years. In 1883, Mr. Lewis, the General Manager of the Society, retired, and the Board of Directors unanimously chose Mr. Hunt to fill that important position. He accepted that offer, and his career since is too well-known to need recapitulation here, since it would be but re-writing the history of the most flourishing part of the career of the Wesleyan and General Life Assurance Society.

Mr. Hunt is one of the best-known and most respected of Industrial Insurance officials in the country, and his popularity among the Agents of the organisation he rules is remarkable.

JOHN HUGHES.

JAMES INWARDS.

Hughes, John, of the Underwriting Staff of the Reliance Marine Insurance Company, first commenced business in the office of Messrs. Price and Cox, Underwriters, of Liverpool. On that firm, in 1864, deciding to turn its private business into a Limited Company, the Maritime Insurance Company was formed, and Mr. Hughes entered the service of the Company, thus becoming thoroughly conversant with the various details of the business. In 1886 he was promoted to be Underwriter, in which capacity his ability, energy, and tact did much to enhance the importance of the Maritime Insurance Company. He resigned his position in 1891, to take up that which he occupies at present with the Reliance Marine.

———

Inwards, James, is the Agency Manager of the British Equitable Assurance Company, with which institution he became connected in 1856, and since which time he has rendered it 35 years' faithful service. He is both capable and genial, and is therefore greatly esteemed by the Company's Agency Staff.

ARTHUR JACKSON.

Jackson, Arthur, the General Manager of the English and Scottish Law Life Assurance Association, of 12, Waterloo Place, London, was born at Wisbeach, Cambridgeshire, in the year 1839. He is the son of the late Mr. Edward Jackson, a very well-known solicitor of that town.

It was originally intended that Mr. Jackson should follow his father's profession; consequently his education was shaped to that end, and at the Final Examination for Solicitors in Michaelmas term, 1860, he appeared in the list as Second Prizeman.

After being admitted, he joined the firm of Charles Druce and Sons, Solicitors, of Billiter Square, London, E.C., afterwards Druces, Jackson and Attlee. As a partner he remained with this firm from the year 1863 to 1883, in which latter year he retired from practice.

He then turned his attention to the higher branch of the legal profession, and four years later (in 1887), he was called to the Bar by the Honourable Society of Lincoln's Inn.

In the month of March, 1888, Mr. Jackson first joined the Board of Directors of the English and Scottish Law Life Assurance Association, and sat as a Director of that Company until the following December, when a certain amount of re-organisation of the staff being decided upon by the Board, Mr. Jackson acquiesced in the general wish of his colleagues, and took the position of General Manager of the Institution—the same appointment that he holds at present.

O. B. JEENS.

RICHARD T. JONES.

Jeens. Octavius Brown, is the late Manager of the Mutual Accident Association Limited, now Manager of the Accident Department of Palatine Insurance Company Limited.

In 1872, upon the death of his brother, the late T. E. Jeens, he succeeded him as District Agent and Surveyor at Gloucester to the Liverpool and London and Globe Insurance Company, which appointment he held until the end of 1877. Early in 1878, he became attached to the London Office of the Mutual Fire Insurance Corporation shortly after its advent to the Metropolis, where he took an active part in securing its present valuable connection. In 1881, after the passing of the Employers' Liability Act 1880, the Directors and Manager (Mr. J. N. Lane) of the Mutual Fire decided to establish the Mutual Accident Association, with its Head Office at Manchester; and Mr. Jeens was selected to be its Manager and Secretary, a post which he held until that Company (following the example of its parent, the Mutual Fire) became merged into The Palatine Insurance Company, of 32, Brown Street, Manchester, and where he is now to be found in charge of its Accident and Guarantee Department.

Mr. Jeens ranks as one of the foremost Accident Insurance Officials in this country, of which business he has an experience extending over a number of years.

Jones, Richard T., the Assistant Underwriter in the Marine Department at the Head Office of the Commercial Union Fire and Life Assurance Company of Cornhill, London, enjoys a very high reputation among his fellow-workers in the science of Marine Insurance.

His business career commenced in the offices of Messrs. Dumas and Wylie, an establishment which has earned for itself the self-explanatory soubriquet of "the cradle of Underwriters." On the staff of this firm he remained for thirteen years, resigning his position then to take up the appointment of Deputy-Underwriter to the National Marine Insurance Company of London. This post he held for five years, vacating it on accepting the offer of his present position with the Commercial Union.

E. D. JONES.

Jones, E. D., Director-General of the British Department of the Mutual Reserve Fund Life Association of New York, has devoted the most part of his life to banking, but was induced by Mr. Prest Harper, of the Mutual Reserve Fund, to identify himself with that undertaking in the earlier years of its existence. In 1887, on the decision of the Directors of the Association to carry its business into the United Kingdom, Mr. Jones was amongst those selected to carry out this important scheme, and the two years of his first sojourn in London show an honourable record for himself and a satisfactory one for the Association. He then removed to Glasgow for another period of two years, where he was equally successful in overcoming the scruples of the cautious business men of Scotland, and the present important post which he holds is a fitting testimony to the appreciation in which his organizing powers are held by the Association.

EDWIN JUSTICAN.

W. KENT LEMON, F.I.A.

Justican, Edwin, F.I.A. and **F.S.S.**, is the Principal of the Actuarial Staff of the Gresham Life Assurance Society of London. He was born on the 10th of October, 1841, so is now in the full prime of his life. His Actuarial career has been a most distinguished one. He was elected a Fellow of the Institute of Actuaries in the year 1869, and he holds the certificate of competency of the Institute. In 1884, Mr. Justican acted as Examiner of the Students of the Institute of Actuaries, and in 1887 he was appointed by the Treasury one of the Actuaries under the Friendly Societies Acts (1875). In 1879, he first entered the service of the Gresham Life, and with them he has since remained.

————

Lemon, W. Kent. F.I.A., is the Secretary of the National Insurance and Guarantee Corporation Limited, which has recently been formed, Mr. Lemon was previously the London Secretary of the City of Glasgow Life Assurance Company, and has had a thorough training in Insurance matters. He is a Fellow of the Institute of Actuaries.

GEORGE KING, F.I.A.

King, George, F.I.A, Actuary and Principal Officer in the Life Department of the Atlas Assurance Company, began his commercial life in the office of a large East India firm. Leaving Commerce for Insurance in 1870, he entered the service of the British Imperial Insurance Company, as Agency Inspector at its London Office. From this, in 1871, he was promoted to be Secretary to the London Board of that Office. It is on record that in both these appointments he rapidly acquired an extensive experience of the practical side of the Insurance work, and gave evidence of his business aptitude by the valuable assistance he gave to his Company in enlarging their connections. In 1874, he accepted the position of Actuarial Assistant in the Head Office of the Alliance Assurance Company, and remained with them in that capacity till 1883, when he was selected as the Secretary to the Glasgow and London Office, which appointment he accepted. This he held until October, 1885, when his abilities were further recognised by the offer of his present post. His career since is known to all Insurance men. Mr. King is, and has been for some time, a very prominent Fellow of the Institution of Actuaries. For a good many years past has been a member of its Council, and in 1891 he was elected Honorary Secretary. He was formerly lecturer at the Institute on the "Science of Life Contingencies," and the Council showed still further appreciation of his abilities by deputing him to write its text book on "Life Annuities and Assurances. and their practical Application," which was afterwards published by the Institute. In addition to this, Mr. King wrote and published a volume which has become a standard work, on "The Theory of Finance" Besides these he is the author of many contributions to Actuarial literature, which have been always recognised as being of the greatest value to students and members of the profession. The effect of his work on the business of the Atlas has been very marked ; it will be remembered that in 1889 the Directors, on his advice, resolved to reduce the rate of interest assumed in the valuations of the Life business of the Company to the unprecedented low figure of $2\frac{1}{2}$ per cent., thus enabling the Office to claim the proud position of being one of the "strongest Life Companies in the World."

THOMAS KYD.

FRANCIS LAING, F.I.A.

Kyd, Thomas, is the Resident Manager at the Aberdeen Office of The Northern Assurance Company. A native of Dundee, and for many years clerk to a firm of linen exporters there, he was, in 1871, appointed Secretary to the Company's branch in that city. The Northern's Fire engagements in the Dundee district had been of considerable magnitude ever since, in 1858, it absorbed the Forfarshire and Perthshire Fire Insurance Company. The latter office, enjoying an influential local connection, had for more than thirty years transacted an important share of the insurance business of the East of Scotland. Under Mr. Kyd's charge the success of the branch was further developed, until, in 1885, he was translated to Aberdeen, the birthplace of the Company, and one of its Head Offices. Mr. Kyd is a Fellow of the Institute of Actuaries, as well as of the Faculty in Scotland. In 1890, he prepared a lecture by request of the Actuarial Society of Edinburgh, choosing the subject of "Taxes on Production and Trade." This title savours quite as much of political controversy as of insurance theory. Mr. Kyd, however, interests himself in things outside of the strict lines of the profession. This is indicated by the offices which he holds in sundry Aberdeen institutions. He is President of the Chamber of Commerce, and Vice-Chairman of the Young Men's Christian Association, and is Treasurer of the Association for improving the condition of the poor, and of the Association for the promotion of technical and secondary education. He is a Justice of Peace for the county of Aberdeen.

———

Laing, Francis, Secretary of the Northern Assurance Company at the office of that Company at Aberdeen, is a native of that city, and received his education at the University there. He commenced his career in the Insurance profession in 1870, in which year he entered the service of the Northern Assurance Company, removing his place of residence to London to work in the Office of the Company there. He remained in London for fifteen years, during which period he was for some time employed in the Secretary's Office; subsequently being transferred to the Life Department, of which he was Head Clerk for a considerable number of years. At the end of that period (in 1885) he was appointed to his present Secretaryship at Aberdeen, which post he has held ever since. Mr. Laing is a Fellow of the Institute of Actuaries (which honour he obtained as the result of examination), and is also a Fellow of the Faculty of Actuaries.

CRAWFORD D. KERR.

ALEXANDER LAWSON.

Kerr, Crawford D., is the Secretary of the Straits Fire and Marine Insurance Companies of Singapore. He joined the Straits Marine about seven years ago, as its agent in Hong Kong, and two years after was appointed Secretary to the Head Office. In 1886, he formed the Straits Fire Insurance Company, which has recently opened a branch in London. Mr. Kerr has had a business experience in the East extending over a period of thirty years; he is most energetic and a good organiser. He will soon come to London, and exchange places with Mr. Murray, the Manager here, who will proceed to Singapore and take up Mr. Kerr's duties at the Head Office.

Lawson, Alexander, is Assistant-Secretary at the Head Office of the Gresham Life Assurance Society. Mr. Lawson began his Insurance career in the Scotch Branch of the Reliance Mutual Life Assurance Society in 1875, leaving that Society in 1878 to join the Head Office staff of the City of Glasgow Life Assurance Company, where he remained till 1881, when he received the appointment of Inspector of Agencies for Scotland and the North of England for the Norwich Union Life Assurance Society, which position he held for nearly four years. Mr. Lawson then entered upon a six years' service in the Sun Life Assurance Society, the first two years of which were spent at the Edinburgh Branch and the remaining four years at the Birmingham Branch as Resident Secretary, relinquishing this position January, 1891, for his present appointment. Mr. Lawson devotes his energies chiefly to Branch extension and organisation, for which work he possesses much ability.

C. G. LAING, F.I.A.

Laing, Claud George, F.I.A., the Manager and Secretary of the Marine and General Mutual Life Assurance Society of London, was born in Fifeshire, in the year 1834.

After receiving a sound commercial and business education he entered the Insurance world in 1856, and made his first entry into Actuarial circles in 1857, when he joined the Institute of Actuaries, receiving the Fellowship of that influential incorporated body in the year 1860.

His knowledge of Life Insurance business both theoretically and practically has been gained by actual and varied experience, and he early made a reputation for himself both for practical knowledge and ability. So much so, that in the year 1867, he was appointed by the Board of Directors of the Marine and General Mutual Life Office to fill the position of Actuary to that Society, and thirteen years later (1880) when its original Secretary and Manager (Mr. W. C. Morgan) retired, he was further promoted to the position he holds to day.

Mr. Laing's reputation is a world wide one, and his friends and well-wishers are exceedingly numerous.

Lane, J. N., is the General Manager of the Palatine Fire Insurance Company at Manchester, into which the Mutual Fire Insurance Corporation has recently been merged. Mr. Lane has all through his business life been engaged in Insurance work. He was born in 1841, and when only eighteen years old, a very early age for a man to be entrusted with such a responsible post, was appointed as Chief Clerk and Surveyor to the Royal Insurance Company at their Branch at Bristol, having previously served a probationary period in the London Office of that Company, and there given sufficient evidence of his abilities and capacity to work to justify the Board of Directors in their selection of him for the higher appointment. He remained at the Royal Insurance Company's Branch for five years, and at the expiration of that period in 1864, became a candidate for and deservedly obtained the appointment to the Resident Secretaryship of the Bristol Board of the Liverpool and London and Globe Insurance Company. His service of this latter Company lasted for a period of thirteen years, when, on the resignation by the late Mr. W. H. Hore of the Management of the Head Office of the Mutual Fire Insurance Corporation at Manchester, Mr. Lane's merits again pointed him out to the Directors of that Corporation for selection as his successor in that post. The Mutual Fire Insurance Corporation had been founded in 1870 strictly as a Mutual Society, with a large guaranteed fund, and owing to the magnitude of the interests which it was promoted to serve, it had speedily secured an important footing in Lancashire and Yorkshire, so that Mr. Lane undertook no sinecure when he entered upon its management; but so competent has he proved himself that the record of

J. N. LANE.

the Corporation, handed over to him as one of almost unbroken prosperity, has in no way been depreciated while under his charge. Mr. Lane's success as a Manager may indeed be said truly to have been most remarkable, and by the unflagging energy and exceptional ability with which he has still further developed the business of the Corporation from what he found it to its present condition of magnitude and solidity, he has not only earned the lasting gratitude of his employers, but has also the gratification of feeling that he has acquired for himself a reputation surpassed by very few of the living members of the Insurance profession. The Corporation, it is true, had done well on the lines on which it had been originally established before he joined it, none of the guarantee fund having had to be called up, but the period of its present rapid, and at the same time sound progress practically dated from his appointment; and as he is still in the prime of life it would hardly be safe here to predict the position which the office may attain to in the course of the next ten years. From the Mutual sprang two off-shoots, the United Fire Re-insurance Company in the year 1877, and the Palatine Fire Insurance Company in 1886, both founded for the purpose of re-insuring the surpluses of the Mutual. Eventually, as stated above, the business of the Mutual Fire was merged into that of the Palatine, and as the United obtained powers to issue fresh policies, Mr. Lane now acts as General Manager for the last of these Companies, which conduct their fire operations in partnership. In 1881, Mr. Lane assisted in the formation of the Mutual Accident Association, which has now become the Accident Department of the Palatine.

W. J. LANCASTER, F.I.A.

Lancaster, William John, F.I.A., the Secretary of the Prudential Assurance Company of Holborn Bars, London, W.C., was born in the old-fashioned town of Lynn, in the County of Norfolk, in the year 1841. For over thirty-three years Mr. Lancaster has been in the service of the office in which he now holds so high and distinguished a position; in fact, the whole of his business life has been spent there.

In 1858 he first joined the staff, and had worked his way assiduously through various departments, gaining the increased confidence of his superiors after every promotion, when Mr. Harben retired from the position of Secretary to the Company in 1873. To succeed Mr. Harben in that capacity was a task from which any man might well shrink, but Mr. Lancaster accepted the post and all its responsibilities ; and, in the opinion of all best capable of judging, has acquitted himself in a very brilliant manner.

During the period that he has held his present office the growth of the Prudential has been of a most phenomenal character, as all the world of Insurance knows, and its limit is apparently by no means yet reached. To this result Mr. Lancaster has contributed in no small measure, and enjoying the full confidence of his *confreres* and also of every one of his subordinates as he does, each year should see substantial additions to a record already so high.

DAVID LAWRIE.

Lawrie, David, the General Manager of the Fire Insurance Association Limited, of London, has had a wide and varied experience in the Insurance profession. In 1860 he commenced his career in a Branch Office in Glasgow—his native city. In January, 1866, when the Scottish Imperial Insurance Company was started he joined its forces and six years later (namely, in 1872,) he was promoted to the position of Secretary of the Company. This appointment he held with credit and success until the amalgamation of that office with the Alliance in February, 1883. On the completion of that arrangement Mr. Lawrie was removed to Edinburgh, as Manager of the Insurance Company of Scotland. This office had also been absorbed by the Alliance many years previous to this date but it still continued to do and carry on business under its own style and title. In the beginning of the year 1887, the Directors of the Alliance finally decided to open a Branch in the United States, and Mr. Lawrie was sent by them to America to make all the necessary arrangements, with the idea that he should remain there in charge and supervise the business. However, the Board did not consider the prospects of the business to be done as being sufficiently promising or encouraging after the receipt of further reports, and the idea fell through for a time. Mr. Lawrie, however, remained for some months in the United States and Canada, spending the time in travelling from centre to centre studying the methods and systems of American underwriting, and the knowledge thus gained has been of great value to him. On his return to England, the Board of Management of the Fire Insurance Association offered him his present appointment, which he accepted, and commenced his duties on July 1st, 1887. What the Company was then is only too well remembered in the Insurance World ; what it is now is equally well-known, and to Mr. Lawrie must be given the credit for this result.

Lewis, Robert, the Chief Secretary and Manager of the Alliance Assurance Company, was born in Denbighshire in the year 1835. His father was a small farmer in that county. His first connection with Insurance was made at the age of eighteen, when he entered the Office of the Provincial Insurance Company at its Head Office at Wrexham. This Company had then only been established two years. In 1862, he was appointed by the Alliance Assurance Company to the position of Inspector of Agents. While holding this office he negotiated the transfer of the business of the Sheffield and Birmingham District Fire Offices to the Alliance, and afterwards also the Fire business of his old Office — the Provincial. From these transactions it will be seen that he had thus early gained the confidence of his Directors, and this was no doubt further strengthened by the manner in which he established the important branches of his Company in Liverpool and Manchester. After founding these he acted as Manager of them until June, 1866. He was called to London and appointed Chief Officer of the Company at the early age of thirty-one. His chief characteristic is probably his power of organisation, and he has proved himself a most efficient trainer of Insurance men, for very many of the most important appointments in the Assurance World are held by men who have served under him at the Alliance. He has done much to make the Alliance the powerful Company it is, and the number of Offices it has absorbed — always with advantage to those concerned — is unexampled by any other Office. Mr. Lewis is a " strong man, " and holds very decided ideas on the position that a Manager should hold. He said once, " The success of a great Insurance Company depends on its entire Management being left to the Manager. When Directors assume part-management, there is sure to be a clash. Insurance is a business that requires the entire attention and continual study of one mind. A successful Manager needs good general knowledge, concentration of thoughts over details, and determination to go through well-nigh endless drudgery."

ROBERT LEWIS.

MACLAREN LEYS.

JAMES LOGIE.

Leys, Maclaren, the Secretary of the Scottish Temperance Life Assurance Company, Limited, dates the commencement of his Insurance experience at the same period as the formation of this Company. He began as an Agent, in which capacity, however, he acted for only a few months, at the end of which he was offered an appointment as Inspector of Agents. This he accepted, to be shortly again promoted to the position of Chief Inspector, in the fulfilment of the duties of which post he effected excellent service to his Company. On the promotion of the late Secretary to the Managership of the Company, at the Annual Meeting in the Spring of 1891, Mr. Leys was selected to fill the vacancy caused thereby. Referring to this appointment, both the Chairman and other Directors of the Board spoke to the admirable and indefatigable devotion of Mr. Leys to the interests of the Company in the past, and their confidence in the happy results of his promotion to the Secretaryship, which confidence has already been amply justified.

Logie, James, Secretary and Underwriter of the Northern Marine Insurance Company, Limited, Dundee, entered the service of the Scottish Sea Insurance Company at Dundee, in May, 1852, and ever since then has been prominently identified with the Marine Insurance business of Scotland.

In January, 1864, Mr. Logie left the Scottish Sea Company to take charge of the Dundee Branch of the London and Caledonian Marine Insurance Company, Limited, whose Head Office was in London, and when that Company resolved on liquidation in April, 1868, Mr. Logie started the Northern Marine, so that his whole life has been devoted to Scotch Underwriting.

The Northern is essentially a provincial Company, and was formed mainly to meet the wants of a wide *clientele* throughout Scotland, and on the whole has had a very successful career; which result has been, to a very considerable degree, due to the personal influence and ability of its Founder and Secretary.

GEORGE M. LOW.

Low, George Macritchie, F.R.S.E., F.F.A., is the Manager of the Edinburgh Life Assurance Company, which position he has held since 1883, previous to which he occupied the office of Secretary. Mr. Low began his Insurance career by entering, in 1863, the Edinburgh Office of the English and Scottish Law Life Assurance Association. In 1875 he entered the Head Office of the Edinburgh Life as Assistant Actuary, and became Actuary and Secretary, and latterly Manager.

He is a Fellow and Member of Council of the Faculty of Actuaries, and was Honorary President of the Actuarial Society of Edinburgh in the session 1883-4. He is the Author of the article on Insurance (life) in the latest edition of the Encyclopædia Britannica. He is a Fellow of the Royal Society of Edinburgh (F.R.S.E.), and a Member of the Royal Company of Archers (Queen's Bodyguard for Scotland).

Lusk, Sir Andrew, Bart., Chairman of the Board of Directors of the General Insurance Company, and also of the Imperial Bank, is an example of what indomitable energy, combined with integrity and business skill, can achieve. Without any advantage in the way of birth, fortune, or education, he raised himself to the highest position in the Corporation of the City of London, and holds a yet higher position in the goodwill and es· teem of his fellow- citizens. His father was a small farmer in the County of Ayr- shire, Scotland, where he was born in 1811. His fam- ily is able to trace their descent back to the time of the Covenant· ers, when their ancestor was one of the most pro· minent members of that body, and a sufferer at the hands of the great Claverhouse. The days of his boy- hood were princ- ipally spent at the plough, but he eventually found employment in Greenock, and while there set himself diligently to work to im- prove his educa- tion, with so much success that he in a few years decided to enter the field of liter- ature, for which he found he had a natural inclina- tion and bent. But

SIR ANDREW LUSK, Bart.

and ship wares in Fenchurch Street. In 1848 he married Miss Eliza Potter, of Grahamstown, Falkirk. His business flourished and increased to such an extent that seven years later (in 1855) he made his first entry into Municipal life, being in that year chosen by his fellow- citizens of the ward of Aldgate, in which his business was situated, to represent them on the Common Council. Here he contin- ued to make his mark, and in 1861 he served the hon- ourable office of Sheriff, and in 1863 he was chosen as Alder- man. Here, in the same way, his energy and abili- ties combined to yet increase his influence and po- sition and to gain him still more of the confidence of those among whom his life was spent, so much so that in 1865, the Bor- ough of Finsbury sent him as its Representative in the Councils of the Nation at the House of Com- mons. His career here was marked with the persist- ence and ability with which he de- fended and upheld the rights of the Ancient Corpor- ation with which he was so closely connected. Eight years later he reached the sum- mit of the Lon- don citizen's am- bition and became

as so many have done before and since, he found the field a very rocky one to cultivate and success very hard to obtain, and after a fair trial he resolved to devote his energies to commerce instead. Consequently, we find him next removed to the great city with the municipal life of which his later years have been so intimately connected, and establishing himself as a dealer in ships' stores

Lord Mayor, receiving in the same year the distinguished honour of a Baronetcy. The text selected by the clergyman who preached before the Common Council and Corporation on the occasion of his election as Lord Mayor was singularly appropriate to the career of this worthy citizen, being—" Seest thou a man diligent in his business, he shall stand before kings."

W. C. LOCKHART.

WILLIAM LUXON, F.C.A.

Lockhart, W. Castleton, the present Underwriter of The Straits Insurance Company Limited, commenced his business career in the office of a Ship and Insurance broker which he left to join the staff of the Consolidated Marine, in which office he remained for over five years, gaining fundamental knowledge of Insurance matters, Policies and Clauses.

Backed up by the excellent recommendations of the Underwriter of the Consolidated Marine, he obtained the position of " Deputy " to the Straits Company in June, 1884, immediately after the Company started in London.   In consequence of the resignation of the late Underwriter (Mr. T. Holroyd Robinson) in 1890, owing to ill health Mr. Lockhart was appointed to the "Chair," but it is only from the 1st January, 1891, that he has the responsibility of the account.

He is blessed with a memory, has abundant energy and a good judgment, is popular and of a genial deposition.

He has published three books entitled " Records of Ships and Steamers Lost with Classified Voyages 1886.90, which are very interesting and useful to members of his profession.

Mackay, Alexander, is the General Manager of the Law Union and Crown Fire and Life Insurance Company.   He commenced his career in the Insurance business as a clerk in the Head Office of the Scottish Fire Insurance Company at Edinburgh where he steadily worked his way through various departments of the office, and, in 1868, was promoted to the position of Chief Clerk in the London Office of the same Company.   After

remaining in that post for some years, during which time he acquired very considerable experience in the business, he was appointed to the District Secretaryship of the Scottish Fire for Birmingham; subsequently being again promoted to be General Agency Superintendent, in which capacity he worked as Inspector and Surveyor in connection with the Head Office and Branches of the Company.   In 1875 Mr. Mackay transferred his services to the Lancashire Insurance Company, having received the appointment of Inspector of Agents, with Fire Survey duties for that Company under the Head Office and the Liverpool, Birmingham and Bristol Branches, his work however in this department lying mainly in Liverpool. After a service of two years' duration with the Lancashire, Mr. Mackay left it, to take up the appointment which had been offered him of Secretary in London for the Scottish Equitable Life Assurance Society, which position he occupied for ten years, eventually resigning it to become Secretary and Chief Officer of the Crown Life Assurance Office.   In July, 1891, he was appointed General Manager to the Law Union, and shortly afterwards, on the amalgamation of the latter office with his former one, the Crown, he was appointed Manager of the combined Law Union and Crown Insurance Company.

Luxon, William, F.C.A., is the Secretary of the Economic Plate Glass Insurance Company, Limited, of Plymouth.   He is a native of that town, and has had considerable experience in the various branches of Insurance.

F. B. MACDONALD.

Macdonald, Francis Bienfait, the Joint Secretary of the Phœnix Fire Office of London, is a son of the late Mr. W. Russell Macdonald, of Chelsea, a gentleman well known in the literary world. He was born in Chelsea in 1831, and like his brother received the first portion of his education at Durham House, Chelsea, proceeding thence to a French College, and finally completing at King's College, London. In 1848 he joined the staff of the office in whose service he has spent the remainder of his life. His work has been almost always associated with the general business of the Company, and in the year 1878 he was appointed Assistant Secretary under the Management of the late Mr. Broomfield. In 1884 he was appointed to his present position of Joint Secretary with his brother, Mr. W. C. Macdonald.

W. C. MACDONALD.

Macdonald, William Chambers, the Joint Secretary of the Phœnix Fire Office of London, was born in Camden Town in 1827, and was educated first at Durham House, Chelsea, and afterwards at a French College. On the 17th of January, 1845, he entered at the same time the Insurance world and the Office to the service of which he has given so many years, and in which he has risen to so high a position. For many years he has been the Chief Financial Official of the Company, and in the year 1884 he was appointed Joint Secretary of the Company with his brother, Mr. F. B. Macdonald,

J. K. MACDONALD.

Macdonald, J. K., is the Secretary of the Scottish Union and National Insurance Company at their headquarters in Edinburgh. Mr. Macdonald is a gentleman of long practical experience and proved ability. He received his early training in the Insurance profession in the Head Office of the Scottish National Insurance Company, where his capacity for business soon brought him to the front, and he eventually received the appointment of Secretary to the Glasgow Branch of the Company. When the Scottish National was united to the Scottish Union Insurance Company, under the title of the Scottish Union and National, Mr. Macdonald continued to act in the same post, having the control of a large business in the West and North of Scotland. On the retirement of the late Mr. Peterswald Pattison from the Secretaryship of the Company, Mr. Macdonald was selected to succeed him.

A. G. MACKENZIE, F.I.A., F.F.A.

Mackenzie, Alexander George, F.I.A., F.F.A., the Manager and Actuary of the Positive Government Life Assurance Company, was born in Edinburgh. In 1867 he entered the Head Office of the Life Association of Scotland in his native city, and remained in the service of that Company until the year 1875, when he was appointed Actuarial Assistant to the late Mr. C. V. Bunyon in the London Office of the Norwich Union Life Assurance Society. This position he held until receiving his present appointment in 1880. He passed the final examination of the Faculty of Actuaries in 1873. Mr. Mackenzie has been a voluminous contributor to Actuarial literature, among his writings being "Notes on War Mortality," which is printed among the Transactions of the Actuarial Society of Edinburgh, and a paper "On the Practice and Powers of Assurance Companies in regard to the Investment of their Life Assurance Funds," which he read before the Institute of Actuaries on January 26th, 1891. In addition to these, Mr. Mackenzie is the author of numerous articles on Commercial and Financial subjects in the "Globe Encyclopædia."

J. S. MACKINTOSH.

Mackintosh, J. S., the present Underwriter of the London Assurance Corporation, assumed the Management of the Marine Department of that Office in 1883.

His London career commenced in the year 1859, when he was appointed to a position on the staff of the Insurance Department of the business of Messrs. H. and J. Johnson and Company (now the Merchant Banking Company). In 1864 Mr. Mackintosh received the appointment to the Secretaryship of the North China Insurance Company shortly after its establishment. He went to Shanghai to take up the duties of the office, and remained there until 1868, when he returned to England to open up a Branch Office of that Company in London, and acted as its Agent and Underwriter here from that time until 1883.

In that year Mr. J. A. Rucker retired from the position of Underwriter of the London Assurance Corporation, and the Board of Directors of that Company offered the vacant post to Mr. Mackintosh. He accepted it, and has even since discharged the duties pertaining to that office.

In the Marine Insurance world Mr. Mackintosh holds a very high position. He is Deputy-Chairman of the Institute of London Underwriters, and he has for several years been delegated by that body to represent it on the Agency Committee of Lloyd's. He has gained the well-earned reputation of being a thoroughly trained Underwriter of sound judgment and keen observation. Certainly his experience has been exceptional and very wide.

PHILIP R. D. MACLAGAN.

Maclagan, Philip R. D., is the Secretary of the North British and Mercantile Insurance Company at their Head Office in Edinburgh. Mr. Maclagan comes of an Insurance family, his father, the late Mr. David Maclagan, having been at one time Chief Secretary to the Alliance Assurance Company, subsequently resigning that post to take the Management of the Edinburgh Life. His grandfather also was Manager of the Edinburgh Life before Mr. David Maclagan, and he is nephew of Mr. Finlay, of the Scottish Equitable. Prior to his appointment to his present post with the North British and Mercantile, Mr. Philip Maclagan acted as Manager in Edinburgh to the Insurance Company of Scotland (The Alliance), and before that as Assistant Secretary in the Head Office of the Edinburgh Life.

J. GRANT MACLEAN.

Maclean, J. Grant, Stock and Share Broker, Stirling, who, for nearly a quarter of a century, has carried on business at his present address in conjunction with his step-son, Mr. Hugh Henderson, has certainly been the medium of bringing before the public the real merit of well-selected Insurance Companies' shares as sound investments in a way not previously thought of.

As a means for permanent investment there is probably no class of joint stock enterprise which should command more favourable consideration on the part of the capitalist than the shares of well-managed Insurance Companies. Comparatively free from the fluctuating influence of trade, and with calculations based upon the most reliable *data*, the value of Insurance Companies' shares generally varies less than those of other branches of business; while a portion of the profit ascertained being in many cases set apart to increase the paid-up capital, the value becomes proportionately enhanced and the risk or liability proportionately reduced.

In these days of telegraphs and telephones Mr. Maclean finds, though Stirling may seem far from the Metropolis, that about a minute will put him into connection with the Edinburgh, Glasgow, or other Stock Exchanges. Besides, a long experience and care in dealing in all parts of the Kingdom have enabled him to form a connection of many thousands among the leading investors and dealers in these securities, which is of great service to his clients and correspondents. The tables of highest and lowest prices for each month, prepared by Mr. Henderson, are well known to the readers of the *Index* and the other Insurance papers, besides the weekly reports and special reports of prices which appear in the Insurance Press generally. Another very interesting publication is the highest and lowest prices of Insurance Companies' shares for each year, a work that involves constant watching of the markets and other special sources of information with great care in preparation to ensure accuracy and completeness.

Although Mr. Maclean transacts all kinds of stock broking business, it will be evident from our remarks that it is more to investors, as distinguished from mere speculators or operators, that he introduces these Insurance Companies' shares and endeavours to keep them posted with all the latest movements.

H. W. MANLY, F.I.A.

Manly, Henry William, F.I.A., the Actuary and Chief Officer of the Mutual Life Assurance Society of London, was born in London in the year 1843.

After receiving a private education, he commenced his Insurance career in the London Office of the Standard Life. His first connection with the Actuarial world was made when he joined the Institute of Actuaries in 1853, and after successfully passing the various examinations was elected to the full Fellowship of the Institute in 1861.

He has held several very high appointments in the Life Insurance world of London, and has always held a very prominent position in the Actuarial circles of the Metropolis. Of the Institute he has filled the offices of Vice-President and member of the Council; while his contributions to the literature of his profession have been numerous and valuable; both to the Journal and Transactions he has sent several papers that rank as standard authorities still on the subjects of which they treat.

HENRY MANN.

Mann, Henry, the present Secretary of the Commercial Union Fire and Life Assurance Company of London, has been employed on the staff of that Corporation for the whole period since 1875.

During that period (which covers the whole of his Insurance career) he has had exceptional opportunities of gaining the experience of organisation and companies' work necessary to fit him for the position he holds. For the greater part of the time previous to receiving his present appointment he was in the Secretary's Office. He did gain some little experience in the Life Department, but, as we have said, throughout his whole career, with this exception, he has been gaining experience in the Executive Departments, and so thoroughly qualified himself that in March, 1889, on the resignation of Mr. Bennett being accepted by the Directors of the Company, they unanimously selected him for the position, which honour he promptly accepted.

Mr. Mann was born in London, and was educated in that city. He has not connected himself prominently with the scientific side of Insurance matters, but has necessarily a good general knowledge of them. His executive abilities, however, are well recognised by his *confrères*, and in their estimation he holds a very high place, as well as in the opinion of his subordinates and his colleagues in the Offices the Commercial Union, where he is extremely popular.

The many excellent reforms he has introduced have all tended to the smoother working of the complicated organisation of so gigantic a Corporation as the Commercial Union, and he has yet others in contemplation, which there is every probability will be equally successful in their operation.

THOMAS W. MANN.

THOMAS SEPTIMUS MARKS.

Mann, Thomas W., is the Secretary of the Hartlepools Steamship Mutual Insurance Association. Mr. Mann is a native of Hull, where he was born in the year 1854, and received his education at North Shields, at which original home of the Ship Clubs it is not surprising that he early imbibed a taste for Marine Insurance and heard the question of Mutual Protection frequently discussed. He entered the office of Mr. G. J. H. Hogg in 1876, where he remained for twelve years, at the end of which period (in 1889) he was offered and accepted the post which he now holds of Secretary to the Hartlepool Steamship Mutual Insurance Association. The Association is mainly composed of the best Hartlepool steamers, though it is open to all 100 A1 or A1*1 Welldeck Steamers, having been founded to prove the erroneousness of the supposition that that type of steamer is unsafe; and Mr. Mann, through his ability, energy and popularity, has done much since his appointment to increase both the magnitude and prosperity of his Club.

Marks, Thomas Septimus, the present Superintendent of the Fire Department of the Liverpool and London and Globe Insurance Company at its London Office, was born in London in the year 1831, and commenced his commercial career in his sixteenth year, when he was appointed to a clerkship in the Customs Department of the London Dock Company. This he left in the following year to enter the profession of his life, joining the staff of the London Assurance Corporation, and remaining in their service until after the great fire at Cotton's Wharf in the year 1861. He was at that time appointed Chief Clerk of the Royal Insurance Company at its London Office, succeeding Mr. Whiting in the post which he had resigned to take the management of the then newly-formed Mercantile Insurance Company, now the North British and Mercantile. Seven years later (in 1868) he was promoted by the Directors of the Royal to be their Assistant Secretary in London, and three years later still, early in 1871, he resigned this post to accept the appointment he at present holds. Mr. Marks has had a large family, and his second son (Mr. G. H. Marks) is the Manager in New York of the London Assurance Corporation, three of his other sons at present holding various junior positions in different Insurance Offices.

E. H. MANNERING.

Mannering, E. H., holds the responsible position of Secretary to the Sun Fire Office, to which he was appointed in the year 1882.

Mr. Mannering's career in Fire Underwriting has been a long and varied one, he having passed through every grade of the business and acquired a practical knowledge of the working of every department, gaining thereby an experience his business capabilities have enabled him to use to its fullest value and extent with the most satisfactory results to his Office.

When scarcely sixteen years of age he made his start in the Insurance profession in the Office of the General Insurance Company, which then bore the name of the Protestant Dissenters and General Insurance Company. He only remained in the service of this office for two years, leaving it then on being appointed to a Junior Clerkship in the Office of the Globe, on the staff of which Company he remained until the year 1858. By that time he had built up for himself a high reputation among Fire Underwriters, as is evidenced by the fact that in the last-named year he was offered by the Board of Directors of the Northern Assurance Company the appointment of Chief Clerk of the Home Fire Department in their London Office, which offer he accepted.

As an active member of the staff of this Company he remained for some years, and in the year 1864 he was promoted to the position of Assistant Secretary, the onerous duties of which he fulfilled for one year. In 1865, on the position of Deputy Fire Manager of the Office becoming vacant the Directors appointed Mr. Mannering to the post.

In the year 1881, after a lengthy service extending over twenty-two years, Mr. Mannering received a further promotion, being appointed by the Directors Joint General Manager of the Company in conjunction with Mr. J. Valentine, who was at that time the Actuary of the office. This position he only retained for a short time, for in the following year (1882) he was offered and accepted the important position he still holds. Four years previous to this, Mr. Mannering received a gratifying proof of the esteem in which he is held by the leading underwriters of the City of London, being on the death of Mr. G. W. Lovell, in the year 1878, elected to the Chairmanship of the London Salvage Corps.

G. W. MANNERING, A.I.A.

Mannering, George Willsher, is the Assistant Secretary of the London and Lancashire Life Assurance Company. His early business career was connected with Banking, first in the provinces and afterwards in London, where he gained considerable experience in financial matters. In 1866, when he was twenty two years of age, he was appointed to the position of Assistant Accountant in the London Office of the London and Lancashire Fire Insurance Company and the London and Lancashire Life Assurance Company, and a few years afterwards was made Chief Accountant. In 1879 he received his present appointment of Assistant Secretary to the London and Lancashire Life Office, and has since taken an active part in the affairs of the Company.

Marshall, Thomas, the Secretary of the Hearts of Oak Benefit Society of London, was born on the 21st of August, 1830. In 1859 he was appointed to the Secretaryship of the Manchester Mechanics' Institution, which he held until July, 1865, when he was offered and accepted his present position. At that time the Hearts of Oak Society had about ten thousand members and a reserve fund of about thirty thousand pounds. Its offices then were on a very small scale, and were located in Greek Street, Soho. Under Mr. Marshall's management the Society soon began to grow rapidly, and in 1875 it was compelled to move its Head Offices to much larger premises in Charlotte Street, Fitzroy Square, and these again had to be much enlarged in 1889, at which date the Society numbered over one hundred and thirty thousand members with a Reserve Fund of nearly a million and a-quarter sterling.

Martin, Martin Luther, J.P., the Manager and Founder of the Scottish Accident Insurance Company of Edinburgh, was born in the month of November, 1848, at Strathmiglo, Fifeshire, N.B. After receiving a thorough commercial education, he commenced his business career in the Branch Office of the Union Bank of Scotland at the town of Auchtermuchty in 1862. The intricacies of banking doubtless proved a very valuable experience to the future Insurance Manager, both as to knowledge of finance, associations made, accountancy, &c.

With the Bank he remained until 1870, when he resigned his position with it to enter the Insurance World. In that year, which witnessed the outbreak of the great war between Germany and France, he joined the staff of the Reliance Life Insurance Company of King William Street, London, at its Glasgow Branch Office. He did not hold this position long, resigning it in the same year to take up a higher appointment in the service of the Life Association of Scotland. With this Corporation he remained for over two years, leaving it in the year 1873, on being appointed to the position of Resident Secretary for Newcastle-on-Tyne and District of the Scottish Commercial Insurance Company.

All these years he was developing his powers of organisation and concentration, and gaining experience in each, and these finally culminated, in 1876, in the establishment of the Scottish Accident Insurance Company (Limited), an office which from the first held a most prominent, if not the leading, position among Accident Insurance Corporations of its country.

Mr. Martin has been largely instrumental in putting into practical working order very many reforms in Accident Insurance, not only in new ideas, but also in amelioration of restrictions, conditions, and again in facilities to agents to secure business, the fruit of all of which is shown by the last published figures of the Office. Many, if not all, of the features he has initiated have become very popular, and if imitation is the sincerest form of flattery, as an old adage declares it is, then Mr. Martin should be a very proud man, for they have all been very extensively copied.

In 1886 Mr. Martin [was elected a member of the Finance Committee of the Edinburgh Exhibition, and this distinction should go far to show the esteem in which his ability and energy are held by his fellow-citizens of 'the historical City of Edinburgh.

MARTIN L. MARTIN, J.P.

Martin, T. Jacques, F.I.A., F.S.S., is the Managing Director of the Colonial Mutual Life Assurance Society, Limited, of which office he was practically the founder, and of which he has been the guiding spirit for many years.

He was born in Liverpool, England, and his early boyhood was spent on the banks of the Mersey, but in his youth his parents emigrated to the Antipodes.

His natural bent towards Insurance soon showed itself, and at a comparatively early age he began his career in the profession in which he is such a prominent figure. His first connection with it was made when he entered the Head Australian Branch Office of the Northern of Aberdeen at Melbourne. He remained here some time, resigning then to join the staff of a local office, the Australasian Fire and Life Insurance Company.

In the year 1859 he started out to commence business on his own account. He still retained a connection, however, with the Australasian Company, which had just then made a departure by adding a Marine Insurance Department to the other branches of business it still

T. JACQUES MARTIN, F.I.A., F.S.S.

carried on. Mr. Martin styled his firm "T. Jacques Martin and Co.," and under this trade name both at Melbourne and at Ballarat a very prosperous business was carried on for many years. Five or six years ago the firm was so prosperous that it was formed into a Limited Liability Corporation under the same name and title, with chief offices in the four great Australian centres of trade—Melbourne, Sydney, Adelaide, and Brisbane. Mr. Martin retains a very large interest in the Company, and holds the position of Chairman of the Board of Directors.

The year 1874 saw the crowning work of Mr. Martin's Life, the formation, foundation, and organisation of the Colonial Mutual Life Office, a Company whose record for progress is unexampled in the history of Life Assurance.

Mr. Martin is a man of untiring energy, and he has personally supervised the establishment, extension, and organisation of the business throughout the whole of the Australian Colonies, New Zealand, Cape Colony, and Natal. It was also at his initiation the British Department which has grown to be so important a Branch was started. The nucleus of the idea was first seen when Messrs. Dalgety and Co. were authorised to collect and receive premiums in England, and in 1881, when Mr. Martin visited England, he laid the foundation for the work he completed in 1886, when the Branch for Great Britain and Ireland was opened in the Company's own building in the Poultry, London.

Mr Martin combines a thorough practical business capacity with a complete knowledge of the *technique* of his profession. He is the Chairman of the Colonial Mutual Fire and Marine Insurance Company, which he also founded, and is the Consul of His Majesty the King of Portugal for a number of the Australian Colonies, and also holds several other important local offices.

W. D. MASSY.

Massy, William Dillon, the Joint Secretary of the Railway Passengers' Assurance Company of London, was born in the ancient and historic City of Bath in the year 1837, and is the only surviving son of the late Hugh Massy, a very well-known surgeon of that city.

He was educated at Christ's Hospital, London (the school that has turned out so many good men in commerce and finance), and after leaving this spent some two years in Egypt. Returning to England he commenced his Insurance career in the service of the Railway Passengers' Assurance Company.

This was in the year 1860, and it was in the "Claim Department," with which he has since been almost exclusively identified. He rapidly mastered all the details connected therewith, so quickly, indeed, that he was very soon promoted to the head of it; and since the first day he took charge of it very nearly one hundred and fifty thousand claims have passed through his hands. This would go far to show that his experience in this respect has been a wide one, if not unique, and the importance of a gentleman with such an experience to an Accident Insurance Company needs no expounding.

J. Corbet McBride.

W., McGavin McCulloch

McBride, J. Corbet, the Manager and Secretary of the Globe Accident Insurance Company at Manchester, was born in 1861, and at the age of sixteen migrated to London, where he remained for four years, three of which were spent in the service of the Standard Life Assurance Company, and the rest of the time in a Stockbroker's office. In 1881 he became Inspector for the Lancashire and Yorkshire Accident Insurance Company. From 1885 to 1890 he acted as their Chief Inspector, besides assisting generally in the management of the Company, during that period visiting practically the whole of the United Kingdom in the furtherance of his Company's business. He was appointed to his present post in August, 1890, on the formation of the Globe Accident Insurance Company, and under his supervision that Office has already made very considerable progress amongst its contemporaries.

McCulloch, W. McGavin, Local Manager of the Glasgow Branch of the Union Assurance Society, has held this post now for nearly twenty years, during which period he has built up a successful business for the Society. Mr. McCulloch deservedly stands high in the regard and esteem of his fellow-citizens, both within and without the Insurance circle; and there is no doubt that his success in business is to be attributed equally to his geniality and private worth on the one hand, and his ability and tact on the other. Like many others, he was unfortunately involved in the disastrous failure of the City of Glasgow Bank, as trustee for one of its shareholders. Heavy as the blow was, however, it failed to undermine the indomitable courage and perseverance of Mr. McCulloch, who struggled bravely through the difficulties with which he found himself surrounded, meeting with warm sympathy and assistance from his friends. He has well earned the success which has since attended his efforts, and which has, besides in a great measure compensating him for his own severe losses, firmly established at the same time the business of the Society with which he is associated. Mr. McCulloch is also connected with the Caledonian Plate Glass Insurance Company, Limited, a well-known local institution of eminence, established under his auspices and those of other well-known local gentlemen in 1871.

J. M. McCANDLISH, F.R.S., F.F.A.

McCandlish, John MacGregor, F.R.S., J.P., F.F.A., late Actuary and General Manager of the Scottish Union and National Insurance Company, was born in Edinburgh, in 1821, where his father was Receiver-General of Taxes for Scotland. He received his education at the University of his native City, and succeeded in gaining the prize for Civil Law. At this period of his life he evidently had the intention of adopting Law for the business of his life, for in 1845 he became a Writer to the Signet, but in 1846 he abandoned the legal profession to be the Secretary of the Scottish National Insurance Company, and in 1853 he succeeded to its management. From then to the year 1877, his whole energy was devoted to the development and success of that Office. In that year (1877) he became also the Manager of the Scottish Union Insurance Company, in view of an amalgamation between the two Offices, and in the following year, when the amalgamation was completed by Act of Parliament, he was appointed General Manager and Actuary of the combined Corporations. He resigned that appointment in 1890, and retired from active business, after a service of more than forty-four years. For many years he was the Chairman of the Committee of the Scottish Fire Offices, and from 1883 to 1886 was Chairman of the Associated Scottish Life Offices. He was one of the original Fellows of the Institute of Actuaries, but resigned his connection with that body on the formation of the Faculty of Actuaries in Scotland, of which he was the first Honorary Secretary ; he was afterwards its first Chairman, and when that body resolved to have a President he was unanimously elected to that office, and twice had the honour of being re-elected to that position.

To Insurance Literature Mr. McCandlish has made many valuable contributions, among them being the article on Fire Insurance in the last edition of the "Encyclopædia Britannica," and also "The Economic Condition of Insurance," which was an address delivered to the Insurance and Actuarial Society of Glasgow, in 1887.

J. H. McLAREN.

McLaren, John H., is the General Manager of the Royal Insurance Company. Mr. McLaren began his Insurance career in the Head Office of the Scottish Union at Edinburgh, from which office he removed to Manchester to take up the appointment which had been offered him of Fire Superintendent to the Lancashire Insurance Company when that Company was first established in 1852. He was next promoted to the more important post of Secretary to the London Branch of the same Company, but not very long afterwards the business of the Royal Insurance Company had increased to such an extent that Mr. Percy Dove, the then General Manager, found it necessary to secure the services of an experienced and reliable lieutenant, and Mr. McLaren was accordingly selected to be his Assistant-Secretary, resigning his appointment with the Lancashire for that purpose. From Assistant-Secretary he was subsequently promoted to be Sub-Manager, and on the death of Mr. Dove, in 1868, Mr. McLaren, as a matter of course, succeeded to the General Managership, which he has held ever since. During the period for which he has acted as Chief Officer the progress of the Royal has been one of uninterrupted continuity, the result almost solely of push and skill on the part of himself, an example being thus also set to those under his authority in the Company.

JAMES McCANKIE, F.S.S.

NEIL McDOUGALL.

McCankie, James, is Managing Director of the Scottish Live Stock Insurance Company, and District Manager for the East of Scotland for the Employers' Insurance Company of Great Britain. Mr. McCankie is well known in Scotland as being specially conversant with the Insurance of all kinds of Live Stock, and has had a long experience in this and all kinds of Accident Insurance Business, having been formerly Manager of the Edinburgh Employers' Liability and General Assurance Company, which Company he did his best to save from its unfortunate collapse both by personal energy and advice, only resigning when he saw that other and more unfortunate counsels were prevailing in its ranks.

He is a Fellow of the Royal Statistical Society and a Member of the Scottish Institute of Accountants, and is a gentleman universally esteemed by all who know him, both inside and outside of his profession.

McDougall, Neil, Managing Director of the British Steam Users' Insurance Society, Limited, Manchester, was educated and served his apprenticeship as a mechanical engineer in Yorkshire. He then entered the service of the Admiralty at Portsmouth Dockyard, and was shortly afterwards promoted to the Admiralty Offices at Whitehall. He gained the prize of the Naval Professional Association for the best essay on "Simple and Compound Engines as applied to Ships of War." He was afterwards promoted to the position of Inspecting Officer at the Admiralty. This position he resigned in 1879 to take the Management of the Boiler Insurance and Steam Power Company, Manchester, and after quitting the service of that Company Mr. McDougall, in conjunction with a number of the most important steam users in Lancashire, started the Society of which he is now Managing Director. As will be seen, Mr. McDougall's experience as an engineer has been a very wide one. He is a Member of the Institute of Civil Engineers, and a Member of the Institute of Naval Architects.

DAVID MACFARLANE.

GEORGE MACGREGOR.

Macfarlane, D., Manager of the Fire Department of the Lancashire Insurance Company at Manchester, enjoys the proud record of having spent nearly a quarter of a century in the service of one Company, that for which he at present acts. He was for the first five years of his connection with the "Lancashire" in the Head Office of the Company, whence he was promoted to the Resident Secretaryship at Leeds, and remained there for seventeen years, raising his office to the position of one of the most successful Branch Offices in the district. He was then transferred to a similar position in charge of the Birmingham Branch, where he was for two years, being subsequently recalled to the Head Office for further promotion to his present position. Mr. Macfarlane has, by his work in all the posts he has held, won for himself a brilliant reputation for first-class business capacity, ability, and thorough practical as well as theoretical acquaintance with the intricacies of his business, which has stamped him as a leading Insurance authority of the present day.

Macgregor, George, is Manager of the West of Scotland Fire Office, Limited. He began business in 1869 in the Edinburgh Office of the Scottish Amicable, passing, after three years, to the Head Office of the Scottish National. After fourteen years' service in Edinburgh and Glasgow with the Scottish National and Scottish Union and National, he, in 1886, originated and floated his present Company—the West of Scotland Fire Office. Mr. Macgregor is locally well known as a rifle shot, and he can shew trophies of Wimbledon.

J J McLAUCHLAN.

D. Y. MILLS.

McLauchlan, J. J., the Secretary of the Scottish Equitable Life Assurance Society, has served during the whole period of his Insurance career in that Office. After completing his education at Edinburgh University, he entered the Head Office of the Scottish Equitable in 1865, then under the management of Mr. George Todd. He worked his way steadily through the various departments of the Office, and during the same period passed the examinations of the Faculty of Actuaries in Scotland, being in 1873 admitted a Member of the Faculty. In that same year, Mr. Sprague having succeeded to Mr. Todd as Manager, Mr. McLauchlan was placed in charge of the Actuarial Department of the Office, and in 1878 received the appointment of Assistant Actuary. He ubsequently acted as the Manager's Assistant in making many important improvements in the business arrangements of the Society, and in 1891, on the retirement of Mr. Finlay, was appointed to his present post. Mr. McLauchlan has contributed various papers to the Transactions of the Actuarial Society of Edinburgh, among which may be mentioned :—" On Joint Life Annuities," 1879 ; "On Life Assurance Bookkeeping," 1887 ; "On some Formulas for use in Life Office Valuations," 1891. In 1874 he communicated to the Journal of the Institute of Actuaries a new formula for use in obtaining the rate of interest yielded by an annuity certain, which is now reproduced in the text books.

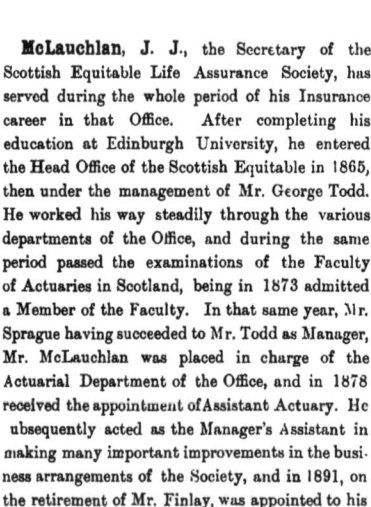

Mills, Daniel Yarnton, A.I.A., is the Assistant Secretary of the Scottish Equitable Life Assurance Society at its headquarters at St. Andrew Square, Edinburgh. Mr. Mills was appointed to his present post in August, 1891, having immediately previous to that engagement held the position of Branch Manager to the Clerical, Medical, and General Life Office at Manchester, the only Branch of that office out of London, having been appointed in 1888. Before that he was Agency Manager to the University Life Office, and before that again Assistant-Manager of the West End Office of the Sun Life in London.

R. K. MITCHELL.

W. M MONILAWS.

Mitchell, R. Kennedy, Manager of the Lancashire and Yorkshire Accident Insurance Company, is a native of Glasgow, where he was born in 1857. Having received his education in Edinburgh, he commenced life in the Royal Bank of Scotland in their branch at Granton, but after three years' service, banking proving uncongenial to his tastes through offering neither rapid promotion nor any great scope to his ambition, he abandoned that profession, and returned to Glasgow. There he entered the service of a firm of dyers, but that engagement was terminated in three years by the collapse of the business ; and it was then that Mr. Mitchell turned his attention to the Insurance profession and, the prospects proving inviting, entered the Head Office of the Scottish Accident Insurance Company as a Junior Clerk. Here he at last found ample field for the exercise of his natural ability, and profiting by his opportunity, he soon won the approval of his Manager, and in a very few months was promoted to the more important and responsible post of Superintendent of Agents for the Edinburgh District. His fidelity and energy were further rewarded in 1880, when he was again promoted to the District Secretaryship at Glasgow, which post he held for no less than eleven and a half years, working during the whole of that period steadily and conscientiously and building up a large and valuable business for his Company. In October, 1891, the Directors of the Lancashire and Yorkshire Accident having determined to transform the Management of their Company into a joint tenancy, with a view to introducing broader views into the conduct of their business, Mr. Mitchell was appointed Joint Manager with the late Mr. McBride, resigning his post with the Scottish Accident, much to their regret. Mr. McBride died in December, 1891, leaving him sole Manager.

Monilaws, W. M., the Chief Inspector of the Scottish Provident Institution, Edinburgh, is the youngest son of the late Rev. Dr. Monilaws, of Peebles, N.B., where he was born in June, 1857. Mr. Monilaws' Insurance experience has been gained almost entirely in the service of the Scottish Widows' Fund Life Assurance Society, he having entered it at the age of fifteen, in 1872, at the Branch Office at Glasgow. His progress was so rapid that only four years later he was transferred to the Dundee Branch in the capacity of Cashier, and two years afterwards, in 1878, he was again transferred, this time to the Head Office Actuarial Department. His abilities in this Department won the confidence of his superiors to such an extent that during the illness of the Resident Secretary at the Newcastle Branch at intervals in 1880 and 1881 he was selected to supply his place. He was then moved to Leeds in 1882, and, after acquiring a good deal of Agency experience there, was appointed in the December of that year Inspector of Agents at the Society's Liverpool Branch, which office he held till 1885, when he returned to Leeds to take up a similar appointment to that which he had held at Liverpool. This he resigned in September, 1887, on undertaking the Liverpool Secretaryship of the Scottish Equitable Assurance Society, but eighteen months later he came back to the Scottish Widows' Fund as their Liverpool Secretary, on the retirement of Mr. A. H. Whytt. This post he relinquished in February, 1890, on receiving the official appointment he now holds on the Head Office Staff of the Scottish Provident. Mr. Monilaws is an Associate of the Institute of Actuaries, having passed his first examination, as well as the first two examinations of the Faculty of Actuaries. He is the author of a work on "The Surplus Funds of Life Offices."

Miller, Thomas R., is the Joint Manager of the United Kingdom Mutual Steamship Assurance Association Limited, the Head Office of which is in London. Mr. Miller became associated with Club Insurance under the able guidance of the late Mr. Joseph Carr, who died in 1865, when Mr. Miller was appointed Manager, or, as it is styled in Newcastle, Secretary, of the North of England Steamship Club, which position he occupied with credit to himself and benefit to the members for the long period of twenty years.

During the time Mr. Miller conducted the affairs of the clubs at Newcastle steam shipping increased to such an extent that the capital of the Club rose from about half-a-million to over three millions, and including the Freight and Protecting Clubs, of which Mr. Miller was also Manager, the aggregate capitals amounted to about thirteen millions, and although several Richmonds came into the field the parent club held its position and always continued a Samson. As time advanced Mr. Miller thought a change would be of advantage to himself, more particularly in the matter of health, and having the offer of Joint Management of the United Kingdom Clubs, he determined to accept the appointment offered to him; and in January, 1886, he left Newcastle for London. Before severing himself from his old office a handsome presentation was made to Mr. Miller and the following resolution passed by the directorate:—

"The directors much regret the resignation of their secretary, Mr. T. R. Miller. They desire to place on record their high appreciation of the ability with which he has conducted the business of their associations during a secretaryship of twenty years, and to express their sense of the regret they feel at the withdrawal of his great and varied experience and sound judgment from their deliberations; at the same time they heartily and cordially wish him success in his new and wider sphere of labour in the metropolis, and hope that the change may be beneficial to him in health, in business, and in every other department of his public and private life."

Mr. Miller since he came to London has been and is now Joint Manager of the United Kingdom Mutual Steam Ship Assurance Association Limited, which, at the time he joined in the management, was composed of three classes, viz., "Insurance on Hulls of Steamers," "Insurance on Freight," and "Protecting," to which has been added "Indemnity." The usefulness of the two latter clubs has been demonstrated frequently in resisting spurious and improper claims of shippers and receivers of cargoes. In fact, without the aid of Protecting and Indemnity Associations no individual shipowner could safely carry on his business, as it is only by co-operation that abuses such as so frequently occur can be remedied.

Mr. Miller is well known in Marine Insurance and shipping circles. He is at

THOMAS R. MILLER.

home when dealing with average claims, salvage claims, and other claims in connection with Marine Insurance business, and for many years he has been looked upon and consulted as an authority.

He is one of those zealous, hopeful, and confident men who are seldom discouraged, and always invaluable and influential in the weak and unpromising beginning of things, he is warm-hearted and sympathising, plain and simple in manner, and is esteemed a kind neighbour, devoted friend, and delightful companion.

Miller, F. Norie, Manager of the General Accident Assurance Corporation of Perth, commenced his career in the Insurance profession in the service of the London and Lancashire Fire Insurance Company, entering the London Office of that Company. Leaving that Office in March, 1880, he transferred his services to the Ocean Accident Company at its Head Office also in London. When the Employers' Liability Assurance Corporation was established, Mr. Miller was selected from among a large number of applicants for the appointment to the Chief Clerkship of the Accident and Guarantee Departments of the Corporation, commencing his duties on the 1st of January, 1882. After holding this appointment for a period of four years, he resigned it at the close of 1885, in order that he might take up the position which had been offered him of Assistant-Manager to the Mercantile Accident and Guarantee Company, then just recently founded at Glasgow. He held this appointment in its turn for a little over twelve months, at the end of which time he was approached by the Directors of his present Corporation with a view to his accepting the post of Manager and Secretary then vacant, which offer he acquiesced in, and accordingly entered upon his duties in February, 1887. He found his task on his first accession to office of a somewhat heavy nature, the whole business of the Corporation being in a most unsatisfactory condition. Though the Corporation had been then established for thirteen months under Mr. Miller it had practically to begin afresh. The remaining old officials were, with one exception, dispensed with, the bad and doubtful risks cancelled as they fell due, and fresh branches and agents appointed, all of which reforms Mr. Miller carried out in the first twelve months of his management. The result on the prosperity of the Corporation needs no detailing here.

Mr. Miller has in the course of his career received more than one testimonial from the various Offices in whose service he has been, both on the occasion of his marriage, of his resigning his appointments with his former Companies, and from his present Company; all of which afford ample testimony of the friendship and esteem which he has so deservedly won among his fellow-workers in Accident Insurance.

F. NORIE MILLER.

C. WILLIAMSON MILNE.

Milne, C. Williamson, the General Manager and one of the Directors of the Security Company Limited, was born in the year 1862. His first business experience was gained in the Office of the great Transatlantic Steamship Companies in Glasgow, but soon evincing a *penchant* for a more active career he very naturally drifted into the Insurance world. His first appointment was that of Secretary for Scotland of the English and Scottish Boiler Insurance Company, and in a very short time, through his indefatigable energy, he established a record over the achievements of his more experienced predecessors in office. Such an appointment, however, could only be regarded as a stepping-stone to something better, and accordingly in 1885 he established, under the auspices of a very influential and representative board, the Mercantile Accident and Guarantee Insurance Company, which, under his management, soon took a forward position as a progressive office in the domain of General Accident Insurance and Fidelity Guarantee business. Shortly before severing his connection with that Company, Mr. Milne made a careful and exhaustive collation of all the available statistics bearing on burglaries and thefts, and formulated a scheme of Insurance against these risks. Although the idea had previously been canvassed it had failed to secure any support, but through the efforts of Mr. Milne the new departure has made rapid strides, and seems destined to rank as one of the most popular and useful of recent applications of the principle of Insurance. London being *facile princeps* the field for developing Burglary Insurance with success, Mr. Milne, towards the end of 1889, started The Security Company there with Mr. Howard Vincent, the well-known M.P., as Chairman, and Sir George Hayter Chubb as Deputy Chairman. Mr. Milne has a considerable reputation for organising capacity, and his suavity of manner goes a long way in the management of the large army of representatives he has secured for his Company in every part of the United Kingdom.

G. C. MORANT.

Morant, George Christopher Assistant Manager of the Fire Department of the Commercial Union Assurance Company Limited, has had a wide and varied experience of the Insurance business. He commenced his career in it by entering the Head Office of the Royal Insurance Company in Liverpool (in 1867), then under the management of the late Percy M. Dove. Here he remained till the year 1869, when he came to London to take a responsible position in the office of the Northern Assurance Company. In 1873 he went up another step of the ladder, being in that year appointed by the Directors of the Guardian Assurance Company to be Superintendent of their then newly-started Foreign Department. This position he held with conspicuous success for fourteen years, when he resigned it to join Mr. E. Roger Owen in the Management of the Fire Department of the Commercial Union Insurance Company. During the present year Mr. Morant has had an extensive trip to the other Hemisphere. On this journey he spent some time in Chili, and was in Valparaiso during a portion of the recent revolution against Balmaceda's Dictatorship. His experiences here and views of the situation he has embodied in a very interesting volume, entitled "Chili and the River Plate in 1891," which was published on his return, and has met with a very satisfactory reception by the press and the public.

Among the many other movements in the Insurance world with which his name is connected, "The Insurance Musical Society of London" will always stand prominent. This Association Mr. Morant promoted in the year 1882, and he acted as Honorary Secretary to it from then till the end of 1886, when the pressure of other work compel'ed him to resign the position.

Mitcalfe, J. Stanley, is the Consulting Secretary of the North of England Protecting and Indemnity Association, and Chairman of Directors of the Northern Maritime Assurance Company. Mr. Mitcalfe has passed the whole of his business career in connection with underwriting and the protection of shipowners' interests generally. He commenced in the office of Mr. Matthew Atkinson, of North Shields, Secretary of the Equitable and Oriental Mutual Marine Insurance Association, then one of the oldest and most influential Mutual Insurance Associations, insuring first-class sailing vessels, where he remained first as Junior and afterwards as Chief Clerk for nearly seven years, subsequently, in 1862, obtaining the appointment of Secretary to the Britannia Mutual Marine Association, an institution for the insurance of sailing vessels of the second class. Three years later he was selected for and accepted the

J. STANLEY MITCALFE.

post of Underwriter to the Northern Maritime Assurance Company of Newcastle, which he worked up to a standard rarely, if ever, attained by Marine Assurance Companies, although starting at a great disadvantage through the previous ill-success of the Company. In 1874 he successfully promoted the Steamship Owners' Mutual Protection and Indemnity Association, the first Association of its kind ever established, and in 1876 the New-

castle Home Trade Insurance Association. In 1880 Mr. Mitcalfe ceased his active connection with the Northern Maritime, in consequence of the pressure of his other business, and was appointed Managing Director. The success of the Steamship Owners' Mutual Association naturally causing the formation of other similar Associations, in 1886 it was amalgamated with the North of England Protecting Association, under the name of the North of England Protecting and Indemnity Association, with Mr. Mitcalfe and Mr. Ralph Carr as Joint Secretaries, Mr. Mitcalfe being appointed liquidator to wind up the affairs of his old Association; the new one soon becoming one of the largest of its kind in the United Kingdom, numbering among its members some of the most wealthy and influential shipowners of the country. The Newcastle Home Trade Insurance Association was founded later for the Insurance of coasting steamers only, at that time not regarded as very favourable risks, but under Mr. Mitcalfe's able conduct proving not to be so unfavourable as had been supposed. In 1890, Mr. Mitcalfe resigned his post as Joint Secretary to the North of England Protecting and Indemnity Association, taking up in its stead that which he now holds of Consulting Secretary, and in 1891 he was, on the death of the late Chairman of the Northern Maritime Assurance Company, elected to fill the vacancy.

J. B. MOFFAT.

Moffat, James B., the General Manager and Secretary of the Manchester Fire Assurance Company, has had a long experience in Fire Insurance business, having entered the service of the Scottish Union at Edinburgh many years ago. Subsequently he became connected with the Northern, with which Company he remained fourteen years, first in its London Office and afterwards as its Local Secretary at Liverpool, a position which he vacated in January, 1879, to become Sub-Manager of the London and Lanca- shire Fire Insurance Company. In 1889 he was offered and accepted his present position, and under his able management the Manchester Fire Office has taken its proper position as the leading Company, and bids fair to become one of the largest and most prosperous British Fire Insurance Companies. It is generally conceded that Mr. Moffat is one of the most able Fire Insurance Managers in the United Kingdom, and his future career will be watched with considerable interest.

ROBERT MUIR.

Muir, Robert, is the late General Manager of the Scottish Alliance Insurance Company at its Head Office at Glasgow. Previous to holding that appointment Mr. Muir for a period of 14 years acted as Manager for Scotland and Ireland for the London and Staffordshire Fire Insurance Company, and on the retirement of the then General Manager of that Company, was solicited by the Directors unanimously to accept the General Managership on account of his long and varied Fire Experience of Home and Foreign Business. He continued to act in that capacity until the transfer of the London and Staffordshire Fire Insurance Company's business to the Lancashire Insurance Company, when he accepted the post which was offered him of the Assistant-Secretaryship at the Scottish Branch of the last-named office; at no very long period afterwards, however, resigning that appoint-ment in order that he might improve his position by undertaking the duties of Manager for Scotland for the London Assurance Corporation upon its opening a Branch Office in Glasgow. Mr. Muir subsequently filled for some years a similar position in connection with the Patriotic Assurance Company till towards the close of 1888, when, on the establishment of the Scottish Alliance Insurance Company by a large and influential body of local gentlemen of position for the transaction of Fire Accident and General business, with the exception of Life business, Mr. Muir was waited on and asked to accept the General Manager-ship, which invitation he accepted, re-signing the post which he held at that time with the Patriotic. Mr. Muir subsequently resigned his position with the Scottish Alliance in 1891.

ALEXANDER MUNKITTRICK, Junr.

Munkittrick, Alexander (junior), the Manager for Great Britain and Ireland of the Equitable Life Assurance Society of New York, was born in the United States, and for eleven years he has been connected with the Branch of the Society of which he is now the official head in this country. He was promoted to his present important position on July 1st, 1889.

THOMAS S. MORTIMER.

A. S. MURRAY.

Mortimer, Thomas S., the Secretary of the Western Provident Association at Exeter, though well known in the Insurance world as the managing spirit of an important Association, has not had a very varied Insurance career, having been brought up solely in the work of the Western Provident Association, namely, Life and Old Age and Sick Pay Assurance. He is the son of the late Mr. William Mortimer, J.P., who, with Mr. Charles Hill, founded the Association in May, 1848, and conducted it through the perils of its first year of existence, and on his death Mr. Thomas Mortimer succeeded him.

— — —

Murray, Alfred S., the Manager of the Straits Insurance Companies, Limited, and of the Straits Fire Insurance Company, Limited, is another example of a gentleman abandoning commercial life for an Insurance career.

His first experience of business life was gained in the office of a Scotch bank, and subsequently in a Ship Insurance Broker's Office.

It was in the year 1878 that his first connection with the Insurance World was made. In March that year he joined the Staff of the South British Insurance Company of New Zealand, at its Head Office in Auckland.

He was afterwards made the Manager for the Company for the Province of Otago, with Head Quarters at Dunedin, and this important position he held for two years. At the expiration of that time he was appointed to be Inspector of Branches, and in this capacity he acted for seven years, and was then offered by the Board of Directors the important appointment of Manager of their Branch, that had for its district the whole of the United States and Canada.

In January, 1891, he was offered the Managership of the London Office of the Straits Insurance Company, Limited, and he accepted it, subsequently to this was added the Managership of the Straits Fire Insurance Company, Limited, and he has had the sole charge of the organising of the business of the latter office in this country.

W. Oscar Nash.

Nash, W. Oscar, is the Actuary of the London Amicable Assurance Company, Limited. He is a Fellow of the Institute of Actuaries, having passed the three examinations in the year 1883, 1884, and 1888 respectively. He joined the Head Office staff of the Marine and General Mutual Life Assurance Society and remained with that Company until appointed Chief Clerk to the London Amicable Assurance Society, Limited, at the date of its commencing business in November, 1887. He was appointed Actuary to the Society at the beginning of 1890.

Newbatt, Benjamin, F.I.A., F.S.S., F.R.G.S., the Actuary of the Clerical, Medical, and General Assurance Company, was born in 1834. He commenced his Insurance career in the Office of the Company of which he is the present chief Officer in 1854. Ten years later (1864) he was appointed to the position of Assistant Actuary which post he filled until 1882, when he was selected by the Board of Directors to occupy his present position.

Mr. Newbatt was elected a member of the Council of the Institute of Actuaries in 1869. In 1871, he retired from that body altogether, but rejoined its Council in 1886, when he was elected a Vice-president of the Institute. When the Life Offices Association was established in 1889, Mr. Newbatt was elected its first President.

SAMUEL T. NICHOLSON.

THOMAS W. NOAD.

Nicholson, Samuel T., the Secretary of the Hull and Eastern Counties Mutual Plate Glass Insurance Company, is a noted man in his own county and those adjoining, for, besides holding the above post, he has the credit of having been the promoter or founder of the Eastern Counties Insurance Company, in which he still takes considerable interest, whilst that immediately under his personal control, has, thanks to his supervision, made great progress and become exceedingly popular in the district.

Noad, Thomas W., is the Manager of the Standard Mutual Steamship Associations, and is a Member of the firm of Charles Taylor and Company, of London.

Mr. Noad, who succeeds his father in the position he now fills, commenced his business career in the employ of a well-known London Marine Insurance firm, who were also the London Agents of a Liverpool Marine Insurance Company, and he had thus exceptional opportunities of gaining a thorough insight into both the scientific and practical sides of the business of Marine Underwriting. With this firm he remained for some years, during the last few of which he did their work in Lloyd's room.

After resigning his position with them he accepted an appointment in the London Office of the Powell Duffryn Steam Coal Company, and with them he remained until the year 1882, when he was offered a position on the staff of Messrs. Charles Taylor and Company, which he accepted. For some years he managed the whole of their Insurance Brokerage Business, but the Standard Mutual Insurance Association grew so fast, and its connections increased so much, that it became necessary for him to devote the greater part of his time to its interests, and in the year 1885, during his father's illness, he was compelled to take the complete management of this Association. The onerous duties thus devolved on him he carried out to the thorough satisfaction of the Board of Directors, who signified their approval and appreciation of his efforts by a very complimentary resolution, which was duly entered on their minutes.

Mr. Noad has always been a very eager student in pursuit of the knowledge of his profession, and has always endeavoured to gain a thorough practical acquaintance with ships by making short voyages whenever time and opportunity would permit. In addition to these he has given much time to the study of the most important text books and decisions relating to the carriage of goods by sea, general average, and such other matters as more immediately concerned his profession, so much so that it may be fairly questioned if there is another man of his age who has acquired such knowledge of his business in so short a time.

W. T. OVERSBY.

Oversby, W. T., Manager of the General Agency Department of the Pioneer Life Insurance Company, Limited, Liverpool, was born at Livesey Hall, Blackburn, Lancashire, February 27th, 1856. After receiving a fair commercial training, he entered the service of the Poor Law under the Local Government Board at Liverpool, where, by dint of perseverance and attention to duty, he was promoted on several occasions, and in 1888 was appointed Assistant-Clerk to the Guardians, and Superintendent of the Out Relief Department of the Sheffield Union.

It was while holding this important position that Mr. Oversby had brought to his notice the principles of the Mutual Reserve Fund Life Association, and after thorough examination and enquiry, he resolved to abandon the Poor Law and throw in his lot with that Association.

Mr. Oversby actively commenced business as an Agent on the 11th January, 1890, and so successful did he become, having written over ¼ of a million of business during the year 1890, that the Management speedily appointed him Sub-Manager at Liverpool, and subsequently he attained the position of District Manager. During this time, besides his personal work, he rendered valuable aid to his office in organizing the district, having established active agencies in all important centres around Liverpool. Mr. Oversby comes of an old Insurance family, several members of which have represented old established Companies for nearly twenty years. He also holds the Silver Medal of the Humane Society for saving life from fire in 1883.

E. ROGER OWEN.

Owen, E. Roger, is the Fire Manager of the Commercial Union Assurance Company at their Head Office. Previous to joining the Commercial Union, Mr. Roger Owen was for a period of twenty years in the service of the Alliance Assurance Company.

Owen, Douglas, Secretary of the Alliance Marine Assurance Company, Limited, is the son of Mr. William Buy Owen, Surgeon, of Cleveland Square, Hyde Park, and was born at Finchingfield, Essex, in 1850. His first entry into Commercial Life was made in the Office of an East India House in Fenchurch Street, where he received the foundation of a good business training. On leaving that office in 1874, he was appointed Examiner of claims to the United Swiss Marine Insurance Companies, of which Mr. Septimus Merriman was the London Manager. Of these Companies he subsequently became, in addition to his other post, Deputy-Underwriter. In the same year (1874) he was appointed Secretary to the Association of Average Adjusters of Great Britain, and he still holds that position. He is an Honorary Auditor of the Institute of London Underwriters, and is the accredited Representative with the same Institute of the National Board of Marine Underwriters of New York.

To the literature of his profession Mr. Douglas Owen has added several valuable works, among them being " Marine Insurance Notes and Clauses," the first edition of which was published in 1883 by Messrs. Sampson, Low and Company, and of a work entitled " Declaration of War : a Survey of the Position of Belligerents and Neutrals, with Relative Considerations of Shipping and Marine Insurance During War," published by Messrs. Stevens and Sons, Limited, in 1889. Mr. Owen is also a Barrister of the Inner Temple.

W. SWAN PARKER.

Parker, W. Swan, Managing Director of the Standard Accident Insurance Company of London, was born in the North of England in 1848, and is consequently one of our younger Insurance Managers. He was educated there, and received there his early business experience. He then went to Glasgow to occupy an important position in the office of a large firm of shipbuilders, when an opening more suited to his special bent presented itself. He at once interested himself in Insurance business, and has had great experience in all classes. But he has always made Accident Insurance his special study.

He has passed through all grades—Agent, Canvasser, Superintendent and London Secretary to the Scottish Accident Insurance Company.

After nine years with this Company he severed his connection with them to become the Managing Director of the Standard Accident Insurance Company, of which, indeed, he is the moving spirit. The Standard is a young Company, but vigorous and enterprising, and has already obtained an excellent reputation for prompt and liberal settlement of claims. Under Mr. Parker's careful superintendence it has shown considerable enterprise, and is not only well represented all over England and Scotland but has established agencies in Amsterdam for Holland, in Antwerp for Belgium, in Paris for the North of France, in Marseilles for the South of France, and has Managers and a Local Board of Directors in Dunedin, New Zealand, for Australasia.

H. S. Patteson, J.P., D.L.

Patteson, Henry Staniforth, J.P., D.L., of Cringleford, President of the Norwich Union Fire Insurance Society, is a son of J. S. Patteson, Esq., one of the Original Directors of the Norwich Union Fire Office, and grandson of John Patteson, Esq., at one time Member of Parliament for the City of Norwich. He has always been recognised in that city as a man of great energy and sound business habits. He was elected a Director of the above Society in 1849. In 1874 he became Vice-President and President in 1877. He is also Chairman of the General Hail Storm Insurance Company, the Norwich and London Accident Insurance Company, the Norwich Waterworks Company, and is officially connected with almost every important institution in the City and County of Norwich. Our engraving is taken from an oil-painting subscribed for by the Directors of the Norwich Waterworks Company, hanging in the Board Room of that Society.

RICHARD JAMES PAULL.

Paull, Richard James, Secretary and Manager of the Ocean Accident and Guarantee Corporation, Limited, entered the service of the Ocean in 1876 as a Junior, and had the good fortune of receiving his early training under two of, perhaps, the ablest men in their respective branches of Insurance business, Mr. R. Dolphin Wood, of whose experience he had for many years the benefit in the Accident Department, and Mr Robert Kelly, who for many years had conducted the Fidelity Guarantee Department for the Old European, and who managed the same business for the Ocean until his death in 1883. Mr. Paull, whom Mr. Kelly had carefully trained, was then entrusted with the Management of the Guarantee Department, with the title of Secretary, that of Manager being added in 1888, on the retirement of Mr. Dolphin Wood through ill-health, since which time he has had the entire management of affairs. Mr. Paull, who is a young man and full of energy, is certainly one of the most able, as well as one of the most popular, Accident and Fidelity Guarantee Insurance Managers in this country, and it is largely due to him that the Ocean Corporation's operations have hitherto proved so successful, and that it still shows such undoubted signs of continued growth in strength and usefulness. Mr. Paull is on the best of terms with his Board, and on the occasion of his marriage (in 1886), was presented by them with a handsome silver salver, bearing the following inscription:—" Presented to Richard J. Paull, Esq., Secretary to the Ocean Accident and Guarantee Assurance Companies, Limited, by the Directors, on the occasion of his marriage, with their best wishes and as a mark of their esteem and regard."

DAVID PAULIN, F.S.S.

Paulin, David, F.S.S., is the Manager of the Scottish Life Assurance Company Limited, the Head Office of which is in George Street, Edinburgh. Mr. Paulin has had a large and varied experience in Insurance matters, and is an official of great ability.

Paterson, D. R., the Manager and Secretary of the Equitable Fire and Accident Office at the headquarters of that office in St. Ann Street, Manchester, commenced work in 1862 under the auspices of the late Mr. Frank Jewsbury, in whose service he remained till 1865. He then became connected with the Northern Assurance Company in the capacity of Agency Inspector to that Company's branch at Manchester, which office he held till 1870, subsequently acting as Principal Surveyor to the Mutual Fire Insurance Company until 1872. In 1873 he established the Equitable Fire Office, which has since developed into the Equitable Fire and Accident Office, of which he has been the Manager and Secretary since its formation.

JOHN G. PHILLIPS.

Pearson, Arthur, F.I.A., the Actuary of the Metropolitan Life Assurance Society, was born on the 5th of December, 1830. His first connection with the Insurance and Actuarial profession was made when he entered the service of the Royal Exchange Assurance Corporation in 1849. With this office he remained for some years, and in 1856 he was appointed to the important post of Assistant Actuary to the Metropolitan, a position he held until promoted to his present appointment in 1873. Mr. Pearson has served the office of Vice-President of the Institute of Actuaries and conferred a lasting boon to the Actuarial world, by (in 1865) publishing the "Mortality Experience of the Metropolitan Life Assurance Society."

Phillips, John George, is the Secretary of the Sceptre Life Association Limited, of Finsbury Pavement, London.

He was born in London in 1837, and was educated privately. After a short experience of Commercial life, he entered the Insurance world, and was appointed to his present position in 1866.

SAMUEL J. PIPKIN, A.I.A.

Pipkin, Samuel J., A.I.A., is Secretary of the Atlas Insurance Company. Mr. Pipkin commenced commercial life in the office of Messrs. Walker, Parker and Co., at their shot manufactory in Lambeth in the year 1866, leaving there to enter the service of the eminent public accountants, Messrs. Kemp, Ford and Co., where he remained for two years. During that time he gained much valuable experience that he has doubtless found the advantage of in later life, for during that historical (financially speaking) period he was engaged on some of the largest liquidations of the time. In March, 1868, he first entered the office of which he is now the head as a Junior Clerk in the Fire Department, where he remained for five years, leaving in 1873 to become the Directors' Auditor of the Commercial Union Assurance Company.. Here he remained, and gained so much of the confidence of the Directors that, in 1881, he was advanced to the Secretaryship, which position he held until February, 1884, when he was appointed to the position he now holds. While

there he has been responsible for the chief developments the Atlas has experienced of late years—the opening of Home Branches, the increase of the Foreign Business of the Company and of its powers of investment, together with several material changes in the Life Department prior to the appointment of the present Actuary. The stimulus given to the Company's business thereby has resulted in an addition to the Reserves of more than £150,000 in the last eight years, while the dividend in that time has been advanced from 15% to 22%. Mr. Pipkin is one of the Trustees of the London Salvage Corps Buildings, and also of the Royal Society for the Prevention of Loss of Life by Fire, a Vice-President of the Insurance Musical Society, and a Fellow of the Royal Geographical Society. In 1890 he made a complete circuit of the globe, the incidents of which journey he published under the title of "A Run Round the World," and the volume was very favourably received by the Press and the public.

W. H. PORT.

HENRY PORT.

Port, William Henry, the Sub-Manager and Actuary of the British Workman's Assurance Company, is the son of Mr. Henry Port, the General Manager of the same Company, and was born in the year 1857. He entered the service of the British Workman's Assurance Company in 1873, commencing at the bottom of the ladder as a Clerk in the Chief Office, but he speedily attained such a mastery over the details of the business that in 1879 he was appointed to the Superintendency of Liverpool and the adjacent districts. Up to that date the district had not been a profitable one to the Company, but, under Mr. W. H. Port's able management, it was not long before it began to recover the ground that it had lost, and made a considerable advance towards the important position that it now holds in the Company's books. In 1884 Mr. W. H. Port, who had given good evidence of his skill in Actuarial matters while supervising the above-mentioned district, was recalled to the Chief Office of the Company at Birmingham to take up the appointment of Assistant Actuary, which post he held for four years, when, in 1888, the higher and more responsible title of Actuary was conferred upon him. In the September of 1890 he again received promotion, being authorised to add the title of Sub-Manager to that which he already held.

Port, Henry, the Managing Director of the British Workman's Assurance Company, Limited, of Birmingham, was born on the 4th of June, 1833. His first connection with the Insurance world, in which he now holds so prominent a position, was made in the year 1851, when he started work as an Agent for the British Protector Life Office. This Company soon came to grief, and during the next few years Mr. Port experienced various changes through the transference and amalgamation of the Protector and other offices that he acted as Superintendent for.

In 1865 he was appointed District Manager at Birmingham for the Sceptre Life Insurance Company of London. His connection with this office, however, was a brief one, for in the following year (1866), he commenced what has proved to be his life work by founding the British Workman's Assurance Company, of which from the start he has been Managing Director.

From very small beginnings this office has grown, till it is to-day in the very front rank of Industrial Insurance Offices, and it is not too much to say that everything is due to the abilities, tact, energy, and remarkable organising powers of Mr. Henry Port.

JOHN E. PHILPOTT.

CHARLES POVAH.

Philpott, John Edward, the City Inspector to the Church of England Assurance Institution, was born in 1865. He began his Insurance career in 1881, by entering the Office of the Edinburgh Life Assurance Company. After passing through several of the Departments at the Head Office, he was placed in charge of the Agency Department, and in January, 1889, he was appointed Chief Clerk and Cashier in the London Office of the Company. This post he held till October, 1890, when he exchanged it for more active out-door work by accepting one of the District Inspectorships attached to the London Office of the Company.

In March, 1891, Mr. Philpott severed his connection with the "Edinburgh" by accepting his present post with the Church of England Assurance Institution.

———

Povah, Charles, A.I.A., Manager of the Life Department of the Lancashire Insurance Company of Manchester, was born in the year 1847, and was educated at Sheffield College. In January, 1865, his Insurance career commenced in the Head Office of the Company in which to-day he holds so distinguished a position. His professional training has been under the able guidance of Mr. George Stewart, the General Manager and Actuary of the Company. He has worked his way through every department of the office work, passing as Junior through each of both the Fire and Life branches, and has been Chief successively in the Foreign, Accountant's and Fire Re-assurance Departments in the Head Office. The ability he had shown, and the experience he had gained, led the Board, in 1871, to give him the appointment of Chief Clerk and Cashier in the Company's Branch Office at Birmingham. This position he held for about three years, relinquishing it in 1874 to return to the Head Office to take up the post of Cashier and Chief Clerk there. Six years later (in February, 1880), he received the appointment of Assistant-Actuary to the Company, and in the same year his professional abilities were recognised by his being elected by the Institute of Actuaries to an Associateship of that learned body. In January, 1889, the Directors of the Lancashire gave him the appointment of Joint Sub-Manager, and twelve months later (January, 1890), they made him sole Sub-Manager, and in October, 1891, he was promoted to be Manager of the Life Department. Mr. Povah is very popular in Insurance circles in Manchester, and is the President for the present year of the Insurance Institute of that City, in which capacity he delivered the opening address of the Winter Session on the 21st of October last, the subject of his address being "Some Modern Features of Fire Insurance."

WILLIAM PROCTOR

Proctor, William, is the Managing Director of the Refuge Assurance Company, Limited, which position he has occupied with signal success since the death of his father. Mr. Proctor is in the prime of life, and has shown great ability in the conduct of the affairs of this important and rapidly-growing Company.

Ronald, Thomas R., A.I.A., General Manager and Secretary of the Law Guarantee and Trust Society, Limited, is at present in his fortieth year. It is eleven years now since he entered the Insurance profession, prior to which he had gained a good insight into the higher ways of Commercial life and considerable experience in Stock Exchange and Banking Business, experiences that he confesses have proved of exceptional value to him in his present position. His first appointment in the Insurance world was as West End Inspector (London) for the Life Association of Scotland. This he left on being selected to be the Resident Secretary in Liverpool of the Scottish Equitable, where he remained five years, resigning the post then to open the present West End Office of the Caledonian in London. In all these positions his record is one of more than usual success. In June, 1888, he was offered the position he now holds, and in which his record speaks for itself. Mr. Ronald is the youngest son of the late John Ronald, Naval Architect and Shipbuilder, and is a Director of a prominent Railway in Nova Scotia, and other commercial undertakings.

BARON ALEXANDER PROFUMO.

Profumo, Baron Alexander, is chiefly known as the founder and the head of the Provident Association of London, an institution which combining all the best principles of Building Societies, was the first Corporation of the kind to combine Life Insurance with its system in such a manner that its members need have no fear of their death causing the loss of their savings. To do this a separate Company had to be formed, and the necessary £20,000 deposited with the Court of Chancery. It will be remembered that there was some confusion over the title of the Office, which was registered on the 4th of July, 1889, but this matter was amicably arranged with the Provident Life Office, and it is now known as the Provident Free Home Assurance Company Limited.

In addition to considerable personal property invested in British Securities, Baron Profumo has recently succeeded to very valuable properties in England through the death of a near relative, and is also the sole heir to very extensive family estates in Italy.

Baron Profumo has been approached by several constituencies, with a view to induce him to represent them in Parliament, but hitherto his duties in connection with the Provident Association have been too onerous to permit of his undertaking any such additional heavy responsibility, but now the organisation of that Corporation and its sister office being complete, he has felt himself justified in acceding to the wishes of his many friends and so recently accepted the offer of the Chief Liberal Organisation of South Monmouth, and has consented to be the candidate for that constituency at the next election. In politics the Baron is a Liberal, but his wide knowledge of men and affairs, of business and organisation, combined with the proved ability and skill that could found, lead and manage such a Corporation as the Provident Institution of London, will be a valuable acquisition to the body of public men of this country.

HENRY JOHN PUCKLE.

Puckle, Henry John, the present Manager and Secretary of the National Life Assurance Society of London, was born at Champion Hill, in the County of Surrey, in the year 1829.

He commenced his business life in 1843 in the service of a London wholesale house. In April, 1849, when twenty years of age, he gave up commerce for Insurance, and entered the service of the National Life. The Secretary of the office at that time was the late Mr. Charles Britiffe Smith. Very shortly after joining the staff of this office, Mr. Puckle was appointed Bookkeeper and Accountant to the Company. In this position he had opportunities of gaining experience in the practical working and management of a large Life Insurance Company, of which, it is hardly necessary to say, he fully availed himself, and which experience he has found very valuable to him in later years. By various promotions in different departments he gained a thorough knowledge of the Society's business, and from the year 1870 to 1874 he practically fulfilled the responsible duties of Secretary to the Board of Directors. In the latter year he received the formal appointment, which he still holds.

In 1886 the Directors of the Society gave him a further promotion by appointing him to the position of Manager to hold jointly with that of Secretary.

All these years he has enjoyed the thorough confidence of the Board, and in consideration of the many and valuable services he had rendered the Society during a service extending over forty years, in the year 1889 that body presented him with a fully paid-up policy of the Society on his life for one thousand pounds.

Mr. Puckle is married to the eldest daughter of the late William Standidge, Esq.

A. J. RELTON.

Relton, Arthur John, the Manager of the Fire Department of the Guardian Assurance Company of London, was born in 1856, and is the son of Francis Boyer Relton, the late Secretary of the Sun Fire Office. He entered the service of the Guardian in 1876, and, after working his way through the Home and Foreign Departments of that office, was appointed Chief of the Foreign Department in February, 1886, from which he was promoted (in February, 1888,) to the responsible position of Sub-Manager of the Fire Department. In October, 1888, on the death of Mr. F. J. Marsden, he received a further proof of the Directors' confidence in him and acknowledgment of his abilities by the offer of the post he at present holds, which he accepted.

Ryan, Gerald H., F.I.A., is the Actuary of the Royal Exchange Assurance Corporation, to which position he was appointed in 1888. In 1882 he became Assistant-Actuary of the Marine and General Life Assurance Society, and from this position he was promoted to the higher one of Actuary in 1886, resigning it two years later to accept that which he at present holds. Mr. Ryan has been a Member of the Council of the Institute of Actuaries, and is a Member of the Actuaries' Club. He is the Author of several contributions to the Journal of the Institute and also of a paper which was read before the Actuarial Society of Edinburgh in 1885.

ALFRED PRICE.

T. S. RODEN.

Price, Alfred, Secretary of the Ocean Marine Insurance Company, commenced his career in the Marine Insurance profession in the office of Mr. William Percival, Average Adjuster, which he entered in 1854, remaining there until Mr. Percival's death. He then went into the office of Mr. Manly Hopkins, and afterwards into that of Messrs. Davison, Son and Lindley for a short period ; at the end of which, in 1861, he became connected with the Ocean Marine Insurance Company in the capacity of Assistant-Secretary. At the end of another fifteen years, the late Secretary died, and Mr. Price, who naturally was more fitted by past practice to succeed him than any one else, was accordingly appointed Secretary in his place. Mr. Price is an official endowed with the highest abilities, and bears a reputation for honesty of purpose which gives him the unqualified confidence of all who have to do with him, whether in business matters or otherwise.

Roden, T. S., Secretary of the Life Association of Scotland, at its Newcastle-on-Tyne Branch, was born in 1846, and after receiving a sound education at Epsom College, Surrey, commenced his business career, at the early age of fourteen, as a Clerk in the National Provincial Bank of England in 1860. He remained in the services of that Bank for twenty-two years, working his way up through the various steps and acquiring a store of financial and administrative experience that has since been of considerable use to him, until in 1882 he was appointed to his present post with the Life Association of Scotland.

Ratliffe, Bernard E., is Joint Secretary of the County Fire Office of London, and was born in the year 1831. He was educated at private schools, and in 1849 entered the service of the Office he is still with. During the time he has been a member of the staff of this well-known Company he has passed through various departments, and for many years filled the position of Surveyor and Inspector of Fire Risks. In 1877 the Directors appointed him Joint Secretary, and he has now entered the fourth decade spent in the service of one Office.

EDGAR RICE.

ISAAC ROGERS.

Rice, Edgar, is the Secretary in London of the Queen Insurance Company. He was born in the old Surrey town of Croydon, where his family have resided for many generations, on the 12th of May, 1852. At the early age of fourteen he commenced his Insurance experience as a Junior in the London Office of the Royal. This was in the year 1866, and he remained in the service of this Company for upwards of seventeen years, passing through the Accountant's Department to the position of Fire Loss Clerk. He was afterwards appointed to the position of Chief Clerk at the Branch Office of the Company, opened at that time in Chancery Lane. In 1882 he joined the Head Office Staff of the Kent Fire and United Kent Life Offices at Maidstone. For these Corporations he opened the London Branch Offices, and received the appointment of Manager in London in 1884. Here he remained until October, 1890, when he was offered and accepted the position he holds at present. Mr. Rice has always been an enthusiastic supporter of outdoor sports and exercise, and for many years he acted as Secretary to the Insurance Companies' Football Team. At football he is an adept himself, and played regularly up to the year 1890. He is also a Member of the Victoria Rifles, and for many years past he has held the Marksman Badge of the Corps.

––––––

Rogers, Isaac, is the Manager of the Fire Department of the Law Union and Crown Fire and Life Insurance Company. He received his early Insurance training in the London Office of the Lancashire Insurance Company, where he remained for five years. He then, in 1857, joined the Staff of his present Company as Chief Clerk, having the superintendence of the Fire Department, of which Department he now holds the more exalted position of Manager. Mr. Rogers is a tried, trusted, and capable official, and one whose services have been of great value to his Company.

JAMES ROBB.

Robb, James, the Manager of the Fire Department of the Northern Assurance Company at its London Office, commenced his Insurance career on the staff of the Guardian Insurance Company at its Manchester Branch Office. Leaving this he received an appointment from the Directors of the Lancashire Insurance Company, with whom he remained some years, a great portion of which period he acted as Surveyor to the Company.

This last position Mr. Robb resigned to start business on his own account as an independent Fire Surveyor, in which business he was very successful, being employed by a number of offices, and frequently by the combined Fire Offices.

In the year 1866 the Board of Directors of the Northern Insurance Company offered him the position of Secretary and Surveyor to their Manchester Branch Office which he opened. Here his record was so good and his abilities so well marked that, in 1882, when the position of Manager of the Fire Department at the London Office became vacant, he was selected by the Management to have the first offer of the position, which he accepted.

Mr. Robb was one of the Founders of the Insurance Institute of Manchester, and was several times elected President of that body; and during the time he was immediately connected with the district he wrote and read before it several papers that proved of great interest and use to the members of that important organisation in the Insurance world.

ADAM K. RODGER.

Rodger, Adam K., the Manager of the Scottish Temperance Life Assurance Company Limited of Glasgow, was educated at the High School of Glasgow.

He entered the Commercial and Insurance world in the latter part of the year 1869, when he received an appointment in the office of Mr. William Smith, an Accountant and the Resident Secretary in the City of Glasgow for the London and Southwark Fire and Life Insurance Corporation of London. In the year 1877 he was admitted as a partner in the business which was afterwards known as Messrs. Smith, Rodger and Company. When the business of the London and Southwark Office was taken over by the London and Lancashire Insurance Company the firm were appointed to be the District Managers in Glasgow of the Law Union Fire and Life Office of London.

In the year 1883 Mr. Rodger commenced the organisation of the Office with which he has ever since been connected. In the founding of this Corporation Mr. Rodger had the active co-operation of the leading Temperance gentlemen in Scotland, and they worked with such will and earnestness that the Company was registered in the month of July, 1883. Mr. Rodger acted as the Secretary of the Office till the spring of 1891, when his title was changed to that of Manager.

J. J. ROBERTSON.

A. B. ROSE.

Robertson, John James, the Assistant Secretary at the Head Office of the Life Association of Scotland, entered the service of the Association in 1881, and from that time, until the close of 1883, acted as Inspector of Agents at the Head Office. At the latter date he went to Glasgow, to succeed Mr. Archibald Hewat (now Secretary at the Head Office of his Company) as Secretary at the West of Scotland Branch of the Edinburgh Life Office. During the latter part of his stay in Glasgow, Mr. Robertson was appointed, in addition to his duties as Secretary there, to take the supervision of the Newcastle Branch and District of the Edinburgh Life Office, which District embraced several of the Northern English Counties, extending as far south as York. He remained in Glasgow until the summer of 1888, when the Directors of the Life Association having decided to create a new post at their Head Office, i.e., Superintendent of Branches, Mr. Robertson was selected to fill that position, and accordingly returned to the service of his original Office; the duties of this position being principally to supervise and organise—under the direction and instructions of the Manager— the Association's Branch and Agency arrangements in the various districts throughout the United Kingdom. In 1890 Mr. Robertson was promoted to be Assistant Secretary at the Head Office of the Association, under which new designation he continues to carry out the work of Branch and Agency Organisation, in addition to the duties which usually devolve upon an Official occupying the position of Assistant Secretary.

Rose, Alexander Benjamin, Adjuster of Claims to the Marine Department of the Commercial Union Assurance Company in London, is one of the most widely-known experts in his own business in the whole of the profession of Marine Underwriters and Adjusters.

He is very frequently appealed to on knotty points affecting Marine Policies, and his opinions are highly valued, his decisions being rarely questioned.

He has been connected with the London Salvage Association for over thirty years, and he was elected to the Chairmanship of that body in 1887, and served in that position till 1890. He is also connected with the Association of Average Adjusters as the Representative Member of the Institute of London Underwriters.

Rowsell, Hubert G., the Secretary of the Mutual Life Assurance Society of London, was born in the Metropolis. He first entered the Insurance world and his present office in 1860 as a Junior Clerk under the late Mr. Ingall, who was then the Actuary of the Society. After passing through several offices he was appointed Head Clerk; and in the year 1885, the office was reorganised, and he was then created Secretary of the Society.

FREDK. W. RUTHERFORD.

ARTHUR RUTTER.

Rutherford, Frederick William, is the Assistant Manager of the Scottish Alliance Insurance Company, Limited, of Glasgow. He was for some time a pupil of the Rev. Dr. Abbott at the City of London School, and his business career was commenced in 1879, when he entered the office of the London Guarantee and Accident Company Limited as a Junior Clerk. To Mr. Laughton Anderson, the Secretary of that Company, he is indebted for the advantage of a sound practical training, and when, after a service of about eight years, Mr. Rutherford occupied a responsible position upon the staff of the Company, he was offered an important post by the Mercantile Accident and Guarantee Insurance Company, Limited, of Glasgow. There he acted as Chief Assistant to the General Manager for a period of two years, and upon a change in the management of the Company, he was appointed to the position of Secretary. For some time previous to his promotion, Mr. Rutherford had been devoting himself closely to the preparation of a scheme for applying the principles of Insurance to Burglary, with the result that shortly after that event the Mercantile announced the introduction of a system of Burglary Insurance. Evidence of the importance of this new feature was soon afforded by the expansion which attended the operations of the Mercantile, and at the present time there are several Companies doing business in the same field.

In May, 1891, a scheme was carried into effect for the amalgamation of the Mercantile with their neighbour, the Scottish Alliance Insurance Company, and Mr. Rutherford was appointed Assistant-Manager of the "Scottish Alliance." In that position he continues to take charge of the Accident, Fidelity Guarantee, and Burglary Departments.

It is the intention of the Directors, however, to transfer the last-named branch to a separate Company with headquarters in London, and it is understood that Mr. Rutherford has undertaken the formation of a Company for the purpose, and is to be its General Manager and Secretary.

Mr. Rutherford is a Fellow of the Statistical Society.

Rutter, Arthur, General Manager and Secretary of the Cambridge University and Town Fire Insurance Company, Limited, was the original founder of that Company, which was started in 1887. It speaks highly for Mr. Rutter's enterprise that the Cambridge University and Town Fire Insurance Company was the outcome of a chance conversation with Mr. W. B. Redfarn, the Chairman of the Company, on the commerce of Cambridge and the possibility of establishing a Company of this sort; acting on which idea, Mr. Rutter floated his Company, induced a number of gentlemen to take up shares, and in a few days registered it to carry on business in the United Kingdom and elsewhere. Since then the career of the Company has been one of uninterrupted success, which is likewise due to the organisation and able management of its affairs by Mr. Rutter. Mr. Rutter is also Secretary to the Cambridgeshire Permanent Benefit Building Society, instituted in 1850, to which post he was elected in 1876, by a large majority over all other candidates, a material testification of his popularity and reputation for business-like qualities. Mr. Arthur Rutter is deservedly esteemed by all who have ever had to do with him.

F. W. P. RUTTER.

Rutter, F. W. P., the Sub-Manager of the London and Lancashire Fire Insurance Company at its Head Office, was born in Liverpool, and educated at the Liverpool College.

He commenced his Insurance career in the service of the Office in which he has risen to so high a position, at the early age of fifteen, when he entered on an apprenticeship to the Company. He worked his way through various departments of the office, gaining experience and practical acquaintance with all the details of Fire Underwriting, until at length he was appointed to the position of Head Clerk in the Foreign Department. While holding this post he travelled very extensively abroad for the Company. His journeys covered the whole of Europe, and among the places he visited were Constantinople and Athens. In addition to these, other journeys on important business connected with the Company's affairs took him to both North and South America, in both of which Continents he had to travel very widely. He has thus had exceptional opportunities of acquiring a very extensive knowledge of men and manners, as well as of the various systems adopted in different countries and centres of the practice of Fire Underwriting.

His next promotion was to the post of Assistant Secretary to the Company, the onerous duties of which he discharged for two years; indeed until July, 1891, when the Board of Directors gave him his present appointment, thus making him the Second Chief Officer of the Company, to which, at a very early age, he brings an experience so ripe and wide as to be unsurpassed in any living Insurance Man.

Saunders, Harris C. L., F.I.A., F.R.A.S., the Actuary and General Manager of the Sun Life Assurance Society, was born in 1847, and is therefore 45 years of age. His whole business career has been passed in that Office, and it has been his agreeable lot to see the rapid growth and development of business follow as the consequences of the several improvements introduced and perfected by him. Passing in early life through the various grades of the Office, in 1882 he was appointed Assistant-Actuary and Assistant Secretary ; in 1883 he was elected a Fellow of the Institute of Actuaries, and shortly afterwards he was appointed Joint Actuary with Mr. John George Priestley. In 1887 the High Court of Justice appointed him one of the Actuaries to value the liabilities of the Sovereign Life Office (in liquidation), the result of his efforts being the introduction of the policy-holders to his own Office on terms satisfactory to both parties. On the retirement of Mr. Priestley, in the early part of 1890, he became General Manager, a title which the Managers of the Sun

HARRIS C. L. SAUNDERS, F.I.A.

Life Office then conferred for the first time as more fully descriptive of the extended functions and responsibilities assumed by him. An examination of the methods pursued since this important Office was created, and a comparison of these methods with those which prevailed some time anterior to the public announcement of the appointment, make it evident that he had been inspiring the many changes which have proved so

beneficial in their results, and he has now the satisfaction of looking back upon a past which he altered and moulded to suit the requirements of the times. Under his Management the conditions of Assurance at the Sun have been completely modernized. Policies are now made world - wide from the outset, claims are paid immediately on proof of death and title, and a complete system has been devised for the maintenance of policies which might otherwise be endangered through omission or inability to pay premiums and to facilitate the transfer of policies and promote rapid and economical dealings with them. His attitude on the assignment of policies, the Life Assurance Companies Acts, and the Married Women's Property Act, in relation to Life Assurance has had an important bearing on the practice of the Office. The system introduced by him in connection with the complete settlement of policies and the registration of titles has tended considerably towards simplifying the contract and rendering policies readily marketable and easily negotiable. He introduced the system of Assurance without Medical Examination under proper safeguards, and this and the double option scheme, which have proved so acceptable, have resulted in great benefit to the Office. The establishment of the Sun Life Assurance Company of India is one of the latest of Mr. Saunders' successes, and he is its Actuary and General Manager.

JAMES CARR SAUNDERS.

Saunders, James Carr, Underwriter of the Commercial Union Assurance Company Limited, is the scion of a family that has been identified with Underwriting in London for considerably over a century. At an early age he commenced his acquaintance with the science and practice of Marine Insurance, entering the service of his uncle, the late Mr. William Saunders, at Lloyd's when only seventeen years old. Here he remained till 1860, when he was offered and accepted the position of Second Underwriter in the London Office of the Thames and Mersey Marine Insurance Company, the Underwriter of which at that time was Mr. Henry Burnand. He took such advantage of the experience and practice this position afforded him, and so increased his reputation among the principals of his profession, that two years and a half later he was selected to fill the appointment he holds now. Since then each year has brought him increased reputation and honour among his *confrères*, and, if the word may be used, rivals. He is the Chairman of the Institute of London Underwriters, thus occupying the highest position possible in his profession, and in addition has been chosen to be the Representative of the London Marine Insurance Companies on the Committee of Lloyd's Register. In Marine Insurance circles, as may be imagined, Mr. Saunders occupies a conspicuous and unique position. It is the great aim of the Brokers to get him to "lead" their risks, more especially perhaps those known as "time risks," as they well know there will be but little difficulty in finishing a risk commenced by him, the Underwriters of London Companies deferring much to his judgment.

JAMES H. SCOTT, F.S.S.

Scott, James Henry, F.S.S., the Secretary of the Gresham Life Assurance Society of London, was born in London, in January, 1854.

After receiving a thorough commercial and general education, he decided to adopt for his life's career the profession in which, by sheer ability, personal qualifications and energy, he has won so high a position.

For sixteen years he was in the service of the English and Scottish Law Life Assurance Association of London at its Head Office in Waterloo Place. He passed in turn through various departments, thoroughly qualifying himself in each, and gaining much knowledge and experience that has been of exceptional value to him in later years. He so gained the confidence of the Management and Board of Directors of the Association that, in the year 1886, they offered him the position of Agency Manager of the Society, and this he accepted. Subsequently, various other responsible duties were added to this office, all of which he carried out with credit to himself and the satisfaction of the Board.

In the year 1888 Mr. Joseph Allen, who had for many years occupied the position of Secretary to the Gresham Life Assurance Society of London, died. As well may be imagined the number of applicants for such a coveted post were very numerous, and consequently the duty of selection a very onerous one for the Board. After careful consideration they decided that Mr. James H. Scott was the man for the post, and he was duly appointed. It is proved that the congratulations of his friends on his becoming announced were merited by the excellent way in which he has since fulfilled the duties such a position entails on its holder.

WILLIAM SCOTT.

Scott, William, is the Agency Manager of the Imperial Life Insurance Company. He commenced his Insurance career in the service of the British Equitable Assurance Company, whence he subsequently removed to that of the Sun Life Office, leaving that again to take up his present duties. He is held in the highest esteem by his Manager and all connected with the Company.

Schooling, Frederick, F.I.A., is the Actuary of the Prudential Assurance Company, Limited, of London, the service of which office he entered in 1867. He passed the several examinations of the Institute of Actuaries in the years 1884, 1885, and 1886 respectively, and in the year 1888 he was appointed Assistant Actuary, being in 1892 promoted to be Actuary.

PHILIP SECRETAN.

Secretan, Philip, Underwriter of the Ocean Marine Insurance Company, comes of a family whose name has for over a century been honourably connected with Underwriting in the City of London. His father, Mr. Philip Secretan, was a well-known Member of Lloyd's, and it was in his office that he commenced his career as an Insurance man, at a very early age, in the year 1854. Having passed through his father's office, Mr. Secretan was afterwards in the employ of the Universal and Oriental and General Marine Insurance Companies successively, subsequently, in 1868, being appointed Assistant Underwriter to the London and Provincial Marine Insurance Company. There he remained till 1883, when he was selected as Underwriter to the City of London Marine Insurance Corporation, and on leaving the London and Provincial Marine, the Directors of that Company presented him with a service of silver, and a resolution expressing their appreciation of, and regret at losing, his services, which had extended over a period of fifteen years. Mr. Secretan, on taking up his new post, found the City of London Marine Insurance Corporation involved in great difficulties; half the capital of the Corporation having been lost, and with it, of course, a great deal of its credit; and its £2 shares depreciated in value to five shillings. He set to work, however, with a good heart, and in five years had not only recovered the Corporation's lost capital but had placed it in such a sound position that in 1888 the Ocean Marine Insurance Company entered into negotiations and finally agreed to purchase its business on the basis of giving £2.1s. for each £2 share and a further sum to be paid when the accounts were finally settled; it being also agreed that Mr. Secretan should become the Underwriter to the Ocean Company. Since then he has had more difficulties to contend with in an unprecedented list of casualties on good business; but notwithstanding that he has done well, and fully sustained his reputation for skill, prudence, and caution.

W. L. SEYFANG.

Seyfang, Walter Louis, the Manager and Secretary of the Kent Fire and Life Offices of Maidstone, is a son of the late Mr. George Bond Seyfang, who was for more than forty years the Secretary to Lloyd's Register in London.

Born in London in the year 1847, his Insurance career commenced in 1864, when he entered the London Office of the Royal Insurance Company of Liverpool, and in the service of that Company he remained until 1881. During those seventeen years he passed through most of the Departments of the Office, thus practically acquiring a wide general knowledge of all that pertains to Under-writing, and the experience then gained he has been able to put to excellent use.

In 1881, when Mr. Lendon, who had held the position of Secretary to the Kent Offices for nearly thirty years, retired, it may well be imagined that the Board of Directors had very many applicants for the post. After very careful consideration, their choice fell upon Mr. Seyfang, and he at once took up the duties he has since discharged so admirably.

Mr. Seyfang stands very high in the opinions of his brother Insurance officials as an expert, and as one always worth following, which is as high a compliment as can be paid him.

GEORGE E. SCHMETTAU.

EDWARD MAPLETON SHEPHERD.

Schmettau, George E., is the Deputy Underwriter of the Marine Department of the Royal Exchange Assurance Corporation of London, to which position he was appointed in the year 1888.

Mr. Schmettau's experience in Underwriting has been a long one, and he has had excellent opportunities of acquiring a thorough knowledge of his profession, of which he has not failed to avail himself. He first entered Lloyd's, twenty years ago (in 1872) in connection with the well-known firm of Messrs. Hogg and Robinson. With them he remained four years, being then (in 1876) appointed by Mr. F. C. L. Rasch to the position of his Underwriting Clerk, and this position he held until the retirement of Mr. Rasch in 1882.

In the year 1884 Mr. Schmettau was appointed Underwriter in London to the Mannheim Insurance Company of Germany, and he held this position until 1888, when he resigned it to accept the one he at present holds.

Shepherd, Edward Mapleton, is the Assistant Underwriter of the Ocean Marine Insurance Company. He has had a good training in Insurance business, and is well known in the profession, having commenced his business life in 1877 at Lloyd's in the service of the important firm of Messrs. Robert Bradford and Company. After being seven years with them, he next obtained an appointment with the London Assurance Corporation under Mr. Mackintosh, which appointment he held until he entered upon his present duties at the end of 1889. He has since then fully justified the confidence placed in him by the Directors of the Ocean Marine Insurance Company when selecting him for this responsible position.

ALFRED B SHELLEY.

Shelley, Alfred B., is the Secretary of the Imperial Union Accident Assurance Company. He was born in 1841, and has passed the whole of his business life in the Insurance profession, having commenced as a Clerk in the Office of the Kent Mutual, and on the absorption of that Company by the Albert, having entered the service of the latter in the same capacity. When the Imperial Union Accident Assurance Company was formed, Mr. Shelley applied for and obtained the post, which he still holds, and, being a gentleman of much ability, under his guidance the Imperial Union has hitherto enjoyed a very prosperous career.

A. GILLIES SMITH, F.F.A, F.R.S.E.

Smith, Adam Gillies, is the Manager at Edinburgh of the North British and Mercantile Insurance Company, and like many another prominent member of the profession North of the Tweed, is the son of a minister of the Church of Scotland. His father, the late Reverend Robert Smith, D.D., was Senior Incumbent of the Cathedral Church of Aberdeen.   Of five sons, the two eldest chose the profession of arms, the survivor having attained the rank of a General in the army, while medicine claimed the two youngest, one being now Medical Superintendent of the Durham County Asylum, and the other, Surgeon-General Colvin Smith, C.B., who organized the Indian Ambulance Corps, which did such eminent service in the Egyptian Campaign. The subject of this sketch, the third son, was born in 1827, and named after his grand-uncle, Lord Gillies, a Scottish Judge of great eminence. Mr. Gillies Smith was for some years partner in the firm of Messrs. McClelland, Son, and Smith, Accountants, of Glasgow. He then transferred his energies to Edinburgh, where, in partnership with a son of Lord Moncreiff, Lord Justice Clerk of Scotland, he was carrying on the business of an Accountant, when he was appointed in 1880 Manager in Edinburgh of both Fire and Life Departments of the North British and Mercantile Insurance Company, of which he was afterwards appointed Registrar.

Mr. Gillies Smith is a Member of the Society of Chartered Accountants in Edinburgh, a Fellow of the Faculty of Actuaries in Scotland, a Fellow and Treasurer of the Royal Society of Edinburgh, Local Treasurer of the Meeting of the British Association to be held in Edinburgh, and a Justice of the Peace for Edinburgh. He married, in 1868, the eldest daughter of S. G. Barrett, Esq., of Barrett Hall, Jamaica.

E. COZENS SMITH.

Smith, E. Cozens, the General Manager and Secretary of the Imperial Fire Insurance Company of London, was born in 1834, and represents an old Hertfordshire family, which settled at St. Margaret's about 1550. He commenced his Insurance career at the early age of seventeen, entering the office of the Phœnix Fire in 1851, under the management of the late Mr. Wilmer Harris. Here he spent six years, gaining a wide knowledge of, and much experience in, his profession which was to bear fruit very early, for in 1857, when he joined the Globe Office under Mr. Newmarch, he was promptly set to work to analyse the business on the books of that Company, in order that the various risks might be separated and classified. This responsible and arduous task he carried out to the entire satisfaction of his superior officer. After about six years the amalgamation of the Globe with the Liverpool and London took place, and at that time Mr. Cozens Smith had been acting for a short period as Sub-Manager of the Unity Fire and Life Company. This position he resigned to accept office in the service of the then newly-formed Commercial Union. At that time this office worked on the non-tariff system, and it was in particular to push this that Mr.

Cozens Smith's services were secured, on the suggestion of Mr. Henry Thomson. The astuteness, energy, and skill with which he worked so successfully at this difficult task, were recognised by his appointment to be Chief Officer of the Company, when Mr. Thomson (in 1865) removed to the Liverpool and London and Globe.

This position he continued to fill until 1873, when the General Managership of the Imperial Fire Office was offered to him, and he accepted it. He has amply fulfilled the expectations of those who invited him to fill the office. In the enormous and daily-increasing business of the Imperial, with its wide and important connections, he has found plenty of field and scope for his energy and fertility of resource. During the last few years he has travelled to all parts of the world to inspect and obtain a personal knowledge of the Foreign Agencies and Risks held by the Company. Thus, besides gaining a first-hand knowledge of Foreign business unequalled perhaps by any other man in his profession, he has likewise acquired that great essential to success as an Insurance Manager,—a thorough acquaintance with the men with whom he has to deal.

J FISHER SMITH, F.S.S.

Smith, J. Fisher, the General Manager of the New York Life Insurance Company for the United Kingdom, is an American, born in Boston in 1839, coming from a good old Puritan stock, his ancestors having emigrated to America in 1630, and his great grandfather having fought in the War of Independence. His father, Captain N. Proctor Smith, was distinguished for having opened up commerce between Turkey and the United States after the Græco-Turkish War in 1826. Mr. J. Fisher Smith, having received his education at Boston, left that city in 1856, and went to California amongst the foremost of the pioneers, where he followed many occupations and endured many privations, in all of which he showed himself worthy of his sturdy persevering ancestors. In 1862 he went to China, and gained fresh experience as purser and chief officer on board steamers running on the Yanghi river, where he remained for three years, at the end of which period he returned to San Francisco. In 1866 he took part in the famous Bregfoyle Expedition to Los Angelos in search of some supposed gold mines of fabulous wealth, in the course of which he and his companions underwent almost unheard-of privations and danger, and which eventually proved futile. On his return from this expedition he settled down to more civilised pursuits, joining the Pacific Department of the Mutual Life Insurance Company as Secretary, and subsequently resigning that position in March, 1870, to enter the service of the New York Life. In April of that same year he was sent over to London to represent his Company as Sub-manager for Europe, which position he held till 1874, during the latter two years of which period he acted as Manager for the United Kingdom. On the 1st of November, 1874, his efforts in behalf of his Company were rewarded by his appointment to his present position of General Manager for the United Kingdom. Mr. Fisher Smith is kind and considerate, though firm in maintaining discipline amongst his staff, and their appreciation of him in their turn is amply shown by their having presented him with a handsome testimonial subscribed for by a numerous body of District Managers and Special Representatives of the New York Life Insurance Company in Great Britain and Ireland.

J. GARNER SMITH.

Smith, J. Garner, is the Secretary of the Travellers' Accident Insurance Company. He has had a long and varied business experience, having commenced as a Clerk in a West India Merchant's Office in 1864, which firm he eventually represented for some years at Lloyd's. He afterwards became London Inspector for the Scottish Accident Insurance Company, thus taking up a new line for his energies, but relinquished that post to become London Manager of the Scottish Assurance Corporation. On that ill-fated Company going into liquidation in 1889, Mr. Smith was appointed Manager of the Accident Department of the Glasgow and London Insurance Company, with a view to making use of his former experience to specially organise that Department, which he succeeded in doing most effectually. Owing, however, to the Economic Fire Office taking over the Fire Business of the Glasgow and London at the close of 1890, arrangements were made for the transfer of the Accident and Fidelity Business to the new-formed Travellers' Accident Insurance Company, with the express understanding that Mr. Garner Smith was to be appointed Agency Manager to the latter Company, which appointment accordingly took place, and on the resignation of Mr. A. C. Macintyre in February, 1892, the Directors decided to promote him to his present position as Secretary of that Company. Mr. Garner Smith's friends and acquaintances speak of him as a remarkably well-informed, shrewd business-like man of the world, besides being widely known for his eminent qualities as a companion and a friend.

J. TURNBULL SMITH, F.F.A., C.A

Smith, John Turnbull, F.F.A., is Manager of the Life Association of Scotland. A native of Peeblesshire, he spent his early days in the Upper Ward of Lanarkshire, and went to Edinburgh in 1857, at the early age of fourteen, to start his apprenticeship with the late Mr. Kenneth Mackenzie, Chartered Accountant. About six months after completion of his apprenticeship, Mr. Turnbull Smith was taken into partnership, and was associated with Mr. Mackenzie until the latter's death in 1880, after which time Mr. Turnbull Smith continued to carry on the business on his own account. As an Accountant, he held various public appointments, such as, Auditor to the Highland and Agricultural Society, to the Leith Dock Commission, to the Royal College of Physicians, and other public institutions, while his private appointments included Auditor to the Earl of Wemyss, the Earl of Zetland, and Mr. A. J. Balfour, M.P. In 1883 Mr. Turnbull Smith became a Director of the Life Association of Scotland, and on the death of Mr. Fraser, Manager of the Association, in 1885, he was asked by his co-directors to accept the post of Manager, since which time the business of the Association has considerably increased, the new business reported in 1891 exceeding one million sterling, being the largest amount transacted in any one year of the Association's history. A Fellow of the Faculty of Actuaries in Scotland, Mr. Turnbull Smith has for the last few years held the office of Honorary Treasurer to that Incorporation. Mr. Turnbull Smith has been associated with various religious and social movements, and as Convener of the General Assembly of the Church of Scotland's Committee on Sunday Schools, he has shewn a deep interest in the welfare of the young. In 1891 he was elected to the honourable position of Master of the Merchant Company of Edinburgh, after having, for a year previously, filled the office of Honorary Treasurer to that important body.

WILLIAM SMITH, LL.D., F.I.A.

Smith, William, LL.D., F.F.A., F.I.A., is a gentleman commanding universal respect, both within and without Insurance circles. For the long period of 45 years he has held the post of Manager at Edinburgh of the English and Scottish Law Life Assurance Association, a term of service now surpassing that of any present Life Assurance Manager in Scotland. The business of the Association has been wisely and surely developed under his care. For the last quarter of a century, he has acted as Chairman of the National Guarantee and Suretyship Association, Edinburgh.

Dr. Smith's name is also well-known in connec-

tion with the Philosophical Institution, Edinburgh, of which he was Vice-President for a long series of years ; and it was largely owing to his influence and guidance that the Institution gained the high position it held as an acknowledged centre of literary and scientific culture. His translation of the popular works of J. G. Fichte, the German Philosopher, has long maintained its position in the philosophic world in Great Britain, and has passed through several editions. At one time a keen pedestrian and traveller, Dr. Smith has visited most parts of Europe. He now resides chiefly at his pleasant country seat near Edinburgh.

WALTER A. SMITH, F.F.A.

DAVID SMITH.

Smith, Walter A., F.F.A., Secretary at Edinburgh to the English and Scottish Law Life Assurance Association, began his business career in the service of the Bank of Scotland, first at Edinburgh, and afterwards at their Office in London. In 1875 the Directors of the English and Scottish Law Life Assurance Association appointed him "Life Clerk" at Edinburgh, in succession to Mr. George M. Low, F.I.A., on the occasion of the appointment of the latter as Secretary to the Edinburgh Life Assurance Company. In 1878 Mr. Smith was promoted to the post of Secretary to the Edinburgh Board of the "English and Scottish," which position he has since held. Mr. Smith is well known in the Insurance world in the North. For some years he acted as Honorary Secretary to the Edinburgh Health Society, and arranged several of the series of the wonderfully successful "Health Lectures," given under its auspices by Edinburgh Physicians. He is a Director of the Scottish Rights of Way and Recreation Society Limited.

Smith, David, is the Agency Superintendent of the Scottish Equitable Life Assurance Society at Edinburgh. Previous to his connection with the Society for which he at present acts, Mr. David Smith was, for a period of upwards of twelve years, employed as Chief Clerk in the Head Office, also located in Edinburgh, of the Colonial Life Assurance Company, of which circumstances have since that time brought about the amalgamation with the Standard Life Assurance Company, and whilst engaged in that Office he received a careful intuition into the details of the Insurance business from its then able Manager, the late well-known Mr. William Thomas Thomson, which has since proved of great value to him in his subsequent career. In the year 1865 Mr. David Smith received the appointment of Superintendent of Agencies to the Scottish Equitable Life Assurance Society, of which first-class office the late Mr. George Todd then held the Managership. For several years subsequent to the date of his joining the Society, Mr. Smith acted as sole Inspector to the Scottish Equitable, but since the accession of Mr. Sprague, the present Manager to the Office, Mr. Smith's chief official duties have been for by far the most part carried on at the Head Office at Edinburgh, the large and steady increase in the business of the Society having rendered it impossible for one man to conduct it in anything like an adequate manner, and having consequently necessitated a correspondingly extensive increase in the number of the Resident Secretaries and District Inspectors, who are now dispersed about the various districts throughout the United Kingdom under the control of the Society.

ARTHUR SMITHER, F.I.A.

Smither, Arthur, F.I.A., is the Actuary and Secretary of the National Provident Institution, in the service of which Corporation he has spent the whole of his Insurance career. He was born in London in 1842, and entered the Office of the National Provident in 1865. In 1879 he received the appointment of Assistant-Secretary, which he held till 1882, when he was made the Actuary of the Institution. The year following he received the additional appointment of the Secretaryship. Mr. Smither has the reputation of being one of the most capable Actuaries in the City of London, and certainly has done much to bring the National Provident to its present high position among Life Insurance Companies.

Sorley, James, F.I.A., the Actuary and Secretary of the Scottish Life Assurance Company, has been Joint Principal Officer at the Head Office of that Company at Edinburgh since 1881. He has also for many years been a partner in the firm of Paulin, Sorley and Martin, Accountants and Actuaries, Edinburgh. Mr. Sorley is a Fellow of the Institute of Actuaries, London, a Fellow of Faculty of Actuaries, Edinburgh, and a member of the Institute of Chartered Accountants, Glasgow, in each case by examination. He is also a Fellow of the Royal Society of Edinburgh and Honorary Treasurer of the Scottish Meteorological Society. He has made several contributions to Actuarial literature in the Journal of the Institute of Actuaries.

EDWARD H. SMITHETT.

Smithett, Edward Henry, A.I.A., the Secretary and Manager of the West of England Fire and Life Insurance Company of Exeter, began his professional and Insurance career in the London Office of the Scottish Provincial Insurance Company, on the staff of which office he remained for five years, and at the end of that period he served for a year on the London Office of the Royal, and was then appointed to the position of Chief Clerk in the London Office of the Company of which to-day he is the official chief. Subsequently he entered the Head office of the Guardian Assurance Company of London as Chief Counter Clerk, and this post he held for six years.

In the year 1883 the London and Provincial Law Life was absorbed by the Guardian, and Mr. Smithett was then promoted to be the Assistant-Manager of the Law Courts Branch Office, and on the subsequent retirement of Mr. Ralph P. Hardy, F.I.A., from the office of Manager of the Branch, he was further promoted to the chief position.

This Management proved very successful, and his reputation was consequently considerably increased. In May, 1888, on the position he now fills becoming vacant, he was selected (from sixty candidates) by the Board of Directors of the Company for the appointment.

WILLIAM G SPENS.

Spens, William G., the Secretary of the Scottish Amicable Life Assurance Society of Glasgow, is a son of the late Mr. William Spens, who was for nearly thirty years the Manager of that Society, holding the appointment from 1839 until his death in the year 1868.

The subject of this article commenced his Insurance career in 1863, as a Clerk under his father, and for five years he remained in the Head Office of the Society, gaining much experience and practical knowledge of the routine work of the Office and practice of Life Assurance, which has proved most valuable to him in later life. Towards the close of the year 1868 Mr. Spens was sent by the Board of Directors to the London Office of the Society, on the staff of which he worked for some months.

Early in the year 1869 he was selected by the Board to fill the appointment of Resident Secretary at the Branch Office of the Society in Edinburgh, and this position he held until the month of March, 1878. At that date he was appointed to the important position he at present holds.

T. B. SPRAGUE, M.A., F.I.A., F.F.A., F.S.S.

Sprague, T. B., is the Manager of the Scottish Equitable Life Assurance Society. Mr. Sprague was for some years Actuary and Secretary to the Equity and Law Life Assurance Society of London, but resigned that post in 1873, when, on the death of Mr. Todd, he was selected by the Directors of the Scottish Equitable to succeed that gentleman in the post which he now holds. Mr. Sprague is a Manager of great energy and organising ability, and enjoys a world-wide fame as an Actuary. His accession to the Management marked a new era in the history of the Scottish Equitable; at once taking means to extend the business by opening Branch Offices and appointing Agency Inspectors, a large body of active Agents being at the same time appointed throughout the United Kingdom, he soon had the satisfaction of seeing the business come in at a considerably increased ratio. The new business now accruing to the Society is something between £700,000 and £800,000 annually, all of which is practically owing to Mr. Sprague's personal genius as their Manager and Actuary. Never behind the times, he has always been amongst the first to introduce every modern and attractive improvement into the methods of his office with a view to increasing its popularity and usefulness.

GEORGE STEWART, F.I.A.

Stewart, George, F.I.A., the General Manager and Actuary of the Lancashire Insurance Company of Manchester, is a native of Edinburgh, in which city he was also educated and commenced his professional career. He received his early training in the office of the late Mr. Holmes Ivory, who was then the Actuary to the Advocates Widows' Fund, and other Insurance Societies. This accomplished gentleman was also for some time the Manager of the Scottish National Insurance Company. Mr. Stewart spent eight years in Mr. Ivory's office, receiving a thorough training in Actuarial science, and gaining an experience which has been of the greatest value to him in his after life. At the end of that time, on being appointed the Manager of the North of England Insurance Company he came to England. He held this position for some time, resigning it a year or two before the Company was amalgamated with the Liverpool and London Insurance Company. On the retirement of the late Mr. James Kennedy, in the year 1858, Mr. Stewart received an offer of the appointment he has now held for upwards of thirty-three years. In that time he has conducted no less than seven Quinquennial Valuations of the Company's Life Business, and has besides negotiated the purchase of five Insurance Companies, namely, the Birmingham Fire Office, the Birmingham Alliance Insurance Company, the Northern Counties Assurance Corporation, the Scottish Commercial Insurance Company, and the London and Staffordshire Insurance Office. Under Mr. Stewart's control and guidance the Lancashire has prospered considerably. In 1858 the Fire Premium Income was £41,926 ; in 1891 it reached the colossal figure of £905,238. During the same period the Fire Reserve Fund which now exceeds £500,000, has been built up ; the Life Premium Income has grown from £19,724 to £86,022, and the Life Reserve Fund from £44,989 to £862,639 sterling. In 1858 the total funds of the Company were £200,000, and they now exceed a million and three-quarters sterling. It must be always universally admitted that the most potent factor in reaching these results has been the conspicuous ability and earnestness which have characterised Mr. Stewart's management, and the honourable and liberal policy which, under his guidance, has marked the Company's career. Mr. Stewart has been a Fellow of the Institute of Actuaries since the year 1859.

WILLIAM SUTTON, M.A., F.I.A.

Sutton, William, M.A., F.I.A., is the present holder of the very important position of Actuary to the Central Office of the Registry of Friendly Societies.

He was born in 1842, and was educated at King Edward's School, Birmingham, whence he went to St. John's College, Cambridge. At the University his career was a prominent one, as he gained various exhibitions and also a Foundation Scholarship, finally graduating in 1865 as thirty-second Wrangler.

In the respective years 1866, 1867 and 1868, Mr. Sutton passed the three examinations of the Institute of Actuaries, to qualify for the Fellowship of that Body. His first practical connection with the Life Insurance world was, however, not made till two years later, when, in the year 1870, he became private Actuarial-Assistant to Mr. T. B. Sprague, F.I.A., who at that time held the position of Actuary and Secretary to the Equity and Law Life Assurance Society.

Three years later (in 1873) Mr. Sutton resigned this position to succeed Mr. T. G. C. Browne, F.I.A., F.S.S. (the present Actuary and Secretary the Guardian Assurance Company, of London),

in the post of Chief Clerk in the Office of the London and Provincial Law Assurance Society. Here he remained until when, in 1876, the Friendly Societies Act (which had been passed the year previous, 1875,) came into full force and operation, Mr. Sutton was selected by the late Lord Iddesleigh, who was then the Chancellor of the Exchequer, to fill the post of Actuary to the Central Office of the Friendly Societies' Registry. Mr. Sutton now acts in addition as Actuarial Adviser to the Board of Trade.

To Actuarial Literature Mr. Sutton has been a prolific and valuable contributor, including, besides Part I. of the Institute of Actuaries' Text-Book, many papers and letters to its Journal, and he has also taken a very active part in the educational and examining work of the Institute. To him the Institute will ever remain specially indebted for his services in connection with the grant of a Royal Charter of Incorporation to that body. Altogether the position he holds in the Actuarial world is a most prominent and important one, and from June, 1888, to June, 1890, when under the bye-laws his term of office expired, Mr. Sutton held the distinguished position of President of the Institute. He is also a Barrister-at-Law.

EDWIN R. SPEIRS, F.S.S.

Speirs, Edwin Robert, is the Comptroller of the British Department of the Mutual Reserve Fund Life Association of New York. Mr. Speirs is one of the most energetic of our young Insurance men. He was born in London of Scottish parentage in 1860, and consequently is now in his thirty-second year. Since boyhood he has been self-dependent, and his present position is one that has been attained by those qualities that go to make the successful man. At an early age he entered the Insurance world in the London Office of the Scottish Equitable. In 1880 he was appointed to a Clerkship in the Head Office of the Clerical, Medical, and General, making advancement through the different grades. Feeling, however, that the Clerical Department was too limited, after a number of years he concluded to take a more active position for this Office, and was very successful in securing business for this office in connection with the City Branch. In August, 1888, he was appointed Secretary of the London Branch of the Provincial Life Office. During the early part of 1889 his attention was attracted towards the Mutual Reserve, and being induced to apply for the Sub-Managership, received the appointment. In October of 1890 he was promoted to his present position. Mr. Speirs is a Fellow of the Royal Statistical Society ; a Member of the Society of Arts ; and he also belongs to a City Company. He is well known in the political world, and is a forcible and effectual platform speaker. His interest in all subjects of an econom. ical or social nature is recognized by the *cognos centi*, and his opinions have weight, to which they are justly entitled.

HENRY STEEL.

D. J. SURENNE, F.F.A., A.I.A.

Steel, Henry, is the Manager of the British Legal Life Assurance Company of Glasgow, which post he has held since the death of his father, the former manager, in 1870.

Mr. Steel has had a large experience in Industrial Insurance, and is an able and conscientious official.

———

Sunderland, A. W., M.A., F.I.A., Actuary of the National Life Assurance Society, before he entered the Insurance world was a Scholar of Trinity College, Cambridge, where he graduated (7th Wrangler) in 1876. Four years after he began his Insurance career as a Clerk in the Office of the National Life. In the beginning of the year 1885, he was appointed to the position of Assistant-Actuary, and later in the same year the Directors further promoted him to his present position.

Mr. Sunderland is the Author of numerous works and papers on various branches of Actuarial Science, most of which are acknowledged as Standard Works, and all as authorities, among them being " Notes on Finite Differences,'

which was written for the use of the Students of the Institute of Actuaries ; also a paper " On Risk Premiums for Survivorship Assurances," and two other papers dealing with the subject of Bonuses, which were both read before the Institute of Actuaries. In addition to these, Mr. Sunderland had contributed sundry other papers and articles to the Journal of the Institute. He is in his 40th year, and holds a very high reputation among his scientific brethren.

———

Surenne, David John, F.F.A., the Secretary of the Caledonian Insurance Company of Edinburgh, commenced his Insurance career in the year 1856, when he entered the service of the Colonial Life Assurance Company. This Corporation was then under the management of the late William Thomas Thomson, of the Standard Life Assurance Company, with which the Colonial was, in 1866, amalgamated. In the year 1869 Mr. Surenne was appointed by the Directors of the Caledonian Insurance Company Assistant-Actuary to that office, and in 1878 Secretary of the Company.

GEORGE J. H. HOGG.

Hogg, George J. H., is the Secretary of the East Coast and Well Deck Insurance Associations of West Hartlepool.

He began his career as a Junior Officer in the Navy, and after serving some years in various parts of the world, received injury to his sight which precluded his remaining in a tropical climate, with the result of his being invalided and subsequently withdrawing from the Service. He then entered the office of a Mutual Insurance Club for Sailing Vessels, and becoming associated with the promoters of the East Coast Association in 1869, was offered the post of Secretary. This Association commenced operations 20th February, 1870, and has now grown into a very large and important Club, Mr. Hogg having built up for it one of the largest Mutual Insurance businesses in the United Kingdom. His name is well-known throughout the country and he is an acknowledged authority on all questions of steamship Insurance.

Nicholls, Edward William, Underwriter of the Alliance Marine Assurance Company, Limited, was born on the 18th of March, 1846, and is the son of Francis Nicholls, a chartered accountant. In the year 1861, he commenced his business life with the Salvage Association which was at that time located at Lloyd's. Here he stayed for about four years, leaving it in 1865, to enter the service of Messrs. Leathley and Hardman of Lloyd's, and he remained with them managing their Insurance brokerage business until 1867. In that year he was appointed Deputy Underwriter to the Marine Insurance Company Limited, and held that position until the year 1878, when he received the offer of his present position and accepted it. Mr. Nicholls was an original member of the Committee of the Institute of London Underwriters and still occupies a seat on that Committee.

Taunton, Frank H., the Secretary of the Royal Liver Friendly Society at the Chief Offices of that enormous collecting organization, in Prescot Street, Liverpool, was born at Rugeley in Staffordshire forty years ago.

He was educated on the Continent, and soon after leaving College went out to Western Australia. In this rapidly growing country he at first held several appointments under the Government, among them being Clerk to the Magistrates. This was followed by higher offices, but Mr. Taunton resigned them to go into various Bush Pursuits and Ranching. When in turn he abandoned this rough life he visited India, Singapore (the Straits Settlements), and also the Dutch East Indies on several occasions. On these journeys he engaged in commercial pursuits, but after being wrecked on the South-West Coast of Sumatra he put a termination to his wanderings for a time and returned to England.

At home he continued his commercial career, and obtained a temporary appointment on the staff of the Mersey Docks and Harbour Board in Liverpool. This position he shortly afterwards resigned to take up an appointment with the Royal Liver Friendly Society, and thus commenced his Insurance career.

For some years with this Society he acted as "Travelling Agent" and in this capacity he had excellent opportunities of learning the practical work of "collecting," of which he availed himself to the utmost possible extent, as his subsequent career has proved. While holding this position he was

FRANK H. TAUNTON.

in charge at different times of Agencies of the Society in Cork, Newcastle-on-Tyne, Warrington, Bangor, and other places.

At this time his brother, Edward F. Taunton, who, it will be remembered, mainly brought about the reform in the management of the Royal Liver, was the Secretary of that Society. This gentleman was taken seriously ill, and Mr. Frank H. Taunton, then Chief Inspector of Agencies, was selected by the Board of Management to act as his *locum tenens* until he could be sufficiently cured to return to his duties. This last event, however, never took place, and, after a long wearying illness, Mr. Edward F. Taunton succumbed. It speaks volumes for the ability his brother had displayed in his temporary position by simply recording the fact that he was unanimously selected by the Board of Management of the Society to take permanently the Chair of the Secretary that he had so ably filled temporarily.

For about two years Mr. Taunton was Honorary Secretary to the Congress of (Collecting) Friendly Societies, but subsequently resigned that office, after having given evidence before the Select Committee on Industrial Insurance of the House of Commons in the year 1889, and before a Select Committee of the House of Lords in the following year.

Mr. Frank H. Taunton has certainly had a more varied and wider experience of men and places than falls to the lot of most Secretaries of Insurance Societies.

J. B. TENNANT, F.I.A.

Tennant, J. B., the Secretary and Actuary of the Friends' Provident Institution, has been in the service of the Institution since December, 1860. Previously to entering the Insurance profession, Mr. Tennant had gained some valuable business experience in the Office of the North-Eastern Railway Company at York, and since entering the service of the Institution he has been engaged in almost every department of the work of the Office. Twenty years ago he was placed in charge of the Actuarial Department, and at the same time he became an Associate of the Institute of Actuaries. In 1883 he was appointed Assistant-Secretary to the Institution, and in 1885 he was promoted to the Secretaryship, in both cases retaining the oversight of the Actuarial Department, and in 1889 he received his present appointment, being officially entitled Secretary and Actuary. Mr. Tennant also takes an active part in Insurance matters outside his Office. In 1890 he was President of the Insurance Institute of Yorkshire, and delivered the Inaugural Address for the Session, which was afterwards published, by request. He has been again elected to the same office for the Session 1891-92. In 1886 he was elected a Fellow of the Institute of Actuaries, of which he had long been an Associate, his election being not as the result of an examination, but on account of his extensive acquaintance with Actuarial principles and the long experience he had had in their application to the affairs of an important Assurance Institution. Both before and since his election as Fellow, Mr. Tennant has been a frequent attendant at the meetings of the Institute.

R. W. THOMPSON. '

W. E. THOMSON.

Thompson, R.W., the General Manager of the Northern Accident Insurance Company, Glasgow, is a native of Newcastle-on-Tyne. He received his first Insurance experience as an Agent of the Northern Accident Insurance Company, at Newcastle-on-Tyne in 1883; in March, 1884, he was promoted to be the Inspector of the Newcastle Branch, and later on was made the Resident Secretary of this branch. In consequence of his success in this district he was, in March, 1886, selected by the Directors as their Assistant-Secretary at the Head Office in Glasgow, and in November, 1888, he was still further promoted to the post of Secretary, and in 1889 he was made General Manager. From this it will be seen that Mr. Thompson has a record of which he may well be proud ; having by degrees worked his way up from an ordinary agent to the entire management of the Company. He is an able and popular official and under his management the Company is making substantial progress and meeting with a large measure of success

———

Thomson, William Edward (Capt. V.R.E.), is the Managing Director of the Crown Accident Insurance Company Limited of Bristol. He was born in the year 1852, and began his business life in the Goods Department of the Great Western Railway (Bristol and Exeter Division) as a junior. He remained in this service for nine years, at the end of which period he had risen to the position of Goods Agent. This he resigned to enter the Insurance profession, and was appointed by the Imperial Union Accident Company its Agency Superintendent for the South of England. With this Company he remained three years, when the Scottish Accident Insurance Company offered him the position of London Secretary, and this, in May, 1879, he accepted. He had a district under his charge comprising no less than twenty counties. For five years he held this appointment, doing a very large business and working entirely on commission. He was then appointed by the same office to be its Manager at Bristol with a district that stretched from Reading in Berkshire, to Penzance in Cornwall, and included South Wales ; his position as London Secretary being filled by his former Assistant, Mr. William Swan Parker. This latter office he held for three years, making a total of eight years spent in the service of the Scottish Accident. In July, 1887, he resigned, and formed the Crown Accident Insurance Company.

In addition to his Insurance work Captain Thomson has done good service in the interests of the Volunteer Forces. He was in 1880 gazetted as 2nd Lieutenant in the 2nd Gloucester Engineers. In 1881 he was promoted to Lieutenant, and in the same year he was attached to the Schools of the Royal Engineers at Chatham (Brompton Barracks), and successfully passed his examinations in Military Engineering ; in 1883 he was promoted to Captain, which position he maintained until 1890, being then appointed by the War Office Captain "Commandant" of the first Sussex Volunteer Royal Engineers, which position he still holds.

F. J. TIMMS.

ALFRED TOZER.

Timms, Frederick Joseph, the Adjuster of Marine Claims of the London Assurance Corporation, has been in the service of that Corporation now for nearly thirty-seven years.

For very many years he served in the Claims Department under Mr. Greathead, gaining much valuable and varied experience, and in the year 1883, when that gentleman retired, the Court of Directors of the Corporation selected him for the appointment, to which he was accordingly promoted.

Mr. Timms has been on the General Committee of the Salvage Association of London for some considerable time, and he is now the Deputy Chairman of the Committee of that Institution. He is also one of the Original Members of the Institute of London Underwriters, and a Member of Lloyd's Agency Committee.

Tozer, Alfred, late Secretary and Average Adjuster of the Universal Marine Insurance Company, Limited, of London, occupied that position from the incorporation of the Company in the month of February, 1860, until the amalgamation of that Company with the British and Foreign Marine last year.

Previous to that he had gained a large and extensive knowledge of Average Adjusting in the offices of Messrs. William Richards and Sons, with whom he was for some years before receiving his present appointment.

Mr. Tozer was a Member of the Committee of the London Salvage Association and also of the Institute of London Underwriters. He stands in very high repute in the Marine Insurance world, and his experience and abilities entitle him to the respect which he receives.

S. C. THOMSON, B.A., F.I.A., F.F.A.

Thomson, Spencer C., is the Manager and Actuary of the Standard Life Assurance Company at its Headquarters in Edinburgh. Mr. Thomson is the son of Mr. William Thomson, the first Manager of the Company, under whom it made such steady and satisfactory progress during the early years of its existence. Mr. Spencer Thomson himself received his training in the service of the Standard, and on the death of his father succeeded him in his post of Chief Officer of the Company. He is still in his early prime, and is a gentleman of high culture and attainments. He is a Bachelor of Arts and a Fellow both of the Faculty and of the Institute of Actuaries.

J. STOCKDALE TOULMIN.

Toulmin, J. Stockdale, the Underwriter of the Royal Exchange Assurance Corporation of London (Marine Department), is the son of the late Dr. Francis Toulmin, of Clapton, who was a very widely-known and honoured Member of the Medical Profession.

Mr. Toulmin first joined the Underwriting fraternity in the year 1862, when he first entered Lloyd's as a Member of that world-wide known Corporation. In the "room" there he quickly made his mark as an Underwriter of exceptional ability, prudence, and sagacity.

In 1888, on the position he now holds becoming vacant, the Directors of the Royal Exchange Assurance Corporation selected him as being the most suitable man for the position, and duly offered it to him. He accepted it, and continues to hold it with the esteem and respect of all working under and with him.

Taylor, R. Aiton, is the Manager and Secretary of the Commercial Fire Insurance Company of Scotland, Edinburgh. Mr. Taylor commenced his Insurance experience on the 1st January, 1870, as a Clerk in the Head Office of the Scottish Commercial Insurance Company, and in 1875 he was promoted to the position of Surveyor and Head Clerk to the Company's branch in Edinburgh. When the Scottish Commercial amalgamated with the Lancashire, he resigned his position, and took an active part in the formation of the Scottish Metropolitan Fire Insurance Company, and on the amalgamation of the Company with the Caledonian Insurance Company he was appointed Assistant Secretary of the latter Company in Glasgow, and afterwards acted as its Joint Secretary in Liverpool. This position he resigned, and was subsequently appointed Manager and Secretary of the Commercial of Scotland on its formation at the beginning of the year 1887.

ROBERT C. TUCKER, F.I.A.

Tucker, Robert C.,\F.I.A., is the Actuary and Secretary of the Pelican Life Office of London.

Mr. Tucker was born in London in the year 1845, and is a son of the late Mr. Robert Tucker who for so many years occupied the position now so ably filled by his son.

Shortly after leaving school, Mr. Tucker entered the service of the office of which he is the present Chief Officer. That was twenty-seven years ago, and under his father's supervision he worked his way through each department of the office, acquiring thereby a thoroughly practical experience of its organisation and of the business of Life Insurance.

In the year 1875, after twenty-one years' service, the Board of Directors selected him to fill the position his late father had so honourably occupied for so many years, and he has since in every way justified that choice, having introduced many reforms into the working of the office, and its system of business, doing also, in addition, very much to increase the popularity of the Company, and keep it thoroughly abreast of the times and well up in advance with modern progress.

Mr. Tucker is a Fellow of the Institute of Actuaries, and is held in high esteem by the members of that body and the Insurance world generally.

Turnbull, Andrew H., is the Manager and Actuary of the Scottish Widows' Fund Life Assurance Society at its Head Office in St. Andrew Square, Edinburgh. Mr. Turnbull commenced his Insurance career in the year 1850 as an apprentice in the Head Office of the Standard Life Assurance Company, and consequently, has enjoyed an experience of over forty years. Thirteen years later (in 1863) while he was still in the service of the same Company, engaged in the Actuarial department, Mr. Turnbull published a work of considerable value to his profession, entitled "A Book of Tables of Compound Interest and Annuities in Decimals and Currency," which was received with much favour at the time of its production, but is now, we believe, out of print, although some of the tables are still extant as part of a book of "Useful Tables," issued during the last few years by the Scottish Widows' Fund. In 1865 Mr. Turnbull, who had previously qualified himself by passing the examination of the Faculty of Actuaries, was appointed to the post of Manager and Actuary of the City of Glasgow Life Assurance Company, a post which he continued to hold with distinguished success both to himself and his Company until 1876. In that year he accepted the offer of an appointment to the Secretaryship and Joint-Actuaryship to the Scottish Widows' Fund, his present Company; and on the retirement of Mr. Raleigh from the management, in 1881, he was chosen to succeed

A. H. TURNBULL, F.I.A., F.F.A.

that gentleman. Mr. Turnbull's success in his present sphere is well known, not only to the Insurance world but to all who have had the good fortune to be brought in contact with him, and there is no need here for any elaborate eulogy on his merits. The records of the Society, since his accession to the management, present an unbroken history of energetic enterprise and progress, modified by prudence and sound judgment; and the result is that at the present time the Scottish Widows' Fund is almost without a rival, and at any rate is quite in the front rank of its contemporary institutions in extent and rapidity of development; while the accumulated funds of the Society have already, in the comparatively short period of seventy-six years that has elapsed since its formation, reached the truly massive amount of eleven millions sterling. Much of this success may with confidence be attributed to the skill with which Mr. Turnbull has conducted the management. Mr. Turnbull's financial abilities are amply testified by the honours that have been conferred upon him. He is a Fellow of the Faculty of Actuaries and a Fellow of the Institute of Actuaries. And besides the position which he deservedly occupies in his own immediate profession, his talents have marked him for selection as a Fellow of the Royal Society of Edinburgh and one of the Directors of the Royal Bank of Scotland.

J. R. TURNER.

Turner, John Randal, the Assistant Secretary of the Positive Government Security Life Assurance Company, was born in the year 1851; and received his early Insurance training in the office of the Provident Clerks' Life Association, with which he was connected from 1867 to the year 1872. In 1873 he received the appointment of Accountant to the Positive Government Security Life Office, and in this capacity he acted for about eighteen years; and in 1890 he was appointed by the Directors to be the Assistant Secretary to the Company, which position he still holds.

Tait, Patrick Macnaghten, F.S.S., F.R.G.S., is the son of the late William Tait, Esq., of Edinburgh, where he was born and received his early education, mainly under the late Principal Tulloch. He entered the service of the Scottish Union Insurance Corporation, as Articled Clerk, at the age of thirteen, where he remained till 1845, removing to the East of Scotland Insurance Office as Accountant, and again, in 1848, to the National Mercantile Insurance Company as Accountant and Deputy-Secretary, which post he retained till 1851. He then took up the Secretaryship of the Medical Invalid and General Assurance Society at their Branch in India, where he remained during the whole period of the Mutiny, doing signal service to his country in the raising of the Rifle Company of the Calcutta Volunteer Guards, in which corps he held a command. In 1860, he became Director of Indian business to the Medical Assurance Company, which post he held till 1869. In 1872 he became Managing Director and Director of the Ocean Railway and General Accident Insurance Company, which post he held for ten years, ultimately resigning on the most friendly terms with all his colleagues. Mr. Tait is a Fellow of the Statistical and Royal Geographical Societies, a late Member of the Institute of Actuaries of Great Britain and Ireland, and a Member of the Council of the East India Association. He is also Member of the Oriental Club, and Honorary Member of clubs in India, China, Japan, Montreal, New York, and Chicago, all of which places he has visited in the course of his extensive travels. He has contributed largely to the contemporary weekly and quarterly press, and is the author of numerous papers read before the British Association and other Societies.

W. J. TRELEAVEN.

WILLIAM THOM.

Treleaven, William J., the Manager of the Metropolitan District of the Gresham Life Assurance Society of London, has had a wide and long experience in Life Insurance business. He made his first connection with it when he joined the staff of the Provident Life and County Fire Offices at their Branch office in Liverpool. From here he was after a time sent to Manchester in the interests of the Provident Life Office. This position he held until receiving an appointment to the post of Resident Secretary at the Liverpool Branch of the Reliance Life Office of London, which he accepted and held until about five years ago.

At that time he was selected by the Directors of the English and Scottish Law Life Assurance Company to open for them a Branch Office in the City of London, which he did on Ludgate Hill, holding himself the position of Resident Secretary.

While occupying this post he received the offer of the appointment he at present holds and which he accepted, and in which he has made a successful and a very progressive record.

Thom, William, is the Treasurer of the Scottish Legal Life Assurance Society at its headquarters at Glasgow. Mr. Thom was born in 1851, in the town of Dalry, Ayrshire, but while he was still very young his father—left a widower when the son was born—removed their residence to Airdrie in Lanarkshire, at the Academy of which town he received the rudiments of his education. Another removal was then made by his family, this time to a rural part of Scotland near the classic village of Torphichen, where he continued his education under one of those typical Scotch masters, who have, by their learning and integrity, made the name of "parish master" an honoured word. At the age of twelve, Mr. Thom was already at work assisting to gain his own living, and at sixteen he was engaged in his father's business at Coatbridge. It was at this time that, with certain other youths of his own standing, all feeling a desire for more of this world's knowledge than they had already acquired, out of his own pocket money, which was naturally scanty enough, he co-operated in engaging a private tutor to coach him and his companions in many subjects and more especially arithmetic. A few years later found him connected with the provincial press, which connection led him first to an engagement on a local paper in the suburbs of Glasgow, and eventually to a better post on the staff of the *Glasgow Evening Citizen*, namely, that of Manager for the proprietors of that paper of their Greenock District. It was while engaged in this latter capacity that in June, 1883, Mr. Thom was elected Treasurer to the Scottish Legal Life Assurance Society by the unanimous vote of the members, which post he has held with honour ever since

JAMES VALENTINE, F.I.A.

Valentine, James, F.I.A., the General Manager of the Northern Assurance Company located at its Head Office in Moorgate Street, London, has spent the whole of his career and received the whole of his Insurance training in the service of that Company, having entered it as a junior immediately on completing his education at school. Since that time he has steadily worked his way through every department of the Company, winning the esteem of all both for his personal qualities and his ready grasp of all the manifold details of the business, which esteem has been amply evidenced by his regular and progressive promotion as opportunity presented itself through the various grades of the office, until he at last attained to his present position at the head of the Company's affairs, which took place in May, 1882. Mr. Valentine was elected to a Fellowship in the Institute of Actuaries in 1868, and has served on several occasions on its Council. He has also contributed to the Literature of the profession, in some very able papers published in the *Assurance Magazine*.

C. H. VENNING, F.S.S.

S. G. WARNER, F.I.A.

Venning, C. Harrison, F.S.S., the Secretary of the Local Government Mutual Guarantee Society, is the son of Daniel Venning, Esq., of Whalesborough, Stratton, North Devon, for many years the Vice-Chairman of the Guardians of the Poor of the Stratton Union. He was educated at the Bedford Grammar School, Tavistock, and at the Queen's College, Taunton, in connection with which latter Institution he afterwards became Honorary Secretary, and Member of the Committee of the Taunton (Queen's College) Old Boys' Union.

At the commencement of his Commercial career, Mr. Venning was more closely associated with Building Societies than with Insurance Offices, and in 1888 published a set of Building Society Rules, containing unique tables of Repayment, for which is claimed a principle of equity—in adjusting the uncertainty and unfairness of the Ballot System—not previously attempted by such Societies.

In 1886 he became the first Superintendent in London of the Mutual Reserve Fund Life Association of New York, in which capacity he achieved a very considerable success.

In 1888 he undertook the Secretaryship of the Leicester Assurance Company, but two years later, being invited to co-operate with some of the leading officials in the Local Government Service to found a Guarantee Society in the interests of Local Government Officers, he severed his connection with the Leicester to become the Secretary of the newly-formed Society, and has since received many marked expressions of the esteem and confidence in which he is held by the Directors and all those connected with the Local Government Mutual Guarantee Society.

He is a Fellow of the Royal Statistical Society, and, being but thirty-five years of age, has a future of usefulness before him.

Warner, Samuel George, F.I.A., is the Secretary and Actuary of the Law Union and Crown Fire and Life Insurance Company.

The Insurance career of Mr. Warner began in the year 1872, when he received an appointment on the staff of the London Office of the Scottish Provincial Assurance Company of Aberdeen (since amalgamated with the North British and Mercantile Insurance Company).

In 1886, when the appointment of Actuary of the Law Union became vacant, Mr. Warner was selected by the Board of Directors to fill the post, and he has since fully justified the choice made, and last year he was also given the additional appointment of Secretary.

Mr. Warner has passed the Final Examination of the Institute of Actuaries.

WILLIAM WALLIS, F.I.A.

Wallis, William, F.I.A., the Actuary of the Union Assurance Society in London, commenced his Insurance career in 1852, when he entered as a Clerk the office of the Star Life Insurance Company. Four years later he began his Actuarial experience by passing the Matriculation Examination of the Institute of Actuaries in 1856, and he successfully got through the second examination in the following year (1857). In the year 1860 he received the appointment of Actuarial Clerk in the Union Life Office, Mr. Ebenezer Wenham, who was then the Actuary to the Company, being in failing health at the time. At the death of this gentleman, which occurred in the same year, Mr. Wallis, then in his twenty-third year, became practically the Actuary of the Company, though the actual title was not accorded to him until some years later. The Union Assurance Society, which dates its establishment from the year 1714, and carried on its business in the good old days when proposers came to the office direct and of their own accord, had, of course, some difficulty in accommodating itself to the vastly different state of things that exists to-day ; but that it has done so is proved by the fact that the new business which, when Mr. Wallis entered the service of the Society, was less than two hundred policies per annum, was last year over five thousand eight hundred policies. Much of this advance is no doubt due to the energy and enterprise of Mr. Wallis, and certainly every step the Society has taken to enable it to keep abreast of the times, if not actually initiated by him, has received his warmest support.

HENRY WARD.

Ward, Henry, F.S.S., the Secretary and Manager of the General Assurance Company, entered that office at an early age, and by his perseverance and industry rapidly advanced from one stage to another, until, in 1880, he was made Fire Manager on the retirement of Mr. Bone, his former chief. Here he still continued to do good work, with the result that though the Fire Loss ratio remained well within the limits of safety, the income was increased 50 per cent. . While Fire Manager Mr. Ward took a very large personal share in the opening of several very valuable direct foreign agencies, whose establishment has, in a great measure, contributed to the above-mentioned results. Mr. Ward was promoted to his present position in 1887, and the energy and aptitude shown in the subordinate have been maintained in the chief position, as is evidenced by facts that speak for themselves, and require no comment. During the five years that have elapsed since his appointment to the helm of affairs, the Income of both Departments of his Company has been raised by over 18 per cent., while the wealth of the Office has been increased by some £300,000.

Fluent and concise in public speaking, Mr. Ward has done much good service in arranging and attending meetings of Agents and Branch Managers in all parts of the Kingdom, a most gratifying accession of business resulting from such demonstrations.

ARTHUR WATERS.

Waters, Arthur, the Managing Director of the London and Provincial Horse and Carriage Insurance Company, Limited, and The Horse Insurance Company, Limited, of Queen Victoria Street, London, was born in Devonshire in the year 1850.

After completing his education and gaining a fairly wide knowledge and experience of Commercial Life he was, in the year 1877, appointed a Member of the staff of this Company, with the position of Secretary. He was subsequently promoted to the position of General Manager, and in 1887, ten years after making his first connection with the office, he was elected to a seat on the Board and appointed Managing Director, the position which he still occupies.

Whamond, J. Robbie, C.A., the Secretary of The Security Company, Limited, is a Forfarshire man. He was born in 1863, and gained his first Insurance experience in the office of the National Guarantee and Suretyship Association of Edinburgh, where he remained for over eight years. He has been in the service of his present Company since it commenced business in 1890, and has acquired a valuable experience in Fidelity, Investment Guarantee and Burglary Insurance. He is a Member of the Chartered Accountants' Society of Edinburgh, having qualified in 1889.

JOHN WAUGH, C.E.

E. A. WELLS.

Waugh, John, C.E., is the Manager and Engineer of the Yorkshire Boiler Insurance and Steam Users' Company at Bradford, Yorks. He is a native of Yorkshire, and acquired his first experience in the engineering profession with the firm of Messrs. Hick and Sons, of Bolton, for whom, after having duly served his apprenticeship, he went to Egypt to carry out a contract for the erection of flour and cotton mills, and pumping works for the Government of that country. On his return to England, Mr. Waugh successively took part in the erection of the Gas Works of the Manchester and Southport Corporations, entirely planning the latter undertaking, after which he became Gas and Water Engineer to the Midland Railway Company. In 1872 he left the service of the latter Company to set up in business for himself as a Consulting Engineer at Bradford, where, in the following year, he successfully promoted and established the Yorkshire Boiler and Steam Users' Company, which he has managed ever since. As evidence of the success of this Company and the conscientiousness with which Mr. Waugh as its Chief Officer has fulfilled the intentions with which it was founded, we may mention that the Yorkshire Boiler and Steam Users' Company is able to boast that it has never in the course of existence had a single explosion of a boiler under its charge. Naturally, the prosperity of the Company has marched with its progress, and its reputation with both ; the latter being as great in the home district as in more distant parts of the kingdom, a fact which speaks for itself,

and must be highly gratifying to the founder. Mr. Waugh has on more than one occasion been employed by the Government and local authorities to examine into the causes of many boiler accidents.

Mr. Waugh is a County Councillor for the West Riding of Yorkshire, he sits also on the Council of the Chamber of Commerce, and of the Bradford Technical College. He is an Associate of the Institute of Civil Engineers, a Member of the Association of Mechanical Engineers, a Fellow of the Institute of Patent Agents, &c., &c.

———

Wells, Ernest Arthur, is the Secretary of the Yorkshire Boiler Insurance and Steam Users' Company of Bradford. Mr. Wells is a native of Manchester, where he was born in 1856, and having received his education at the Grammar School at Leeds, commenced his business career in the service of Messrs. H. W. and J. Blackburn, Accountants, a firm having a very large connection in the two great centres of Leeds and Bradford. He subsequently served for a number of years in Messrs. William Williams, Brown and Company's Bank at Leeds, and on leaving them, having by this time acquired a thorough knowledge of accounts and financing, he started an Accountancy and Insurance Agency business on his own account in Leeds. Nineteen years later, the Secretaryship of his present Company being vacant, he applied for the post, and was selected from among 116 candidates.

JOHN WAINWRIGHT.

JAMES GRAHAM WATSON.

Wainwright, John, the Secretary and Manager of the Federative Insurance Company of Oldham, in the formation of which Company he was the chief mover, was originally engaged in the cotton business, and had served in more than one office of that trade. In 1875 the Insurance rates on cotton mills were so high that they were a serious drain on the profits of the owners, no allowances being made by the Tariff Officers for even the newest premises fitted up with the best possible fire appliances. This was felt to be a great injustice, and accordingly Mr. Wainwright, whose manifold experience of the business and the risks thereby incurred pointed him out as the fittest person to undertake the work, was deputed to form a special Insurance Company to meet the requirements of the trade. This he effected most successfully, issuing circulars to the Directors of Cotton Mills in Oldham and District, calling meetings to discuss the matter freely, and in a very short time the Federative Company was formed with a Board of seven Directors, each representing a cotton mill and elected by the Shareholding Companies. The capital is £51,010 in shares of £1 each, of which four shillings and three-pence have been called up, subscribed entirely by Policy-holders, who consist of Cotton Mill Companies and Co-operative Societies. The Company, under Mr. Wainwright's able management, has fulfilled all the expectations which were formed of it at its formation, the reserve fund being £20,000.

Watson, James Graham, the Manager of the Scottish Provident Institution, was born in 1850, the son of the late Manager and co-founder, Mr. James Watson, and having been educated at Edinburgh Academy, was trained for business in the Office of Mr. Gillies Smith, Chartered Accountant, now Manager of the North British and Mercantile Insurance Office. Mr. Watson qualified as a Chartered Accountant in 1874, in which same year he entered the Office of the Scottish Provident Institution. Here he gradually worked himself up, fortunate in being under the carefully guiding eye of his father, and successively became Assistant-Secretary, Joint Secretary, and Secretary, from which last duties he was promoted to his present position, on the retirement of his father in 1890. Mr. Watson, previous to his appointment, had already on more than one occasion, when circumstances required his doing so owing to the absence or illness of those then above him, had to take upon himself the whole duties of the management of the Institution, and it was the efficient manner in which he discharged these duties as a *locum tenens* that justified the Directors in their selection of him to carry them on, when the time came, on his own responsibility. Mr. Watson was for many years an Officer in the Forfar and Kincardine Militia, from which he retired with the rank of Major. He has visited the Australasian Colonies in connection with the business of the Institution. His wife is a daughter of Colonel Boothby, of St. Andrews.

FIRE LOSS ASSESSORS.

HENRY DANIEL.
(Alexander, Daniel, Selfe & Co.)

T. V. SELFE.
(Alexander, Daniel, Selfe & Co.)

Daniel, Henry. The professional life of Mr. Henry Daniel (Alexander, Daniel, Selfe and Company) began as a lad with the late Mr. Samuel Alexander and his father, as Messrs. Alexander and Son in 1840. A slight break having occurred, his connection was resumed in 1850, and subsequently entering into partnership with Mr. Alexander, his duties became rapidly more and more important, until the Fenian Rising in March, 1867, involved him in very risky and responsible investigations in Ireland. This formed the commencement of a vast increase in this branch of the business, extending to all parts of the United Kingdom. The result of this extensive work rendered Mr. Daniel's experience exceedingly valuable, and he was requested to give evidence upon Fire Insurance questions before a Committee of the House of Commons.

Of late years the increasing responsibilities of the general Auctioneering and Valuing Business of the firm, added to the late Mr. Samuel Alexander's failing health, have rendered it imperative upon Mr. Daniel to largely withdraw from more active work in Fire Loss Assessing, his principal duty in connection therewith being almost wholly confined to advising generally with his partners upon the treatment and direction of cases as they have arisen.

The Firm of Alexander, Daniel, Selfe and Company, of Bristol and London, of which Mr. Henry Daniel is now the senior partner, consists also, in Bristol, of Messrs. Charles A. Alexander, H. A. Hood Daniel and W. S. Hawker, and in London of Messrs. T. V. Selfe and E. W. Ball.

The business was founded by Mr. John Alexander nearly 150 years ago, but the Firm date their establishment from 1790, having a complete series of books from that year. In connection with losses by fire at the time of the Bristol Riots, in 1831, the then head of the firm was employed by the City to assess the damages sustained, and the present firm of Alexander, Daniel, Selfe and Company date their connection with the Fire Insurance Companies from this time. The London Branch was established in 1883.

Selfe, T. V. (Alexander, Daniel, Selfe and Company), was born in Bristol in the year 1845, and educated in that city. At an early age he entered the offices of Messrs. Alexander and Daniel, Fire Loss Assessors, subsequently joining these gentlemen in partnership.

H. A. H. DANIEL.
(Alexander, Daniel, Selfe & Co.)

W. S. HAWKER.
(Alexander, Daniel, Selfe & Co.)

Mr. Selfe is now an Assessor of close upon twenty-five years' standing, and during this time he has been continually engaged in the settlement of important losses throughout the United Kingdom. He has also had valuable Foreign experience, amongst the more important of his trips being those to Buenos Ayres, Turkey, Spain and Belgium. Much of his time is occupied in sitting as Arbitrator.

For the more convenient working of the firm's business, Mr. Selfe, in the year 1883, left Bristol for London, where he was joined by one of his partners, Mr. Ball. Mr. Selfe is also assisted by his son, Frederick V. Selfe, who will doubtless eventually be admitted as a member of the firm.

Daniel, H. A. Hood, F.S.I. (Alexander, Daniel, Selfe and Company, Fire Loss Assessors), who is 38 years of age, entered the office of his father in January, 1870, and was admitted to partnership in January, 1878.

Mr. Hood Daniel's professional experience has been acquired in the several departments of his firm's widespread practice, and in addition to the adjustment of Fire Claims his attention has been largely directed to that branch of the business comprising the Survey, Valuation and Transfer of Properties. He was in 1883 admitted a Fellow of the Surveyors' Institution.

Hawker, William Seymour, of the firm of Alexander, Daniel, Selfe and Company, who was born at Weston-super-Mare, is 43 years of age. He was educated at a private school in Clifton, and upon leaving spent six years in a large Manchester Warehouse in Bristol. In January, 1871, he entered the offices of Messrs. Alexander, Daniel and Company, and was admitted a partner in January, 1878. Mr. Hawker has been concerned in the adjustment of many very heavy fire losses in various parts of the Kingdom, and since Mr. Selfe went to reside in London in 1883 his time has wholly been devoted to assessing.

CHARLES A. ALEXANDER.
(Alexander, Daniel, Selfe & Co.)

E. W. BALL.
(Alexander, Daniel, Selfe & Co.)

Alexander, Charles A., F.C.A., of the firm of Alexander, Daniel, Selfe and Company, Fire Loss Assessors, who is 37 years of age, entered the office of his late uncle in January, 1870, and was admitted to partnership in January, 1878. He is a great grandson of the founder of the firm, who practised as an Auctioneer and Valuer in Bristol nearly 150 years ago. Mr. C. A. Alexander has had the advantage of careful training in every department of the extensive business of his firm, but for several years past his attention has been chiefly devoted to the Assessment of Fire Losses; he is also a Fellow of the Institute of Chartered Accountants.

Ball, E. W. (Alexander, Daniel, Selfe and Company, Fire Loss Assessors), was born in Bristol in 1859. He was educated at Clifton College, and in 1876 was articled to the firm in which he is now a partner, having been admitted in 1883. In the same year Mr. Ball came to London. where (at 34, Old Jewry, E.C.,) the Branch business is carried on.

J. C. GULLILAND.
(Robert McTear & Co.)

JOHN LAIRD.
(Robert McTear & Co.)

Gulliland, J. C., is partner to Mr. John Laird, in the firm of Robert McTear and Co., Fire Loss Assessors, Auctioneers and Valuers, Royal Exchange Salerooms, Glasgow. After fifteen years' experience in the firms of J. Davidson and Co., and John and James Morrison, now Morrison, Dick and McCulloch, Auctioneers, Glasgow, he joined the present firm in 1878, and in conjunction with his partner, Mr. Laird, has conducted this extensive business most successfully in all its branches.

Laird, John, Fire Loss Assessor of Glasgow, is the Senior Partner of the firm of Messrs. Robert McTear and Co., the oldest firm of Fire Loss Assessors in Scotland, founded by the late Mr. Robert McTear, the well-known Liberationist, in 1840, and by him kept level through all the changes in Fire Loss Assessing to the requirements of the time. Mr. John Laird entered Mr. McTear's employment in 1863, and rapidly rose to the position of Manager; succeeding to the business on Mr. McTear's death in 1886. The business rapidly extending, he, two years back, took into partnership Mr. J. C. Gulliland, a gentleman of consider-

able experience in his profession, by whom and a large staff of experts he is ably supported. Although still a young man, Mr. Laird by his unassuming manner and devotion to business has earned the entire confidence of his clients. His broad grasp of general principles and steady application to details, added to a suavity of manner, which he has the happy gift of retaining even under the most trying circumstances, enable him as a rule to carry his point in face of all difficulties. Among his fellows in the profession he is held in high esteem, and his services are, therefore, greatly in demand for the office of arbiter in difficult cases all over the country. He is an art expert of wide experience and an extensive contributor to Art journalism, and his acquirements in that line have frequently stood the office in good stead.

Messrs. Robert McTear and Co. are also Surveyors for the American and Continental Underwriters, and carry on a large business as Fine Art Auctioneers and Valuers. Their Art Galleries are the finest suite of Auction Rooms out of London.

ANDREW GRAY.

A. HEATON.

Gray, Andrew, Sole Partner of the firm of Messrs. A. and G. Gray, Wrights and Builders, succeeded to his father's business in 1863. Shortly afterwards he commenced Fire Loss Assessing, devoting himself entirely to building losses. While carrying on a considerable Assessing business he has always had on hand several large contracts and taken in hand the entire work. For the Fire Offices he has re instated several large buildings to their entire satisfaction. Making a speciality of building losses, he has during the past twenty years had most of the large losses of this class in Glasgow and the West of Scotland passing through his hands, notably the buildings in the extensive Buchanan Street conflagrations of 1883 and 1888. In the building trade he has reached the top of his profession, being Ex-Deacon of the wealthy Incorporation of Wrights and presently a Trade's Liner in the Dean of Guild Court.

We may also state that Mr. Gray joined the Volunteer Movement in 1859, and is still an efficient officer of the 4th Volunteer Battalion Cameronian Scottish Rifles.

———

Heaton, Alexander, is the Senior Partner of the firm of Messrs. Heaton and Company, Fire Loss Assessors, of Manchester. He was originally educated as a Millwright and Engineer, but left that line of business to take up that in which he has now been engaged for nearly thirty years, and in which he has found his former experience of great service. He first started in conjunction with his brother, Mr. James A. Heaton, of Manchester, with whom he carried on business for seventeen years.

WILLIAM MITCHELL.

WALTER HUME.

Mitchell, William, Fire Loss Assessor of Manchester, commenced his business career in the cotton mill of Messrs. A. and G. Murray, of Ancoats, where his father was Manager, and thence transferred his services to the shipping warehouse of Messrs. Robert Barbour and Brother, and the whole-sale millinery and general drapery establishment of Messrs. Falkner Brothers, of Manchester, succes-sively. Thence he passed into the office of Messrs. Fullalove Brothers, Auctioneers and Valuers, whose connection was at that time the largest and the most varied in all the Manchester District, where he remained for fourteen years, gaining a thorough experience of the value of every sort of property— Agricultural, Trade, Manufacturing, Building, etc., this with his former employments being of good service to him in the business which he afterwards took up and which he now carries on. He com-menced business for himself as an auctioneer and valuer in 1860, and in the following year Mr. Kennedy, the Manchester Secretary of the Liverpool and London and Globe, first pointed out the value of the training he had gone through for Insur-ance purposes. Soon afterwards Mr. Mitchell was entrusted with his first settlement by the Liver-pool and London and Globe, and others quickly followed; and these bringing him in contact with other offices, he soon became well-known. Since

that time he has settled nearly four thousand claims for no less than fifty-five different Insurance Companies in every District of the Northern Counties, in the Midlands, and in Scotland, Wales, and Ireland, from Bristol to Inverness, and from Sunderland to Cork. The principal offices for which he has acted are the Liverpool and London and Globe, London and Lancashire, Alliance General, Northern, Norwich Union Royal, Royal Exchange, Queen, Manchester, Westminster, West of England, Yorkshire, Caledonian, Scottish Union and National, the Royal Farmers', and others.

———

Hume, Walter. Among the Assessors of Fire Losses in Dublin, Walter Hume takes a promi-nent position, although he has not been established there many years. Previous to coming to Ireland, Mr. Hume was assistant to Mr. Cruickshank, the well-known assessor at Edinburgh, from whom he received a strong testimonial when leaving his service. Mr. Hume has had a large and valuable experience in all classes of settlements, especially as regards losses on mills and manufactories; and as he is popular with the Companies to whom he is known, he doubtless has a prosperous career before him.

WILLIAM MONTGOMERY, JUNR.

JOHN F. POWELL.

Montgomery, Wm., Junr., is the Junior Partner in the firm of Wm. Montgomery and Son, Fire Loss Assessors and Auctioneers, of Belfast and Dublin. He commenced his commercial career by serving an apprenticeship in one of the leading manufacturing concerns in Ireland, or, indeed, in the kingdom—W. Ewart and Son, Belfast. In 1882 he went out to America, residing for a year at Chicago, where he was employed in one of the principal Insurance Brokers' offices of that city. He then went "out West" in search principally of adventure and health, and spent the greater part of a year amongst the cow-boys of Colorado, on the prairies, and in the foot hills of the Rocky Mountains. In the latter end of 1883 he returned to the old country, and joined his father and brother, whose business at that time showed signs of considerable expansion, devoting all his time to the assessing department ever since.

This firm has of late years been entrusted with the settlement of the largest fire losses occurring in Ireland. Mr. W. Montgomery, junr., has for over a year been resident in Dublin in charge of the Dublin office of the firm.

————

Powell, John Frederick, Fire Loss Assessor, of Bristol, commenced his Insurance career as a Salvage Assistant with Messrs. Alexander, Daniel and Co., of Bristol, in April, 1879, and during the eleven years he was in their employ had most valuable experience both in his special capacity and as Assessor, his field of operations covering a large area, embracing England, Ireland, Scotland, and Wales ; and he has been engaged upon losses of almost every description. He resigned his appointment in May last, and commenced business as an Assessor of Fire Losses, in partnership with Mr. Halse, of Queen Anne Buildings, Baldwin Street, Bristol, under the style of Halse and Powell.

GEORGE UNSWORTH.

Unsworth, George, Fire Loss Assessor at Manchester, has not been very long engaged in that profession. He is an Auctioneer, Valuer, and Estate Agent. His experience in this capacity having given him a considerable insight into the proper adjustment of claims upon Insurance for losses from Fire, he has determined to turn his experience to account, and accordingly has taken up the business of Fire Loss Assessor in addition to his present vocation. His particular line is in connection with farm property and implements, his family having been farmers for several generations, so that there is little if anything in the farming business with which he cannot be said to be personally and perfectly acquainted.

BRANCH OFFICE OFFICIALS.

A. ABSELL.

J. J. ACASON.

Absell, A., is a well-known London Fire Insurance Broker and Agent. He has had abundant experience in the Insurance profession, having commenced his career in the year 1862 at the Phœnix Fire Office, where he remained for a period of three years, eventually leaving the Phœnix to take service with the Royal Insurance Company at Liverpool. After two years passed in the employment of that Company,. he again transferred his services in 1867 to the London and Lancashire Fire Insurance Company, being appointed to a more important position than he had hitherto occupied, and in 1874, on the appointment of Mr. Fothergill to the Managership of the London and Lancashire Fire, Mr. Absell was promoted to the post of Foreign Superintendent. In 1880 he left the London and Lancashire to accept the post which had been offered him of Fire Superintendent to the Fire Insurance Association, which was just then starting in London under the auspices of the London and Lancashire Life Company, in which post he remained until 1887, when, on differences arising between the two Companies, which had up to that time, and were for a brief period afterwards, worked under the same roof and the same management, Mr. Absell resigned his position, in the hope of averting the impending separation of the two Companies. The self-sacrifice, however, proved unavailing, for the separation shortly afterwards

took place, Mr. Absell himself receiving from several members of the Board the warmest expressions of their appreciation of the efforts he had made for the interests of the Fire Insurance Association, and also of their regret for the unfortunate circumstances which had resulted in the loss of his services. He is now established in London as a Broker and Agent, and has charge of the interests of several of the most important Foreign Insurauce Companies, besides fulfilling the duties of Local Secretary to the Commercial Fire Insurance Company of Scotland.

Mr. Absell has travelled extensively in the interests of the various Companies which he has served. He is well and favourably known to a wide circle of friends in the Insurance profession in all parts of the world.

Acason, J. J., Resident Secretary of the Birmingham Branch of The Fire Insurance Association, has passed the greater part of his Insurance career in the service of that Association, having entered their service in 1882 at the Head Office in London, where he remained for six years, for the greater part of the time at the Head of the Guarantee Department. In 1888 he was transferred to Bristol in the capacity of Local Surveyor, which post he held until 1890, when he received his present appointment at Birmingham.

THOMAS ADAMS.

DAVID ADAMS.

Adams, Thomas, the Secretary of the Norfolk Street (London) Branch of the Alliance Assurance Company, was born in 1845, and in 1863 entered the service of the Royal Farmers' and General Insurance Company as a Junior Clerk. In this office he remained for a period of fourteen years, rising step by step till, in 1887, the Board of Directors appointed him to the position of Secretary of the Company, which position he held until the amalgamation of the Royal Farmers with the Alliance Assurance Company, when he received his present appointment.

Adams, David, is the Secretary of the Alliance Assurance Company at their Branch Office at Birmingham, to which post he was appointed on the retirement through ill-health of Mr. J. H. Wright. Mr. Adams commenced his Insurance career in the service of the Scottish Imperial at their Head Office at Glasgow, whence, at the end of twelve years, he was promoted to the Management of the Newcastle-on-Tyne Branch of the same Company. On the Fire business of the Scottish Imperial being transferred to the Alliance in 1883, Mr. Adams retained his post as District Secretary at Newcastle to the latter Company, which post he held for about three years, until his removal to Birmingham.

FREDERIC A. ADEY.

EDWARD ADENBROOKE.

Adey, Frederic A., is the Resident Secretary at Bristol of the County Fire Office. Mr. Adey entered the Bristol Branch of the Liverpool, London and Globe in 1866, which was then under the management of Mr. J. N. Lane. Sometime after this he left England, and occupied some 12 or 13 years in visiting nearly all parts of the world, the latter part of which time he served as an officer on board the vessels of the Peninsular and Oriental Steam Navigation Company. After this, he again settled in England, and entered the service of the Mutual Fire Insurance Corporation at its Head Office in Manchester, and later on, at its Bristol, South Wales, and Liverpool Branches as Surveyor, Inspector of Agents, &c. In 1885 he entered the Bristol Branch of the Commercial Union, and in the following year was appointed Manager of the Bristol Branch of the County Fire Office, which position he now holds.

———

Adenbrooke, Edward, is the District Manager at Bristol of the British Law Fire Insurance Company, Limited, and the Eagle Life Office. He commenced his Insurance life in the Head Office of the Mutual Fire Office at Manchester, under Mr. J. N. Lane, in 1877, and spent six years in the office and five years out-of-doors, inspecting agents, surveying risks, &c. In August, 1887, he was appointed Resident Secretary to the Fire Insurance Association, Limited, in the Midlands, which post he held until the beginning of 1890, when he went to Bristol as the District Secretary of the British Law Fire Office, combined with an appointment under the Eagle Life Office.

A. ALISON.

A. T. ALEXANDER.

Alison, A., Local Manager to the Royal Exchange Assurance at its Branch Office at Newcastle-on-Tyne, has been associated with the Insurance business in that town since 1874, having served the Lancashire, the Scottish Commercial, the Northern, and the Scottish Provincial Companies successively, remaining with the latter Company for a period of eight years in the capacity of Local Secretary and Inspector. Mr. Alison was appointed to his present post with the Royal Exchange Assurance in 1889, since which time he has managed the business of the Branch to the entire satisfaction of his Directors.

———

Alexander, Alexander T., the District Manager of the Glasgow and West of Scotland Branch of the New York Life Insurance Company, commenced his business life as an accountant, serving his time with a Glasgow firm, and subsequently obtaining a position as cashier for another Accountant's firm, who were at the same time acting as Branch Managers for several Insurance Companies. Here he gained considerable experience in the Insurance business, and next became Manager of the Insurance Department of another like firm, devoting himself more especially to the outdoor work amongst Agents. Proving successful in this capacity, he received the offer of the Head Inspectorship at the Head Office of the Northern Accident Insurance Company of Glasgow, which he accepted. Here he was again very successful in introducing a large volume of business throughout their various Branches, and whilst with this Company he was offered his present position, which he has now held for over two years with credit to himself and the Company.

DAVID ANDERSON.

J. C. ANDERSON.

Anderson, David, District Manager of the Economic Life Office at their Manchester Branch was born in 1851, the son of a Perthshire schoolmaster. He was educated by his father and subsequently at Dundee High School. Having served his apprenticeship in the Dundee Branch of the National Bank of Scotland, he was selected as Cashier of the Scottish Widows' Fund Dundee Branch by Mr. J. W. Miller, who was then in charge of that Branch. On the Society opening a Branch at Bristol, Mr. Anderson was transferred thither as Cashier, and soon after to a similar, but more remunerative, position at the Glasgow Office under Mr. T. Muir Grant. Mr. Muir Grant having been appointed Secretary of the Norwich Union Life Office, Mr. Anderson was selected to superintend the business department and the extensive Agency connections of that Society, which had through long indifference become very unproductive. His work there for over three years was successful, and his efforts met with the appreciation of the Directors; but having allowed his health to suffer, he found it necessary to recruit it, and accordingly visited Australia and New Zealand, on an important mission for the Norwich Union Fire Office, involving points of delicacy and special enquiry. This mission was performed to the full satisfaction of the Board, who, on Mr. Anderson's return, gave suitable expression to their estimate of his services. Soon afterwards he was appointed Head Office

Inspector to the Caledonian Company at Edinburgh. Mr. Anderson was subsequently again associated for four years with the Norwich Union Life Office as District Manager at Birmingham, again leaving that Society's service to take up the District Managership of the Economic Life Office at Edinburgh for the North and East of Scotland and the Northern Counties of England, whence he was promoted to the more important post which he at present holds.

Anderson, James C., the District Manager of the Commercial Union Assurance Company at their Irish Branch at College Green, Dublin, commenced his Insurance career in the service of the Royal Fire and Life Insurance Company at their Edinburgh Branch. In the year 1863 he was transferred to the Dublin Branch of same Company. There he remained until 1879, in which year the Commercial Union Assurance Company, on the re-organization of their Irish business, being in want of a new District Manager, their choice fell on him from amongst a large number of candidates, and he was accordingly appointed to the post. During the period of twelve years that he has now been in charge of the Dublin Office, he has been most successful, having worked up the business of his Company, which before his appointment had not been of the most plentiful, to a very high standard both of quantity and quality.

W. H. ANDERSSON.

A. R. ANDERSSON.

Andersson, William Henry the Senior District Manager of the Norwich Union Fire and Life Insurance Societies at their Branch, the common property of the two Societies, in Norwich Union Buildings, Castle Street, Liverpool, was born on the 26th of June, 1822. He is the eldest and only surviving son of the late Mr. John Ulric Andersson, who was also connected with the Norwich Union at Liverpool for thirty-five years, and who subsequently met his death at the Stanley Dock fire in that city in the year 1860. Mr. W. H. Andersson received his early education at St. George's House, Everton, Liverpool, and was afterwards apprenticed to the soap-boiling business. He then made a voyage to the West Coast of Africa ; and eventually, in the year 1844, entered the service of the two Norwich Union Societies in Liverpool as Assistant to his father ; having thus at the present time completed forty-eight years of Insurance work in the service of the same employers. Mr. W. H. Andersson has been very successful in his work, not the least instance of his zeal and goodwill in the behalf of his employers being the special recommendation laid by him before them that they should effect the purchase of the present handsome premises which their offices now occupy, which purchase took place twenty-seven years ago in 1865. Mr. Andersson now in his turn his son for his assistant, in the superintendence of the two Insurance businesses, the firm being known as Messrs. W. H. Andersson and Son. Mr. W. H. Andersson takes some considerable part also in local affairs, and in the April of 1889 was appointed one of Her Majesty's Justices of the Peace for the County of Lancaster.

Andersson, Arthur Robert, is the Junior District Manager of the Norwich Union Fire and Life Insurance Societies Branch in Liverpool, and is the eldest son of Mr. William Henry Andersson, with whom he is associated in the business of that Branch. Mr. A. R. Andersson was born on the 12th of July, in the year 1854, and is thus at present in the thirty-eighth year of his age. He was primarily educated at the Royal Institution School in his native town of Liverpool, and when of sufficient age to commence the more serious business of earning his own livelihood was apprenticed to one of the principal firms of cotton brokers of that city. He continued after the expiration of his term of apprenticeship in the same line of business until 1876, in the month of February of which latter year he gave up cotton broking in order that he might become associated with his father in the Joint Office of the Norwich Union Fire and Life Societies. It was not, however, until after the expiration of five years, in 1881, that Mr. A. R. Andersson was appointed to the post which he at present holds of Joint District Manager in conjunction with his father, the appointment being made at the time when the branch arrangements of the Norwich Union Societies were first being taken into consideration by the Board of Directors. Mr. A. R. Andersson has proved himself to be a thoroughly able and energetic Assistant to his father, and the father and son now transact an important and ever-increasing business in the locality over which they together exercise the superintendence.

W. ANDREWS.

JONAS ANDERTON.

Andrews, W., District Manager to the Marine and General Mutual Life Assurance Society at Bristol, has for upwards of twenty-five years represented various offices as Insurance Broker, and for many years assisted the late Mr. Cornelius Walford in adjusting claims for the Accident and Colonial Insurance Companies. In 1866 he undertook the representation of the Sovereign Life Office, subsequently becoming Agent for the Lancashire Life and Fire Offices. In 1870, and for many years subsequently, he was Superintendent of the West of England Fire Brigade at Bristol, doing besides a very good business as Agent for the Fire Department of that Company, while at the same time he represented the Carriage Accident Insurance Company, the Provident Fire Office, and the Continental Insurance Agency. In 1875 he became Agent for the Imperial Union, a post which he held for many years, and at other different periods he has acted for the London and Southwark Life and Fire and the London and Lancashire Insurance Companies. He received his present appointment in 1889.

———

Anderton, Jonas, is the District Agent of the British Equitable Assurance Company at Bradford, Yorkshire, with which Company he has been connected for more than 15 years, during which time he has placed a very large amount of business on its books. He is a native of Bradford, in which town he occupies an influential position.

HON. F. W. ANSON.

Anson, The Honourable Frederic William, Manager of the West End Branch of the Commercial Union Assurance Company, is the fourth son of the late Earl of Lichfield, and was born in 1862, his mother being the eldest daughter of the 1st Duke of Abercorn. Mr. Anson was appointed to his present position in the Spring of 1886, then being but twenty-four years of age, so that he may no doubt claim to be the youngest Branch Manager of an influential Insurance Office. His Management has been marked with conspicuous success. The year of his receiving this appointment he married Florence, the eldest daughter of Colonel Bagot Lane, Coldstream Guards, of King's Bromley Manor, Lichfield, and Lily Hill, Ascot, and his home is in Hertfordshire. Mr. Anson is also a Director of the Securities Insurance Company, Limited.

Watson, James, was, until his retirement in March, 1890, the Manager of the Scottish Provident Institution, with whose career from its commencement his own has been practically identified. He was born in Edinburgh in 1811; and, having received his education at the High School and the University, served his apprenticeship to business in an accountant's office. He then entered into partnership with Mr. James Cleghorn, one of the highest authorities on Actuarial business of his time; and, though Mr. Watson always attributes the credit of the original idea to Mr. Cleghorn, it was virtually the two together who started this remarkable Mutual Life Assurance Society in 1837. On the death of Mr. Cleghorn in the following year, Mr. Watson was appointed to the sole management; and under his able administration, the history of the Scottish Provident may be said to have been one unbroken record of prosperity. The leading idea of its founders was, that —while as a nonproprietary Society the profits should belong solely to the members —in consideration of its low premiums, those only who survived to pay up in premiums the amount of their policies and secure the Bonus Fund from loss should be entitled to participate; and to this principle the Office has adhered since its commencement. From the first it attracted considerable attention to itself, from the difference between it and the usual type of Insurance Office then existing; and it has been the subject of many and repeated attacks, mainly on the ground of the novelty of its principle, but Mr. Watson has never given way to these, but has quietly pursued his own course; thus convincing his opponents against their will by his success. Indeed, it may safely be asserted that it

JAMES WATSON, F.F.A.

has been for the most part due to Mr. Watson's individual efforts that the business of the Scottish Provident has outstripped most others of a like nature; the accumulated funds now amounting to over seven millions sterling. Mr. Watson, in 1874, did great service to the public when he exposed many of the fallacies propounded by the American Insurance Companies which had established branches in England and hoped thereby to attract custom. He has always set his face steadfastly against the too reckless expenditure of commissions, which was formerly no inconsiderable item in the cost of Insurance.

The career of Mr. Watson as an Insurance official may be well said to be unique. He has never been associated with any other Office than the Scottish Provident; closely associated with its original founder, and the calculator of its tables when it was founded, he has not merely held office in it, but has been its Manager, practically, from its commencement to his recent retirement into private life. His rare abilities, decision of character, breadth of mind, and unfailing tact, have greatly served to enhance the popularity of his Office. His directors and his staff have always placed the greatest confidence in him, and, in 1888, the year of his jubilee as sole Manager, he was presented with two handsome testimonials, one from the Branch Secretaries of the Institution throughout the kingdom, and the other from his directors, the latter causing to be placed on their Minutes a special record of his services, and an expression of their appreciation of the unsparing devotion with which he has given the services of a life-time to the interests of the Institution.

T. WILKINSON WATSON, F.S.S.

Watson, Thomas Wilkinson, F.S.S., is the Manager of the Scottish Imperial Insurance Company of Glasgow. He was born in the ancient and historical Scottish Metropolis in the year 1843. He is a son of the late Mr. George Watson, who, at the commencement of a highly-promising career as a Writer to the Signet, gave up the legal profession for religion, and became a Minister of the Apostolic Church. While filling this position he married a daughter of a clergyman of the Church of England. Their union was blessed with a large family, one member of which is the subject of this article. His early training was certainly somewhat Draconian. His education was practically begun at the early age of five, when he was entered at the Circus Place School in his native city. At the age of seven he was transferred to the High School, Glasgow, where he remained until he reached the age of thirteen, and at that early age he began his professional and commercial career, being then apprenticed to a Chartered Accountant in Glasgow. Four years later, when only seventeen, his health completely broke down, and he was an invalid, with very shadowy hopes of recovery. When he was twenty years old the doctors were compelled to amputate one of his feet. After this he did somewhat improve in health, gradually, it is true, but in such way that when he was twenty-two he was able to resume work. He then entered the service of the Scottish Imperial Insurance Company. This was in the year 1866, when that office was just commencing business. Here he was successively appointed to the responsible positions of Cashier, Accountant, Assistant-Actuary, and eventually to be Actuary to the Company. The Board of Directors of the Scottish Imperial finally determined to relinquish its fire business altogether, and on the necessary arrangements for this being completed and carried out, Mr. T. Wilkinson Watson was by them appointed to the position of Manager, holding that appointment in conjunction with that of Actuary. Mr. Watson holds a high reputation in the Actuarial world, and has been twice elected the President of the Insurance and Actuarial Society of Glasgow.

ALFRED WEAVING

A. E. WHITE.

Weaving, Alfred, the Secretary of the Employers' Liability and Workpeople's Insurance Company, Limited, of Newhall Street, Birmingham, was born in Warwickshire in the year 1859.

The whole of his Insurance experience has been gained in the service of the Office in which he now holds so responsible and onerous a position. On its foundation in 1881 he was appointed to the post of Chief Clerk, and in this capacity he acted until the death of the late Mr. W. H. Greening (the first Secretary) in 1889. The Board of Directors of the Company, after due consideration of the claims of the various candidates for the vacant post, unanimously selected Mr. Weaving to fill it in conjunction with Mr W. F. Greening, and he has discharged the duties, thereby entrusted to him to the utmost satisfaction of all concerned.

———

White, Auckland E., is the Agency Manager of the Pelican Life Insurance Company, having been appointed to that position in September 1890. Previously to his entering the service of the Pelican, Mr. White was for over nine years in the Head Office of the Crown Life Assurance Company, and has had altogether over ten years' Life Assurance experience.

THOMAS H. WELLS.

Wells, Thomas H., late Underwriter of the Universal Marine Insurance Company, Limited, of London, has been connected (with one lapse) with that Company since it originally started in the year 1860.

Mr. Wells had previously received some training in the science of Marine Insurance in the offices of Messrs. Ryan and Dale, Insurance Brokers, of Lloyd's. He left this firm to join the Underwriting Staff of the office he has been almost ever since connected with. For several years he occupied the position of Deputy-Underwriter to the Company, serving under both Mr. Rutherford and Mr. J. L. Fisk.

In 1870 he was appointed London Underwriter to the British and Foreign Marine Insurance Company, and this position he held for eleven years. At the end of that time, on the death of the late Mr. John L. Fisk, he was offered and accepted an appointment with his old office, with which he remained up to the time of its amalgamation with the British and Foreign Marine last year

White, F. A., Underwriter and Manager of the Marine Insurance Company Limited, received his Marine Insurance training at Lloyd's, the great school for successful Company Underwriters. After a preliminary probation of some years under the auspices of Mr. Arthur Burnand, brother of his predecessor in the Marine Insurance Company, he became an Underwriter for himself and two or three other gentlemen in Lloyd's, and at once acquired for himself, by his activity and aptitude for business, the position of a man of mark and influence in the career which he had chosen. In 1874 his diligence was rewarded by his appointment to his present post; and putting himself strenuously to work, he rapidly succeeded in the task that had been set him of regaining the position for his Company which it had temporarily lost in the interval which had elapsed between Mr. Burnand's retirement and his own appointment. It is stated—and, from a close examination into statistics, there is

F. A. WHITE.

rank of his branch of the profession, the outlook of Marine Insurance was very gloomy. Foreign agencies were multiplying fast in the City, to the extent of at least three times their former number, not to speak of Colonial, Australian, China, and Indian Offices. To popularize their business, many of these adopted a system of offering large bonuses to their clients at the end of each financial year; and for a time this attractive prospect of sharing in the profits strongly tempted even some of the first-class houses to desert the older institutions. To meet such competition in the open market required a man of exceptional boldness and resource, but such an one was fortunately forthcoming in the person of Mr. White, to whom one and all of the older Companies, as well as the firms which had established themselves at Lloyd's will ever owe a debt of gratitude for his services during that trying time. His method of attack was to reduce the rates of Insurance from India and the East, and thus

every reason to believe that the statement is thoroughly trustworthy—that under Mr. White's skilful and prudent management the profits of the Marine Insurance Company have, in the comparatively brief period of fourteen years, exceeded one million and a quarter sterling. But Mr. White did even more than this for the Marine Insurance fraternity generally. At the time when he had established himself in the front catch the bonus Companies in the most vulnerable point of their system; these rates having been, up to that time, the principal source whence the bonus that they distributed was derived. It was a bold stroke to win back the former power of the old Companies, but it was well calculated, and the result has borne ample testimony to its wisdom, few of the clients having failed to have been eventually convinced that after all " the old is better."

WILLIAM GEORGE WILKINS.

Wilkins, William George, holds the important position of Fire Manager of the old established Union Fire and Life Assurance Society of London, to which he was appointed in the year 1888.

Mr. Wilkins commenced his business life as a Clerk in the office of his father (who carried on an extensive business as a Russian Merchant) in the year 1850. Two years later (in 1852) he deserted commerce for Insurance, then entering the service of the Monarch Insurance Company of London. At that time the offices of this Corporation were at Adelaide Place, London Bridge.

It was not long after this that this Company was amalgamated with the Liverpool and London and Globe Insurance Company, and Mr. Wilkins's next appointment in the Insurance World was on the staff of the Head Office of the Union Assurance Society as a Clerk in the Town Department. Year after year of conscientious work in the various departments, each bringing knowledge of the practical working and organization of so important an office, with the corresponding experience, also brought well-earned promotions, and the year 1884 saw Mr. Wilkins at the head of his department in the office.

In 1886, on the death of a colleague on the staff, the Directors appointed Mr. Wilkins to the important post of Chief of the Agency Department. In discharging the duties of this post he was successful, and in the year 1888, on a certain amount of re-organization of the staff of the Society being thought advisable, and also being carried out, he was promoted to the position he has now ever since occupied.

F. B. WILLIAMS, F.S.S.

Williams, Frederic Bessant, F.S.S., the Managing Director of the London and General Plate Glass Insurance Company, Limited, of Leicester Square, London, was born at Hackney, Middlesex, in 1836. He was educated at Oxford, and first entered the Insurance profession in the year 1854. Seven years later (in 1861) he was appointed to the position of Secretary to the office of which he is the present official head, and after holding that position for twenty-five years, he was in 1887 elected to fill the office of Managing Director, which position he still holds.

In the year 1864 Mr. Williams was elected a Fellow of the Royal Statistical Society, and is in addition a Member of the Courts of two of the Livery Companies of the City of London, namely, "The Paper Stainers" and "The Blacksmiths."

H. E. Wilson.

Wilson, Henry Edward, is the Secretary of the London Office of the Northern Insurance Company, and has spent a considerable portion of his life in the service of that Corporation.

It was in the year 1866 that he first joined its staff, and he spent several years in working his way through various departments and acquiring the necessary knowledge and experience to qualify him for his present position.

In 1878 he was promoted to the position of Assistant-Secretary, a post which he filled to such advantage that when, in the year 1881, the Secretaryship became vacant, he was selected by the Board of Directors of the Company for the appointment which he at present holds.

Whittall, William Joseph Hutchings, F.I.A., is the Assistant-Actuary of the Clerical, Medical, and General Life Assurance Society, and was born on the 23rd of June, 1857. He commenced his Actuarial career by joining the Institute of Actuaries in the year 1873, and in the following year his practical Insurance experience began, when he entered the service of the office he is still with. He passed the several examinations of the Institute of Actuaries, receiving the Certificate of Competency from that body in 1880, and in that same year was admitted to its Fellowship. Five years later (in 1885) he was appointed to his present position. He has contributed several papers to be read before the Institute of Actuaries, and has also collaborated with other gentlemen in the same object.

He is the Honorary Librarian of the Institute of Actuaries.

R. RIDDELL WILSON.

Wilson, R. Riddell, is the Secretary of the London and Provincial Horse and Carriage Insurance Company, Limited, and the Horse Insurance Company, Limited, of Queen Victoria Street, London. He was born in 1860, and is a native of Aberdeenshire. He was appointed by the Board of Directors to his present position in the year 1887.

His first connection with the Staff of the Companies was made in the month of March, 1880, and he was afterwards raised to the position of Assistant-Secretary, from which post he was promoted to his present appointment.

———

Weiland, Walter, is the Secretary of the London Amicable Assurance Society, Limited, the Head Offices of which are at 3, Regent Street, London, S.W. Mr. Weiland has had a wide experience of Life Insurance, having been Director for France and Italy and Inspector-General for the Continent for a large English Company. He is a native of London.

PHILIP WINSOR.

A. A. WOOD.

Winsor, Philip, Foreign Sub-Manager of the North British and Mercantile Insurance Company, received his English education principally at the Collegiate Institution at Liverpool, but in 1855 went to Germany and France, remaining a year and a-half in each country to acquire a knowledge of the respective languages. He commenced his Insurance career in 1859 in the Imperial Fire Office under the late highly-esteemed Mr. Andrew Baden, the then Fire Superintendent, from whom he received the greater part of his Insurance training. Early in 1863 he obtained the appointment to the Chief Clerkship of the Foreign Department of the North British and Mercantile London Office, which appointment he held till 1875, when he was promoted to his present post. He makes frequent official trips to the Con-

tinent and elsewhere, and is well-known in Insurance circles in Berlin and Vienna, which cities he most frequently visits in connection with the Company's important Continental Branches.

***

Wood, Andrew A., entered the Assurance Profession in 1886, as an Inspector for The Scottish Life Office. In February, 1888, he was appointed to an Inspectorship in The Standard Life Assurance Company, and in July of the same year he succeeded Mr. George Edwards, as Chief Inspector. In June, 1890, he was appointed General Superintendent of Branches and Agencies for England, which appointment he now holds. He was educated at the Edinburgh Academy, and began his business career in The National Bank of Scotland, at the Head Office.

ARTHUR B. WOODS, A.I.A.

Woods, Arthur B., A.I.A., the Actuarial Assistant of the Rock Life Assurance Company of London, is on the threshold of what promises to be a remarkable Actuarial career.

He was born at Godalming in the year 1857, and after completing his education was appointed to a position on the staff of the Rock Life Assurance Company in the year 1874, since which time he has remained in the service of that Company.

Mr. Crisford early recognised the abilities he displayed, and after watching his progress, and the way in which he utilised the opportunities afforded him of gaining both practical and theoretical experience in his profession, he advanced him to the position of Chief of the Staff of the Office in the year 1890.

Mr. Woods is an Associate of the Institute of Actuaries by examination, and is also one of the Auditors of that body. This fact proves the extent of the confidence the members of the Actuarial Fraternity have in his abilities, and also justifies the promise we have mentioned as to his future.

ERNEST WOODS, F.I.A

Woods, Ernest, F.I.A., the Actuary of the Westminster and General Life Assurance Association of London, was born in the year 1855.

He received the first portion of his education at the Royal Grammar School of Guildford, in the County of Surrey, under Dr. Merriman, and completed his early studies at the College Galliard, Lausanne, France.

His Insurance career was commenced by the appointment to a Clerkship in the Westminster Fire Office in the year 1872, and while fulfilling the duties of that post he had charge of the Guarantee Department of the Company. Six years later (in 1878) he resigned this office on being appointed Actuarial Assistant at the Head Office of the Guardian Life Assurance Company in Lombard Street, in which capacity he acted until December, 1888, when he left the service of this Company on being selected by the Board of Directors of the Westminster and General Life Office to fill the same appointment. This he held until the month of October, 1890, when he was appointed to the post of Actuary to the Association, in succession to the late Mr. Edward Cutbush.

Mr. Woods passed the Final Examination of the Institute of Actuaries in 1884, receiving his Fellowship the same year, and has been selected by the Council of that body to act as Examiner five times since that date

WILLIAM WOODWARD.

Woodward, William, is the Joint Managing Director with Mr. Grayling of the London and Manchester Industrial Assurance Company. Mr. Woodward devoted his earlier years to commercial pursuits. which, however, he soon relinquished from choice for the calling of Life Assurance. The scene of his labours was at Sheffield, as representative of the Friend in Need, where, by the exercise of the qualities of industry and perseverance, he was rewarded by seeing his efforts result in a rapidly increasing and thriving Agency.

When the London and Manchester was started, Mr. Woodward was invited to become a Director of it, which offer he accepted. It soon became evident to all concerned that no better choice could have been made. His hearty re-elections to the Board of the Company to which he has attached himself testify in no small degree to the appreciation in which his services are held, as also does his election to the post which he now holds conjointly with his old friend Mr. Grayling. Mr. Woodward was born in 1835.

ALFRED WRIGHT.

Wright, Alfred, who holds the responsible position of Treasurer of the Royal Liver Friendly Society, was born at Liverpool in 1851, and was educated at Liverpool Institute in that city. In 1868 he entered the employ of the Society as a Junior Clerk. He soon showed a remarkable capacity for accounts, and rapidly rose above his contemporaries. The year 1880 saw him entrusted with the position of Deputy-Treasurer, a post which he filled to the satisfaction of every-one ; and he ultimately succeeded the late Treasurer (Mr. Stephenson) in 1882.

The post of Treasurer is no sinecure. There is no harder worker in the Society's interests than Mr. Wright, the nature of his occupation tying him down closely to the office. But his heart is in his work, and, as a consequence, there is never any hitch in his Department. Mr. Wright's gentlemanly and courteous manner is appreciated by all who come into contact with him.

Mr. Wright is Chairman of one of the most flourishing of the Starr-Bowkett Societies, and was for many years intimately connected with the promotion of Penny Savings Banks in Liverpool. His views are Liberal, and, although not an ardent politician, he is always ready to sacrifice time and convenience for the service of his party.

S. WIGHTMAN.

JOHN DRUMYOND YOUNG.

Wightman, S., of the Head Office of the Guardian Assurance Company, entered the service of that Company in 1875, after having been connected for some time with one of their principal Agencies. He was employed for nine years in the Fire Department of the Head Office, for the last seven years of which period he occupied the position of Chief Clerk of the Guarantee Department. In 1886 he was appointed Resident Secretary of the West of England and South Wales Branch of the Company at Bristol, having under his charge the counties of Gloucester, Somerset, Wilts, Dorset, Devon and Cornwall, and the whole of South Wales. Under his management the Branch made steady progress, especially in the Fire Department.

In November, 1891, Mr. Wightman resigned his position at Bristol to take up the special appointment which he now holds in the former scene of his operations, the Fire Department in the Company's Head Office.

Young, John Drummond, is the Managing Director of the Scottish Boiler Insurance and Engine Inspection Company, Limited, of Glasgow and Manchester. Mr. J. D. Young has occupied his present responsible post since the establishment of the Scottish Boiler Insurance Company in 1881, and its subsequent success is mainly due to his personal efforts, his history in fact being since that date entirely that of his Company.

Young, T. E., B.A., F.I.A., the Actuary of the Commercial Union Assurance Company Limited, was born at Newcastle-on-Tyne, in 1843. Before leaving School he distinguished himself by taking Honours in the Junior Middle Class at an Oxford University Local Examination. In 1859 he entered the service of the London and Provincial Law Assurance Society, under Mr. Archibald Day. While here he continued his studies, and won a scholarship at New College. In 1865 he re-entered the Insurance world under Mr. W. P. Pattison, of the Commercial Union, acting, in addition to his official duties, as Assistant to that gentleman in his private practice. While acting thus he was engaged on what will be by many considered the most important work of his life, viz.—the Life Assurance Act of 1870. With the Right Honourable Stephen Cave and Mr. Pattison he was employed on this from its first drafting to its passing the Houses of Parliament. The year previous to this he passed the Final Examination in the University of London for the Degree of B.A., and the same year and the following one he added to his learned honours by passing the First and Second Examinations of the Institute of Actuaries. The year following (1871) he accepted the Life Managership of the Guardian Life Assurance Company, which, however, he only held for twelve months, retiring from it on being appointed to the same position in the Commercial Union. During these twelve months he was called in by the Board of Trade, during Mr. Pattison's absence from England, to advise on the Returns of the Act of 1870 that he had so much assisted in, and the expiration of that twelve months saw him a Member of the Convocation of the University of London, and also Auditor to Marlborough College. From that year to 1874 his career was comparitively uneventful; then he became a Fellow of the Institute of Actuaries, and three years later a Member of its Council. Nine years afterwards (in 1885) he accepted the position of Joint Honorary Secretary and Editor of the Journal of the Institute. In 1888 the Institute recognised the work he had done in the interests of Life Insurance by electing him one of its Vice-Presidents, and in the same year he was appointed Consulting Actuary to the Provident Clerks' Life Office. Of all the work Mr. Young has done we have not space here to speak— he has acted several times as Examiner for the Associate and Fellowship Examinations of the Institute of Actuaries ; he was one of the Founders and is now the Honorary Secretary and Treasurer of the "Life Managers' Association"; he is also Auditor and Vice-President of the Insurance Musical Society ; and has contributed numerous papers to the Journal of the Institute.

T. E. YOUNG, B.A., F.I.A.

HENRY G. ANDREWES.

THOMAS AITKEN.

Andrewes, H. G., is the Resident Secretary at Glasgow of the Scottish Union and National Insurance Company. He received his early training in the Birmingham Office of the Royal Insurance Company, and afterwards in the Glasgow Branch of the Imperial Fire Office. In 1875 he was appointed Resident Secretary of the Scottish National at Newcastle-upon-Tyne, and in 1878, when the Birmingham Branch of the Scottish Union and National was established, it was placed under his management. In this capacity he was remarkably successful, and the Directors of that Company, after some years' experience of his qualifications, selected him for the management of the more important Glasgow Branch.

Aitken, Thomas, Resident Secretary of the West of Scotland Branch of the Gresham Life Assurance Society in West Regent Street, Glasgow, is an old and devoted servant of the Gresham, having become connected with it early in the seventies. He was formerly Local Secretary at the Edinburgh Branch, the business of which he built up and established on a sound basis. Since his appointment to Glasgow, in 1886, the business of the Gresham in the West of Scotland has shown a very considerable increase.

H. W. ARKCOLL.

W. V. ARROWSMITH.

Arkcoll, H. W., is the Resident Secretary of the Lancashire Insurance Company at Hanley, Staffordshire. Mr. Arkcoll commenced his Insurance career in the Head Office of the Staffordshire Fire Insurance Company at Hanley in 1872. In 1880, on the capital of the Company being enlarged and the name changed to the London and Staffordshire, the Head Office was removed to London, whither Mr. Arkcoll was likewise transferred in the early part of 1881 as one of the Company's chief officials. Towards the close of the same year, however, he returned to Hanley in the capacity of Resident Secretary to the now Branch Office there; and in the following year, on the home business of the Company being sold to the Lancashire Insurance Company, Mr. Arkcoll was continued by the latter Office in the same capacity.

———

Arrowsmith, William Vallack, is the Resident Secretary at Birmingham of the Caledonian Insurance Company, which position he has occupied since August, 1888, having been previously associated with the Scottish Equitable and the Scottish Widows' Fund Life Offices. Mr. Arrowsmith has been very successful in the Insurance field, and is an energetic and popular member of the fraternity.

WILLIAM ATKINSON.

W. C. ASPINALL.

Atkinson, William, is the Local Secretary and Surveyor of the Phœnix Fire Office at their Midland Branch at Birmingham. Mr. Atkinson dates his experience in the Insurance profession back to 1863, when he entered the service of the Lancashire Insurance Company at their Head Office. He subsequently joined the Royal, and until taking up his present appointment had secured his wide experience in the Lancashire District with these two Companies. In 1882 he was selected to take charge of the Birmingham Branch of the Phœnix, the district under his charge including the counties of Warwick, Worcester, Stafford, Nottingham, Leicester, North-ampton, Rutland, and part of Oxfordshire and Derbyshire. Under Mr. Atkinson's management the business of the Phœnix has largely developed in the Midlands, so much so that they have been compelled to increase both their Office and their staff.

———

Aspinall, W. C., Resident Secretary at Liverpool of the Ocean, Accident and Guarantee Corporation, Limited, 46, Castle Street, is a member of one of Liverpool's oldest and most respected families. He has a large and influential connection in that city, and has succeeded in building up a very profitable business.

W. G. BADDELEY

JAMES BAILEY.

Baddeley, W. G., the District Manager to the Norwich Union Life Insurance Society at their Branch Office at Bristol, commenced Insurance work in 1875 in the Head Office of the Liverpool and London and Globe Insurance Company at Liverpool. After remaining in the service of that Company for a period of over ten years, during which time he served in all departments of the office, and acquired a thorough knowledge of all the details of the Insurance profession, he applied for and obtained the Inspectorship for the South Western District, comprising six counties, of his present Society, and in this capacity gave uch satisfaction to his employers that he was ventually promoted to be District Manager of the Branch then just formed of the amalgamation of his former District with the South Wales District, consisting of seven counties, making thirteen counties in all. Since then Mr. Baddeley has done a large and constantly-increasing business.

———

Bailey, James, is the Manager of the Dublin Branch of the Equitable Life Assurance Society of the United States, which appointment he took up in 1890. He had previously had a very long and successful experience in the Life Insurance business. Mr. Bailey is an able and energetic official, and is building up a large business for his Company in Ireland.

J. T. HERBERT BAILY.

R. BALBIRNIE.

Baily, J. T. Herbert, F.S.A.A., is the Resident Secretary of the Law Courts Branch of the Sun Life Office at 40, Chancery Lane, W.C. He was born at Broughtey Ferry, Forfar, and educated at Bussage House School, Stroud, Gloucestershire, and Leeds Grammar School. He first entered business as a Junior Clerk in the firm of Messrs. Colthurst, Symons and Company, of Bridgewater, Somerset, but shortly afterwards, in November, 1882, received an appointment in the Head Office of the Guardian Fire and Life Assurance Company, where he remained for a period of eight years until January, 1891, when he relinquished it for his present position. Mr. Baily is an Accountant by profession, having passed his Final Examination in December, 1889.

Balbirnie, Robert, is the Inspector of the Caledonian Insurance Company at its Branch Office at Dublin. Mr. Balbirnie commenced his career in the Edinburgh Agency of the Sun Fire and Life Offices, and afterwards accepted an appointment in the Guarantee Department of the late Scottish Fire. When the latter Company was taken over by the Caledonian, he remained for six months at the Head Office, when he was transferred to their Glasgow Branch, to take up the duties of Chief Clerk and Assistant to the late Mr. Adam Knox, Fire Superintendent. After about seven years in that Branch, he was offered the post which he now holds at their Dublin Branch. Through his stay in Glasgow Mr. Balbirnie gained large experience of the various risks in that district, having had almost the whole of the surveying to do during his last two years owing to the illness of the Fire Superintendent.

C. C. BALLINGALL.

G. HAMPTON BARBER.

Ballingall, Charles Campbell, the Secretary of the Lancashire Insurance Company at Edinburgh, was born and educated in Scotland, and entered the office of his present Company at Glasgow when quite a youth. After twelve years' service there, having during that period gone through all departments, he became Chief Clerk at the Company's Branch in Birmingham. Four years after that he received the appointment of Local Secretary at the Inverness Office of the Company, in which capacity he acted till the year 1890, when he was promoted to his present post of Assistant-Secretary on the staff for Scotland with charge of the Edinburgh Branch.

Barber, G. Hampton, is the Manager for Scotland of the Pioneer Life Insurance Company, Limited. Mr. Barber began his Insurance career in connection with the Lancashire Department of the Mutual Reserve Fund Life Association of New York, and for some time remained with this Association in that field, after which he was made the Manager of the Yorkshire Department of the Mutual Reserve, with his headquarters at Leeds, which post he resigned to accept his present appointment   Mr. Barber has been very successful as a Life Insurance man, having done a very large amount of business for the Companies with which he has been connected.

G. W. W. BARCLAY, J.P.

J. M. BARR.

Barclay, George W. W., M.A., J.P., F.R.S.E., commenced a career which has been singularly active and varied in the service of the Indian Government. Official employment not proving congenial to his taste, he left it to take the Editorship of the Calcutta *Englishman*, the leading daily newspaper in India. This position he occupied for five years, during a portion of which period he also acted as the Editor of the *Calcutta Review*. While residing in the Metropolis of our Indian Empire, his abilities were widely recognised, and he was connected with many public bodies. Among other honours he was made a Justice of the Peace for the City, and also a Fellow of the University of Calcutta.

Owing to ill-health Mr. Barclay had to return to England, and then turned his attention to Insurance matters. The Alliance Insurance Company of London was the first to secure his services, and the Management of this Corporation appointed him to the position of District Manager of its Branch Office in Glasgow. After holding this post for some months he was appointed Local Manager for the Sun Fire and Life Offices in Edinburgh, and this appointment he held for nine years.

In the beginning of the year 1890 the North British and Mercantile Insurance Company appointed Mr. Barclay their Local Manager at Aberdeen—a Branch which controls and directs the business of the Company, not only in that City but in a large tract of the North of Scotland. Additional importance attached to the appointment on account of the recent amalgamation of the Scottish Provincial with the North British and Mercantile, the latter Company now occupying the Head Offices of the former in the "Granite City."

When he left Edinburgh, to take up his present appointment, Mr. Barclay was a Member of the Town Council, and he is also a Justice of the Peace for the City of Edinburgh, and for the County of Aberdeen, and is a Director of the Scottish Accident Insurance Company.

———

Barr, J. M., is the Branch Manager at Glasgow of the Atlas Assurance Company, to which position he was appointed in 1890. Previous to this Mr. Barr was Manager for Scotland of the London and Lancashire Life Assurance Company, and the Fire Insurance Association, Limited, having formerly held the post of Surveyor to the Royal Insurance Company at its Glasgow Branch, and officiated as Assistant Surveyor to the Glasgow Fire Rate and Salvage Committee.

J. BARTLETT.

E. P. BARTLETT.

Bartlett, J., is the Resident Secretary of the Reliance Life Office at their Branch Office at Bristol. Mr. Bartlett also opened a Branch of the Manchester Fire Assurance Company in 1875, the business of the Company having been formerly worked by Agencies, and has retained charge of it till a few months ago, to the utmost satisfaction of his Directors. He is one of the most respected residents in Bristol.

Bristow, H. J., Manager of the London Branch of the New Zealand Insurance Company, is the London Managing Partner of the firm of Messrs. Bowley and Bristow, Merchants and Underwriters, who have been the representatives of the New Zealand Insurance Company in London since its formation in 1859, first as its Agents and subsequently as its Managers. The New Zealand Insurance Company was the first Institution of a corporate character of any magnitude established in that colony, and since its foundation has been undoubtedly successful almost beyond the most sanguine expectations of its promoters, in the attainment of which result Mr. Bristow is certainly entitled to a large share of the credit. Mr. Bristow is also Chairman of the Australian and New Zealand Underwriters' Association, which originated in a suggestion made by him in January, 1875, to establish a tariff of minimum premiums, which was done, and chiefly through the influence of the Association founded to support it, loyally adhered to for three or four years. The proverbial incoherency of Underwriters, however, reasserted itself once more, and the war of rates recommenced. Still the Association has done good work of multiform kinds under the able direction and tactical skill of its chairman, and is always well to the front whenever anything affecting the interests of Underwriters needs attention. The existence of the Institution of London Underwriters, a very similar body, established by the English Companies, is in a great measure due to the good example set by this Association. Mr. Bristow has been a Member of Lloyd's Agency Committee since 1882, and of the Book Committee since 1883 ; he has also been on the Committee of the Institute of London Underwriters since its formation and of the London Salvage Association since 1881.

Bartlett, Edward P., is the Local Secretary to the Gresham Life Assurance Society at their Nottingham Branch. Mr. Bartlett has risen from the ranks to his present position, having first entered the service of the Gresham in 1883 as an Agent in Nottingham. He was appointed to his present position in 1887, and has since increased the business of his District to a very great extent. Mr. Bartlett is an enthusiastic cricketer, as well as a Volunteer, in both of which capacities he has obtained considerable distinction. He also takes an active part in politics, being Honorary Secretary to one of the Local Conservative Clubs, and holds a seat on the Nottingham Board of Guardians in the Conservative interest.

HENRY W. BARKER.

THOMAS BARTON.

Barker, Henry W., is the District Superin-tendent of the British Equitable Assurance Company at Sheffield, which position he has occupied or upwards of ten years. Mr. Barker is a member of the Wesleyan Methodist Church, a class leader and local preacher, and possesses the confidence of his fellow citizens in an eminent degree.

Bristow, William, Assistant Underwriter in London of the New Zealand Insurance Company, began his commercial career in the office of Messrs. Rowley and Bristow. Thence he went to Calcutta to take temporary charge of the Company's Branch there, and after discharging the onerous duties which devolved upon him in that position in a most efficient manner he returned to London to assume the appointment which he now holds.

Barton, Thomas, is the Resident Secretary of the English and Scottish Law Life Assurance Association at its Branch Office at Leeds. Mr. Barton only commenced his Insurance career towards the latter end of 1890, when he was appointed to his present position. Before that he was for some ten years with one of the leading firms of Land and Estate Agents in Leeds. He

is well known and has a large circle of friends and acquaintances among whom he is extremely popular.

Blair, Archibald, Manager for Scotland of the London and Lancashire Fire Office, with his office at Glasgow, gained his early Insurance experience in the service of the Royal Insurance Company and later in that of the North British and Mercantile, first in both cases, in their local Branches at Glasgow, where he was Secretary to the latter Company for some years, and afterwards at their respective Head Offices, in Liverpool and Edinburgh. While with these offices he had ample opportunity to acquire a considerable knowledge and experience in the details of his profession, of which opportunity he fully availed himself. In 1878 Mr. Blair accepted the offer of the General Manager of the London and Lancashire Fire Insurance Company to undertake the duties of his present post, and since his appointment he has worked most successfully to bring his Branch to a position worthy of its parent Company, and place it in the front rank of similar institutions in Scotland. Mr. Blair has a very extensive connection at home and abroad, having visited all parts of the globe in the interests of his Company, towards the extension of which he has done much in India, China, Japan, the West Indies, &c

DAVID BELL.

WALTER BELL.

Bell, David, the District Secretary to the Scottish Amicable Life Assurance Society at Manchester, commenced his Insurance career in the Liverpool Branch of the Equitable Fire and Accident Offices in 1884. After a short stay of six months, he was transferred to the Companies' Head Office in Manchester, where his three years of inside work were marked by a speedy acquirement of knowledge of Fire Insurance Business, he acting as head of one of the responsible departments for the last twelve months of this period. In January of 1888 he was appointed to the post of Inspector of Agents for Newcastle and the North of England for the Equitable Fire and Accident Offices, in which position he met with well-merited success. In May of the same year he was promoted to the Inspectorship of the Midlands for the same Offices. In October he left the Equitable with the good wishes and recommendations of the Manager and Branch Managers under whom he had worked, and undertook the task of organising the Scotch business of the Crown Life Company, the results of his eighteen months' labour in Scotland being highly satisfactory.

In April, 1890, the Scottish Amicable Life Assurance Society extended their operations in Lancashire and Yorkshire, and appointed Mr. Bell their first Manchester Secretary. Since the appointment the Branch has made that headway which at the time was generally anticipated.

Bell, Walter, Joint District Manager of the Equitable Fire and Accident Office at their Branch Office at Liverpool, was born at Ecclefechan in Dumfriesshire in 1859, and is therefore a fellow townsman of Carlyle. He was educated as a teacher, but after having qualified for that profession abandoned it for the more congenial one of Insurance, entering the service of his present Company at the Head Office in 1879. After five years' experience in various departments, Mr. Bell was, on the opening of a Branch Office in Liverpool, appointed District Representative to the Equitable in that City, and in 1888 promoted to his present rank of District Manager, then being the sole occupant of the post; but in 1890, on the British business of the South British and National being acquired by his Office, he was associated with Mr. Clarke, the local Manager of the absorbed Companies, in the joint exercise of the duties. Mr. Bell's career in Liverpool has been very successful, especially in the Accident Department.

ROBERT W. BELL.

GEORGE WM. BELSHAW.

Bell, Robert W., is the Liverpool Secretary of the Scottish Equitable Life Assurance Society. He has had considerable experience in life insurance, having been previously Agency Inspector at the London Office of the Scottish Equitable.

Brookes, Albert D., Secretary to the Alliance Assurance Company at their Branch in Corn Street, Bristol, was the first to open that Branch in 1885, and has remained in charge of it ever since. Mr. Brookes started in Bristol under good auspices, for the Alliance Assurance Company had already extensive connections in the West of England and South Wales both in the Life and the Fire business before the opening of the Branch, but none the less is credit due to him for the perseverance, energy, and good tact with which he has, since being put in charge of the District, conducted the Company's operations, so that the Alliance has now fully established its claim to be regarded as one of the first Insurance Companies in Bristol. Mr. Brookes for a long time carried on business as District Secretary, but this, owing to the importance he has conferred on his post, has since been changed for the title of Secretary.

Belshaw, George William, is the District Manager of the Scottish Employers' Liability and Accident Insurance Company of Aberdeen, at their Branch Office at Manchester. During his early years Mr. Belshaw was apprenticed to an Architect and Surveyor, and after serving his time became Surveyor, under the Manchester Branch, to the Staffordshire, afterwards the London and Staffordshire Fire Office, which post he held for a period of five years. He then became a General Surveyor, and was employed by several of the leading Fire Offices to make reports to them. He was also at this period District Agent for the Ocean and General Accident Company, and Hamburg Bremen Insurance Company. In 1889 he was appointed District Manager to the Scottish Employers' Liability and Accident Insurance Company, the post which he still holds, and a year later, accepted in addition the District Agency of the Glasgow and London Fire Insurance Company ; but upon the amalgamation of that Company with the Economic he continued to represent that particular Fire Office as Special Agent. Mr. Belshaw has also for several years been the Resident Secretary to the Liverpool Plate Glass Insurance Company.

T. BERESFORD.

FRANK G. BENNETT.

Beresford, T., is the District Manager at Norwich of the United Kingdom Temperance and General Provident Institution, which appointment he has held for 23 years. He is a prominent citizen of Norwich and has been a member of the Board of Guardians for several years. He also occupies other positions of importance.

Barrett, W., is the District Secretary of the English and Scottish Law Life Assurance Association at their Branch Office at Manchester. Mr. Barrett is a Manchester man, and received his education at the Grammar School there. After a few years of commercial experience he entered the Insurance profession, taking service in the Manchester Branch Office of the Scottish Union and National, where he acquired a thorough practical knowledge of Branch Office work. After paying a visit to Canada, he accepted

an appointment as Superintendent to the Provident Life Office at Manchester, subsequently acting in a similar capacity for the National, also at Manchester, and for the Imperial at Manchester and Liverpool. In the summer of 1891 he entered upon his present duties, since which date he has been further selected to act conjointly for the Straits Fire Insurance Company.

Bennett, Frank G., District Manager at Manchester to the Positive Government Security Life Assurance Company, began his Insurance career as Agency Superintendent to the Manchester Branch of the Mercantile Accident and Guarantee Assurance Company, now amalgamated with the Scottish Alliance Fire and Accident Company; subsequently becoming Agency Inspector to the Manchester Branch of the Provident Life and County Fire Office.

J. COTTRELL.

THOMAS A. BENTLEY.

Cottrell, J., of the Birmingham Branch of the Mutual Life Insurance Company of New York, is a gentleman in the prime of life, possessing an excellent business training and a very considerable experience in the most aggressive department of Life Assurance work.   Prior to joining his present Company he held responsible appointments with several of the largest Life Companies, and on the Mutual Life of New York opening up the Birmingham District, his reputation was quite sufficient to justify his selection for the post which he has since held.   Mr. Cottrell's connection with the Mutual Life of New York is not yet of very long standing, but already the result of his past record and present aggressiveness has been good.   He is a writer on Assurance matters of ability and weight, and some of his works on various phases of the business are in current everyday use among the members of the profession.

Bentley, Thomas A., is the Local Manager of the London and Lancashire Fire Insurance Company, at its important Manchester Branch.   Mr. Bentley, who is one of the most respected Insurance Managers in Lancashire, has been in the service of the London and Lancashire since it was established in 1862, and acquired his early Insurance training in the Manchester Branch of the Liverpool and London and Globe Insurance Company, which office he left to accept the position of Managing Clerk to the Manchester Branch of the London and Lancashire, on the formation of that Company.   He afterwards became Surveyor to the Company, and in 1875 was appointed Local Manager of the Branch, which position he still holds with credit to himself and profit to the Company.

E. C. BLACKALL.

T. H. B. BLACK.

Blackall, Edward C., the District Manager of the North British and Mercantile Insurance Company at its South Devon and Cornwall Branch at Devonport, has been known for many years both in London and Devonshire as a very successful Accountant, Appraiser, Insurance Agent, and Building Society Manager. He received his present appointment in March, 1882, since which date he has chiefly devoted his energies to pushing the business of the Company which he represents. Mr. Blackall is a reliable and energetic business man in every way, and holds several local appointments, being, amongst other things, a Member of the Devonport County Council, a Guardian of the Poor, and a Member of the Devonport School Board.

Black, T. H. B., is the Local Secretary at Glasgow of the Standard Life Assurance Company and is a native of Glasgow, his Insurance experience having commenced with the Crown Life Office as Inspector of Agents for the Counties of York, Lancaster, Nottingham, Lincoln, and Derby. In this position, which he held for some years, Mr. Black gained a large amount of valuable practical experience in out-door work, and was extremely fortunate in being able to show good results from his operations on behalf of the Crown. Six years ago the Directors of the Standard were induced by his high reputation to appoint him to his present post, in which he has distinguished himself by a large and yearly increasing development of the Company's business. Mr. Black is held in much esteem in his native city, as an evidence of which it may be mentioned that he was elected a member of the Finance Committee of the Glasgow Exhibition.

GEORGE M. BLAND.

J. R. BLANDFORD.

Bland, George M., the District Manager of the Economic Fire Office at Manchester, received his first Insurance experience in the Manchester Office of the Royal Insurance Company in 1868, whence he went to the Head Office of the Manchester Fire Office, and remained there for ten years. He was then transferred to the London Office of the same Company, when, on the establishment of the City of London Fire Office, in 1892, he was appointed Chief Clerk in the Town Department at the Head Office, which position he held until 1886. He was then made District Manager of the Manchester Branch of the City of London Fire, and remained there till March, 1891, when he was appointed to his present post, with supervision over portions of Lancashire and Cheshire, and the whole of Derbyshire, Cumberland, and Westmoreland.

Blandford, J. Richardson, is the West o England Branch Manager of the Hand in Hand at Bristol. He commenced his Insurance career at the age of eighteen with the West of England Insurance Office, which Company he left after four years, to undertake the charge of the London and Southwark Fire and Life Company's Bristol Office. During the two years up to the time of its amalgamation with the London and Lancashire Mr. Blandford considerably advanced the connections of his Office in the West of England and South Wales District. His services were then immediately transferred to the Hand in Hand Fire and Life Insurance Society's West of England Branch Offices in Bristol, where, for the last ten years, Mr. Blandford has conducted the business of this old-established and influential Company to the entire satisfaction of his Directors.

J. HEADON BOOCOCK.

JOHN G. BOSS

Boocock, John Headon, is the District Manager of the Commercial Union Assurance Company, Limited, at its Branch office at Birmingham. Mr. Boocock commenced his Insurance career in 1875 in the Surveyor's department at the Head Office of the Manchester Fire Assurance Company, and remained in the employ of that Company at their offices in Manchester and Birmingham until 1882, when he was appointed Local Manager for the Midlands for the Fire Insurance Association. He relinquished the last-named appointment in 1884 to take up the duties of his present important position. Mr. Boocock is a member of the Manchester Insurance Institute, and also of the Birmingham Insurance Institute, having a seat on the Council of the latter; indeed he may practically be considered its founder, as it was upon his suggestion that an Institute for the discussion of Insurance questions was established, instead of an Athletic and Social Club, as had been formulated by the original promoters. He has always taken a very lively interest in the affairs of the Institute, and at its inauguration delivered the opening lecture to its members, the subject he chose being a very appropriate and inspiring one, viz.: "British Insurance Offices, their Power and Influence." Mr. Boocock is a gentleman universally esteemed by all who know him, both inside and outside his profession.

Boss, John G., is the Resident Secretary of the North of England Branch of the Queen Insurance Company at Newcastle-on-Tyne. Previous to obtaining his present appointment, Mr. Boss was for many years connected with the Northern Branch of the Royal, becoming Resident Secretary to the Queen in 1874. Mr. Boss was one of the promoters of the Newcastle Insurance Institute, being its first Honorary Secretary, and subsequently occupying the positions of Vice-President and President. In the Session 1877-78 he contributed a paper on the Chemical (Alkali) Works on the Tyne. Under the Royal-Queen amalgamation scheme, Mr. Boss has been appointed Joint Local Manager of the Northern District Branch of the Royal.

J. P. BOURNE.

R. DE K. BOULGER,

Bourne, James P., District Manager to the Star Life Assurance Company at Liverpool, came to Liverpool in June, 1869, an old friend, the then Secretary of the Star Life Office, having persuaded him to leave a lucrative position in the West of England with a view to becoming his successor in the post. Mr. Bourne has represented the same Company in Liverpool ever since, and has largely extended its business in his district, enjoying the confidence of his Board, while at the same time his well-known tact and benevolence have earned him the merited esteem of all who know him. Mr. Bourne has written very extensively for the press, his talents embracing most subjects of interest in the present day. In 1880 he was compelled for health's sake to make a trip to America of seven or eight months, his business being meanwhile left in charge of his sons. On his return, though much benefited, he was compelled, greatly to his regret, to relinquish much of his former outside work. Prior to his illness he had been connected with several philanthropic and public works in Liverpool, including the School Board, and had been Secretary or Treasurer of various Societies, all of which had had his individual and enthusiastic [attention. He is a Director of the Liverpool Reversionary Company, much of whose success is attributed to his efforts. He has often been consulted by various Companies on Actuarial Subjects, and has published several little books on such matters, the most recent being "Life Interests or Annuities" and "Reversionary Values." He is an Associate of the Institute of Actuaries, and a Member of the Liverpool Reform Club.

Boulger, R. de K., is the Resident Secretary of the Royal Exchange Assurance Corporation at their Branch Office at Birmingham. Previous to entering upon the duties of his present position, Mr. Boulger was for many years in the Head Office of the Corporation in London; and on their adoption of the Branch system, and deciding to open a Branch at Birmingham, where they had already been for many years transacting a considerable business through their local Agents, Mr. Boulger was selected to establish the Branch, which undertaking he successfully carried out in 1888.

F. W. BOWEN.

DOUGLAS BOWLEY.

Bowen, Francis William, the District Manager in Birmingham of the West of England Fire and Life Insurance Company of Exeter, was born in London on July 26th, 1847. His Insurance career commenced in the Head Office of the Liverpool and London Insurance Company, where he received an appointment as Clerk in 1863 in the Agency Department, being afterwards transferred to the Town Department. He left the service of this Office in 1876, on being appointed Chief Clerk at the Liverpool Branch of the National Assurance Company of Ireland. With this Office he remained for some time, and for about five years was engaged as Surveyor and Inspector of Agents in the Liverpool, North Wales, and Midland Districts. In 1882 the Management of the Edinburgh Fire Insurance Company offered him the appointment of Resident Secretary of their Birmingham Branch, which he accepted. In the following year (1883) he was appointed Local Manager for the Midland Counties for the National Fire Insurance Corporation, which position he held until the amalgamation of that Office with the Royal Insurance Company, when

he received the appointment to the position he holds at present. Mr. Bowen has made a wide reputation for himself as an experienced Surveyor of Fire Risks.

Bowley, Douglas, Inspector of Agents to the National Provident Institution for their South of England District, commenced his Insurance career in the service of a Fire Insurance Company now passed out of human ken, with which he remained for some years, eventually leaving it to join the Crown Life Office. He remained with that Company for seven years, during six of which he was engaged on the staff and one in the capacity of Town Inspector of Agents. In 1884 he entered the service of the National Provident Institution to undertake his present duties, which he has carried on with considerable success.

In private life Mr. Bowley is well known to Rugby football players as an enthusiast in the game, and he was at one period for some years a Member of the Kent County Committee for Football.

E. J. BRADLEY.

E. BRAIMBRIDGE.

Bradley, E. J., is the District Secretary of the British Law Fire and the Eagle Life Companies at Birmingham, where the former Company possesses a good connection and an unusually influential local Board of Directors. He received the appointment early in 1891, having previously been associated with the County and Manchester Fire Offices.

Mr. Bradley commenced his career in 1879, in the Office of the County. He was afterwards appointed Surveyor and Inspector in connection with the Birmingham Branch of the Manchester Fire, having supervision of the Midland Counties and South Wales.

Braimbridge, Edward, is the Superintendent of the British Equitable Assurance Company for the Yorkshire District. He commenced his Insurance career in 1865, as a local Agent for the Company he now represents. He was so successful that at the end of twelve months he was appointed District Agent for Bradford, which appointment he held until 1879, when he was appointed to his present position.

In 1879 a testimonial, in the form of a gold watch, was presented to Mr. E. Braimbridge by the Agents of the Company, prior to his entering upon his present appointment.

G. W. M. BREMNER.

CHARLES F. BRENAN.

Bremner, G. W. McEwen, the Resident Secretary at Glasgow to the Northern Assurance Company, commenced his business career in the Insurance Company of Scotland, Edinburgh, under the management of the late David Maclagan, Esq., who was afterwards Chief Secretary to the Alliance Assurance Company, London, and finally Manager of the Edinburgh Life Assurance Company, Edinburgh.

After four years' service as apprentice and clerk, Mr. Bremner was appointed to his present Company, in which he acquired large and varied experience during the many trying years through which most of the Fire Offices passed in connection with risks in Glasgow. The experience thus gained proved of great value, and in 1871 he was appointed Secretary to the North British and Mercantile, Glasgow, in which service nearly two years were passed, when, on the death of Mr. George Cruikshank Smith, Secretary to the Northern, the Directors of that Office did Mr. Bremner the honour to offer the vacant post for his acceptance. Mr. Bremner rejoined the Northern in the winter of 1872. He enjoys the support and co-operation of an influential local Board of Directors, and under his management the business of the Glasgow Office has made good progress, and proved of great value to the Company.

Mr. Bremner's whole life has been devoted to Insurance, primarily the Fire Department, and while a thoroughly trained Fire Underwriter, he is also a good all-round man, whose experience, practical knowledge, and ability, are valued by many friends within and without the Insurance business.

———

Brenan, Charles F., is the Resident Secretary at the Manchester Branch of the National Assurance Company of Ireland. Born in Dublin, he was educated there at one of the schools founded by Erasmus Smith. He subsequently matriculated at Queen's College, Cork, in the School of Engineering, where he studied for over twelve months, when he was reluctantly compelled to abandon his intended profession owing to his father sustaining some serious monetary losses. He entered the service of the National Assurance Company of Ireland on the 1st March, 1872, as Guarantee Clerk. The following year he was sent to London to assist in opening the Company's Branch there, and in 1875 he was appointed to the Chief Clerkship of the Liverpool Branch, being recalled to Dublin the following year to take charge of a department at the Head Office. In 1881 Mr. Brenan was appointed to the position he now holds.

He is Member of the Council of the Insurance Institute of Manchester, and ex-President of the Insurance Association.

F. A. BRINGLOE, C.A.

. G. J. BRODIE.

Bringloe, Francis A., C.A., is the Resident Secretary of the County Fire and Provident Life Office at Edinburgh. Mr. Bringloe, who has held his present appointment since 1874, has been a member of the Society of Chartered Accountants since 1871, and is the senior partner in the firm of Bringloe and Graham.

Brodie, George J., Manager for Scotland of the Mutual Life Insurance Company of New York at Edinburgh, began life as a sailor, and from 1872 to 1874 was on board Her Majesty's School Frigate "Conway," where he became Senior Petty Officer, and obtained the highest possible certificate for seamanship and general good character. For about a year thereafter he served as apprentice on the "Rokeby Hall,"
belonging to Messrs. Balfour, Williamson, and Co., of Liverpool, but ultimately left the sea, owing to inability to get into the Royal Navy, caused by an alteration in the age of admission. He then entered the office of his uncle, the late Mr. John Clerk Brodie, of Idvies, C.B., Deputy Keeper of the Signet, with whom he remained until the death of that gentleman, which took place in 1888. Mr. Brodie had meanwhile (in 1881) become a Member of the Society of Writers to Her Majesty's Signet, and in 1889 he entered into partnership with Mr. A. H. Cooper, W.S. He was appointed to his present post with the Mutual Life Insurance Company of New York in September, 1891, and has already succeeded in organising an influential Board of Reference, and in extending the business to various parts of Scotland. .   . .

L. H. BROOK.

J. PEARSON CALLUM, C.A.

Brook, Leonard H., Resident Secretary to the Alliance Assurance Company at their Leicester Branch, commenced his Insurance career in 1880 in the Nottingham Branch office of the Commercial Union Assurance Company. He remained in the service of that Company in the same Branch until 1891, acting for eight years as Chief Clerk and Surveyor, when, on the opening of a Branch office at Leicester of the Alliance Assurance Company, he was appointed to take charge of it.

Bowker, Charles E., the Superintendent for Ireland of the Lancashire Insurance Company in Dublin, has gained the whole of his Insurance experience in the service of that Company, having joined the Head Office staff in the year 1873, at the age of sixteen, as Junior Clerk. From that time until December, 1890, he passed through all the various Departments in connection with the Home business, his last post before receiving his present appointment being the responsible one of Chief Surveyor. His present appointment was made at the last-mentioned date.

Callum, J. Pearson, C.A., is District Manager at Edinburgh of the London and Provincial Horse and Carriage Insurance Company, Limited, and the Horse Insurance Company, Limited, which appointments he has held since May, 1887. Mr. Callum is a Chartered Accountant, and being a gentleman of energy and ability, has succeeded in building up a large business for these Companies in his district.

WILLIAM J. BROWN.

GEORGE W. BULFORD.

Brown, William J., District Manager of the Kent Fire and Life Insurance Offices at their Branch Office at Liverpool, began life as a merchant, and had already acquired a considerable reputation as a business man on the Liverpool Exchange, when he took up Insurance business, being, in 1878, appointed Resident Secretary at Liverpool to the Scottish Imperial. This position he held for three years, resigning it in 1881 on being offered the appointment to open a Branch Office in the same city for the London Assurance Corporation. This undertaking he carried through satisfactorily, and remained in charge of the Branch till June, 1888, when he withdrew himself from his connection with the London Assurance and accepted his present post to open a

Branch of the Kent, which the Directors had decided to establish at Liverpool. Under Mr. Brown's management this Branch Office of the Kent has largely prospered.

— —

Bulford, George W., is the Agency Superintendent of the British Equitable Assurance Company for the Birmingham District. He has passed the whole of his Insurance career in the service of the British Equitable, having been appointed by the Directors District Agent for the County of Worcester in 1859. Having held that position for four years he was in 1863 promoted to his present post of Agency Superintendent at Birmingham, where he has remained ever since, doing good work for his Company.

G. R. BURGESS.

GEORGE BUNYON.

Burgess, G. R., Acting Secretary of the Imperial Fire Office at Manchester, has been connected with the business of that Company for over twenty years. Before being appointed to his present post, he was Assistant-Secretary at the same Branch Office of the Company.

Bunyon, George, is District Manager of the Norwich Union Fire and Life Office at Bristol. Mr. Bunyon comes of an old Insurance family, and has spent the greater part of his life in the service of the Norwich Union Offices, by the Directors of which he is held in great esteem. He has held his present appointment since 1859, and is, therefore, one of the oldest Insurance officials in Bristol.

H. J. A. I. DE BURIATTE, F.S.L.

JAMES BURNHAM

De Buriatte, Henry J. Allan Isaac, F.S.L., the Resident Secretary of the Northern Branch of the Ocean Accident and Guarantee Corporation, Limited, at Newcastle-on-Tyne, is the son of the late Rev. W. Isaac, of Ealing, and commenced his business career in the Claims Department of the Great Western Railway Company. He entered the Ocean Railway and General Accident Assurance and Guarantee Companies' service in 1879, spending four years (with the exception of an absence of over a year through illness), in the Head Office, there gaining a thorough insight into all the details of the working of the business. In 1884 he became Superintendent of Agents for the Metropolitan District; working from the Head Office for a year and nine months; and in 1886 he was appointed Resident Secretary to organise and manage the newly-inaugurated Eastern Counties Branch, where he remained for four years and a-half, meeting with great success, and having at the end of that period raised the Branch to a highly satisfactory and very remunerative position. He left that post to take over that which he holds at present in the April of 1891.

Upon the occasion of his marriage, in 1890, the Directors of the Ocean presented Mr. de Buriatte with a handsome silver salver, suitably inscribed, as a mark of their esteem. In 1891 he was elected a Fellow of the International Society of Literature.

Burnham, James, District Inspector of the Norwich and London Accident Insurance Association, for some years occupied a responsible position in a well-known building firm in West Kensington and only started as Agent for the Royal London Friendly Society in 1885. Here he met with so considerable a success that he was in a few months promoted to be Assistant-Superintendent of the London District, subsequently being drafted to Sheffield, from which latter post he was promoted to the Superintendency of the Barnsley District. Here he did much to increase the Society's business, at the same time winning the esteem of all who were brought in contact with him, so much so that on his resigning his post in 1888 he was presented by his staff with a handsome clock as a testimonial of their regard. At that latter date he took up the District Inspectorship for the North of England District of the Norwich and London Association, but that district not suiting his health he obtained his removal to his present post with the supervision of the South Central District, the headquarters being at Reading.

G. B. CARRUTHERS.

FRED. BUTLER.

Carruthers, G. Burfield, is the Branch Manager of the Imperial Fire Insurance Company at their West End office. Mr. Carruthers commenced his Insurance career in 1864, when he entered the office of the Commercial Union Assurance Company, remaining there for a period of eight years, during which time he acquired a thoroughly practical experience in the details of the profession under the auspices of the late Mr. Thomson, and his present General Manager, Mr. Cozens Smith. In 1872 Mr. Carruthers was offered, and accepted, an appointment in the Head Office of his present Company, where he remained till 1879, in which year he was selected by Mr. Cozens Smith to fill a vacancy in the West End Branch of the Company as Chief Clerk and Surveyor. This post he held till the following year, when, on the death of the late Branch Manager, he was appointed to succeed him, since which time he has been most successful in his labours on behalf of his Company.

———

Butler, Fred, is the London Manager of the Boiler Insurance and Steam Power Company, Limited, of Manchester. Mr. Butler has had a very large experience in the boiler insurance business, having represented his present company for upwards of 20 years.

EDWARD T. CLIFFORD.

A. W. COUSINS.

Clifford, Edward T., is London Secretary of the Scottish Metropolitan Life Assurance Company, and Manager of the Royal National Pension Fund for Nurses. Mr. Clifford, who is a native of Devon, commenced his business life in the National Provincial Bank of England. His first appointment in the Insurance world was as Inspector to the Life Association of Scotland. In 1885 he was appointed Secretary in London of the Scottish Economic Life Assurance Society, which Office ultimately amalgamated with the Scottish Metropolitan, at which time Mr. Clifford accepted his present appointment. Mr. Clifford is a Captain in the First Middlesex Volunteers Royal Engineers, Commanding a Railway Company.

————

Cousins, A. W., is the District Manager of the Chancery Lane Branch of the Sun Fire and Life Offices. He is also the Hon. Secretary of the Insurance Musical Society of London. Mr. Cousins has had a long experience in the Insurance business and is very popular among the fraternity.

J. BRUCE CAIRNIE.

GEORGE LEOPOLD CAIRD.

Cairnie, John Bruce, is Joint Resident Secretary of the Manchester Branch of the Liverpool and London and Globe Insurance Company. He commenced his Insurance life in 1860 at the age of sixteen, in the service of the Alliance Insurance Company at their Edinburgh Branch, and three years later was promoted to a clerkship in the Foreign Department of the Head Office of that Company. Further experience was gained in the Home Department as Chief Clerk of the Manchester and Sheffield Branches. In 1873 he accepted the post of Chief Clerk of the Manchester Branch of the Liverpool and London and Globe, which appointment he held until July, 1890, when he was appointed to his present position in conjunction with Mr. R. A. Kennedy. Mr. Cairnie is a thorough and earnest Insurance official, and has gained his present position by close application to the business.

———

Caird, George Leopold, is the Agency Inspector to the Sun Life Office at their Irish Branch at Dublin. He formerly acted in the same capacity for the Queen Insurance Company in the Midland District of England, and afterwards for the Lancashire and Yorkshire Accident Company in the same district. He joined the Sun Life Office as District Inspector in the South Wales District, whence he was transferred to his present position at Dublin.

J. W. CALVERLEY.

A. P. CALEY.

Calverley, J. W., the District Superintendent to the Mutual Life Insurance Company of New York, at the Branch Office of that Company at Bradford, is a native of Leeds, where he was born in 1853, and formed his first connection with the Life Insurance profession in 1884, in which year he entered the service of the Bradford Office of the Prudential Assurance Company, then under the charge of Mr. Joseph Wardle.   He very speedily acquired a thorough mastery of all the details of the business, and was eminently successful in his operations in behalf of the Prudential Assurance Company, which Office he continued to represent for six and a-half years, at the end of which period, in August, 1890, Mr. Calverley was offered and accepted the post which he now holds of District Superintendent for the Mutual Life Insur-ance Company of New York, working the district in conjunction with Mr. Boyd, as District Manager.

Caley, Arthur Pelham, West End Manager of the Norwich Union Life Insurance Society, is a member of a well-known Norwich family.   His Insurance education began in the office of Mr. Pocock, the successful London Insurance broker, where he remained for ten years, and acquired a very extensive experience.   In the October of 1890, when the Norwich Union opened its Piccadilly Branch, Mr. Caley was selected by the Directors to take charge of it, first as Superintendent, and subsequently under his present title.   In 1892 he was promoted to his present position.

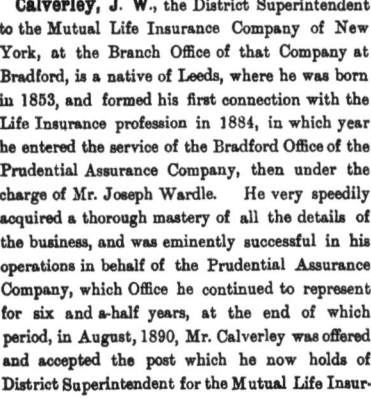

HUGH FLETCHER CAMPBELL.

JAMES CAMPBELL.

Campbell, Hugh Fletcher, is the Superintendent of the Mutual Life Insurance Company of New York for the Yorkshire District. His first connection with Life Insurance business was in the capacity of Local Secretary to the Scottish Provident Institution at their Branch Office at Leeds, which post he took up in 1877, retaining it for eleven years, at the end of which period, in 1888, he was selected by his present Company for the appointment of Leeds District Manager, resigning his former post accordingly. He was promoted to his present post of Superintendent for Yorkshire at the beginning of 1891.

————

Campbell, James, of the firm of Smith, Campbell and Company, Glasgow, is Joint Resident Manager for Scotland of the Lion Fire Insurance Company, Limited, which appointment he has held since 1885, prior to which he had been for several years Joint Local Manager in Glasgow of the Law Union Fire and Life Insurance Company.

WATSON CARLILL.

EDWARD HOWARD CARLILL.

Carlill, Watson, is the Senior Partner of the firm of Watson Carlill and Son, Local Secretaries to the Phœnix Fire Office at their Branch at Hull. His father was first appointed Agent to the Protector Office, on the establishment of that Company, and when it was subsequently merged into the Phœnix Fire Office, he continued to represent the latter Company. Mr. Watson Carlill succeeded to the Agency in 1848, and afterwards on the business being made into a Branch office, in 1880, he became Local Secretary. Mr. Edward Howard Carlill, his son, who had been working in the office since 1878, was taken into partnership in 1883, and the firm has since been carried on under its present denomination. Messrs. Carlill and Son are very highly esteemed throughout their District, a fact which has been of immense advantage to the Phœnix in extending its business and connections.

————

Carlill, Edward Howard, is the Joint Local Secretary at Hull of the Phœnix Fire Office. He has been connected with this Office since 1878, and in June, 1883, he was taken into partnership by his father, Mr. Watson Carlill, who had been Local Secretary of the Company since the Branch at Hull was established.

HENRY E. CASHMORE.

HENRY R. CARR.

Cashmore, Henry E., is the Resident Secretary of the Yorkshire Insurance Company at their Branch Office at Birmingham. Mr. Cashmore commenced his Insurance career at Birmingham in 1879, first entering the Branch office of the Queen there, and subsequently joined the City of London and Commercial Union successively. Having, at the conclusion of his service with the latter Company, gone through and acquired experience in every department of the business, Mr. Cashmore was, in 1886, selected by the National Assurance Company of Ireland to open a new Branch at Nottingham, which he successfully accomplished, taking charge of the Branch. He afterwards carried out the same undertaking for the National in Birmingham, and took charge of that Branch, still, however, retaining control of the Nottingham District, which duties he fulfilled until he was eventually appointed to his present post with the Yorkshire Insurance Company.

———

Carr, Henry R., is the Secretary of the Eastern Counties Insurance Company, Limited, of Hull. Mr. Carr commenced his Insurance career at the Leeds Branch of the Royal Insurance Company. He next became Chief Clerk at the Leeds Branch of the Union Assurance Society, where he remained until he received his present appointment. He is a young man of much energy, and is well known to the Insurance profession of Yorkshire.

THOMAS D. CHALLONER.

W. H. H. CASSON

Challoner, Thomas D., is the Local Manager at Newcastle-on-Tyne, of the Fire Insurance Association, Limited, which position he has held since within twelve months of the formation of that Company. He is a native of Newcastle, having been born there in 1856, and educated at Chester College. He is a member of the Institute of Chartered Accountants, and has compiled several works, including Dividend Tables, and Mortgage Tables containing over 15,000 calculations.

Casson, William H. H., the Branch Manager of the Royal Exchange Assurance at Leeds, was born and educated in Liverpool, and has been in the Insurance profession since 1873, when he entered the service of the County Fire and Provident Life Offices. The greater part of his experience has been gained in the manufacturing centres and seaport towns of the North and Midlands, an excellent school for practical Insurance work, and Mr. Casson has profited by his training. Besides the County Fire and Provident Life Office, he has been in the service of two other Companies previous to obtaining his present appointment, which was in 1886.

GEORGE CHAPPELL.

GEORGE CHAPMAN.

Chappell, George, is the Resident Secretary of the Midland Counties Insurance Company at their Branch Offices at Liverpool and Manchester. Mr. Chappell has passed the whole of his Insurance career in the service of the Midland Counties Office, having entered the Head Office at Lincoln in 1878, and two years later having been appointed to the Resident Secretaryship at the Branch Office at Manchester. In 1883 he was deputed to open the Liverpool Branch for his Company, since which time he has continued to work both Branches.

Chapman, George, Agency Superintendent of the Life Association of Scotland for Nottingham and the adjacent district, commenced his Insurance career in 1856, with the establishment and management of the Briton Life Office in Leicester. Two years later his success caused him to be selected to remove to Derby, to undertake the organization of the business of the Society in Derbyshire and North Staffordshire. Here he remained till 1860, subsequently removing again on the same mission to the East Midland District. The measure of his success while working for the Briton Medical and General Association may be estimated from the fact that on the institution of an enquiry into the affairs of the Office, Mr. Chapman was found to have introduced more policies than any other of its representatives. He remained steadfast to the Briton Medical and General Office throughout all the attacks made upon it, and never ceased to work for it until it collapsed in 1886. When that Office, in 1874, closed its doors to new business, he, by his large influence and connection, aided very materially in the establishment of the Briton, now absorbed by the Marine and General. On his becoming disengaged, a large number of Offices sought after his services, with the eventual result that he chose the Life Association of Scotland, for which he is now working with all his old energy.

HENRY CHARD.

HERBERT CHEETHAM.

Chard, Henry, the Inspector of Agents for the Scottish Amicable Life Assurance Society at Bristol, was, when he first entered the Insurance profession, attached to the staff of the Royal Exchange Assurance Corporation at their Branch at Bristol, of which town he is a native. He subsequently became Inspector of Agents for the Bristol District of the Scottish Life Office, and continued in that post until the summer of 1889, when on the London Amicable Assurance Company opening a Branch at Bristol he was offered and accepted the post of District Manager to that Company. This post he held until towards the close of 1890, when he was appointed Inspector of Agents for the Scottish Amicable Life Assurance Society in connection with the London Branch, his District comprising Bristol, the West of England, and South Wales.

Cheetham, Herbert, Resident Secretary to the Scottish Accident Insurance Company at Middlesbro', commenced his business career at the age of sixteen in the commercial firm of Messrs. Bolckow, Vaughan and Co., Limited, with whom he spent two years at their steel-works at Gorton, Manchester, and twelve at their Head Office at Middlesbro'. In 1884 Mr. Cheetham first became acquainted with Insurance business as an Agent to the Scottish Accident, in which capacity his success was so great, and his relations with the Head Office so satisfactory, that in 1886 he was offered a Resident Secretaryship, which, after full consideration as to the advisability of leaving one profession for another, he accepted. Since then he has been one and a-half years at Brighton, in charge of the Southern Counties District, and three and a-half at Middlesbro' North Eastern District. That the results have warranted Mr. Cheetham's promotion, the fact of the Company's interest in the Middles-bro' District having more than doubled since his appointment fully testifies

D. D. CHRYSTAL, A.F.A.

EDWARD R. CHURCHWARD.

Chrystal, D.D., is the Resident Secretary of the Lancashire Insurance Company, at their Branch Office at Bristol. Mr. Chrystal, who is a Scotchman by birth, is a gentleman of long and varied experience, having served some of the most important Companies, both Fire and Life, in Edinburgh, Glasgow, and Manchester. He was appointed to his present post on the death of the late Mr. Scott, who had managed the Bristol Branch since its commencement, and he has most ably carried on the work so well begun by his predecessor, the Bristol business being now of very large dimensions and drawn from a large area; no less than fifteen counties being worked from Bristol.

Mr. Chrystal is a Member of the Faculty of Actuaries, having passed the necessary examination when in Edinburgh in the service of the Scottish Provident Institution.

———

Churchward, Edward R., is the Local Manager of the Royal Insurance Company at its Newcastle-on-Tyne Branch. Mr. Churchward commenced his Insurance career in the Head Office of the Liverpool and London and Globe Insurance Company in 1870, and was appointed Surveyor to the Newcastle Branch of the Royal Insurance Company in October, 1879. He succeeded to the Management in 1883.

ANDREW CLARK.

J. COURTENAY CLARKE.

Clark, Andrew, is the Resident Secretary of the Imperial Fire Office at its Glasgow Branch, to which post he was appointed in 1870. Mr. Clark resigned the Imperial, and entered the service of the Guardian Assurance Company at its Manchester Branch in 1874, and subsequently at its Glasgow Branch, where he remained Glasgow Secretary of the Guardian until he accepted his present appointment in 1885.

Collings, John B., the Manager for the North of England of the Scottish Temperance Life and Accident Assurance Company, Limited, was born on the 25th of February, 1848, at Kingston-on-Thames, Surrey. His first experience as an Insurance man was gained in the capacity of Agent for the United Kingdom Temperance and General Provident Institution, which position he occupied for some years. In the year 1879 the Briton Life Office gave him the post of District

Manager; this he subsequently resigned, and in 1885 was appointed to his present position.

Clarke, J. Courtenay, is the Joint Manager for London, Liverpool and Glasgow, of the United Swiss Marine Insurance Companies, an amalgamation of five Swiss Marine Companies for the purpose of transacting larger business than could be effected by each individual Company.

Previous to entering the service of the United Swiss Companies, Mr. Courtenay Clarke was engaged in the underwriting room of the Trident Marine Insurance Company. His colleague in office is Mr. Emil Schött, and they have been with the United Swiss Companies during the whole period the Companies have been operating in this country, and, on the resignation of Mr. Septimus Merriman in 1885, became the Joint Managers of the English business. Mr. Courtenay Clarke acted as Deputy to Mr. S. Merriman for several years prior to his appointment as Underwriter.

J. N. CLYMER.

T. B. CLARKE.

Clymer, J. Nicholas, the Resident Secretary of the Manchester Fire Assurance Company at Leeds, received his first insight into Insurance business at the Head Office of the British Reinsurance Company in Manchester. He was then engaged for a period of six years in the service of the Scottish Union and National Insurance Company at their Manchester Branch until the September of 1890, when he was appointed Chief Agency Inspector in connection with the Head Office district of the Manchester Fire Assurance Company. In the Spring of the following year, the Leeds Resident Secretaryship to the Company having become vacant, Mr. Clymer was nominated to fill the post.

———

Clarke, Thomas B., Joint District Manager of the Equitable Fire and Accident Office at their Branch Office at Liverpool, is a native of that city, and after receiving the principal part of his education in Switzerland and Germany, acquiring a considerable acquaintance with foreign languages, was occupied for several years in Liverpool as a Merchant and Shipowner. In 1877 he was offered and accepted an appointment as Special Agent to the Head Office of the London and Lancashire Fire Insurance Company, which he retained for ten years, at the end of which period, in 1887, he was selected for the post of Local Manager to the South British and National. This post he held until 1890, when, on the business of those Companies being taken over by the Equitable Fire and Accident, he was appointed to his present post of Joint District Manager with Mr. Bell to the latter office. Mr. Clarke is a gentleman highly respected by all who know him, and enjoys the personal friendship both of the Directors and Managers of the several Companies with which he has been associated.

WILLIAM EDWARD COATES.

P. IVER COGHILL.

Coates, William Edward, is District Manager of the Star Life Assurance Society at Newcastle on-Tyne. Mr. Coates commenced his Insurance career in the office of his father, who had for many years represented the Star, and in 1882 was admitted to the firm of William Coates and Son ; and on the death of his father, in 1888, he became sole Manager for the District.

Coghill, P. Iver, is the District Manager of the New York Life Insurance Company at its Branch Office at Manchester. Mr. Coghill is the son of John Coghill, Esq., J.P., C.C., Thurso, and was at first intended for a legal career, being apprenticed to and receiving a valuable training with the well-known Peter Keith, Solicitor, Thurso. He was induced, however, to adopt the Insurance profession, and, after spending a few years in one of the leading Fire and Life Offices in Edinburgh, accepted an appointment at the Head Office of the Royal Insurance Company,

Liverpool, where he remained about four years. Subsequently, Mr. Coghill went to London, and then to Newcastle-on-Tyne, where his luck in securing a large volume of profitable business, as well as numerous personal friends, followed him. It was with much regret that he severed his connection with the Tyneside district, where he was known as an able and successful Fire and Life Manager ; but, being desirous of experience in a larger and more important centre, he accepted the voluntary offer of his present appointment, where his success has been uninterrupted.

Socially, and in business, Mr. Coghill is very popular, and we congratulate him on the fact that his district last year produced far and away more business than was ever secured in a like period through the Manchester Branch, which was opened about twenty years ago. When we add that, almost single-handed, Mr. Coghill wrote over £100,000 new business during 1891, our readers will appreciate our congratulations.

E. Tenison Collins.

W. R. Collinson.

Collins, E. Tenison, Resident Secretary at the Dublin Branch of the North British and Mercantile Insurance Company, was, previous to his connection with Insurance business, the Secretary to the Irish North-Western Railway Company, and on the amalgamation of that Company with the Great Northern Railway of Ireland, was appointed Secretary and Manager of the Dundalk and Newry Steam Packet Company, which mainly owes its present sound position to his energetic management. While in Dundalk he conducted the Marine Insurance business of that port, and acted as Local Agent for the Scottish Provincial Assurance Company, of which he subsequently became Irish Secretary, which post he held until that Company's amalgamation with the North British and Mercantile, when he became Resident Secretary to that latter office.

Collinson, William Robert, District Manager of the New York Life Insurance Company at their Yorkshire Branch, was born in London in 1859, and educated at the Birkbeck Schools, Peckham. In 1876 he entered the New York Life's London Office, and was deputed to open up the West of England District for his Company prior to their opening a new Branch at Bristol in 1881, by visiting the chief towns in Gloucester-

shire, Somersetshire, and South Wales, to secure agents and business for the office. Though much good pioneer work was done, the immediate results were scanty, and Mr. Collinson returned somewhat disheartened with his prospects as an Insurance man. He met with encouragement, however, from the General Manager, and in the autumn of 1881 was again selected to push the business in the south-western counties. This venture proved more successful, and he was appointed the regular district representative of the Company for the counties of Devon and Cornwall. His headquarters were first at Plymouth, but on his marriage in 1884 he shifted them to Exeter, only quitting it in 1887, on being promoted to the important position of Manager of the Midland Counties District, at the Birmingham centre. Mr Collinson had much preliminary work to get through when he first joined this district, the new business having, consequently on changes in the district representatives, fallen off very considerably, but Mr. Collinson's efforts soon raised it to a higher standard than it had ever attained before. After four years' work in this field he was selected to fill the still more important post of Manager of the Yorkshire District, where the Company has a very large and influential connection. The Branch Office is at 13, Park Square, Leeds.

S. P. COLMAN.

E. B. CONSTERDINE.

Colman, S. P., Local Manager to the London and Lancashire Fire Insurance Company at its Birmingham Branch, commenced his career in the Insurance profession so far back as 1853, in which year he entered the Globe Office in London in the capacity of Surveying Clerk. Ten years later, in 1863, he joined the staff of the London and Lancashire Fire Insurance Company, then just established in the preceding year, and a few years later, on the opening of the Company's Birmingham Branch Office, he was transferred to it as Local Manager, which position he still continues to hold. The London and Lancashire does a large and lucrative business through its Birmingham Branch, which happy condition of things is mainly due to Mr. Colman's admirable business qualities and experience. Mr. Colman is universally recognised as one of the leading members of the Insurance profession in Birming-

ham, and has held the highly honourable position of President of the Insurance Institute of that city.

———

Consterdine, Ernest B., the District Manager of the Standard Accident Insurance Company at their Branch Office at Manchester, commenced his connection with the Insurance profession in 1880, in which year he entered the New York Branch of the Lancashire Insurance Company. Finding, however, that the climate of New York was not suited to his health, he resigned his position with the Lancashire, after about four years' service, in September, 1884, and returned to Manchester, whence he had gone out. From October, 1884, he was engaged in the service of the Manchester Fire Office in various capacities until April, 1891, when he applied for and obtained his present appointment with the Standard Accident.

WALTER COWLEY.

DOUGLAS COLQUHOUN, A.I.A.

Cowley, Walter, is the London Secretary of the Scottish Temperance Life Assurance Company, Limited. Mr. Cowley gained his first Insurance experience in the service of the Gresham, and subsequently in the British Empire, Norwich Union, and Standard Offices. He has held his present position over five years, during which time he has succeeded in building up a large business for his Company in the Metropolitan District.

Colquhoun, Douglas, A.I.A., was born in 1863, and educated at University College, London. He commenced his Insurance career in 1882, with the London, Edinburgh and Glasgow Assurance Company, and in the same year was elected an Associate of the Institute of Actuaries. In 1884 he was appointed a clerk in the Sun Life Office, which position he relinquished in 1889, in order to commence the business of an Insurance Broker. On the formation of the British Branch of the Phœnix Life Assurance Company, towards the close of 1890, Mr. Colquhoun was offered and accepted the position of Secretary to the London Board of Directors.

T. COOP.

J. A. COOK

Coop, Thomas, is the District Superintendent of the United Kingdom Temperance and General Provident Institution, at its branch office, Bennett's Hill, Birmingham. From 1866 Mr. Coop has been an official of the Office, but in the year 1874 yielded to the many urgent requests of the late Mr. John Rutherford, who was the Birmingham Superintendent of the above Office, to become his colleague, and from 1882 he has had the sole management of the Birmingham District. Mr. Coop has proved himself an efficient Life Insurance Manager, having made an annual return of new business much in excess of any other superintendent of the Institution with which he is connected, and there are but few, if any, other district managers in Birmingham or England who have been able to complete such a large amount of business within the time Mr. Coop has represented the United Kingdom Office.

Cook, James Allan, is the Edinburgh Manager of the Alliance Assurance Company, or, as it is known there, the Insurance Company of Scotland, which position he has held since the amalgamation of these two companies. Previous to that event Mr. Cook had been in the service of the Alliance for upwards of 12 years.

———

Cooke, George, the Manager of the London Branch of the West of England Insurance Company of Exeter, was born on the 30th of March, 1826. He commenced his Insurance career in the service of the Globe Insurance Office in 1842, and with this Company he remained until 1869, when he received his present appointment.

WILLIAM COOTE.

W. H. COOPER.

Coote, William, is the Resident Secretary at Dublin of the Sun Fire and Life Offices. Mr. Coote received his early Insurance training in the office of the Royal Insurance Company, afterwards becoming agency clerk and then chief clerk in the Belfast Branch of the Queen Insurance Company, which Office he left to take a position in the Ætna Insurance Company. Passing from there to the Northern for a short time, he was next appointed to a position in the Guardian, where he rose to be Inspector of Agents, and after eight years' service in that Company he became Assistant-Secretary of the Caledonian. Two years later he was Dublin Secretary of the Northern, a position which he left in 1888 to take up his present appointment. Mr. Coote has a large practical and personal knowledge of Irish business, extending over a period of thirty years, and is one of the most widely known and popular men in that country.

Cooper, William H., is the District Manager of the Patriotic Assurance Company at its Liverpool Branch. Mr. Cooper was previously Assistant District Manager at the Liverpool Branch of the Commercial Union Assurance Company, with which office he had a long experience, having entered its service in 1868.

J. L. G. CORKILL.

O. C. COX.

Corkill, James L. G., is the Local Manager of the London and Lancashire Life Assurance Company at their Manchester Branch. He is a native of the Isle of Man, and was educated at King William's College, Castletown. After some years' experience in the General Manchester business, he became connected with the London and Lancashire Life Assurance Company in 1875, and early in the following year received the appointment he has since continued to hold. Under his management the Branch has become a very important one, transacting a large and increasing business.

Cox, Otway Cooper, late Secretary of the Gresham Life Assurance Society at its Portsmouth Branch Office, was, previous to entering the Insurance profession, in her Majesty's Navy, from which he retired in 1882, having held the appointment of Chief Petty Officer for twenty years. He commenced his Insurance career as Agent to the Imperial Union Accident, the National and Provincial Plate Glass, and the Atlas Fire and Life Insurance Companies, which post he held for six years, at the end of which time he was selected by the Directors of the Gresham Life Assurance Society for the post of Local Secretary for Hampshire, with his headquarters at Portsmouth, which post he held till recently. Mr. Cox is well known and respected throughout the South of England by all his contemporaries in the Insurance profession.

C. CHEVALLIER CREAM.

JAMES CROCKER.

Cream, C. Chevallier, Branch Manager to the North British and Mercantile Insurance Company, has derived the whole of his Insurance experience from his service with that Company, having joined the London staff in 1869. After remaining in the London Office for twelve years, during which he passed through the various departments of the business, acquitting himself in all with credit, his industry was in 1881 rewarded by his appointment to the Branch Managership of the important centre of Liverpool, where he had an influential local Board in authority over him, composed of prominent gentlemen of the district. Under his charge the business of his Branch in Liverpool made very substantial progress, and after occupying his post for ten years, he was, in April, 1891, removed to his present similar posi-

tion at Manchester, where he has since continued to act for the North British and Mercantile with all his former success.

———

Crocker, James, is the District Manager at Newcastle-on-Tyne of the West of England Insurance Company. Mr. Crocker is one of the oldest and most respected District Managers in the employ of the West of England Company, having been connected with it since 1862. He is a native of Cornwall, and commenced his Insurance career in 1854 as Superintendent of Agents in the West of England for the Merchants' and Tradesmen's Mutual Life Assurance Society of London.

He has built up a very large and prosperous business for the West of England in his district.

E. CRICK.

H. L. CROFTS.

Crick, E., the District Manager of the Sun Life Assurance Society at their Midland Branch at Birmingham, received his early training in the Branch Office of the Guardian Assurance Company in Manchester, with which body he remained for fifteen years, occupying during that period the positions of Chief Clerk and Inspector of Agents successively. He resigned this latter post in the October of 1887 on being offered the post of Resident Secretary of the Fire Insurance Association at their Branch in that city. After a period of three years in the latter position he obtained the appointment in 1890, which he now holds.

Cocks, Llewellyn Jameson, is Manager of the Leeds Branch of the Atlas Assurance Company, which district includes the whole of the counties of York, Durham, and Northumberland. Mr. Cocks entered the service of the Atlas in 1875, and after fifteen years, spent at the Head Office in London, was appointed to his present post in 1890, in succession to the late Mr. F. H. Potter.

Crofts, H. Ludlow, District Superintendent to the Mutual Life Insurance Company of New York, at the Nottingham Branch, was, after leaving school, apprenticed to a grocer, and at the age of twenty-three started in business on his own account. He first began making enquiries into Insurance matters with a view of taking a policy himself, and, curiously enough, one of the gentlemen who first approached him was the gentleman with whom he is now associated in his business. After his marriage, the knowledge which he had acquired induced him to take up two Agencies for the New York Life and the Scottish Provident, but, finding the former the most profitable, he abandoned the other, remaining Agent until he was promoted to be District Sub-Manager to the New York Life at Nottingham, and subsequently to his present higher position.

JOHN Y. CROWE.

JAMES CROMPTON.

Crowe, J. Y., Assistant-Superintendent to the National Provident Institution at Bristol, assumed the management in Bristol for the London and Lancashire Life Assurance Company in 1878, with which he combined that of the Fire Insurance Association, on its formation in 1880. He had previously gained a good knowledge of Fire business in the Bristol office of the London and Lancashire Fire. At the end of 1884 he left the service of the London and Lancashire Life, and early in 1885 he was appointed Chief Agent in Bristol to the National Provident Institution, whose members in that city comprise a numerous and influential body. In 1886 that Institution appointed him Assistant-Superintendent for the West of England district, to aid Mr. Fisher, the District Superintendent. Mr. Crowe also represents the Yorkshire Insurance Company (Fire department only) as District Agent for Bristol and the West of England.

Crompton, James, the District Manager of the General Assurance Company, at their Lancashire District Offices, 34, South John Street, Liverpool, is an old and widely-respected member of the Insurance fraternity, having been entirely devoted to the work of Life and Fire Insurance for upwards of forty years. He is a warm advocate for the addition of a Life Policy to the provisions of every household as a great increase to the general home comforts, and by his earnestness in the good cause has been instrumental in inducing many thousands of his fellow-townsmen and friends to join the ranks of Insurers. Having laboured in the Lancashire district since 1850, it can naturally be supposed that he has seen many changes and advances in the progress of Insurance work, but he has always kept abreast of the times, and is an honour to the profession.

W. F. CROXTON.

HERBERT CROOKE.

Croxton, W. F., Resident Secretary of the Colonial Mutual Life Office at Cardiff, was born at Stratford, Essex, in 1859, and after being educated at Bromley, in Kent, was at the age of sixteen ordered abroad for his health, and travelled for three years in New Zealand. Returning to London, he entered into business with his father, being for five years Junior Partner in the firm of George Croxton and Son. In 1880, whilst so engaged, he was induced to undertake an Agency for the London and Lancashire Life Office and the Fire Insurance Association, for both of which he did a considerable business. In 1882 he went to Australia to join a proposed expedition to New Guinea, under General McIvor, but the expedition not coming off, he made his way to the Queensland Gold Fields, where, however, he met with but very moderate success. He next joined a Government Survey party, with which he remained till the completion of the work in hand, and then again turning his attention to Life Assurance, obtained the District Managership for Central Queensland to the Mutual Life Assurance Society of Victoria. This appointment he held for two years, only resigning it on account of the death of his father, which necessitated his return to England. A few months after his arrival in London, in 1887, he was offered, and accepted, an appointment with his present Company as District Manager for South Wales, with headquarters at

Cardiff; and in 1890 the business had increased to such an extent that the Company found it necessary to establish a Branch at Cardiff, of which Mr. Croxton was made Secretary.

Crooke, Herbert, District Manager for Lancashire, Cheshire, Shropshire, and North Wales, for the National Life Assurance Society of London, was born in 1860, and after receiving a technical and commercial education in the iron trade, and acting as commercial representative over Lancashire, Yorkshire and parts of Lincolnshire, Scotland and Ireland, for a Liverpool firm of iron merchants and manufacturers for about seven years, he entered the Insurance profession, first as a general broker, then, successively, as special representative and Inspector of Agents for the Norwich and London Accident Insurance Association. In 1889 he was invited to take the Superintendence of Agents in West Lancashire for the National Life Assurance Society, and at the close of that year was promoted to the Joint Management of the same Society in the above-mentioned district, in conjunction with Mr. John Marshall, where he has largely contributed to the development of that Society's more recent schemes of Whole Life and Endowment Assurance. Subsequently, on the retirement of his colleague, Mr. Crooke was appointed District Manager as above.

FRANK DALTON.

H. D. CURNICK.

Dalton, Frank, is the well-known District Manager in Birmingham for the Norwich Union Fire Office. The position is an important one, the Office having old and numerous Agencies in the district. Mr. Dalton commenced his Insurance career as far back as 1860, in the Head Office of the Midland Counties Insurance Company at Lincoln. In 1865 he entered the London Office of the Royal Insurance Company, and remained there until 1870, when his services were transferred to the London Office of the Norwich Union, where for 16 years he assisted Mr. C. J. Bunyon, the well-known author of the works on the Law of Fire and Life Insurance, in the conduct of that Office, and where he had practically the working management. Since Mr. Dalton has been in Birmingham he has been to the fore in all matters connected with the Insurance profession. He took a prominent part in the founding of the Birmingham Insurance Institute, and has a seat on the Council of that body. In February, 1891, he was unanimously appointed a Vice-President of the Norwich Insurance Institute. His late father was well-known in the County of Lincoln as Head Master for many years of Christ's Hospital, Lincoln, and an ardent supporter of the national game—cricket.

———

Curnick, H. D., is the District Manager of the Norwich Union Fire Office at their Manchester Branch, which Branch he opened in 1886, the business of the Company having previously been carried on through a Chief Agency. Mr. Curnick's former Insurance experience had extended over a period of twenty years, and had been acquired in the service of some of the leading Fire and Life Companies of the United Kingdom, amongst them being the Liverpool and London and Globe, the Scottish Widows' Fund, and the Mutual Fire. He has now under his charge the whole of Lancashire, except the Liverpool district, Cheshire, and Derbyshire, in which area is situate many of the most important risks in the British Isles.

A. T CUFLEY.

Y. R. ECCLES, F.I.A.

Cufley, Alfred T., is the London Manager of the Norwich and London Accident Insurance Association. He received a great part of his education at the University of London, where he had already successfully proceeded to the intermediate stage of the Arts degree, when he turned his attention to business matters, adopting Insurance as his particular profession, and entering the service of the Norwich and London Association, at its Chief Offices at Norwich, in 1874. There he continued for a period of fourteen years, during a great part of which time he held the position of Chief Clerk in his Office, and on the retirement of the late London Manager, Mr. Powell, in 1888, Mr. Cufley was appointed to succeed him. Mr.

Cufley's early education well adapted him for the hard mental labour required in the performance of his duties, which, added to his natural energy and his great powers of organization, has no doubt contributed in no small degree to the great success which has followed him throughout his career.

———

Eccles, Y. R., is the London Secretary of the Scottish Amicable Life Assurance Society, which position he has occupied for the last 23 years. He received his early Insurance training in the Office of the old Britannia Company. He is a Fellow of the Institute of Actuaries, as well as an energetic and popular official.

R. W. CAMPBELL DAVIDSON.

RHYS DAVIES.

Davidson, Robert William Campbell, Branch Manager of the Fire Insurance Association at Manchester, entered the service of the Royal Insurance Company in 1877, in which office he remained for nine years, leaving it at Christmas, 1886, to take up the duties of Head of the Town Department at the Head Office of the Fire Insurance Association. Since that time he has continued in the service of the same Company, acting in various capacities both in London and the provinces, until the end of 1890, when he was offered and accepted his present post. Mr. Davidson has in the course of his Insurance career travelled very extensively, having at various periods visited almost every part of Europe, besides Egypt, and on the other side of the Atlantic, Canada and the United States.

Davies, Rhys, the South Wales and Monmouthshire District Manager to the London and Lancashire Life Assurance Company, commenced as an Agent to the Standard Life Assurance Company, acting at the same time in a similar capacity for the Provincial Assurance Company. He then undertook the District Managership to the English Fire and Life Insurance Company, which he held for one year; after which he accepted his present appointment with the London and Lancashire, which office he has now served since 1868. Mr. Davies was appointed by the Presbyterians of Glamorganshire and Monmouthshire as their Moderator for the year 1891.

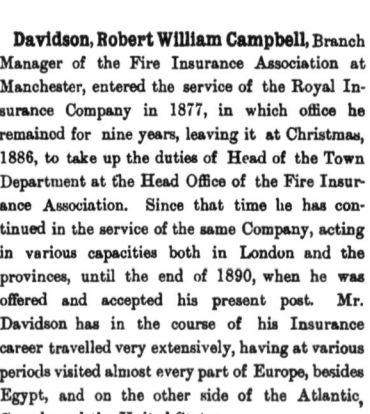

J. B. DAVIS.

JOHN C. DE VOY.

Davis, J. Burton, is the Resident Secretary of the Sun Life Assurance Society at Nottingham. He commenced his career in the Insurance profession in the Head Office of the Engine, Boiler, and Employers' Liability Insurance Company, of Manchester, where he remained for five years, working steadily through all the departments of the office. He next became Inspector of Agents to the Northern Accident Insurance Company for the Lancashire District, and after having gained a little further experience at Newcastle-on-Tyne, working the counties of Northumberland and Durham therefrom, he was appointed Resident Secretary to the same Company at their new branch at Leeds, with supervision over the whole of Yorkshire. After having held that post for nearly two years, during which time he placed his Branch on a most successful footing, Mr. Davis accepted the District Managership to the Pelican Life Office at Birmingham, to establish that Branch, in which undertaking he was also successful. He left the Pelican about the middle of 1890 to take up his present duties at Nottingham for the Sun Life Office.

———

De Voy, John C., is District Representative of the Mutual Life Insurance Company of New York at its Dublin Branch. Mr. De Voy has had a long and successful Insurance experience.

G. DUNCAN DEUCHAR.

JAMES DICKIE.

Deuchar, G. Duncan, is the General Agency Superintendent of the Rock Life Office.   Mr. Deuchar, who is a native of Forfarshire, in Scotland, received his early Insurance training in the London office of the Scottish Provincial Assurance Company, which he left to become Inspector at the London office of the Scottish Metropolitan Life Office, after which he accepted an appointment to open up the Eastern counties for the West of England Fire and Life Insurance Company.   He joined the Rock in January, 1888, and was promoted to his present position two years later.

Dickie, James, is the Manager for Scotland of the Sun Life Assurance Society.   He was appointed to his present position in the February of 1891, with control of the Society's Branches in Edinburgh and Glasgow, having for several years previous to that date been Resident Secretary for the Society at its Glasgow Branch.   He was trained in the Head Office of the Edinburgh Life Assurance Company, and also spent a number of years in the London Office of the same Company.   When the Sun extended the sphere of its operations, he started that Society's Yorkshire Branch at Leeds, and remained there for two or three years previous to his removal to the "second city."

WALTER DICKINSON.

THOMAS DICKINSON.

Dickinson, Walter, Branch Manager to the Economic Life Assurance Company at Birmingham, was, previous to taking up Insurance work, engaged in the Banking profession, being for nearly twelve years in the Birmingham, Dudley, and District Bank, now the Birmingham District and Counties Bank. He left that to take up an appointment for the Ocean, Railway, and General Accident and Guarantee Companies, working for them for some time in the North of England up to Carlisle, and eventually settling in Manchester, where he opened a Branch office for those Companies. There he worked successfully for three and a-half years, eventually leaving the service of the Ocean Companies to take up the District Inspectorship to the Birmingham Branch of the Scottish Provident Institution, in which capacity he had his first real experience of Life Insurance work. After being with the Scottish Provident Institution for some time, on the District Managership of the Economic Life in Birmingham becoming vacant, Mr. Dickinson accepted it in 1889.

———

Dickinson, Thomas, is the District Manager at Birkenhead of the Star Life Assurance Society. Mr. Dickinson has had an experience of 30 years in the Life Assurance business, 23 of which have been spent in connection with his present Office, for which, we understand, he does a large business, the district under his supervision embracing Cheshire, Shropshire, and North Wales.

A. A. DIXON.

THOMAS DOW.

Dixon, A. A., the Resident Secretary of the North of England Branch of the Northern Accident Insurance Company at Newcastle-on-Tyne, has been connected throughout the whole of his Insurance career with his present Company, having commenced work for it in the August of 1887 in the capacity of Inspector of Agents. After a period of three years he was appointed to his present post at the chief Branch, after London, of the Company, having a Local Board of Directors, and extending over the whole of the East and West Coasts district between York and Berwick. Mr. Dixon's Branch has a large and influential connection, with a constantly increasing business, much of which has been due to his own personal exertions.

Dow, Thomas, the District Manager of the London Assurance Corporation, at their Office for Scotland, at 99, St. Vincent Street, Glasgow, received his early training in the Edinburgh Branch Office of the Alliance Assurance Company, where he gradually worked his way up until he was transferred to the Glasgow Branch of that same Company, to undertake the duties of Surveyor. He eventually left the service of the Alliance on obtaining his present appointment with the London Assurance Corporation, with control of its business over the whole of Scotland, and since then he has succeeded in building up a considerable and increasing business of a good class in both the Fire and Life Departments of the Corporation in the North.

GEORGE DUTHIE.

R. B. DUNCAN.

Duthie, George, is the Secretary for Scotland of the Equitable Fire and Accident Office, Limited. Mr. Duthie commenced his career in the Insurance profession in the Office of one of the principal Agents of the Scottish Union at Glasgow, where he remained for eleven and a half years, receiving a thoroughly sound practical training in all the details of the business. He then transferred his services to the Northern Assurance Company in the capacity of Chief Clerk to the Manchester Branch of that Office, then under the management of Mr. James Robb, from whom he acquired more experience of the most valuable description ; and after a period of three years with the Northern, on the establishment of the Equitable Fire Insurance Company, he was offered and accepted the post of Surveyor to their Head Office. In 1874 the Equitable opened a Scottish Branch in Glasgow under the control of an influential Board of Directors, and Mr. Duthie was appointed Secretary, which post he still continues to hold. He has since then worked up a large and profitable business for his Company in Scotland.

———

Duncan, R. B., the Local Secretary of the Standard Life Assurance Company at their Branch at Newcastle-on-Tyne, was, prior to his connection with that Company, Examiner of Accounts for Guaranteed Railways to the Government of India at Calcutta, in which capacity he acquired an experience of life and business generally which has been of great service to him in enabling him to represent effectively the interests of the Standard, with its large *clientèle* in the North of England. He opened the Branch of which he is the Secretary in 1880, the office being first situate in Grey Street, but in 1884, owing to the increase of business, removing to the larger premises it now occupies in Neville Street.

DAVID DRIMMIE, JUNR.

GEORGE DRIMMIE.

Drimmie, George, David and Arthur, are the partners in the firm of David Drimmie and Sons, the representatives in Ireland of the Phœnix Fire Office, the English and Scottish Law Life Association, and the National Guarantee Association. Their father, Mr. David Drimmie, the founder of the firm, was connected with the English and Scottish Law Life Assurance Association for twenty-eight years in all, first as an Agent at Londonderry, and for the last twenty-five years as Secretary for Ireland at Dublin. In 1876, on the Phœnix Fire Office re-commencing to do business in Ireland, Mr. Drimmie obtained the management of its affairs, and succeeded in working up a very large business for that Office. In 1867 he was appointed Secretary for Ireland to the National Guarantee Association, and transacted a large and profitable business on their behalf as well. He also held the appointment of Secretary to the Accident Association of Scotland, and on that Company's business being amalgamated with that of the Lancashire and Yorkshire Accident Company he took an Agency for the latter Office. In 1883, after some years' careful training under their father, and with the cordial consent of all his Directors, Mr. Drimmie took his two elder sons, George and David, into partnership with him, under the title of David Drimmie and Sons, in the management of his extensive and growing Insurance business, and since his death these sons have taken their younger brother into the firm, and continue the business under the same title.

ARTHUR H. DRIMMIE

E. J. DUXBURY.

Duxbury, Ezra John, is the late Local Superintendent at Blackburn to the National Life Assurance Society, in charge of the sub-office to their Manchester District Office. Mr. Duxbury is himself a native of Blackburn, having been born there in the year 1854, and the whole of his experience in Insurance business has been acquired there. He began his Insurance career in the year 1878 as Agent at Blackburn for the Wesleyan and General Assurance Society, in the service of which office he remained for a period of eleven years, bringing in a great deal of business to the Society. In the year 1889 he was offered and accepted the appointment to the Superintendency of the Blackburn District for the Universal Insurance Company of Leeds. In the exercise of the functions of this post he still continued to make himself so conspicuous that only twelve months later, in the January of last year, when the Board of Directors of the National Life Assurance Society of London had considered it advisable to still further extend their business to the district of North East Lancashire, by opening a new Branch Office at Blackburn, he was selected by them as the most fitting person to fill the post of their Local Superintendent, to carry on his duties under the control of their District Manager in charge of the Branch Office situated at Manchester.

F. W. H. DURANT.

A. C DURANT.

Durant, A. C. and F. W. H., of Leeds, are the partners of one of the most important firms of Insurance Brokers in Yorkshire ; their business being very large and far-reaching. They have now been established nearly fifteen years, and transact every description of Insurance, having every facility for placing lines to any amount. They have worked up the system of their firm to a high pitch of thoroughness and completeness even in the minutest details, and the plans and specifications prepared by them are famous throughout the profession for their accuracy. Messrs. Durant make a specialty of large lines, and the handling of the entire Insurance of large establishments, and count some of the most important firms in Yorkshire among their clients.

RICHARD EARLE.

WALTER EASTON.

Earle, Richard, the Resident Secretary of the Royal Insurance Company at their Yorkshire (Queen) Branch Office at Leeds, has spent the whole period of his Insurance life in the service of the Queen, now merged in the Royal Insurance Company, having entered its service as a Junior Clerk in 1863. From that position he gradually worked his way up step by step through all the various Departments of the office, till he arrived at his present post, which he has now occupied for some years. He has under his control the business of the whole of Yorkshire.

Easton, Walter, the Resident Secretary of the Phœnix Fire Office at their Glasgow Branch, was formerly an Agent for that Company in the same City ; and upon the adoption by the Company, some years ago, of the modern system of organisation in the place of the former system of representation by Agents, he was selected for the duties of his present post, being, in fact, one of the first Resident Secretaries appointed by the Office. Mr. Easton, who is a gentleman of good social position and very highly esteemed, is also a Marine Underwriter of experience, a Member of the Glasgow Underwriters' Association, and one of the Committee of Lloyd's Registry of British and Foreign Shipping, London.

A. S. M. EATON.

B. H. EBERHARD.

Eaton, A. S. Molesworth, is the District Manager to the Sun Insurance Office (Fire), at their Branch Office, Bennett's Hill, Birmingham. Mr. Eaton's first introduction to Insurance life was in the Scottish Provident Institution, and he subsequently served his apprenticeship in the Fire Department of the Scottish Union and National. He afterwards received the appointment of Resident Secretary in Birmingham to the Scottish Metropolitan Fire and Life Offices; and upon the absorption of the former by the Caledonian Insurance Company, he transferred his services to them in the capacity of Fire Surveyor and Superintendent and Life Inspector. The directors of the Sun Insurance Office subsequently conferred upon Mr. Eaton the appointment of District Manager in Birmingham, which he continues to hold.

———

Eberhard, B. H., is the District Manager at Birmingham of the Leeds and North of England Boiler and Accident Insurance Company, Limited, and Scottish Plate Glass Insurance Company, Limited. Mr. Eberhard, who has had a large and successful Insurance experience, also represented until recently the City of London Fire Insurance Company, Limited.

ARTHUR ROBERT ELAND.

J. P. EDDISON.

Eland, Arthur R., Resident Secretary and Inspector of Agents to the Sun Life Assurance Society for their Bedford District, is the son of a banker at Thrapston, Kettering, in Northamptonshire, in whose office he first commenced his business life, remaining there for nineteen years. On leaving that he entered the service of the Union Discount Company, of London, with whom he remained for eighteen months, eventually abandoning the banking profession altogether to take up that of Insurance in November, 1890, when he was appointed to his present post. The district over which he has supervision comprises the counties of Bedford, Cambridge, Huntingdon, and Northampton.

Eddison, J. P., the Local Manager of the Leeds district of the North British and Mercantile Insurance Company, originally intended to be an Estate Agent and Land Surveyor, and served his articles to that profession in an office at Leeds. In 1883 he abandoned his original profession to adopt that of an Insurance man, and from that year till 1887 he acted as Surveyor to the Leeds Branch of the North British and Mercantile Insurance Company, subsequently removing to the same position at the Head Office of the Company at Edinburgh. He was appointed to his present post in the February of 1891.

REGINALD EVERILL.

ROLAND ELLIOT.

Everill, Reginald, Resident Secretary to the Western Branch of the Ocean Accident and Guarantee Corporation at their Branch Office at Bristol, has spent the whole of his career in the service of that Corporation, formerly known under the compound name of the Ocean, Railway, and General Accident Assurance and Guarantee Companies. After being engaged in various capacities in other districts, Mr. Everill came to Bristol in 1884 to open his present Branch, since which time it has become one of the largest and most important that the Corporation possess. This is entirely due to Mr. Everill's personal energy and ability, which, combined with the large experience he had acquired in dealing with claims under the three departments of the Corporation business, General Accident, Employers' Liability, and Fidelity Guarantee, could hardly fail to bring about satisfactory results. He has received many offers of employment from other Companies, but has always remained staunch to his first allegiance.

Elliot, Roland, is the Local Secretary of the Manchester Fire Office at their Law Courts Branch at the Clock House, Arundel Street, Strand. Mr. Elliot commenced work in 1881 in the Accountants' Department of the Briton Life Office, where he remained for about twelve months, eventually leaving that Office to go through a two years' training in Surveying and Advanced Drawing at one of the South Kensington Art Schools. In 1884 he entered the service of the London and Provincial Fire Assurance Company as Assistant-Surveyor, and continued there till the opening of the Economic Fire Office when he transferred his services to that Company in the same capacity. From 1889 to 1891 he combined office work with his surveying, and for the last eighteen months of his time with the Economic he held the position of head of their Town Department, having practically the charge of the London business, including the revision of the town business of the Glasgow and London when it was taken over by the Economic. He was appointed to his present post with the Manchester Fire at the beginning of 1892.

G. H. EMMET.

CAUSTON FREETH.

Emmet, George Henry, is the Manager of the London Branch of the Norwich Union Life Office. He was born at Leeds in 1857, and educated at the Whitgift Grammar School, Croydon. He was admitted a Solicitor in 1884, and was shortly afterwards appointed Inspector of Agents for the Life Association of Scotland at its West End Office, where he remained about three years, leaving there to become West End Inspector for the Norwich Union. On the retirement of Mr. Bunyon, who was then Actuary of that Company, he was soon after appointed Assistant-Manager at the London Branch of the Norwich Union, and, on the retirement of Mr. Grant, in 1889, in consequence of ill-health, Mr. Emmet was then appointed London Manager.

————

Freeth, Causton, is the Manager of the Oxford Street Branch of the Sun Fire and Life Offices, the headquarters of which are situated in Oxford Street, W., at the corner of Vere Street. Mr. Freeth entered his father's office in 1871, and under him received his Insurance training; his Insurance life has therefore been entirely devoted to the interests of the Sun Offices.

A. P. FABIAN.

JOHN FERNEYHOUGH.

Fabian, Augustus Phillips, Superintendent for Wales and Monmouthshire of the Gresham Life Assurance Society, is a son of the late Captain George Fabian, R.N., his mother being a native of Pembrokeshire, and was born in 1824. He commenced commercial life at the early age of sixteen, being indentured to the principal merchant at British Accra, on the West Coast of Africa, where he remained for five years, being in the course of his sojourn there despatched on an important commission to Coomassie, the capital of Ashantee, then scarcely known at all to Europeans, and requiring ceremonious preparations by the native priests. At the end of his term he returned to England, and was appointed Manager of the London and County Bank at Leighton Buzzard, where he remained for some years. He then joined the Hampshire Banking Company, obtaining an appointment as Branch Manager, and, after holding that post for a considerable period, entered upon his present duties in behalf of the Gresham, with which Office he has now been connected since 1878. Mr. Fabian is a man of strict integrity and great business capability, and

to him is due much of the Gresham's success in Wales. He has been a Freemason for thirty-five years, and has passed through all the higher orders of that mystic body.

Ferneyhough, John, is the Local Secretary to the British Empire Mutual Life Assurance Company at its Branch Office at Nottingham, succeeding his father, who retired in the year 1887, after a very successful career extending over a period of more than 35 years ; he consequently has a large and varied connection to superintend. Mr. Ferneyhough was formerly and for many years the Manager of an influential newspaper in the district, which he conducted with marked success ; consequently he has numerous friends, and is widely respected and esteemed. The name, therefore, of the Company's representative for the district of Nottinghamshire, Derbyshire, and Lincolnshire, remains unchanged. The connection is an extensive one, and must necessarily command very close attention and careful management by the Local Secretary.

CAPTAIN GEORGE FERRIER.

F. FIELDER.

Ferrier, George, Captain, is Senior Member of the firm of Ferrier and Company, Insurance Agents, Liverpool. He has been connected with Insurance business many years, and until recently was District Manager at Liverpool of the Whittington Life Assurance Company. This firm acts as Insurance Brokers for the leading Insurance Companies of the Kingdom of all kinds.

———

Fielder, F., Agency Superintendent at Portsmouth to the Imperial Life Office, commenced his Insurance career as an Agent for the Gresham Life Assurance Society, in which capacity he soon gave evidence of his fitness for the business, and was promoted to the post of District Agent, laying the foundations for the present Branch of the Gresham at Portsmouth. On leaving the service of that Society he was for some time connected with a well-known firm of In-

surance Agents, where he acquired considerable experience in all branches of the business. He then undertook the Resident Secretaryship of the Scottish Metropolitan Life Assurance Company, in which post he proved eminently successful, and on the transfer of the business of the Scottish Economic Assurance Company to the Scottish Metropolitan, he was appointed District Inspector under the London Office, with the additional charge of the former Agents of the transferring Company. Not foreseeing any great prospects from this post he transferred his services, after a period of less than a year, to the Imperial Life Office, and was appointed to his present post in 1890.

Mr. Fielder also acts as Agent to the Equitable Fire and Accident Company, the Phœnix Fire Office, the Scottish Employers' Liability and Accident Insurance Company, the Imperial Fire Insurance Company, the Boiler Insurance and Steam Power Company, etc., etc.

MONTAGUE G. FISHER.

THOMAS FLEMING.

Fisher, Montague G., District Superintendent to the National Provident Institution for Bristol and the West of England, entered the Head Office of that Institution in 1872, where he remained for ten years, being subsequently promoted to superintend the Agencies in the North of England and Scotland, which duties he efficiently carried out for a period of two years and a-half. That District being at the end of that time in thorough working order, the Directors of the Institution divided it into three Districts, and Mr. Fisher then applied for and obtained the supervision of the Bristol West of England District, where he has now been Superintendent since September, 1884.

———

Fleming, Thomas, is the Secretary of the Caledonian Insurance Company at Newcastle-on-Tyne, which appointment he has held over nine years, previous to which he had eleven years' Insurance experience in Scotland. The district Mr. Fleming now occupies includes the counties of Northumberland, Durham, and the North and East Ridings of Yorkshire. He is a most able, energetic and hard-working official, and is one of the most popular Resident Secretaries in the North of England.

A. S. FLETCHER.

GEORGE H. FOSTER.

Fletcher, Alfred Sullivan, Resident Secretary of the Law Union and Crown Fire and Life Insurance Company, at Manchester, entered the service of the Scottish Fire Insurance Company at their London Branch in 1872, where he remained for a stipulated period of four years. At the end of that period he received an appointment to the Chief Clerkship of the West End Branch of the Scottish Union, and on the amalgamation of that Company with the Scottish National he was transferred to the City Branch of the joint Companies. After some three years' service in the City he again made a change in his Office, this time joining the Millers' and General Fire Office as Resident Secretary to the London Branch of that Company, which position he occupied for about two years. He subsequently made two further changes, the first to the Northern Fire and Life Office as Inspector to their Manchester Branch for three years, and the second to the Crown Life Assurance Company, for which, previous to undertaking the duties of his present position, he acted as Resident Secretary to the Leeds Branch. He now has the control over the Manchester District of the Law Union and Crown Fire and Life Insurance Company. Mr. Fletcher

may be said to have enjoyed a uniform success throughout the whole of his career.

Foster, George H., is the District Manager at Bristol of the London and Lancashire Life Assurance Company, which position he has held for upwards of seven years. He has had a large and successful experience in the Insurance business, having first acted as Inspector for the Scottish Imperial and subsequently as Local Secretary at Bristol of the Gresham Life Assurance Society, which appointment he resigned to accept the post he now holds.

Fligg, William, the District Manager to the Pelican Life Insurance Company at their Yorkshire Branch at Leeds, has spent the whole period of his Insurance life in that town, having entered the service of the Royal Insurance Office there in 1871. After remaining there for fifteen years, during the last three or four of which he acted as cashier, he became a candidate for, and was selected to undertake the duties of, his present post, which he has now successfully held since 1886.

G. FRAME.

JOHN FREESTONE, F.S.S.

Frame, George and James, are the Local Managers of the Royal Insurance Company at their Glasgow Branch. These gentlemen, both of whom take an active part in the management of the office, are possessed of excellent practical experience, and transact an important and thriving business for their Company. They enjoy considerable popularity in local Insurance circles.

Freestone, John, F.S.S., of West Bridgford, Nottingham, although not purely an Insurance man, yet is stamped by his publication, "Where to Insure," as an enthusiast in Life Assurance, and as having such a thorough knowledge of the position and prospects of each Office as is seldom, if ever, met with outside the upper ranks of professional Insurance men.

In 1889, wishing to take out a policy in some Office of better repute than that in which his life was then assured, and being dissatisfied with the grounds on which Agents canvassing him based their several pleas for preference, Mr. Freestone purchased copies of the Government Blue Books relating to the Life Assurance Offices, and compiled therefrom several tables, shewing each Office's percentage of surplus funds, of bonus allotted, expenses, &c.

The mode of allotting bonuses on Endowment Assurance Policies also was tabulated.

After devoting the leisure time of many months to this research, and having arrived at unquestionably solid grounds on which to base the selection of an Office for Life or Endowment Assurance, Mr. Freestone considered that the public ought to have the benefit of his investigations, so he published the tables, with explanatory letterpress, under the title of "Where to Insure." Mr. Freestone has for twenty-three years been engaged in the hosiery trade in Nottingham, and for the last ten has had the management of the business of a large firm in that town.

SIDNEY FULLER.

G. F. FURNISS.

Fuller, Sidney, who holds an appointment in connection with the London, Edinburgh and Glasgow Assurance Company, Limited, is a gentleman of many years' experience in the Department of Accident Insurance to which he is specially attached. Mr. Fuller began his career as an Agent of the Railway Passengers' Assurance Company in Devonshire; but afterwards transferred his services to the Ocean Railway and General in the same district. He was subsequently appointed District Manager for the counties of Hants, Wilts, and Dorset, to the Briton Medical and General Life, and the Ocean Companies. He continued his connection with the Ocean Accident, as Superintendent for the South and West of England, subsequently including the Midlands, and, at last, the whole of Great Britain as far north as Dundee. Mr. Fuller afterwards resigned his connection with the Ocean, on his acceptance of the similar post, which he continues to occupy, with the London, Edinburgh, and Glasgow Company.

Furniss, George Frederick, the Chief Agency Superintendent of the Imperial Life Office at Leeds, commenced his career as Agent for the Edinburgh Life Office at Huddersfield, which post he held for some years with considerable success, subsequently joining the Life Association of Scotland, as Agency Superintendent in connection with the Leeds Branch. In 1884 he removed to Nottingham and the Eastern Counties in behalf of the Imperial Life Office, in which capacity he proved so successful that, as an acknowledgment of his merits, he was invited to undertake his present duties as Chief Agency Superintendent for Yorkshire and the North of England, together with his former District, to which have since been added the Midlands. Mr. Furniss's present position partakes chiefly of the nature of a Head Office appointment, he being responsible for a great deal of the country business. He is very enthusiastic in the cause of his Company, his delight in his work almost amounting to a passion.

JOHN T. FYFE.

W. COUTTS FYFE.

Fyfe, John T., is Resident Secretary at the Glasgow Branch of the North British and Mercantile Insurance Company. Mr. Fyfe has been engaged in Insurance business for many years, and was for a long time connected with the Head Office of the Scottish Provincial Assurance Company, the Glasgow Branch of which Company was also under his management for over 20 years. He is held in high esteem by the Insurance fraternity of Scotland.

Fyfe, William Coutts, is the latest importation from Scotland to a leading position in the Metropolis, having been, in March last, appointed Assistant Secretary to the venerable Westminster Fire Office. Mr. Fyfe was formerly Resident Secretary at the Scottish Branch of the Office in Glasgow, where he succeeded in building up a large and profitable business during the brief period, about six and a-half years of his residence there. Previous to his appointment to the Glasgow Branch, Mr. Fyfe was engaged on the Head Office staff of the Scottish Provincial at Aberdeen, where he received his training, under the disciplinarian eye of the late Mr. Thomas Yuille Wardrop, the Manager of the Company, who, at an early stage, forecasted for Mr. Fyfe a highly successful career. While in Glasgow, Mr. Fyfe was Honorary Secretary of the Insurance and Actuarial Society, and it is well known that his services to that body have brought the Society to the front rank among kindred institutions, its published transactions, which appear periodically, being regarded as important educational contributions to contemporary Insurance literature.

J. GURNEY FOX.

J. A. GREIG, A.I.A

Fox, J. Gurney, the Secretary of the West End Office of the North British and Mercantile Insurance Office at 8, Waterloo Place, London, S.W., was born in 1850, the son of Robert Barclay Fox, Esq., of Grove Hill, Cornwall, and comes of an old family which has been settled in that county since 1645. Previous to his appointment to his present post, which took place in 1890, Mr. Gurney Fox was for a year with the Crown Life Assurance Company.

Greig, J.A., A.I.A., is the West End Secretary at the Charing Cross Branch of the Sun Life Office. He is a native of Edinburgh, and was educated at St. Andrew's, at a public school in that city, finishing at the Edinburgh University. Mr. Greig, as well as being an able Insurance Official, is an Associate of the Institute of Actuaries, and being an old St. Andrew's boy is well-known in golfing circles, and is the Hon. Treasurer of the London Scottish Golf Club.

W. B. GALBRAITH, C.A.

WALTER GALBRAITH, C.A.

Galbraith, William Brodie, is the Junior Partner of the firm of Walter and W. B. Galbraith, Chartered Accountants in Glasgow, who are the Resident Secretaries for Scotland, of the Rock Life Assurance Company. Mr. Galbraith having finished the usual curriculum at the Glasgow Academy, joined the local University, and completed his studies there in 1874. From this point his Insurance career commenced, and since joining his father's firm in 1880, he has been continually before the Insurance world, and has already gained a reputation amongst his fellow-citizens which older men may well envy. Although gentle in manner, his plans are well defined, and carried through with dauntless vigour and characteristic skill. Under his fostering care the Company which he represents has made great strides in Scotland during the past year. The new ground has been opened under the guidance of Mr. Galbraith, and this, although always a tedious and often a thankless operation, has been done with a completeness, and resulted so profitably as to speak volumes for the management.

Mr. Galbraith is a prominent member of the Institute of Actuaries and Society of Chartered Accountants in Glasgow. He inherits all the marked talents and ability of his family; and it may be truly said that he is the worthy son of a worthy sire.

Galbraith, Walter, is the Senior Partner of the firm of Walter and W. B. Galbraith, Chartered Accountants in Glasgow, who are the Resident Secretaries for Scotland of the Rock Life Assurance Company. He has had a long and varied experience as an Accountant and Actuary in Glasgow, where his business career extends over a period of fully forty years. During all this time, embracing many great mercantile calamities, Mr. Galbraith has been constantly before the public. He has attended mainly to the Bankruptcy Department of his firm's business, bringing him continually into contact with most of the practising solicitors in Scotland, amongst whom he has earned the reputation of being complete master of our Bankruptcy Laws. His advice is much courted by the younger members of his profession, and his *dicta* accepted without criticism. Mr. Galbraith's firm is one of the best known in his city, and represents locally many of the largest Dry Goods Firms in the United Kingdom. While they have represented several of our best known Insurance Companies for many years, it is only since their appointment as Secretaries for the Rock Company that they have come more prominently before the Insurance Public. Their good work for this Company in Scotland is already bearing fruit, and promising well for future years. For this good result the senior partner is entitled to a fair share of credit. He is a model Scotchman of the Carlylean type, his whole life stamped with shrewdness, ability, and tenacity of no ordinary kind. He is an ideal representative of an Insurance Company—suave in manners and venerable in appearance; from experience well able to speak of the wisdom of insuring, and by his age competent to point the moral. Mr. Galbraith is a prominent citizen of Glasgow, and held in respect by all with whom he comes in contact.

W. H. GARBETT.

C. GARDINER.

Garbett, W. H., the Local Manager of the Birmingham Branch of the Law Union and Crown Fire and Life Insurance Company, commenced his Insurance career in the service of the Guardian Assurance Company at their Birmingham Branch, which office he entered in 1878. He there remained until the beginning of 1882, when, on the Phœnix Fire Office opening a Branch in Birmingham, he applied for and obtained the post of Chief Clerk to the Branch. His period of service with the Phœnix lasted for a period of nearly nine years, during the last five years of which he performed the duties of Surveyor and Agency Inspector to that office, resigning that post in November, 1889, to take up the appointment of Local Manager to the newly-opened Branch of his present Company, with authority over the seven Midland Counties.

———

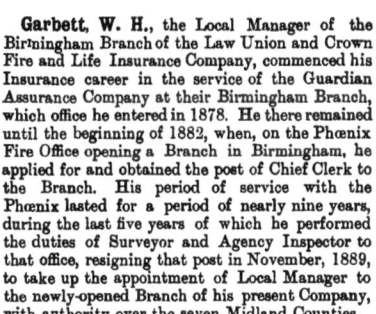

Gardiner, C., is a prominent Insurance Broker of Leeds. His Insurance life commenced in the service of the Sovereign Assurance Company, for whom he acted as General Superintendent for the North of England, in which capacity he so won the esteem both of his subordinates and the policy-holders of his district that, on his resigning his post on the amalgamation of the City with the Sovereign, to take up the duties of Yorkshire Manager for the County Fire and Provident Life Offices, he was presented with two separate testimonials from these two bodies, with an expression of regret at his leaving them. He commenced business for his new company in Leeds, opening their office in that town, and remaining in charge of it for thirteen years. He then transferred his services to the West of England Insurance Company, still as District Manager for Yorkshire, and with his headquarters at Leeds, and occupied that position for ten years, he built up a very important business and connection for the two Companies, and at the same time increased the high reputation and wide feeling of respect which he had already established for himself. Mr. Gardiner finally retired from the West of England Office in 1890, and set up on his own account as Insurance Broker.

He has also taken considerable interest in both religious and political affairs, and was elected one of the fifteen members of the Leeds School Board, on which he was of considerable service; was also for many years one of the managers of the Leeds and Skyrack Savings Bank, and also a member of the Committee of the Leeds Young Men's Christian Association, and a very active and useful Methodist Local Preacher for over thirty years— and in both social and benevolent movements has been a prominent personage.

ROBERT ALEXANDER GARDNER.

JOHN T. GARDNER.

Gardner, Robert Alexander, is the Manager for Scotland of the Norwich Union Life Office, which appointment he has held since the formation of this Branch over 15 years ago. Mr. Gardner, who is a most successful Life Assurance Official, had formerly represented the Life Association of Scotland as Glasgow Resident Secretary.

Gardner, John T., was, until lately, the Local Secretary of the Gresham Life Assurance Society at their Northampton District Office. Mr. Gardner is a native of Northampton, where, previous to his appointment with the Gresham, he was engaged for a period of upwards of eight years in the capacity of a solicitor's clerk. He resigned that position in February, 1891, to accept an offer from the Gresham Life Assurance Society.

JAMES GEMMILL.

J. CLEMENT GEORGE.

Gemmill, James, is the Manager at the Glasgow Branch of the Royal Exchange Assurance, to which post he was appointed in 1889. Mr. Gemmill received his professional training in the West of Scotland Branch of the Scottish Union Insurance Company, after which he added to his Branch experience in Belfast and Leeds as Secretary to the North British and Mercantile. He is a Fire Insurance official of ability and energy.

———

George, J. Clement, is the Resident Secretary to the Scottish Accident Insurance Company at its Branch Office at Bristol. Previous to accepting his present appointment, Mr. George was for five years engaged in the service of the Lancashire and Yorkshire Accident Insurance Company as their West of England Inspector, so that he has had ample experience both of the special line of Insurance in which he is now engaged and of the district which he now superintends, which includes the West of England and South Wales. He was appointed to his present post with the Scottish Accident Insurance Company in 1887, and since then has considerably extended and increased the business of the Company. He is active, zealous and able, and popular with all who come in contact with him, as was shown on his leaving his appointment with the Lancashire and Yorkshire, on which occasion he was presented with a handsome testimonial by the Agents of that Company.

WILLIAM GIBBS.

PERCY GIBBS.

Gibbs, William, is the District Manager at Birmingham of the Employers' Liability Assurance Corporation, Limited. He is an old and esteemed citizen of Birmingham, and has most successfully represented this Company in this District for many years, his field of operations embracing the Midland Counties of Staffordshire, Worcestershire, Warwickshire, Shropshire, and Derbyshire.

Gibbs, Percy, is the Resident Secretary at Birmingham of the Scottish Boiler Insurance Company, Limited. Mr. Gibbs is a young gentleman of marked ability, and under his energetic management the business of this Company in the Midland Counties has grown to very large proportions. He is the son of Mr. William Gibbs, in whose office he received his Insurance training.

HOWARD GLANVILL.

A. G. GILLESPIE.

Glanvill, Howard, Resident Secretary of the Manchester Fire Office at the Birmingham Branch, commenced his career in the Insurance profession in the Head Office of the West of England Fire and Life Insurance Company at Exeter, in which Company he eventually rose to the position of Inspector of Agencies at the Head Office. He subsequently transferred his services to the Commercial Union Assurance Company, where he was employed successively in the Head Office and the Branches at Birmingham and Nottingham, as Chief Clerk and Surveyor. He was appointed to his present post with the Manchester Fire Office in the December of 1890.

———

Gillespie, A. G., is the Secretary of the Edinburgh Branch of the Northern Assurance Company, which post he has held since 1873, previous to which time he was connected with the Head Office at Aberdeen. Mr. Gillespie is highly esteemed in Insurance circles and regarded as a most competent and able Fire Insurance Official.

EVERARD GOADBY.

JAMES H. GOFFE.

Goadby, Everard, Agency Inspector to the London Office of the Commercial Fire Insurance Company of Scotland, was appointed to that position in the latter part of 1891 to work the Accident Department in conjunction with Mr. Absell, the Resident Secretary in London for the Company. Mr. Goadby is the eldest son of the late Professor Goadby, B.A., Principal of the Baptist College, Nottingham, and spent several years in Mercantile pursuits in London, Birmingham, Nottingham, and Derby. He commenced his Insurance career in 1886 with the Provincial Life Office, and afterwards with the Marine and General Life, and Provident Plate Glass Insurance Companies, working from Nottingham. At the same time he was interested as a Fire Insurance Broker, in the same town.

————

Goffe, James H., is the Resident Secretary of the Northern Accident Insurance Company. Mr. Goffe's early Insurance training was received in the service of the Royal and the Scottish Accident Insurance Companies at their respective Birmingham branches, so that he has acquired a very considerable experience in the Accident business. Immediately previous to obtaining his present appointment he held the post of Resident Secretary to the Birmingham Branch of the Scottish Alliance Insurance Company.

W. G. GODDARD

THOMAS GOODWILLIE

Goddard, W. G., is the Resident Secretary of the Star Life Assurance Society, at its Branch Office at Norwich. Mr. Goddard has succeeded in placing his branch on a most prosperous footing, having, by his quiet perseverance secured his full share of the Life Insurance business of the district.

Goodwillie, Thomas, is the Resident Secretary of the Liverpool and London and Globe Insurance Company at that Company's Irish Branch, College Green, Dublin. He has passed the whole of his career in connection with the Liverpool and London and Globe Insurance Company, having entered its service in 1869, and having held his present post since 1870.

CHARLES GOOD.

ALEXANDER GOOD.

Good, Charles, is the Local Manager at Bristol of the Phœnix Fire Office, which position he has held since the opening of the Branch in 1882, previous to which Mr. Good had been District Manager of the Commercial Union Assurance Company, both in Bristol and Southampton. He has had a large and successful experience in Fire Insurance matters, and is regarded as an expert of great ability. He is a B.A. of Exeter College, Oxford, and from 1859 to 1876 held the responsible position of Deputy-Provincial Secretary in the Colony of British Columbia.

Good, Alexander, is the District Inspector of the Pelican Life Office for Bristol, West of England, and South Wales. He is the son of Mr. Good, of the Phœnix Fire Office. After passing some years in the service of the Commercial Union, the Phœnix, and the South British and National Offices successively, he was, in April, 1885, appointed to the post of District Manager to the London and Provincial Fire Insurance Company for their West of England and Wales Branch at Bristol, which Branch he conducted successfully up to the time of the amalgamation of the London and Provincial with the London and Lancashire. Mr. Good was appointed to his present duties at the end of 1891.

JOHN GRAY, A.I.A.

WILLIAM GRANT.

Gray, John, A.I.A., Resident Secretary to the Scottish Widows' Fund Life Assurance Society at its Branch Office at Bristol, was born in Edinburgh in 1848, and entered the Head Office of the Scottish Widows' Fund in 1865, from which he was transferred, in January, 1871, to the Dundee Branch of that Society as Cashier; being again transferred to the Glasgow Office in the same capacity in September, 1871. In June, 1874, he was appointed Cashier and Chief Clerk at the Head Office of the London and Lancashire Life Assurance Company, and remained with that Company, latterly acting as Assistant Secretary, until December, 1879, when he returned to the Scottish Widows' Fund, entering the London Office of that Society as one of the Inspectors. He then was, in 1881, appointed Secretary for the North of Ireland of the Scottish Widows' Fund, where he remained, till, in May, 1888, he was promoted to a similar position for the West of England and South Wales, the headquarters of the Branch being at

Mr. Gray is a gentleman of excellent attainments, and a Life Insurance official of much more than ordinary ability.

———

Grant, William, District Manager to the Sun Life Assurance Society at its Manchester Branch, was born in Invernesshire in 1857, and after being educated there and in Glasgow entered the head office of the Scottish Imperial, then a Fire and Life office, and passed through all the departments of the Fire business, especially acquiring a sound experience in surveying. He then became Chief Clerk at the Liverpool Branch of the Union office, where he remained for some years, subsequently being appointed Superintendent of Agents at the head office of the Scottish Life Assurance Company. Previous to his present appointment he acted as Agency Inspector to the Birmingham Branch of the Guardian Assurance Company. He is now in charge of what is the most important provincial branch of the Sun Life Office.

WILLIAM BIRD GRAY.

W. T. GRAY, F.I.A.

Gray, Wm. B., is a Partner of the firm of Messrs. Gray and Suggit, Secretaries of the Whitby Mutual Marine Iron Steamship Insurance Company, which Company was established in 1873 and registered in 1876, with an influential Board of Directors, comprising most of the principal local steamship owners and some others. The career of the Company under Messrs. Gray and Suggit's management has been very prosperous.

Gray, William Thomas, F.I.A., is the Resident Secretary in London of the Scottish Equitable Life Assurance Society, of Edinburgh, and was born on the 4th of May, 1851. He was educated first at Huntingdon Grammar School, and after-wards at the Lycée Bonaparte, Paris. In 1868 he made his first entry into the Insurance profession as a clerk in the General Reversionary and Investment Company, Limited. It was while with this company that he formed his first connection with the Institute of Actuaries, joining it as a student, and following it up until he became a Fellow by Examination in 1876. In 1878 he was appointed to the position of Assistant Secretary in the London Office of the Life Association of Scotland, which post he held until receiving his present appointment in January, 1886. As a member of the Institute of Actuaries Mr. Gray has contributed several papers on " Valuations " and " Mortality " to the Journal of the Institute.

FRANK GRIFFITH.

G. FEATHERSTONE GRIFFIN.

Griffith, Frank, Secretary of the Edinburgh Life Assurance Company at their London Office, is the son of the late Charles Fox Griffith, for head office of that Company. red the London Office of the

Clerk, and was later on pro- of the Manchester Branch of that Company as Resident Secretary. In 1881, on the Edinburgh Life Assurance Company being in want of an officer to undertake the management of their Branch at Birmingham, Mr. Griffith was offered the post, and, having accepted it, held it for four years, when the management of the London Office becoming vacant in November, 1885, he was selected by the directors to fill it. Mr. Griffith's record in his present post has been an extremely satisfactory one : not only had he the good fortune during his first year of office to show a larger amount of policies than had ever before been obtained in the history of the London Office, which extended over a period of forty years, but he has been able to surpass even that first record every successive year.

Griffin, G. Featherstone, is the Manager of the West End Branch of the Union Assurance Society at 55, Charing Cross, S.W. Mr. Griffin, who is a descendant of Stonestreet Griffin, one of the founders of the Phœnix Fire and Pelican Life Offices, received his first Insurance training in 1879 in the Standard Fire Office, and in 1883 he entered the service of the Guardian under Mr. Marsden, where he gained considerable experience in surveying and loss assessing ; he also appointed Agents for this Company, and aided in generally developing its outdoor business. In 1887 he entered the service of the Commercial Union as Inspector of Agents, where he remained until 1889, when he received his present appointment with the Union Assurance Society. Mr. Griffin has been very successful in increasing the business of the Companies with which he has been identified.

B. R. GRAYSTON.

W. McQUIE GREEN.

Grayston, Bertram R., is the Resident Secretary at Bristol for the West of England Branch of the Sickness and Accident Assurance Association, Limited, of Edinburgh. Mr. Grayston was originally in the scholastic profession. At the earliest possible age he successfully passed all the examinations required by the Government for the qualification of a schoolmaster, and for some years afterwards followed that profession with distinguished success at Stockport. From 1887 to 1889 he devoted the whole of his time and energies to the work of the Manchester City Mission, and, together with Mr. J. Wakefield MacGill, the Secretary, succeeded in establishing the society so well known in Manchester and the district—"The Bible Students' Society." In January, 1889, he accepted the post of Inspector of Agents to the Yorkshire Branch of the Sickness and Accident Assurance Association, but was speedily promoted to the Resident Secretaryship of the Bristol Branch, which post he now holds. As a proof of Mr. Grayston's energy and business capacity in the way of Insurance, we may mention that the amount of new business passed through his Branch in 1891 was more than double that of 1890.

Green, W. McQuie, is the District Manager of the County Fire and Provident Life Offices at their Liverpool Branch. Mr. Green is by birth a Liverpool man, and received his early Insurance training in the Alliance and London Assurance Offices in that town. In 1885 he removed to Birmingham, having obtained an appointment as Surveyor for the Guardian Assurance Office, and about eighteen months later he was promoted to the Agency Inspectorship of the same Branch. This post he held till March, 1888, when he resigned it to take up the Resident Secretaryship, also at Birmingham, of the Yorkshire Insurance Company, whence in April, 1891, he returned to his native city to take up the duties of his present position.

WILLIAM GRIFFIN.

F. W. GRIFFIN.

Griffin, William, is Joint Local Secretary at Bristol of the British Empire Mutual Life Assurance Company, which Company he has represented in or near Bristol for upwards of 40 years. Mr. Griffin is a prominent citizen of the West of England, and has built up a very large business in this District for the British Empire Company.

———

Gilfillan, John, is the Resident Secretary of the Guardian Fire and Life Assurance Company at their Branch Office at Glasgow. Mr. Gilfillan, previous to obtaining his present appointment, held that of Agency Inspector in connection with the Glasgow Branch of the North British and Mercantile Insurance Company. He has now been Resident Secretary to the Guardian since 1885, and has been highly successful in largely developing and extending the business of his Branch, which controls the Company's operations throughout Scotland and some portions of the North of England.

———

Griffin, F. W., is the Joint Local Secretary at Bristol of the British Empire Mutual Life Assurance Company, which office he represents in connection with his father, Mr. William Griffin, whom he joined in the management of this Company in 1883. He is wideawake, able and energetic, and very popular with the local Agents throughout his District.

H. S. Greenwood.

Charles Griffith.

Greenwood, Henry S., Resident Secretary of the Yorkshire Branch of the Church of England Assurance Institution at Leeds, received his early Insurance training in the Office of the Lancashire Insurance Company in Leeds, with which Company he remained nearly nine years. He was subsequently offered the Secretaryship of the Leeds Branch of the Northern Accident Insurance Company, which post he accepted and held for nearly two years. He was appointed to his present position in the service of the Church of England Assurance Institution in August, 1890, his field of operation extending over Yorkshire and Durham.

Griffith, Charles, holds an important position in connection with the London Office of the Edinburgh Life Assurance Company. Previous to receiving this appointment he was the Resident Secretary at Liverpool of the same Company. Mr. Griffith, who is a member of an Insurance family, began his career in the London office of the City of Glasgow Life Company, from which he transferred his services in 1882 to the Crown Life Office, as Agency Inspector. Two years later he received the appointment of Resident Secretary at Newcastle-upon-Tyne to the Edinburgh Life. From this position he was promoted, in December, 1885, to the charge of the more important Branch at Liverpool, and in 1890 he received his present appointment.

WILLIAM HALLETT.

ROBERT HARDMAN.

Hallett, William, is the Resident Secretary of the Colonial Mutual Life Assurance Society at their Edinburgh Branch. Mr. Hallett, previous to taking up the duties of his present position, had acquired a considerable experience in the service of several of the leading Insurance Companies, and latterly represented the Colonial Mutual in the South of Scotland. He opened the Edinburgh Branch of the Society in 1886, and, being a gentleman of much energy and very zealous in the cause of his Society, has succeeded in building up a large business for them in the district.

Hardman, Robert, is the District Manager to the Commercial Union Assurance Company, at their Branch Office at Liverpool. Previous to becoming connected with the Commercial Union, Mr. Hardman was for many years associated with Mercantile pursuits in Liverpool. He was appointed to his present post in 1888.

WILLIAM A. HARRIS, F.R.S.S.A., F.S.S., F.S. Sc.

P. E. HANSELL.

Harris, William A., is the Secretary to the Liverpool Branch of the Phœnix Fire Office. He has had a very long and varied experience: after a grammar-school curriculum, some service with his father, an architect and surveyor in Bristol and London, and a preliminary training at King's College, London, in building construction and applied science, under Professors Hosking and Moseley, he served articles with Thomas Lloyd Evans, Esq., C.E., of Luton, Bedfordshire, and subsequently had a valuable experience as chief clerk in the office of Daniel Watney, surveyor, of London. In 1863 he was appointed Secretary and Surveyor to the Commercial Union in Liverpool, which he held till 1871, and after that he was engaged, for ten years, as Surveyor to the Imperial, and as chief or independent Surveyor to many of the leading Fire Companies, reporting on risks of the most varied character and over the whole kingdom, having his head-quarters meanwhile at Manchester. In 1881 he was appointed Inspector of Agencies on the Head office staff of the Phœnix, with the special object of opening and superintending Branches. These duties, and the inspection of agencies, he fulfilled till December, 1885, since which date he has devoted his energies to his own particular Branch, still, however, retaining his Head Office appointment. Mr. Harris is the author of " A Technical Dictionary of Fire Insurance," published in 1886, and received with great favour both in this kingdom and abroad, and of " A Technological Dictionary of Insurance Chemistry," published in October, 1890. So large has been the sale of these works that only a few copies now remain on hand. He is a Fellow of the Royal Scottish Society of Arts, and of the Royal Statis-

tical Society ; also a member of the Royal United Service Institution, and of the Franklin Institute, Philadelphia, U.S.A.

Hansell, P. E., is the Managing Director of the Norwich or Eastern Counties Branch of the North British and Mercantile Insurance Company, which Branch he himself started in the year 1872, and has superintended the working of it to the present date. He now has a local Board of Directors, consisting of four members, to assist him, the business of the Company being carried on at his office, in the Close, Norwich. During his period of office he has widely developed this Branch, his district comprising not only the town of Norwich but the whole county of Norfolk, together with the adjacent ones of Suffolk and Cambridge ; having in all under his control about 120 agents, who transact the business of the Company exclusively through the Norwich Branch. It is chiefly owing to his efforts that his Company is now as well known and patronised as any other which has a Branch in the same district. Mr. Hansell is a very keen advocate of the Insurance business, both as a provision against death and loss of property through fire, and he never loses an opportunity of impressing on his clients the great advantages that accrue to them on making such a provision. Mr. Hansell, besides his Insurance business, also carries on that of a solicitor, his offices being situated at Norwich as above and also at Cromer, in the same county. He is also agent for the estates of several landowners in the counties both of Norfolk and Suffolk.

S. J. EYRE HARTLEY.

W. H. HASTINGS.

Hartley, S. J. Eyre, is the Resident Secretary at Manchester of the Imperial Life Insurance Company. Mr. Hartley commenced his Insurance life in connection with the Life Association of Scotland, which Company he represented for several years as Local Secretary at Manchester.

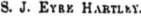

Hartung, F. M., is General Agent in Great Britain and Ireland of the Patriotische Insurance Company of Hamburg, to which he was appointed in 1890. Mr. Hartung commenced his Insurance career on the staff of the Imperial Fire Office in 1864, and remained with them for some years, being eventually promoted to the position of chief clerk of the Foreign Department. This he resigned in 1875 to take up an appointment with the Jakor, of Moscow, which he held till that Company withdrew from this country in 1889.

Hastings, William Hairby, is the District Manager of the Marine and General Mutual Life Assurance Society at its Manchester Branch. After a commercial training in Liverpool he entered the head office of the Royal, at the age of 20, and remained in the service of that Company for about five years. Whilst there he was chiefly engaged as Assistant Private Secretary to the Managers, and had the supervision of the appointments of Agents for the United Kingdom (London Branch excepted), and the development of the Agency system. He also assisted with the advertising, and had over twelve months' experience in the Foreign Fire Department. In order to acquire a practical knowledge of outdoor work he transferred his services to the Atlas Fire and Life Assurance Company, where he had three years' successful experience as Inspector of Agents to their Manchester Branch. He resigned his position with that office at the end of 1890 to take up the improved position which he at present holds. His geniality of manner and characteristic energy give promise of a successful career.

| A. R. HARVEY.!

Harvey, A. R., who is the Manager of the Department of the Mutual Reserve Fund Life Association at Liverpool (which embraces Lancashire, Cheshire, North Wales, and the Isle of Man), though not yet thirty years of age, has achieved great success in the Life Insurance world.

Mr. Harvey, who was born at Liverpool, until a few years ago was engaged in a business entirely different to that of Insurance, but happening to be acquainted with the then Manager of the Liverpool Department of the Mutual Reserve, Mr. Harvey was induced to try his 'prentice hand as an agent of that Association. His aptitude for the work was such that, before long, he was duly enrolled as a member of the regular corps, and in the course of a few weeks it was discovered that he had found his real vocation in life, as in the remarkably short space of twelve months, his energy, organising skill, and wonderful personal success in obtaining business, warranted his appointment to the position of Manager of the Department.

Shortly after attaining this post, a prize was offered by the Association to the Manager of any of its Departments in the world who should do the largest amount of paid and completed business in three months, and this was won by Mr. Harvey in October, 1890, when he topped the list with the surprising total of a quarter of a million sterling.

For his success, however, Mr. Harvey by no means appropriates the whole credit to himself, but, on the contrary, is grateful to the zealous and enthusiastic staff by whom he was surrounded.

He was then persuaded to accept the office of Director of Agencies for Great Britain and Ireland, but as this was not congenial work, he took an early opportunity of returning to his former post at Liverpool, which he now holds.

Mr. Harvey possesses an instinctive knowledge of men, a rapid judgment, great decision of character, and intense enthusiasm for his work.

JOHN R. HASWELL.

W. G. HOON.

Haswell, John R., is the Resident Secretary of the London Branch of the Scottish Accident Insurance Company. Mr. Haswell commenced his business career in Edinburgh, and shortly afterwards proceeded to India, where he was engaged in commercial pursuits for some years, till he returned home. He then accepted the above appointment, in which he has been established for the last three years, and under his management the business of the Branch has increased to a great extent.

Hoon, W. G., Manager of the Holborn Branch of the Mutual Life Insurance Company of New York, commenced his Insurance career in 1881, in the service of the Gresham Life Assurance Society, with which Office he remained three years. He was then appointed Assistant Secretary in London for the Scottish Metropolitan Life Assurance Company, which position he resigned to take up the Management of the London and Lancashire Life Assurance Company for the Midland District at Birmingham. Shortly after the Mutual Life Insurance Company of New York opened a business in England, he received an appointment from that Company in London, opening the Holborn Branch for the Company at the end of 1890.

THOMAS HARPER.

F. J. HALLOWS, F.I.A., F.F.A.

Harper, Thomas, the Resident Secretary of the Liverpool Branch of the Colonial Mutual Life Assurance Society, Limited, is a native of the Midland Counties, where he was born in 1842. In 1886 he undertook an Agency in the Prudential Assurance Company with the intention of ultimately working up a Special Agency. In this post he worked successfully both as regarded the Industrial and Ordinary business of that Company; but not liking the Industrial business, in 1888 he eventually applied for and obtained a Special Agency of the Colonial Mutual, foreseeing the prosperous career that this young Office had before it. He devoted all his powers to the endeavour to increase the business in Liverpool and district, and succeeded to such an extent that when a vacancy occurred he was appointed to his present post. Since his promotion he has, by perseverance and tact, built up a reputation for the Society amongst the assuring public of the district, which promises still further successes in the immediate future of the Society.

Haslam, James, is the District Superintendent of the Scottish Accident Insurance Company at their Nottingham Branch. For some years he was Cashier and Counting House Manager for a firm of Lace Curtain Manufacturers in Nottingham. It was while here that he was introduced to Insurance business, by the then Nottingham District Manager of the London and Provincial Fire Insurance Company, for which Company he did a large and profitable business, besides placing large risks with the Lancashire, Norwich Union Fire, Commercial Union, and other well-known Fire Offices. Later on Mr. Haslam added an Agency for the National Provident Institution, and proved very successful in that branch. His Accident Insurance experience began with the Imperial Union Accident Assurance Company. He resigned his commercial situation in 1889 to take up his present appointment, in which he has given every satisfaction. His District comprises Nottinghamshire, Derbyshire, Lincolnshire, and Rutland. Mr. Haslam attributes his success to his having had the Agencies always before him, and to the many introductions he obtained through his former business engagements. He is one of the best known Insurance men of his District.

ROBERT HATTON.

H. S. HAYWARD.

Hatton, Robert, is the late Local Secretary of the North British and Mercantile Insurance Company at Dublin. Mr. Hatton acquired his first professional experience in the office of Mr. F. G. P. Neison, the eminent London Actuary, and assisted that gentleman to a very considerable degree in the compilation of the tables in his work on Railway Accidents, while associated with him in the office of the Medical, Invalid and General Insurance Company, in which he received an appointment. During the same period Mr. Hatton also passed the first and second examinations of the Institute of Actuaries, but was debarred from entering for the third examination by reason of his removal to Liverpool to take up the duties of Assistant Actuary to the Royal, in which capacity he did good work for the latter Company. After a service of some years' duration with the Royal Mr. Hatton became Actuary to the London and Southwark Insurance Corporation, and drew up the premium tables for that Office. He removed to Dublin a few years later as Resident Secretary to the Life Association of Scotland, resigning that after seven years to take up a similar post for the North British and Mercantile, which he held for a period of fourteen years until May, 1890. Mr. Hatton's retirement was greatly regretted by his Directors. He enjoys the advantage of an acquaintance with most of the leading European languages.

Hayward, H. S., Agency Inspector and Surveyor to the Economic Fire Office, Limited, at its branch at Norwich, is a native of Norwich, and after receiving his education in the Octagon Higher Grade School and School of Art, was apprenticed to a firm of surveyors, valuers, and accountants in that city. After serving his time he was employed in the same profession on several of the largest estates in Norfolk and Suffolk, and then commenced his Insurance career with the Commercial Union Assurance Company by opening up a branch for that Company for the Eastern Counties, in which he served first as surveyor, and after two years as chief clerk, surveyor, and assistant inspector of Agents. He afterwards started business for himself as estate agent and surveyor, and then joined the Glasgow and London Insurance Company for a time, finally taking service with the Economic Fire Office, Limited, at their Eastern Counties Branch, for which he still continues to act.

JOHN HEGGIE.

A. W. HENRY.

Heggie, John, the District Manager to the Marine and General Mutual Life Assurance Society for Glasgow and the West of Scotland, was born in Kinrosshire, Scotland, in 1859, and commenced his business life at the age of sixteen as clerk in a large Commercial establishment in Glasgow. After four years' service he obtained an appointment in the Head Office of the Scottish Amicable Life Assurance Society at Glasgow, where he remained for ten years, during which time he received a valuable training in Actuarial, correspondence, and general routine work under the late Mr. Marr. He left the Scottish Amicable Life Assurance Society in the early part of 1889, having received testimonials from the Manager, Secretary, and Head Office Staff, and took up outdoor work in Belfast for various American Companies. So successful was he in this business that it was not long before he received an offer of an appointment from the Scottish Metropolitan Life Assurance Company, which he accepted, and, as Resident Secretary of that Company's Belfast Branch, undertook the opening up and supervision of its Irish business. He was appointed to his present post on November 1st, 1891.

Henry, Arthur W., is the District Manager of the Manchester Branch of the Provident Life Office, which position he has held for several years, and, until recently, held the dual appointment of District Manager for both the Manchester and Liverpool Branches, including the County Fire Office at the latter Branch. The Liverpool Branch is now a separate charge. Mr. Henry has had a varied and successful experience, and enjoys the esteem and confidence of all with whom he has been associated.

HENRY HERDMAN.

W. E. HERBERT.

Herdman, Henry, is the Local Secretary at Belfast of the North of Ireland Branch of the North British and Mercantile Insurance Company, a post which he has held for over four years, having been appointed to it in 1887.

Mr. Herdman is a member of a family who have long been identified with the staple trade of Ulster, as flax spinners, &c., and after a considerable business experience, gained in connection with the linen industry, he ultimately devoted his attention to Insurance work, for which he first had some training as Agent for the West of England Fire and Life Insurance Company, afterwards becoming Secretary for the Local Branch of the Standard Fire Office. When the latter Company relinquished business in 1884, Mr. Herdman secured an agency from the Royal, acting at the same time as that Company's Surveyor for Ulster, a position which he occupied until becoming connected with the North British and Mercantile.

———

Herbert, W. E., is the District Manager at Glasgow of the Mutual Life Insurance Company of New York. Mr. Herbert, who received his Insurance training in English offices, was in 1872 appointed Superintendent of Agencies for Great Britain for the New York Life Insurance Company, from which post he was promoted in the following year to that of Manager of the Company's Branch for Scotland, resident in Glasgow. This position he held till 1887, when he joined his present Company as District Manager for Glasgow and the West of Scotland, commencing operations in January, 1888.

EDWARD ERNEST HESLEWOOD.

A. HEYWARD.

Heslewood, Edward Ernest, is the Resident Secretary at Hull of the Yorkshire Insurance Company, who was appointed to this position in 1880, at which time the district was made into a Branch, the Company having previously conducted its business here through agents. Mr. Heslewood had previously been a member of the important mercantile firm of T. W. Flint and Co., in which he had gained an experience and business connection that has since been invaluable in his business with the Yorkshire of this district. He is a gentleman of much ability and great personal popularity, and under his able direction this Branch has become one of the most important tributaries of the Yorkshire.

————

Heyward, A., is the Local Secretary at Bristol of the Scottish Provident Institution, and who has been connected with this Office for over 20 years, during the early part of this time as a highly successful Agent, and latterly in his present position. Mr. Heyward was formerly in the banking business, which he left for the purpose of giving his entire attention to Life Insurance.

GEORGE HICKS.

J. D. HILL.

Hicks, George, is the District Manager at the Manchester Branch of the London Assurance Corporation. About thirty years ago Mr. Hicks entered the office of a firm of Ship and Insurance Brokers and Underwriters at Lloyd's. In 1872, when the Trident Marine Insurance Company was formed, Mr. Hicks was appointed its first Deputy-Underwriter. He afterwards held a similar position in the London Office of the North China Insurance Company under Mr. J. S. Mackintosh, who, in 1883, was appointed Underwriter to the London Assurance Corporation. In 1875 Mr. Hicks was offered and accepted the Manchester Agency of the North China Insurance Company. In the twelve years during which he looked after the interests of its Manchester Agency, Mr. Hicks largely developed the connection of the North China. In 1887 Mr. Hicks was appointed Manager at the Manchester Branch of the London Assurance Corporation, an Office transacting Fire, Life and Marine business, and with a long and honourable career.

Mr. Hicks is well known in Manchester in connection with the Manchester Ship Canal, a project the importance of which he endeavoured as early as 1876 to impress upon the citizens of Manchester and surrounding towns. In the spring of 1877, in response to an influentially-signed requisition, Mr. Hicks and the late Mr. Hamilton H. Fulton, C.E., of London, were specially invited to lay before the Directors of the Manchester Chamber of Commerce their views as to the practicability of constructing a waterway to Manchester, available for ocean-going vessels, and as to the commercial prospects of such waterway if completed. After the interview the Directors of the Chamber of Commerce passed a resolution in favour of the scheme, providing it could be carried out without prejudice to existing interests. Mr. Hicks was one of the first and most active promoters of the movement, which resulted in the formation of the now historic Provisional Committee and of the Ship Canal Parliamentary Subscription Fund. At the first meeting of shareholders, after the passing of the Manchester Ship Canal Act of 1885, Mr. Hicks was appointed one of the Auditors of the Company, his colleague being Mr. Bodin T. Leech, now known as Mr. Alderman Leech, present Mayor of Manchester. These two gentlemen still retain the confidence of the shareholders as Auditors of the Company.

Mr. Hicks is also known in Manchester as an active supporter of various social and educational movements.

Hill, J. D., Secretary to the Alliance Insurance Company at its Sheffield Branch, commenced his Insurance career in the service of the Liverpool and London and Globe Insurance Company, at their Manchester Branch in 1872. There he remained till 1875 when he joined the staff of the Branch Office of the Alliance Insurance Company in the same city, till 1877, when he was transferred, still as a subordinate, to the Sheffield Branch of the same office. In 1885 he was appointed to the position of Secretary to the Alliance at their Branch at Newcastle-on-Tyne, which post he held till 1887, when he was again promoted, going back to his old office at Sheffield, as Secretary. Mr. Hill is an able official and thoroughly understands the business, which has considerably increased under his management.

The district of the Alliance under the management at Sheffield, is a wide and important one, embracing the whole of Yorkshire and Derbyshire, and portions of Notts and Lincolnshire.

EDWARD HILL.

B. H. HILTON.

Hill, Edward, is the Underwriter of the Marine Department of the South British Insurance Company of New Zealand at its London Head Office. He is a member of Lloyd's of very considerable standing, having entered it in the year 1857, where he received his early training under Mr. Hyslop, the father of the present Underwriter of the Merchants' Marine Insurance Company. After a period of about seven years, Mr. Hill then obtained the appointment of Deputy-Underwriter to the National Provincial Company, which post he held from 1864 to 1868, subsequently serving the Globe Marine Insurance Company in the same capacity from 1870 to 1882. He commenced his connection with the South British and National Insurance Companies in 1883, and on the retirement of the latter Company from its association with the South British in June, 1892, he continued to act for the last-named Company.

Hilton, B. H., is the Resident Secretary at Liverpool of the Crown Life Office, now the Law Union and Crown, which post he has held since 1865. Mr. Hilton is a Liverpool man by birth, and when he commenced his Insurance career there were but very few Life Offices represented in the Liverpool District, and he may be said to have been a pioneer of organised and systematic local effort in that department of Insurance. He has been very successful, and has succeeded in building up a very large business for his Company in Liverpool and its vicinity.

HENRY HOARE.

MATTHEW C. HINSHAW.

Hoare, Henry, the District Manager to the Scottish Alliance Insurance Company at Manchester, first entered the Head Office of the Lancashire Insurance Company, at Manchester, as an apprentice, in 1871. There he remained for eighteen years, during which period he passed through the various departments in the Home and Foreign Fire business, finally becoming the Chief Surveyor. Mr. Hoare, during the whole of his career with the Lancashire, had the advantage of serving under the able supervision of Mr. Stewart, who enjoys the credit of having trained many of the leading Insurance men of the day; and that this service had good results in his case was amply shown by his being selected from amongst a large body of candidates for the post which he now holds of District Manager to the Scottish Alliance Insurance Company, when that Company opened business in Manchester, in 1889.

———

Hinshaw, Matthew C., is the Chief Agent and Branch Manager for the Atlas Assurance Company, and the National Assurance Company of Ireland, at their Chief Office for the Dominion of Canada at Montreal. Mr. Hinshaw is a gentleman well and favourably known to the Insurance fraternity, and previous to his removal to Canada in the above capacity, occupied the post of Resident Secretary to the Atlas at their Glasgow Branch.

GEORGE HOBSON.

JOHN HOBBS.

Hobson, George, is the Agency Superintendent of the National Provident Institution for their Midland Counties District. Mr. Hobson commenced his Insurance experience in the Yorkshire Branch of the Life Association of Scotland, with which office he remained until 1880, when he obtained the appointment of Agency Inspector for the Edinburgh Life Office. This post he held for four years, gaining great credit for himself with the Directors for the large amount of new business which he obtained for the Association, but at the end of that period in 1884, he resigned his post in order to take up his present duties with the National Provident Institution. He has since, by his energetic supervision, succeeded in very largely increasing the business of the Institution, as well as very widely extending their Agency connection. Mr. Hobson is a Member of the Council of the Birmingham Insurance Institute, and has contributed an Address on "Life Competition" at one of its meetings.

———

Hobbs, John, Resident Secretary of the Bristol, West of England and South Wales Branches, at Bristol, of the Imperial Insurance Company, Limited, has been in the service of the Company since 1851, first as its Agent, and subsequently, when in 1885 the Imperial Insurance Company, owing to its increasing business determined to open a regular Branch at Bristol, in his present capacity of Resident Secretary. Mr. Hobbs also acts as Resident Secretary to the Imperial Life Office, carrying on business in the same building.

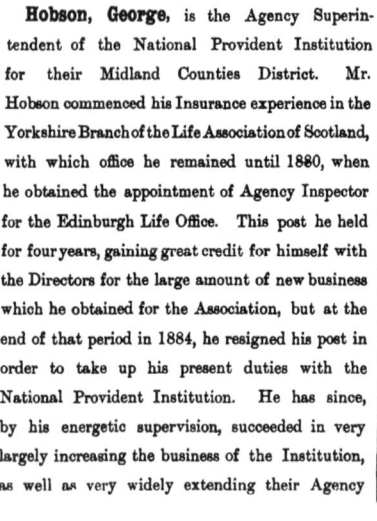

JAMES HOPPER

GEORGE E. HORE.

Hopper, James, is the District Manager at Newcastle-upon-Tyne of the Sun Fire and Life Offices. Mr. Hopper has had twenty-five years' Insurance experience, having entered the service of the Leeds Branch of the Liverpool and London and Globe Company in March, 1867 ; subsequently he was with the Scottish Commercial and other Offices in Manchester. He has held his present appointment since the opening of this Branch, upwards of four years ago, previously having for some time held an appointment as District Inspector to the Sun Life Office in the Northern counties.

Houston, Robert M., is the Local Secretary of the National Assurance Company of Ireland at their Branch Office at Leeds. He commenced his career in the Insurance profession in the service of the Scottish National at Glasgow in 1876, and on that office not very long afterwards becoming part of the Scottish Union and National, Mr. Houston, who had by that time received a thoroughly efficient training under the able supervision of Mr. J. K. Macdonald, the present Chief Secretary

of the company, he was recommended by that gentleman for the appointment to the Chief Clerkship of the Company's Yorkshire branch, situate at Bradford, whither he removed in 1880. He remained there for a period of three years, and having subsequently acted as Surveyor to the Leeds branch of the Norwich Union for another two years, joined the National of Ireland in his present capacity in 1885. Mr. Houston's district comprises North Yorkshire, Durham, and Northumberland, and his appointment has proved very profitable to his company.

Hore, George E., is the Resident Secretary of the Queen Insurance Company, at their Midland Branch at Birmingham. Mr. Hore has passed the whole of his Insurance career in the employment of the Queen, having joined the Head Office staff in Liverpool in 1865, whence after serving the Company there in various capacities, latterly as Surveyor, he was promoted to his present post at Birmingham in 1876. The results of his appointment have since been very satisfactory to the Company.

G. W. HORSFIELD.

T. ABBOTT HOWE.

Horsfield, George William, the Eastern Counties Manager for the Mutual Life Insurance Company of New York, comes from an Insurance family, being the eldest son of Mr. George Horsfield, of Hitchin, a well-known Hertfordshire Insurance Broker and Superintendent to the Railway Passengers' Assurance Company. He received his education partly at Hitchin, completing it with two years spent in France, and two in Brussels and Bonn. He was then for a time in the Consular Service in Beyrout, Syria, whence he had the opportunity of visiting various parts of Turkey, Russia, Spain, and the north coast of Africa. He finally adopted his father's profession, and after an apprenticeship under that gentleman, he was in 1886 appointed Inspector of Agents under the London Office of the Provincial Life Insurance Company. Leaving that Office in 1889, he became Agency Inspector to the Provident Life Office, in which capacity he succeeded by energetic work in effecting a material increase of the business of the District under his charge. This appointment he held till late in 1891, when

he accepted his present post with the Mutual Life of New York, having under his supervision the counties of Norfolk, Suffolk, Cambridge, Essex, Hertfordshire, Bedfordshire, and Huntingdonshire, with his headquarters at Ipswich.

Howe, T. Abbott, the Local Secretary of the Suffolk and Essex District of the Gresham Life Assurance Society, was born at West Hoe, Plymouth, in 1841, being the eldest son of Mr. Thos. P. Howe, late Head Master of Christ's Hospital Boarding School at Ipswich. He served for upwards of twenty years in the Ipswich Bank of Messrs. Bacon, Cobbold and Co., subsequently becoming District Superintendent at Ipswich of the British Equitable Life Assurance Company. This post he held for three years and a half until the beginning of 1891, when he was appointed to his present one. Mr. T. Abbott Howe is the author of several interesting works, amongst them being "Homely Readings for Leisure Hours," "Characteristics of Human Life," "Every-day Philosophies," &c.

CAPT. C. E. M. HUDSON.

THOMAS HOWELL.

Hudson, C. E. Mogridge, is Chief Inspector of the Scottish Metropolitan Life at its London Office. Born of an old Worcestershire county family, at the age of fourteen he started in life as Midshipman in an East Indiaman; at seventeen Officer of a Watch, then through the different grades to command, passing from sailing ships to the Mail services, and then to the Queensland Navy, on retiring from which, in 1886, he took up Life Assurance, commencing as Inspector at the London Office of the Scottish Economic, just then opened by Mr. Edward T. Clifford, the Resident Secretary. He remained an official of that young but energetic office until it was amalgamated with the Scottish Metropolitan, when he transferred his services to the absorbing office, where he has remained until the present time.

During his service at sea, Mr. Hudson was always known as a good organizer and correct navigator, and in 1880, in consequence of an essay read before the Society upon "The Probable Path of Cyclones on the Mozambique Coast," which paper the Portuguese Admiralty had translated in Portuguese for distribution to the ships of their Mozambique Squadron, he was offered the Fellowship of "The Royal Meteorological Society."

Twenty years passed at sea, and in every country of the world, amongst all kinds and classes of people, is not to anyone of observation a bad training for gaining a knowledge of men and their actions and cultivating that nice tact which are such valuable qualities in the Inspectional work of a Life Office; and the subject of our sketch, of good address, courteous manners, and happy conversational power, has turned such knowledge to good account since he has been in the Assurance world.

Howell, Thomas, Assessor of Losses by Fire at Birmingham, commenced his career as an Auctioneer and Valuer in 1848, and having acquired extensive experience in bankruptcy and general work, in 1863 turned his attention to the Assessment of Losses by Fire, the first business of that kind being entrusted to him by the Royal Insurance Company. His theoretical knowledge of most of the trades of the Midland district has been of essential service to him in that capacity, and having gradually gained the confidence of other Insurance Companies, he has built up for himself a reputable position in the Insurance world. He is now the senior partner in the firm of Thomas Howell and Co., 112, Colmore Row, Birmingham (his colleagues being Mr. F. R. Sutton, formerly connected with the Lancashire Insurance Company, and his brother, Mr. Frederick Howell), and there are few provincial offices enjoying a larger practice.

R. W. HUIE.

F. HUTCHINS

Huie, Richard William, Resident Secretary of the Northern Accident Insurance Company, Limited, at Edinburgh, the first and only Secretary the Company has had there, was appointed to the post in 1882, a few months after the Company commenced business, and is therefore one of its oldest officials. Previous to obtaining the appointment his Insurance experience was that of an Agent, and he very successfully represented and still represents a number of Fire and Life Insurance Companies—the National Provident Institution, the North British and Mercantile Insurance Company, the Norwich Union Fire and Life Insurance Company, and the Alliance Assurance Company being his chief Companies.

Mr. Huie is not only an Insurance official but also occupies the post of Joint Agent of the Commercial Bank of Scotland, Limited, Greenside Branch, Edinburgh ; he is also a Director of the Edinburgh and Portobello Cemetery Company, Limited, and Managing Director of the Edinburgh Solvo Laundry Company, Limited. The fact that he occupies other posts of importance, besides being Secretary of the "Northern," has in no way acted injuriously to its interests, Mr. Huie's character being such that the more there is for him to do the more thoroughly it is done.

Mr. Huie is a retired Major of Artillery Volunteers, and is Honorary Treasurer of the East of Scotland Tactical Society.

Hutchins, F., Branch Manager of the Royal Exchange Assurance in Bristol, entered the insurance profession at the age of 20 as a junior in the head office of the Commercial Union Assurance Company, and after two years' service was promoted to the Chief Clerkship of that Company's Branch at Dublin. There he spent seven years, undertaking in addition the duties of Life Inspector and Surveyor. During that period he had opportunities of acquiring a useful practical experience of branch work, especially in surveying, as, during his stay in Ireland, his Office revised the whole of its fire business, which necessitated the furnishing of plans and reports of all risks of importance on the books. In 1887 he was transferred to a similar position in the same Company's Bristol Branch, and in the following year was successful in securing, against much competition, the appointment of Manager to the newly-opened Branch of the Royal Exchange Assurance, which he now holds. Since then, under his management, the development of the Branch has been rapid and the working successful.

MATTHEW IRVING

W E. C. HUTTON.

Irving, Matthew, is the joint Resident Secretary at Manchester of the Royal Insurance Company. Mr. Irving was appointed Fire Surveyor at the Manchester Branch of the Queen Insurance Company in May, 1862, and in June, 1872, was promoted and associated with the late John Kingsley as joint Secretary, under the style of Kingsley and Irving, and on the death of his colleague, in February, 1888, he assumed the sole management of the Branch, which he held up to the time of the amalgamation of the Queen with the Royal, at which time he received his present appointment. Mr. Irving is acknowledged to be a gentleman of much skill as an Insurance expert,

and of large practical knowledge of the special risks with which the district abounds.

Hutton, W. E. C., the Resident Secretary to the Imperial Fire and Imperial Life Offices at their joint Branch Office at Imperial Buildings, Liverpool, was educated at Cheltenham College, and obtained his Insurance training at the Head Office of his present Company; where he remained until 1882, when he was transferred to the staff of the Liverpool Office; and, in the following year, received the appointment of Resident Secretary. Under Mr. Hutton's supervision, the high position always held by the Imperial in Liverpool has been fully maintained.

J. M. C. JOHNSTON.

A. K. HOLROYD.

Johnston, John M. C., is the Secretary in London of the Yorkshire Insurance Company. Mr. Johnston is the son of Mr. J. B. Johnston, the first London Manager for the Royal Insurance Company, which Company he himself entered in 1869, and worked his way up to be head of their agency department in 1876. In 1880, he was selected by the Scottish Commercial Insurance Company, as Secretary to their London Board ; and in the same year, on the amalgamation of that Company with the Lancashire Insurance Company, was sent over to Ireland on a special mission to consolidate the agency connections of the two Offices, and to take charge for a time of the Irish Branch. Whilst in Dublin, he received an offer from the Yorkshire to return to London to open a Branch there for that Company, and to take charge of their business in the Southern half of England. He accepted the offer, and became the first Secretary of the Yorkshire London Branch in 1880, where he has since remained, largely developing the Company's Southern business.

Holroyd, Arthur Kirkby, the Secretary in London of the Equitable Fire and Accident Office of Manchester, was appointed to his present position on the resignation of Mr. L. Beecher Cowin, in 1887. His Insurance career commenced in 1865, in which year he became a member of the staff of the Yorkshire Office (at Leeds) of the Liverpool and London and Globe Insurance Company (Fire Department). He resigned his position here in 1873, to join the Head Office Staff of the Mutual Fire Office in Manchester, and was subsequently promoted to be their Assistant Secretary. This he left on receiving his present appointment.

A. C. IMRIE.

HAROLD V. JAMES.

Imrie, Andrew C., is the Resident Secretary of the Scottish Temperance Life and Accident Assurance Company at its Manchester branch. His first connection with Insurance was when residing in the North of Scotland he was attracted by the special benefits to abstainers given by the Scottish Temperance. He became an active agent of the Company, and on his removal to Glasgow in 1888, he received the appointment of Inspector of Agents at the Head Office. Mr. Imrie, by perseverance, was able to show a good record of proposals completed, and when in the beginning of 1891 the Directors decided to open a branch in Manchester, he was appointed Resident Secretary.

Since his appointment he has made the Scottish Temperance well known in Manchester ; after carefully preparing the ground, he is beginning to reap the fruits of his labour, and they have proved to be most satisfactory. Lancashire men are appreciating the benefits of reduced rates to abstainers.

James, Harold V., the Resident Secretary at Bristol of the Scottish Alliance Insurance Company, Limited, received his Insurance training in the office of Grahame H. Wills, Insurance Broker, Bristol, and in the Bristol Branch of the City of London Fire Insurance Company, Limited.

WILLIAM JOPSON.

J. MUIR LEITCH.

Jopson, William, London Manager of the Scottish Alliance Fire and Accident Insurance Company, has now occupied that important position since October, 1889. Previous to taking up his present appointment, he was for a period of seven years Manager and Secretary of the London and County Fire Office. On his resignation of that post to enter the service of the Scottish Alliance, Mr. Jopson was presented by his late directors with a handsome testimonial of plate, together with an illuminated address, which we quote in full, as evidence of Mr. Jopson's work, and of the esteem in which he has been always held by those whom he has served :—

"To WILLIAM JOPSON, ESQ.

"We, the undersigned directors, forming the whole board of the *London and County* Fire Insurance Company, Limited, desire to testify our high appreciation of the invaluable services you have rendered to the company during the period of nearly seven years in which you have held the office of secretary.

"By your energy, perseverance, tact and shrewdness, you have succeeded in increasing the company's business to twenty-five times the amount of premiums acquired at the time you took office, and this in spite of the great disadvantages under which you laboured through the smallness of the capital, and our congratulations are due to you on the general character and results of the business obtained by you under such trying circumstances. You have crowned your work by conducting in the most able manner the delicate negotiations required to bring the company to a satisfactory and honourable end, by amalgamating with a larger and more important company, and thus deserved and obtained the best thanks of the board and shareholders.

"In conclusion, we beg to tender our best wishes for your success in your new position and the whole of your professional career, which our thorough knowledge of your experience, attainments and natural ability, leads us to confidently anticipate will be an unusually brilliant one.

"London, the 31st of October, 1889.

"(Signed,)   *John Cronkshaw,* Chairman. *Hugh Hyslop, Thomas Moreton, G. F. Turtle, John Stephenson, R. B. Starr, P. E. Roberts.*"

Leitch, J. Muir, is the London Secretary of the Scottish Provident Institution, which appointment he has held for over 34 years. Mr. Leitch is held in high esteem by his Directors and by the Insurance fraternity at large.

ARTHUR LAWTON.

CHARLES LEES.

Lawton, Arthur, the Secretary of the West End Branch (London) of the Caledonian Insurance Company of Edinburgh, was born in London in the year 1852. At the age of 20 (in May, 1872) he joined the staff of the London Office of the Standard Life, with which he remained for over five years, leaving in November, 1877, on being appointed a member of the staff of the West End Office of the Life Association of Scotland. On this he remained till he received his first outdoor appointment, which was the Inspectorship of Agents of the Sun Life Office. Two years later he was appointed Superintendent of Agents for the Eastern Counties by the National Provident Institution. In May, 1888, he was offered and accepted his present appointment, commencing his duties on the first of July of that year, and has made a very successful record, having been able through his energy, influence, and connections to largely increase and extend the business of the Company in the district of which he has charge.

Mr. Lawton has taken advantage of every oppor-

tunity his various appointments have given him to acquire a thorough knowledge of the theoretical as well as the practical business of Life Insurance, and the results of the knowledge thus acquired are now apparent. Among his colleagues thus fairly universally acknowledged, it is generally understood that he is on the threshold of a high career.

———

Lees, Charles, is the Secretary in London of the Caledonian Fire and Life Insurance Office of Edinburgh. His business and Insurance career commenced in 1863, when he entered the office of the Lancashire Insurance Company. Six years afterwards (in 1869) he was appointed the Surveyor of the Manchester Office of the Alliance Insurance Company, which position he resigned in 1878 to become Secretary to the Manchester Branch of the Caledonian, and this he held until the year 1884, when he was appointed to his present position.

W. J. JEFFERSON.

HUGH S. JEFFERSON.

Jefferson, W. J., Resident Secretary to the Royal Insurance Company at their Belfast Branch, commenced in 1863 as a Clerk in the North of Ireland Branch of the North British and Mercantile at Belfast, at a time when Insurance work was carried on in all the old-fashioned semi-organized fashions now scarcely known in the profession. He remained for five years with the North British and Mercantile, at the end of which period he accepted an appointment as Agent to the Scottish Imperial Fire and Life Company, which post he held till 1870. In 1871, the Liverpool and London and Globe, which had previously retired from the North of Ireland, resumed operations there, and Mr. Jefferson had an important position in connection with their Belfast agency. In 1879, the Queen Insurance Company, which retired from Ireland in 1869, likewise returned to business there, and appointed Mr. Jefferson Resident Secretary, the district under his control being subsequently extended to embrace Dublin. Since then he has transacted a most satisfactory business for the Queen in both the Fire and Life Departments, while at the same time he has won golden opinions for his readiness to assist all who come to him for advice about insuring, and for the general courtesy and consideration of his manner towards everyone with whom he is brought into contact, whether rivals or otherwise. In the changes which have followed the amalgamation of the Royal and Queen offices, Mr. Jefferson has succeeded to the Resident Secretaryship of the Royal at Belfast.

Jefferson, Hugh S., is the Resident Secretary of the British Empire Mutual Life Assurance Company at Belfast. Mr. Jefferson is an Ulster man, the son of a gentleman engaged in the linen trade, and after having completed his education at Foyle College, Londonderry, joined his father until the retirement of the latter from business owing to ill-health. On that event taking place, Mr. Jefferson undertook the Chief Agency at Londonderry, for the English and Scottish Law Life Office, which was then vacant, acting at the same time as Agent for the Phœnix Fire and the Northern Accident Insurance Company. In 1887 the Resident Secretaryship of his present Office becoming vacant, he was appointed to it, and has continued to occupy it ever since. Mr. Jefferson's relations with his Directors have always been of the most friendly character, and owing entirely to his exertions on behalf of the British Empire Mutual Life Assurance Company, that Office is daily increasing in popularity and confidence in the North of Ireland district over which he has the supervision.

T. W. JAMIESON.

JOSEPH A. JENKINS.

Jamieson, Thomas W., is the Local Manager of the North British and Mercantile Insurance Company at their Birmingham Branch. He received his early training in the Newcastle Branch of his present Company, where he remained for thirteen years, at the end of that period being appointed Resident Secretary in that city to the Guardian Assurance Company. He subsequently resigned that position to return to the North British and Mercantile in his present capacity in 1886, in succession to the late Mr. M. Smart, since which time the Birmingham Branch has made very satisfactory progress under his supervision.

Jenkins, Joseph A., is the Resident Secretary of the Midland Branch of the Scottish Union and National Insurance Company at Birmingham. He was, previous to obtaining his present appointment, for many years first in the Birmingham Branch and afterwards in the Head Office of the Alliance Assurance Company. He succeeded to Mr. Andrewes in his present post in 1886, on that gentleman's promotion to the management of the Company's Glasgow Branch, since which time Mr. Jenkins has succeeded most satisfactorily in maintaining both the growth and the quality of the business bequeathed to him by his predecessor.

M. PENNANT JONES.

R. G. JENKINSON.

Jones, Myddleton Pennant, is the District Manager of the Wrexham Branch of the Economic Fire Office, Limited. He was educated at the Royal Institution School, Liverpool, and commenced his Insurance career in 1883 in the Liverpool Branch of the Alliance Assurance Company. In 1885 he was appointed a Clerk in the Chancery Lane Branch of the Alliance. This position he relinquished in 1886 to enter the office of his father, Mr. William Jones, a Land and Estate Agent and leading Fire Assessor and Surveyor in Liverpool. Here he obtained valuable experience in the assessing and surveying of all classes of fire losses, and the knowledge so gained has since stood him in good stead. In 1888 he was appointed Chief Clerk and Surveyor to the Liverpool Branch of the Economic Fire Office, Limited, and in June of the same year Acting District Manager. This position he continued to hold until September, 1889. Early in 1890 the Company promoted Mr. Jones to the office of Agency Inspector for Wales, with offices at Wrexham, and this appointment was enlarged the following year to District Manager of the Wrexham Branch.

Jenkinson, R. G., is the Resident Secretary of the General Accident Assurance Corporation of Perth, at its Branch Office at Manchester. He commenced his career in the Insurance profession in 1885, as Inspector of Agents to the Scottish Accident Insurance Company, under the Manchester Branch of that Company, then under the management of Mr. Arthur B. Scholfield, who is now again his District Manager for the General Accident Assurance Corporation, a mutual confidence then springing up between the two men which has never since been relaxèd. Mr. Jenkinson then left the Scottish Accident Insurance Company to take up the duties of Inspector of Agents to the Pelican Life Office, which post he held till December, 1888, when he was appointed to his present position under his former chief. Mr. Jenkinson works hand in glove with Mr. Scholfield, the satisfactory result of their unanimity being shown in the fact that they have together worked up their branch to be one of the most important belonging to the Company, their district, which originally included only a portion of Lancashire, now embracing the greater part of four counties, and the business being of a most flourishing and productive nature.

G. J. JOHNSON.

SIDNEY JEWSBURY.

Johnson, George James, is the Local Manager at Manchester of the General Assurance Company. Mr. Johnson, who is a native of London, went to Manchester as a boy, and subsequently entered the service of an eminent firm of calico printers, with whom he remained for some years. At that time, the General was locally represented by an Agency, held by the late Alderman Bancroft. In 1886 a Branch office was opened in Market Place, under Mr. Johnson's management.

Mr. Johnson is well known and highly respected in the city of his adoption. During the twenty-two years of his connection with the General, he has been very successful in extending its business in both departments, the average loss ratio being very moderate, and the average result profitable to the Company.

Jewsbury, Sidney, the Resident Secretary of the West of England Fire and Life Insurance Company at Manchester, is the grandson of the founder of the original Agency of the West of England in that city, and son of the late Mr. Thomas Jewsbury, who, with his brother, Mr. Frank Jewsbury, did much in their time to extend and make popular the business which their father had built up for their Company. Mr. Sidney Jewsbury at first succeeded to the Agency, but a few years after his accession to the post, the Directors determining to transform the Agency into a Branch Office on the modern system, he was promoted to his present position. Mr. Sidney Jewsbury has received the whole of his Insurance education in the service of the West of England Insurance Company. He has also occupied a seat at the Board of the Lancashire and Yorkshire Accident Insurance Company since its formation, and is Chairman of the Guardian Plate Glass Insurance Company. He is well known as a practical Insurance Expert, and is a gentleman of very considerable scientific attainments.

OWEN D. JONES.

R. D. JONES.

Jones, Owen D., is the Resident Secretary at Newcastle-on-Tyne of the London and Lancashire Fire Insurance Company. The Insurance experience of Mr. Jones dates from 1876, when he entered the service of the Northern Counties of England Fire Office, with which Company he remained until 1879. From 1880 to 1885 he was Chief Clerk in the Newcastle Branch of the Northern Assurance Company, and from 1885 to 1887 he was Chief Clerk and Surveyor in the Liverpool Branch of the Northern, which post he left in August, 1887, to accept his present appointment.

Jones, R. D., is the Local Manager of the Royal Insurance Company at its Branch Office at Shrewsbury. Mr. Jones is a native of that town, having been born and educated there; and when his education was completed joined the staff of the Shropshire and North Wales Fire Office in the early part of the year 1880. From 1883 to 1889 he held the position of Chief Clerk of that Company. When the Shropshire and North Wales and its contemporary, the Salop, became the property of the Alliance, in 1889, Mr. Jones was appointed as Manager of the Branch then opened by the Royal in Shrewsbury, which position he now holds.

W. S. JONES.

W. R. JONES.

Jones, W. Southwell, the Local Manager of the South Wales and Monmouthshire Branch of the North British and Mercantile Insurance Company, has passed the whole of his Insurance career in the service of that Company, having entered the London Office in 1878. Here he remained for ten years in the Town Office, at the end of which period he occupied the position of second clerk in that department. In 1888 the Directors of the Company having decided to open a Branch Office for the South Wales and Monmouthshire District with a Local Board of Directors, Mr. Jones was sent to carry out the work, and on its accomplishment and the opening of the Branch was promoted to his present post.

Jones, William R., is the Resident Secretary of the Caledonian Insurance Company at their Branch Office at Liverpool. Mr. Jones was not originally destined for the Insurance profession, but for the shipping trade, and was for a number of years partner in the firm of Messrs. Robertson, Cruikshank and Co., shipowners, of Liverpool. That firm, however, also acted as Resident Secretaries for the Caledonian, but resigned on the dissolution of the partnership in April, 1889. Mr. Jones was then appointed Resident Secretary, working in conjunction with Mr. James Murray, the Resident Manager of the Company for the Manchester, Liverpool and Leeds districts. Mr. Jones is well-known and highly respected both in Insurance and Mercantile circles at Liverpool, and his personal influence and his wide connection have enabled him to secure his Company a good share of the business of the District.

T. J. JONES.

JAMES KEDDIE.

Jones, T. J., is the Resident Secretary of the Gresham Life Assurance Society at Birmingham. Mr. Jones was for some time Local Manager of the London and Lancashire Life Assurance Company also at Birmingham. He next joined the English and Scottish Law Life Assurance Association as District Secretary of their Bristol Branch, in which position he remained for a period of two and a half years, eventually returning to Birmingham in June, 1888, to take up the post of Local Manager there for the same office. In that capacity he still further increased the business of the Branch, already large when he took it over, and very largely extended the Agency connection. He resigned his post with the English and Scottish to accept his present appointment with the Gresham.

Keddie, James, is the Resident Secretary of the Scottish Equitable Life Assurance Society at their Manchester Branch. Mr. Keddie is a Scotchman by birth, and received his early training in the Insurance profession in the Edinburgh and London Offices of the City of Glasgow Life Assurance Company. He subsequently left the service of that Company to accept the appointment of Agency Inspector of the Scottish Equitable, from which post he was promoted very shortly afterwards to that which he now occupies. This was in 1879, and since that time Mr. Keddie's success in the Manchester District has been very great, he having made his Branch one of the most progressive of those possessed by the Society.

WALTER KEMBER, F.I.A.

BRUCE KELLY.

Kember, Walter, F.I.A., is the Resident Secretary at Liverpool of the Scottish Amicable Life Assurance Society. Mr. Kember, who received his present appointment in 1884, upon the opening of the Branch, is a gentleman of considerable theoretical and practical experience ; and, with the support of an influential Local Board, we understand he has been very successful in building up and maintaining a business. He was formerly, for sixteen years, in the London office of the same Society ; and he has the distinction of being a Fellow (by examination) of the Institute of Actuaries.

———

Kelly, Bruce, is the Resident Secretary at Newcastle-on-Tyne of the Northern Assurance Company. Mr. Kelly commenced his early Insurance career at the Head Office of the Scottish Union in Edinburgh, 'and was subsequently appointed District Manager to the Commercial Union at Bristol, which latter city he left to take up the responsible position he now holds at this important Branch.

R. A. KENNEDY, J.P.

ALEX D. KENNEDY.

Kennedy, Robert A., is Resident Secretary of the Liverpool and London and Globe Insurance Company in their Branch Office at Manchester. When, in 1854, the Company instituted its Manchester Branch, with a local Board of Directors, the management of the Branch was put into the charge of Mr. Robert A. Kennedy, and ever since, under his fostering care, the business of his Branch has been one of steady and continuous growth. Mr. Kennedy is a Manchester man, coming of an old family which has long been established in that town as cotton spinners. He is a gentleman of influence and position in the district, and one of the Magistrates of the city. Few men are better known in the higher circles of Manchester society than Mr. Robert A. Kennedy, J.P., and there cannot be the slightest doubt that the Liverpool and London and Globe have derived many advantages from the influential connection and the perseverance and energy which he has, perhaps more so than most men in a like position, been able to apply to the extension of an important business in an important district. Over two years ago Mr. Kennedy was elected to a seat at the Board of the Lancashire and Yorkshire Accident Insurance Company, and has, ever since its formation, taken a warm and consistent interest in the Manchester Insurance Institute, in which Institute he has on more than one occasion filled the offices of President and Vice-President—a practical and substantial testimony to the estimation in which he is held by his colleagues in the Insurance world.

Kennedy, Alexander D., the Manager for Ireland (excepting Ulster) for the Norwich Union Life and Fire Insurance Societies, has been in charge of their business since 1861, first in the capacity of Chief Agent for Ireland, and afterwards as Manager for Ireland. He has an influential connection in the Sister Isle, and through that and the cordial co-operation of a judiciously chosen staff and agents, he has succeeded in building up a substantial and well-selected business in both Branches. The Irish Branch has contributed in no slight degree to the recent advance in the new business of the Societies. Mr. Kennedy is also Chairman of the Irish Civil Service Permanent Building Society and a Vice-President of the Insurance Institute of Ireland.

EDMUND M. KEYES.

HERBERT KIDSON.

Keyes, Edmund M., is the Resident Secretary at Liverpool of the Gresham Life Assurance Society, which appointment he has held since 1878. Mr. Keyes has had large experience in the Life Insurance field, and has met with much success in the prosecution of this business.

Kerr, James A. S., District Manager to the West of England Insurance Company at St. Vincent Place, Glasgow, has been connected with the Company at that same Branch since 1877,

having received his training from Mr. James Macdonald, who had been Agent to the West of England for some years before the conversion of its Glasgow business into a Branch, and who, on the establishment of the Branch, preceded Mr. Kerr in the District Managership.

Kidson, Herbert, is senior partner in the firm of Kidson and Murray, Chartered Accountants and District Managers of the British Law Fire Insurance Company, Limited, at Manchester.

RICHARD DUNCAN KING.

JOSHUA A. KING.

King, Richard Duncan, J.P., is Joint Manager for Ireland of the United Kingdom Temperance and General Provident Institution, and Joint Local Secretary to the Manchester Fire Office at Dublin. Mr. King commenced his connection with the United Kingdom Temperance and General Provident Institution as far back as 1849 as a policy holder. While engaged in the service of one of the principal Dublin banks, and soon after assuring his own life, he began to bestir himself in behalf of the Institution by introducing new business, eventually developing into one of its most zealous agents. His zeal proved so productive of good that in 1863 he resigned his position at the Bank and undertook the important and honourable duties of Manager for Ireland to the United Kingdom Temperance and General Life Office, which post he has now held for upwards of a quarter of a century to the mutual satisfaction of himself and the Board. Mr. King's connection with the Manchester Fire Assurance Company commenced by his taking up an Agency for that Company in Dublin, which he held till 1884, when a Branch was established for Ireland, and he and his son were appointed first Resident, and afterwards Local Secretaries.

——

King, Joshua A., Joint Manager for Ireland of the United Kingdom Temperance and General Provident Institution, and Joint Local Secretary to the Manchester Fire Office, is son of Mr. Richard Duncan King, J.P., with whom he is associated in both these offices. He began his connection with the Insurance business by spending some time in the Head Offices of both his present Companies at London and Manchester respectively, since which he has joined his father in the conduct of their Irish business.

JAMES KNILL.

VERNON KYRKE.

Knill, James, is the District Agent at Exeter of the Sun Fire Office. Mr. Knill has been connected with this Company for 36 years, during 22 years of which he has held the Exeter Agency, and in the course of this time he has built up a very large local business for it.

Laidlaw, David L., is the Manager of the Glasgow Branch of the North British and Mercantile Insurance Company. Mr. Laidlaw received his early business training in the office of a Chartered Accountant in Glasgow, where he acquired a considerable amount of experience of the utmost value to him in the profession which he has now adopted. After several years' experience of Fire business in the Glasgow Office of his present Company and in another Office, he obtained an appointment as Surveyor to the Scottish Branch of the Queen Insurance Company, subsequently being promoted to the Secretaryship of the same Branch. This latter position he resigned in 1872, when he was appointed Secretary to his present Office; and in 1890, on the retirement of the late Manager, Mr. Snodgrass, Mr. Laidlaw was appointed to fill his post. The

Branch of the North British and Mercantile under Mr. Laidlaw's management is one of the most important which that Company possesses, and its importance has, since his appointment, been still further augmented by the acquisition of the local business and staff of the Scottish Provincial Insurance Company.

Mr. Laidlaw is a gentleman of great popularity and influence in Glasgow, and he is intimately acquainted with the Insurance risks and requirements of his district. He has for two different terms been Chairman of the Glasgow Rate and Salvage Committee, and has also been President of the Insurance and Actuarial Society of Glasgow.

Kyrke, Vernon, is the Secretary of the Alliance Assurance Company at its Dublin Branch, to which post he was appointed in 1883. Mr. Kyrke was originally in the London Office of the Provincial Insurance Company, and entered the service of the Alliance at the Head Office in 1874. He was Chief Clerk at the Edinburgh Branch of the Company in 1877-78, and joined the Dublin Branch on its establishment in 1880.

ARTHUR H. LAMONT.

CHARLES LAMSDALE.

Lamont, Arthur H., Local Manager of the Union Assurance Society at Bristol, is the son of the late Deputy Commissary-General, W. R. A. Lamont, Chelmsford, Essex. He was, previous to taking up his present appointment, for fifteen years in the service of the Life Association of Scotland, and Edinburgh Fire Company (the latter of which is now amalgamated with the Caledonian Office), in both of which Offices he acquired a considerable and valuable experience. He was appointed to his present post in 1884, since which time the business of the Branch has largely increased, necessitating the removal to more commodious premises than it has hitherto occupied.

Lawrence, Herbert Starmer, the Resident Secretary to the Sickness and Accident Assurance Association, at their Nottingham Branch, has been in charge of that Branch since 1888, and since taking it up has met with considerable success on behalf of the Association. He commenced business in the mercantile profession in London, but left it to take up his present position, being appointed by the Founder and then Manager of the Company, J. Byers Black. The present Manager has fittingly recognised the appointment by extending Mr. Lawrence's district to cover some five or six counties, and Mr. Lawrence has

fully justified his position ; the Association has now a very firm footing in his district and a rapidly-increasing business.

Lamsdale, Charles, is the Senior Partner of the firm of Lamsdale and Son, Insurance Brokers of Birmingham. He started in 1865 to select three substantial Insurance Companies for which to do business, and chose the Railway Passengers' Accident Assurance Company, the United Kingdom Temperance and General Provident Institution, and the Royal Insurance Company, representing the three branches of Insurance, Life, Fire and Accident, and since then has worked all these three most successfully. Accident Assurance however has been his special *forte*, and few men have done so much to popularise that branch of the business. The Railway Passengers' Assurance Company received an immense impetus in South Staffordshire by the prompt payment of a claim on the death of a well-known colliery manager, who had only paid his first premium to Mr. Lamsdale thirteen hours before he met his death. In spite of many offers from other Companies Mr. Lamsdale has never wavered from his allegiance to the Railway Passengers' Accident Assurance Company, and the Temperance and General Life Office.

H. LANGRIDGE LANE.

THOMAS LAND.

Lane, H. Langridge, District Manager of the Commercial Union Assurance Company, at its West of England Branch at Bristol, has been in that position since 1885. Mr. Langridge Lane has had a wide business experience, having previously to entering upon the duties of his present post, held other appointments of importance, and the results of his work in his present position have been eminently satisfactory, both to his Directors and those of the public who have dealings with the Commercial Union Assurance Company through his Branch.

Land, Thomas, is the Local Secretary at Manchester of the Phœnix Fire Office. He has held this position since 1882, and he has previously represented the Company as Agent for this District, having been connected with this Company since 1852, first as Junior Clerk, then as Chief Clerk, Agent and Local Secretary. He is an agreeable gentleman, and an upright, energetic and able Insurance official, qualities which have won golden opinions for himself and a large and profitable business for his Company. Mr. Land has a long and varied experience in surveying risks and arranging large insurances.

PAUL LANGE.

JOHN LARGE.

Lange, Paul, is the Local Secretary of the Westminster Fire Office at their Branch Office in Liverpool. In 1865 Mr. Lange was connected with the Berlin Office of the Royal, from which he was afterwards transferred to the Head Office in Liverpool. He subsequently represented for some years the German and Swiss Fire Re-insurance Association, for which he did a very extensive business; and, upon the retirement of the Association from this country, he received his present appointment for the Westminster on that Company substituting a Branch Office in lieu of their old system of agencies. Mr. Lange, who is very popular in business circles in Liverpool, has done a successful business for his present Office, to which his long experience and high-class connection are necessarily of great service.

Large, John, Manager for Scotland at the Glasgow Branch of the Norwich Union Fire Insurance Society, served his apprenticeship in the Glasgow Branch of the Scottish Provincial, whence he transferred his services to the Scottish Fire for a period of six years, until the merging of that office into the Caledonian. On that event taking place Mr. Large joined his present office. When Head Office Inspector he visited many of the Foreign and Colonial Branches and principal Agencies of the Norwich Union Fire Insurance Society.

M. J. LAVALLIN.

JAMES LAW,

Lavallin, Michael J., is the Resident Secretary of the Gresham Life Assurance Society in the South of Ireland. The Branch extends over the whole of Munster. He has now been nine years connected with the Society in Cork, six years of which were spent as an Agent. After leaving school he spent four years in an Insurance and House and Land Agency Office, but left for a more remunerative employment in a wholesale and retail Drug House, in which place he spent four years also. During his stay there he used to employ his dinner hour canvassing for advertisements for local almanacks and one of the local railways. This gave him such an anxiety to develope agency work that he applied for a position in the office of the Cork Gas Company so as to have a prior claim to one of the collectorships which was likely about that time to be vacant. In twelve months afterwards his anticipations were realized and his forethought rewarded by obtaining the coveted position, though he was pitted against a skilled collector, who was also a man of great influence. Immediately on getting this appointment he applied for an Agency to the Gresham and worked it in conjunction with the collectorship for six years, until a vacancy arose for the Local Managership, when Mr. Lavallin was induced by Mr. Elliott, the then Superintendent of the Gresham for Ireland and Scotland, to accept the responsibilities of the office. Since his appointment the Directors of the Society have erected a very pretty office building in Cork, which is considered to be the nicest of its kind in the South of Ireland.

Law, James, the District Manager of the Union Assurance Society at Manchester, is one of the best known and most popular Insurance men in Manchester and Dublin. He commenced his business career with a Greek shipper, and entered the Insurance business in the Manchester Branch of the Liverpool and London and Globe in 1874 as Guarantee Clerk. He migrated for a short time to the London Assurance under Mr. W. W. Page, when first the Manchester Branch of that Corporation was opened. He then became Chief Clerk and Surveyor at the Head Office of the Co-operative in April, 1878, receiving an appointment as Agency Inspector and Surveyor in the Dublin Branch of the West of England in 1880. After a successful service he was approached and engaged by the Crown Life Office as Superintendent for Ireland, taking full charge of that Company's Irish business. Mr. Law was transferred to Manchester in 1888 as that Company's Resident Secretary, retaining at the same time his Irish appointment. The Manchester appointment of the Union Assurance Society becoming vacant, Mr. Law was selected out of a very large number of applicants for his present post.

Mr. Law promoted and organised the Insurance Institute of Ireland, and was its first Hon. Secretary, succeeding to the Treasurership. After holding these offices he was elected almost unanimously a member of the Council, and on his leaving Dublin a complimentary dinner at the Gresham Hotel was given to him, at which the leading Insurance men and some of the principal citizens attended. He is an Hon. Member of the Insurance Institute of Victoria, N.S.W., a member of the Insurance Institute, Manchester, and was elected a Fellow of the Statistical Society, London.

JOHN LECKIE.

A. P. LEDWARD.

Leckie, John, is the Resident Secretary of the Scottish Temperance Life Assurance Company, Limited, in Edinburgh. At an early age he entered the service of a banking and mercantile firm in his native place, there acquiring a knowledge of counting-house and banking business. Afterwards he transferred his services to a firm of Paper manufacturers, passing from the office to the duties of representative on the journeys. He was subsequently placed at Glasgow in the same capacity, and after some years there he accepted a new appointment in Edinburgh. The experiences thus gained have served to extend his knowledge of men and methods of business.

Shortly after the Scottish Temperance entered upon its career, Mr. Leckie was appointed Resident Secretary in Edinburgh in 1874. Prior to this period he was closely identified with the Temperance cause, taking a steady interest in the education of the people in this direction. He has been Chairman of several Associations in the city, and still is an active public speaker. In this connection the prominent feature of the Company is not forgotten. Mr. Leckie has given close attention to the development of the Branch, and has drawn around him a body of agents whose efforts he superintends; and by his guidance the inducements offered by the Company are proving more and more attractive to the temperance and provident classes of the insuring public.

Ledward, A. P., Resident Secretary of the Scottish Provident Institution at Manchester, was born in 1856 of a well-known Manchester family, and was educated at Manchester Grammar School, in France, at the Owens College, and the London University. After taking the first examination for a medical degree at the London University, he graduated there as Bachelor of Science in 1876, and is a member of Convocation. He was elected the same year an Associate of the Owens College, and has since been chairman of that distinguished body. He received the degree of the Victoria University in 1880, since which date he has constantly been a member of the Committee of Convocation. He is a member of the Court of Governors of the Owens College, and a Governor of the Girls' High School. Mr. Ledward takes a keen interest in Volunteer matters, having been for many years Captain, and for some time Acting-Adjutant, of the 2nd Manchester Rifle Volunteers. He was a founder, and at one time President, of the Manchester Tactical Society. In 1884 he organised the Manchester Cadet Corps for the training of poor boys of the city in gymnastic and military drill, which corps has since been constituted by the War Office an independent battalion as the First Cadet Battalion the Manchester Regiment, of which he is Honorary Major-Commandant. He is an Associate of the Institute of Actuaries, and since he took the appointment of Resident Secretary to the Scottish Provident Institution in the year 1883, he has been most successful in maintaining and extending the business of the branch in his district.

JOHN R. P. LEGGATT.

THOMAS LEMAN.

Leggatt, J. R. P., is the Resident Secretary of the Lancashire Insurance Company at its important Branch Office at Liverpool. Previous to obtaining his present appointment Mr. Leggatt had acquired considerable experience in Insurance matters abroad. He became Resident Secretary to the Lancashire in 1876, on the resignation of Mr. J. A. Cunningham now General Manager of the Yorkshire Insurance Company. The Lancashire being a native Company of the County Palatine, with a large section of its proprietary concentrated in Liverpool, the establishment of a Branch in that city with an influential Local Board of Directors rapidly followed the formation of the Company in 1852, and naturally a large business was soon accumulated. This Mr. Leggatt, by his general courtesy and ability, has been very successful in both maintaining and extending, at the same time increasing the popularity of his Company in both the Life and Fire departments. Mr. Leggatt himself, as may be supposed, holds a prominent position amongst Liverpool Insurance men.

Leman, Thomas, is the District Agent at Nottingham of the Scottish Widow's Fund Life Assurance Society. Mr. Leman, who is a chartered accountant of high standing, also represents several first-class Fire Insurance Companies as Agent for his District.

THOMAS D. C. LEVERITT.

H. D. LEWIS.

Leveritt, Thomas D. C., is the Manager for the Midland Counties of the Mutual Life Insurance Company of New York, with Branch Offices at 1, Bennett's Hill, Birmingham, which appointment he received early in 1892. Mr. Leveritt was previously the Local Secretary at Bristol of the Gresham Life Assurance Society, with which Office he first became connected in 1879, and with which he remained until he received his present appointment, his field of operations being the West of England. Mr. Leveritt has been most successful in Life Insurance, and has succeeded in building up a large business wherever he has been located.

Lee, James, is the Resident Secretary of the Imperial Fire and Life Offices, at their Yorkshire Branch at Leeds. Mr. Lee commenced his Insurance career in the service of the Unity Office, which he joined soon after its organization, and remained with it until it was amalgamated with the Liverpool and London in 1862. He next went to Liverpool, early in 1863, as Chief Clerk in the Head Office of the London and Lancashire Fire Office, subsequently receiving his promotion to the Assistant Secretaryship in the same office. In 1865 he was again promoted, this time to the Resident Managership of the Leeds Branch of the London and Lancashire, with a Board of Directors, which position he held until 1870, resigning it to become Chief Clerk to the Imperial. After remaining in this capacity for five years he was, in 1875, appointed Resident Secretary at Leeds. Mr. Lee is the Senior Resident Secretary now in Leeds, and is justly regarded by his con-

temporaries as an authority on Insurance matters. He is very popular, and enjoys the esteem, not only of his agents, but of all with whom he has in any way to do.

Lewis, Hugh D., the Secretary of the Northern Assurance Company at their Birmingham Branch, began his Insurance career immediately on leaving school, entering the service of the Liverpool and London and Globe Insurance Company at their Birmingham Office, where he served as Junior Clerk for three years. He then removed to his present Office, where he has now been for five years, first as Clerk and being promoted to his present position in the February of 1891 on the resignation of the late Secretary, Mr. Richard Walton, now London Manager to the Manchester Fire Office. Mr. Lewis is a Welshman.

Lecky, C. C., the Belfast District Manager of the New York Life Assurance Company, is son of the late Mr. W. S. Lecky, a well-known Dublin merchant. Having finished his education he entered the service of the Ulster Bank, at the Branch in Dublin, but not finding the work congenial to his tastes he left the Bank to enter the linen trade, in which business he remained for over ten years, in connection with one of the principal Belfast firms. He accepted his present post, controlling the whole of the Ulster district, in August, 1890. Mr. Lecky is hardly over thirty years of age, and the energy which he has already shown gives great promise of success for him in the future.

R. D. LIVINGSTONE.

E. S. LISLE

Livingstone, R. D., is the Resident Manager of the Dublin Branch of the Manchester Fire Assurance Company. He began his Insurance career in 1877 in the Branch Office at Dundee of the Standard Fire Insurance Company, and at the same time received a thorough business training in the staple industry of the town of Dundee. When the Standard was taken over by the Fire Insurance Association, Mr. Livingstone was induced to transfer his services to the latter Company, and shortly afterwards he accepted an appointment from the Northern Assurance Company at their Branch Office in the same town, which he held for about three years, being then appointed by the Company as their Chief Clerk and Surveyor for Ireland with Dublin as headquarters.

When the Manchester Fire Office, about two years past, decided on consolidating their business in Ireland, Mr. Livingstone received the appointment as Resident Manager, and during his term with them has been able to show a substantial improvement in their Irish business.

Lisle, Edwin S., is a well-known Accountant, House Agent and Insurance Broker at Exeter, where he represents several Insurance Companies as Agent, including the Phœnix Fire Office, the Scottish Equitable Life Assurance Society, the Lancashire Insurance Company, the Lancashire and Yorkshire Accident Insurance Company, the Guardian Plate Glass Insurance Company, the Engine Boiler and Employers' Liability Insurance Company, the Imperial Live Stock Insurance Association, and the West of England Insurance Company. He also holds the appointment of Assistant Overseer and other public positions in the large and important suburb of St. Thomas, and was previously for nearly eighteen years in the banking establishment of Messrs. Sanders and Company, the Exeter Bank, which he left with the good wishes of the firm in order to obtain more outdoor employment.

E. L. LLOYD.

E. PRYSE LLOYD.

Lloyd, E. L., is the Resident Secretary of the Alliance Assurance Company at their Branch Office at Manchester, to which post he was appointed in 1888 on the resignation of his predecessor, Mr. Henry F. Cutler, to take over the general management of the British Law Fire Insurance Company. Mr. Lloyd commenced his career, in 1856, as a clerk in the London office of the Lancashire Insurance Company, and in 1860 was appointed book-keeper at the Head Office of that Company in Manchester. In 1862 he returned to London to enter upon the duties of Chief Clerk to the Provincial, whose London business was at that time under the management of Mr. Lewis (now Chief Secretary of the Alliance). Upon Mr. Lewis' removal to another sphere, Mr. Lloyd was chosen to succeed him in his post of London Secretary, and he continued to hold the same position until the Fire business of the Provincial was absorbed by the Alliance ; when he was appointed to act as District Secretary to the latter Company at their Branch Office at Wrexham. He remained in the conduct of that Branch for sixteen years ; and at the end of that time he was promoted to the management, which he now holds, of the more important Branch in Manchester.

Lloyd, E. Pryse, is the Resident Secretary at Newcastle-on-Tyne of the Lancashire Insurance Company, and has been connected with this Company for over 30 years. Mr. Lloyd was for nineteen years at the Head Office in Manchester, and in July, 1880, he was appointed Resident Secretary at the newly-established Branch in Dublin, which position he continued to hold until December, 1889, when he was promoted to the more important Branch of the Company at Newcastle-on-Tyne.

Lawson, William, District Manager of the Marine and General Mutual Life Assurance Society, at their Branch Office at Lord Street, Liverpool, commenced his Insurance career in May, 1879, at which date he entered the service of the Liverpool Branch of the Alliance Assurance Company, in which Office he remained for a period of no less than ten and a half years, during which period he acquired a varied and comprehensive experience in all branches of the business. He was appointed to his present position with the Marine and General Mutual Life Assurance Society in November, 1889.

G. J. LLOYD.

D. LLOYD.

Lloyd, G. J., is the Resident Secretary at Birmingham of the Edinburgh Life Assurance Company. Mr. Lloyd commenced his Insurance career in the Head Office at Wrexham of the "Provincial," from which he was subsequently transferred to their London Branch. In the early part of 1874—on the purchase of the Provincial Fire business by the Alliance—Mr. Lloyd was appointed Inspector of Agents at the London Branch of the Edinburgh Life Office, under Mr. John Duncan, F.I.A.; continuing in that post until November, 1878, when he was promoted to the Liverpool Secretaryship of the same Company. In December, 1885, he was promoted to the more important position in Birmingham which he now holds.

Lloyd, D., the District Manager of the Mutual Life Insurance Company of New York at their Branch Office at Norwich, has not been very long in the Insurance profession, having entered it in 1888. He had previously acted as representative to a British Office, but in March, 1890, he was appointed to his present post with the supervision of the Eastern Counties business, and since then his career has been a very prosperous one. He has done much to increase the business of the Mutual Life of New York in his district, where on commencing he found the Company had very few policy-holders.

BENJAMIN LAMB.

JOHN LOUDON.

Lamb, Benjamin, is the Senior Metropolitan District Manager of the Star Life Assurance Society. He received his early education at Queen's College, Taunton, and originally commenced life in the Banking profession, which he subsequently exchanged for that of Insurance. Having by his abilities attracted the notice of the late Sir William McArthur, the Chairman of the Star Life Assurance Society, he was induced to accept a position of responsibility in that office. The selection was soon amply justified, for in a short time he gave confirmatory proof of his capabilities by the valuable work that he did in the East Riding of Yorkshire ground, at that time anything but productive to the Society. He has also on various occasions visited and reported upon other parts of the kingdom, amongst them being the County of Cornwall and the Brighton and South Coast Districts. In the year 1878 he settled permanently in London, and from that time to the present has continued his successful career.

Loudon, John, is the Manager of the Manchester Branch of the Royal Exchange Assurance Corporation. Mr. Loudon began his Insurance career in the Glasgow Branch of the Queen; afterwards filling the post of Chief Clerk in the Local Branch of the Westminster Fire, which he held for four years. He left this position to become Surveyor in the North of England for the Commercial Union; and, at the end of four years, accepted the appointment of Head Office Agency Superintendent to the Caledonian; devoting his attention, for about four years, principally to the Life department in England and Scotland. At the end of that period, Mr. Loudon was promoted to the position of Secretary to the Manchester Branch of the same Company; and he conducted the business in that district with such marked success, that after the lapse of some years he was further promoted to the Secretaryship of the more important Glasgow Branch, where he remained till February of the present year, when he received his present appointment.

ROBERT LOUDOUN.

A. G. LUCAS.

Loudoun, Robert, District Manager of the Union Fire and Life Assurance Society at their Branch Office in Baker Street, Portman Square, is a Scotchman, born in 1856, and educated at Dumfries, in which town he also commenced his Insurance career, entering the Office of the Border Counties Fire Office there, when it was established in 1870. He remained in the service of the Border Counties Office until the transfer of its business to the London and Southwark Insurance Office in 1875, when he obtained an appointment in the Head Office of that latter Company. After three years at that Office Mr. Loudoun was appointed Resident Secretary to the Newcastle-on-Tyne Branch of the same Company, which he held until the further transfer of the London and Southwark's business to the London and Lancashire. He was then offered an appointment with the London and Lancashire, but refused, accepting instead the position of Local Manager at Newcastle-on-Tyne to his present Office, which he held till November, 1886, removing from it on his promotion to his present position.

———

Lucas, A. G., is the Resident Secretary of the Queen Insurance Company at Bristol, which Company he has represented for about 18 years. Mr. Lucas is also a Chartered Accountant, and is held in high esteem in the West of England.

JAMES MACDONALD.

JAMES S. MACK.

Macdonald, James, is the District Manager at Glasgow of the West of England Insurance Company. Mr. Macdonald has had a very extended Insurance experience and has been connected with the West of England Insurance Company for a very considerable period.

Macleod, Mackenzie, the Local Manager of the Law Union Insurance Company at Liverpool, is a son of the late Rev. Dr. Macleod, of Birkenhead, Ex-Moderator of the Presbyterian Synod. He received his Insurance training in the Head Office of the Royal Insurance Company, and on the Law Union in 1885 deciding to change its former system of representation by Agents to that of a Branch Office, he was selected to take charge of the Branch. Since then the business of the Company has been largely developed under Mr. Macleod's management. He also represents the Northern Accident Office in Liverpool.

Mack, James Smith, S.S.C., Joint Local Manager of the General Life and Fire Assurance Company at the Head Office for the East of Scotland in Edinburgh, entered the office of the Agent of that Company, then known as the Protestant Dissenters and General Assurance Company, in Edinburgh in 1842. In 1856 he was appointed Joint Agent to the Company for Edinburgh and Leith, and in 1858 Local Manager for the Eastern District of Scotland, his son, Mr. J. L. Mack, being subsequently associated with him in that capacity. Mr. Mack has for many years been a Director of the General Assurance Company. He is by profession a solicitor, and is the President of the Society of Solicitors in the Supreme Courts of Scotland. He is a Justice of the Peace for the counties of the City of Edinburgh and of Berwick, and a Member of the County Council of Berwickshire, of which body he is Vice-Convener.

M. J. MACKIE.

D. MACKINTOSH.

Mackie, M. J., District Manager to the Employers' Liability Assurance Corporation at Liverpool, is a native of London, where he was born in 1855, and educated at Christ's Hospital. Immediately on leaving school at the age of sixteen, he entered the service of the Life Association of Scotland, at their London Office, where he remained till 1876, leaving it to enter the Life Department of the Commercial Union Assurance Company. On the formation of the Employers' Liability Assurance Corporation in 1881, he was appointed Chief Clerk at the Head Office in London, which position he held till 1886, when he was appointed to his present post, with supervision over West Lancashire, West Cheshire, and North Wales. Since his appointment he has largely increased the local business of the Corporation.

Mackillop, J. F., Resident Secretary to the County Fire and Provident Life Offices at their Yorkshire Branch Office at Leeds, commenced his Insurance career in 1867, as District Manager for Lancashire and Yorkshire to the London and Lancashire Life Insurance Company; subsequently serving for five years in the same capacity and in the same District for the Norwich Union Life Insurance Company. He has occupied his present post for the County Fire and Provident Life since 1879. Mr. Mackillop is a distinguished man in Yorkshire Insurance circles, and has been elected Vice-President of the Yorkshire Insurance Institute for three years.

Mackintosh, D., is the Resident Secretary of the Sun Fire Assurance Society at their Glasgow Branch. Mr. Mackintosh is a native of Glasgow, where he was educated at the Established Church Normal School, afterwards becoming for some time a teacher in the same school. He was subsequently apprenticed by his parents to a Measurer, the name given in Scotland to the person who draws out the specifications for any work and measures up the work of the various artificers after the building is completed, answering in a great degree to the English Surveyor, under whose supervision he received the usual training in building construction. His employer, besides being a Measurer, was also Surveyor to several Fire Offices, and it was thus that Mr. Mackintosh received his first insight into the details of the Insurance business. He remained for five years with the Measurer, subsequently entering the Glasgow Branch of the Imperial Fire Office for a few months, after which he obtained an appointment as Clerk to the Glasgow Rate and Salvage Committee. After spending two years in the service of that Committee, Mr. Mackintosh was invited by the Manager of the Scottish Imperial Insurance Company to undertake the duties of Surveyor to their Head Office, which invitation he accepted, retaining the post when the Alliance took over the Scottish Imperial's business, and later on joining to his former duties those of Chief Clerk. He eventually left the Alliance to take up his present post with the Sun Fire in 1885 on Mr. Blair's retirement.

ROBERT MACMILLAN.

G. C. MACLEAN.

Macmillan, Robert, is the Resident Secretary of the Scottish Union and National Insurance Company at the Bradford Branch, as well as at the Leeds Branch of the Company. He has been connected with the Scottish Union and National Insurance Company for nearly thirty years, and when in 1875 the Bradford business, which had for a quarter of a century been conducted through a District Agency, was transformed into a full Branch, he was put in charge of the Branch. Mr. Macmillan found the business already accrued from the Agency a very large one; but, being a gentleman of undoubted ability and sound judgment, succeeded in building the business up to still greater dimensions, until now it has attained the rank of being the largest done by any Company in the District.   Mr. Macmillan has trained more than one distinguished Insurance officer now at Bradford or elsewhere.   He is an acknowledged authority on the risks peculiar to his District.

Maclean, G. C., is the Resident Secretary at Edinburgh of the Scottish Amicable Life Assurance Society, which post he has held since 1878. Mr. Maclean was previously connected with the Life Association of Scotland, first at its Head Office in Edinburgh and subsequently as its Secretary at Dublin.

PATRICK MACNEIL.

W. MARRIOTT.

Macneil, Patrick, is the Resident Secretary of the Caledonian Insurance Company at their Glasgow Branch. He is a gentleman of very extensive experience in the department of the Insurance business in which he is engaged, having commenced his career so far back as in 1868, in which year he entered the service of the Scottish Fire Insurance Company at their Head Office. When nine years later the business of that Company was transferred to the Caledonian Insurance Company in 1877, Mr. Macneil received an appointment on the Head-Office Staff of the latter Company, where he remained until he was promoted to be Fire Superintendent at Glasgow in 1886, and Resident Secretary in 1892.

———

Marriott, W., is the Resident Secretary at Nottingham of the Imperial Fire and Life Offices, which Companies he has represented in this district for over 30 years. Mr. Marriott has had a very large Insurance experience, and is acknowledged an authority on the fire risks peculiar to this district.

J. W. MARSDEN.

H. E. MARRIOTT.

Marsden, John Wilberforce, Branch Manager at Liverpool for the Atlas Fire and Life Assurance Company, was appointed in 1886, when, under the new *régime* at the Head Office, which began with the accession of Mr. Pipkin to the management, the Branch system was extended to Liverpool.

The Atlas had previously done a good business in the District under the old Agency system; but the increase in the returns since 1886 has more than fully demonstrated the advantage to the Company of having established a Branch Office in the important City of Liverpool, and the appointment of a popular and energetic gentleman like Mr. Marsden as their representative.

Marriott, Henry Edward, is the District Manager of the North-West of England for the Scottish Metropolitan Life Assurance Company. His connection with that Company extends over a period of thirteen years. Previous to joining the Scottish Metropolitan Mr. Marriott was for five years in the office of Messrs. Niven and Cowan, chartered accountants of Edinburgh. His first appointment with the Scottish Metropolitan Life Office was as Chief Clerk, but after three months he was appointed Inspector of Agents. Filling this office with considerable success, he was appointed General Superintendent of Agents and Branches. In 1886 he was appointed to the post he now holds, while still retaining his Head Office appointment. These duties and the Inspection of Agencies have given Mr. Marriott a wide and varied experience, extending over the whole of Scotland and nearly the whole of England.

SETH MARSHALL.

A. MARSHALL.

Marshall, Seth, is the Resident Secretary for the British Empire Mutual Life Assurance Company at its Branch Office at Birmingham. Mr. Marshall, after representing the Midland Counties Company for four years in Lincolnshire, became connected with the British Empire Office. His efforts to secure business for this Company were very successful, and a few months after his appointment the Directors offered him an Inspectorship for the Nottingham district, which he accepted. In April, 1890, he was appointed to his present important position.

———

Marshall, Alfred, is the District Manager to the Mutual Life Insurance Company of New York at their Branch Office, Nottingham. For some six years, previous to his acceptance of this position, Mr. Marshall was in the employ of the British Empire Mutual Life Assurance Company,

the last two occupying the position of Inspector of . Agents in the Manchester, Norwich, and Nottingham Districts. Towards the end of the year 1889, he was offered the more important post which he now occupies. The district which he manages is a large one, comprising the whole of the counties of Nottingham, Lincoln, Leicester, Derby, and Rutland, and since December, 1889, when he entered upon his present position, he has done a good business for his Company. We congratulate Mr. Marshall on the success he has attained by sheer hard work and sound business capacity. The Mutual Life of New York may be congratulated in having obtained so valuable an addition to its working staff, and Mr. Marshall may be considered no less fortunate in finding employment with a Company which affords abundant scope for his energies and abilities, and one which, he may be assured, knows how to appreciate a good servant.

A. MATHISON.

ALBERT V. MARTINDALE.

Mathison, A., is the Resident Secretary at Birmingham of the Guardian Assurance Company, which appointment he has held for upwards of 12 years. Mr. Mathison had previously been in the service of the Caledonian as Inspector of Agents for Scotland.

— — —

Martindale, Albert Victor, is Manager of the Branch of the County Fire Office at Birmingham. Mr. Martindale commenced his Insurance career in 1879 in the Birmingham Branch of the London and Lancashire Fire Office, and in 1886 he visited India on behalf of that Company. Mr. Martindale was appointed District Secretary of the Local Branch of the British Law Fire Office soon after his return from India in 1889, but the position of District Manager of the County Fire Office becoming vacant early in 1891, he transferred his services to his present Company. Mr. Martindale, who is a member of the Council of the Birmingham Insurance Institute, has had a very varied experience in Insurance business, and he is to be congratulated upon the success achieved so early in life, as his present appointment ranks as one of the most important in the profession in Birmingham.

ARTHUR B. MAYHEW.

JOHN McINTOSH.

Mayhew, Arthur B., Standard Life Assurance Company, Bristol, has not had a very long career in the Insurance profession, having entered it, in 1887, when he was selected for the post of Inspector of Agents in the West of England for the Scottish Accident Insurance Company. Here he continued till the following year, when he became associated with the Royal Insurance Company, and was appointed to act as Inspector in the Life Department of that Company in the same District, and subsequently at their Midland Branch at Birmingham. In 1891 the Directors of the Standard Life Assurance Company appointed Mr. Mayhew to the management of their Bristol Branch.

McIntosh, John, is the Resident Secretary at Edinburgh of the Liverpool and London and Globe Insurance Company. Mr. McIntosh is one of the best known Fire Insurance men in Scotland, has had a large and varied experience in the business, and has been connected with his present Company for many years.

A. ROLLINS McLEISH.

R. C. McINTYRE.

McLeish, A. Rollins, the Agency Superintendent of the Imperial Life Insurance Company at Liverpool, is by birth a Scotchman. He originally started his business career in the shipping trade, but, after nine years' experience with the Anchor Line at their head office at Glasgow, he changed his mind; and, being at that time twenty-two years of age, entered the service of the Provident Life Office at their Branch in the same town. After six months with that Company, he received the appointment of Inspector of Agencies for the General Assurance Company, with the supervision of Glasgow and the whole of Scotland except Midlothian. During the two years and eight months that he was acting in this capacity, he acquired sufficient experience and reputation to justify the Imperial Life Office to appoint him to his present post.

———

McIntyre, Robert Cowan, is the Local Secretary of the National Assurance Company of Ireland at their Branch Office at Dundee. Mr. McIntyre, previously to his present appointment, was for many years employed in the Branch Offices of the Royal and Guardian Insurance Companies at Glasgow, and was selected to take charge of the Dundee Branch of the National of Ireland on the opening of that Branch in 1889.

J. H. McNEILL.

THOMAS McPHERSON.

McNeill, James Henry, London Secretary of the Sickness and Accident Assurance Association, Limited, at their Branch Office, 64, Moorgate Street, E.C., commenced his Insurance career as an Agent with his present Company in the beginning of the year 1888, at Manchester. He was so successful that, in November of the same year, the Company offered him their Leeds Secretaryship, which he accepted. Finding the work so congenial, and being endowed with energy, tact and perseverance, he succeeded in developing the business of the Yorkshire Branch in so satisfactory a manner that, in March, 1892, the Directors promoted him to the position of London Secretary.

McPherson, Thomas, is the Resident Secretary of the General Accident Assurance Corporation of Perth at Liverpool, to which post he received his appointment in 1887, when that enterprising Company, not very long after its formation, began to establish Branches in the various chief towns of the United Kingdom. Mr. McPherson commenced his Insurance career as Resident Secretary of the Mercantile Accident and Guarantee Insurance Company, and resigned that position for the purpose of representing his present Office. He has proved a most efficient Resident Secretary, having, by his judicious choice of Agents and general management of the business, secured a good local position and popularity for his Office. He is personally a great favourite amongst the Insurance men of Liverpool.

W. J. McWean.

Thomas Melvin.

McWean, W. J., is the Local Manager at Liverpool of the London and Lancashire Life Assurance Company, which appointment he has held since 1888. Mr. McWean has been very successful in the Life Insurance business, and had been for many years previous to receiving his present appointment one of the most valued of this Company's Agents.

Melvin, Thomas, the District Manager of the Star Life Assurance Society, at their Branch at Leeds, has passed the whole of his Insurance career in the service of that Office, having been connected with it since 1882. He commenced as Inspector of Agents in connection with the Glasgow Branch, whence he was promoted to be District Manager of one of the Metropolitan Districts, being subsequently transferred to his present post at Leeds in 1888.

R. I. METCALFE.

THOMAS MIDDLEBROOK.

Metcalfe, Robert Ives, who was appointed London Manager of the Scottish Imperial in October of 1891, has achieved a distinctive position early in life, being now but in his thirtieth year. The county in which Mr. Metcalfe first saw the light of day is Lincolnshire, and he is the son of Dr. Robert Ives Metcalfe, now of Beccles in Suffolk. Previous to his induction into the Life Assurance world, he had a strong predilection for military matters, and, in fact, at one time it was thought that he would be connected with the Irish Constabulary; but the Fates ordained it otherwise, and his present profession has gained what the Constabulary lost. For some seven years he was connected with the Life Association of Scotland in various capacities, attaining to the position of Chief Inspector of their West End office when the present advanced position was secured by him. Mr. Metcalfe possesses all the elements of a successful man, and unites in his character decisive action and marked urbanity of disposition.

Already, under his able management, the London Branch is showing improvement, and there is little doubt regarding its successful future with him at the head of its affairs.

————

Middlebrook, Thomas, Secretary to the Bradford Plate Glass Mutual Insurance Company, is a native of Bradford, and is very well known and popular in that District. He has held his position with the Bradford Plate Glass Mutual Insurance Company since the first year of its existence, and it is owing to the skill and sagacity with which he has selected the Company's business and managed its affairs generally that although its operations are limited to Bradford and the immediate neighbourhood, it is in a highly flourishing condition of prosperity. Mr. Middlebrook also acts in the capacity of Agent to various Fire and Life Insurance Companies, for all of which he does a very considerable business.

T. BRAND MILLER.

WALTER MILLER.

Miller, T. Brand, is the Resident Secretary of the Guardian Assurance Company at its Bristol Branch. Mr. Miller commenced his career in 1874 in the office of a large esparto importing firm in Glasgow. In January, 1875, he joined the Glasgow Branch of the Scottish Provincial, and remained in that Company's service upwards of twelve years, gaining during that period a valuable experience in all the departments of Branch work. In 1887 he was appointed by the Royal Exchange as their Surveyor and Inspector of Agents (Fire and Life) at Manchester, and was subsequently offered and accepted the Resident Secretaryship of the Newcastle Branch of the Guardian, from which he has recently been promoted to fill a similar post at the more important Branch of that Company at Bristol.

—————

Miller, Walter, is the Resident Secretary of the Bradford (Yorkshire) Branch of the Equitable Fire and Accident Office, Limited. His Insurance experience has been extensive, and covers a period of twenty-two years. Mr. Miller was trained in the office of Messrs. Warden and Miller (now Messrs. Miller and Son), the well-known Manchester Insurance Surveyors, with whom he served nine years, of which period six years were spent surveying Fire Risks over the whole of the North of England. In 1878 he was appointed Surveyor to the Alliance

Assurance Company at Manchester, for which Company he took Lancashire and Yorkshire (West Riding) surveys, besides specially reporting upon risks in other parts of England and Wales. In 1884 Mr. Miller accepted an offer from the South British and National Fire and Marine Insurance Companies to open a Branch at Leeds for Yorkshire and the North of England, and in the following year obtained an additional appointment as District Secretary to the Rock Life Office for the same district. Mr. Miller's was the first Branch appointment made by the Rock and marked a new era in the experience of that old Office, which at the time was under its present able Actuary, Mr. G. S. Crisford. At the request of the Directors of the South British and National Mr. Miller on January 7th, 1887, took over the control of their Manchester Branch (which hitherto had had a most unfortunate experience) in conjunction with that of Leeds, and was successful in re-organising and placing the Branch upon a paying footing. He remained with the South British and National Companies until the latter part of last year (1890), when the English business of those Companies was transferred to the Equitable. Mr. Miller resigned his appointment with the Rock Life Office in 1887, as he found it desirable to remove to Manchester in order to give his full attention to his Fire appointments.

ALEXANDER MILNE.

J. H. MILLS.

Milne, Alexander, Local Secretary of the Gresham Life Assurance Society at their Aberdeen Branch, is a native of that city, and having received a sound Grammar School education entered a mercantile office immediately on leaving school. His father, however, was anxious that he should learn a trade, and accordingly a friend, a magistrate of Aberdeen, who carried on one of the largest building businesses in the North of Scotland, having offered to take him, he was apprenticed to that trade, and duly served his time. Trade, however, at that time being bad, and there seeming to be little prospect before him in his special line, Mr. Milne gave it up, and in 1881 started in the Insurance business as an Agent to the Gresham. His energy soon marked him for promotion, and he was accordingly appointed Assistant to the Local Secretary, subsequently receiving a further step to the post of Agency Inspector to the Gresham for Aberdeen and the North of Scotland. Three years later, on the retirement of the late Local Secretary, Mr. Mackintosh, Mr. Milne was appointed by the Board to succeed him in July, 1890.

———

Mills, J. H., the Resident Secretary of the Yorkshire and North Eastern District of the Palatine and United Fire Insurance Companies at Huddersfield, joined the Mutual Fire Office as Co-District Manager in Ireland in 1878, leaving that post in 1887 to go to Huddersfield to take up his present duties. The district comprises the counties of Rutland, Lincoln, York, Durham, and Northumberland. Mr. Mills has an extensive business under his charge, Huddersfield being the twin birthplace of his old Company, the Mutual Fire Office, now merged into the Palatine.

CHARLES MILNE.

GEORGE MILNE.

Milne, Charles, is the Resident Secretary at Newcastle-on-Tyne of the City of Glasgow Life Assurance Company. Previous to receiving this appointment Mr. Milne was for fourteen years in the Edinburgh Branch of this Company, where he served his apprenticeship, and during the last eight years of this time he held the position of Cashier and Book-keeper. He also for one year acted as Inspector of Agents, in which capacity he was very successful, and was afterwards promoted to his present position.

————

Milne, George, is the Agency Inspector of the British Empire Mutual Life Assurance Company at its Head Office. Mr. Milne has been in the service of this Company over twenty years, during six years of which time he was its Branch Manager at Birmingham.

R. S. MILNE.

J. D. MILNE.

Milne, R. Stephen, is the Manager of the Scottish Branch of the Kent Fire and Life Offices at No. 68, St. Vincent Street, Glasgow, which appointment he received in November, 1890. Mr. Milne had previously been connected with the Scottish Branch of the South British and National Insurance Companies, his early training having been received in the Head Office of the Scottish Imperial and at the Glasgow and Edinburgh Branch of the Alliance Assurance Company.

Milne, James Dingwall, Resident Secretary for the City of Glasgow Life Assurance Company at their Branch Office in Manchester, like many more Scotchmen engaged in Life Assurance work, received his early training in one of the Scotch Banks. His first active experience of Life Assurance was gained in the service of the Life Association of Scotland in Edinburgh, acting in the capacity of Inspector of Agents. Ten years ago he was appointed to the position which he now holds. Mr. Milne is known as a genial and business man.

D. MITCHELL.

R. G. MOFFET.

Mitchell, David, is the Resident Secretary at Glasgow of the Yorkshire Insurance Company, which appointment he has held since 1887. Mr. Mitchell had previously been connected with several first-class Companies, and since he has been in charge of the Glasgow District of the Yorkshire its business here has been very largely increased in both its Fire and Life Departments.

Moffet, R. G., is the Resident Secretary to the Belfast Branch of the Gresham Life Assurance Society. He was educated at a private school, and commenced his commercial career in a mercantile office engaged in the shipping trade, afterwards entering the service of the Irish Post Office, where he formed his first connection with Insurance work, having obtained an Agency to the Guardian Fire and Life Assurance Company in connection with their Dublin Branch.

In 1886 Mr. Moffet was appointed Resident Secretary at Belfast to the Scottish Temperance Life Assurance Company, the sphere of his work at that time being confined to Ulster, but about three years ago Mr. T. W. Russell, M.P., resigned the Dublin Branch of that Company owing to excessive Parliamentary duties, and the whole of the Irish business was placed under the control of the Belfast Office.

In August of last year Mr. Moffet was appointed to his present position, a vacancy having been made for him by the promotion of his predecessor to the Manchester Branch of the Gresham. He is a gentleman universally esteemed by all who know him.

PATRICK MUNRO.

G. McKAY MORANT.

Munro, Patrick, the Local Secretary of the Scottish Provident Institution at their Branch Office in Leeds, entered the service of the Institution in January, 1882, as Chief Clerk in the Glasgow Branch. Here he remained till 1886, when he was promoted to the position of Agency Inspector at the Head Office, which post in its turn he held till 1889, when he was appointed to his present office.

Morant, G. McKay, the London Manager of the North German Fire Insurance Company of Hamburg, is the son of Mr. George C. Morant, of the Commercial Union Assurance Company. He has had an extensive and varied Insurance training, for, in addition to having been in the service of several of the principal London Companies, he was engaged for several years in Fire Insurance business in various parts of the Continent. Besides his London business, he is also a partner in the firm of Haine and Morant, of London and Antwerp, and of Haine, Morant, and Moreau, of Paris, which latter firm act as the

representatives of the Commercial Union Assurance Company in that capital.

———

Montgomery, H. C., District Manager to the Insurance Company of North America and Agent for the Northern Fire and Life Office for the North of Ireland at Belfast, commenced in 1878 in an Agency Office of the Sun Fire Office, whence he transferred his services to the Belfast District Branch of the Norwich Union Fire as Chief Clerk. In 1880 he applied for and obtained the District Agency of the newly-formed Fire Insurance Association, for the North of Ireland, which post he held until that Company took over the business of the Standard Fire Office, when he resigned his position, and, in conjunction with his brother, took up the business of the Glasgow and London for the same district. This position the brothers resigned in 1890, and Mr. H. C. Montgomery applied for the District Managership, which he now holds, for the Insurance Company of North America, for which Company he has already done a very considerable business.

A. H. MORGAN, F.F.A.

JAMES MURRAY.

Morgan, Andrew Henderson, the Resident Secretary to the Scottish Equitable Life Assurance Society at their Branch Office at Glasgow, entered the service of the Society in May, 1870, at their Head Office in Edinburgh, and has thus been connected with the Society for a period not very far short of a quarter of a century. He worked his way steadily up through all departments of the office to the satisfaction of his directors and his own advancement in the Insurance world, he himself attributing much of the success he has achieved in his profession to the valuable experience which he acquired during the earlier years of his career while working in the Edinburgh Head Office, under the able administration of the well-known Manager, Mr. Thomas Bond Sprague, from whom he received a most useful part of his official training. He was appointed to his present post in Glasgow in 1881, on the death of the late Resident Secretary, Mr. Hugh Gibson, and has done much since his appointment to increase the business and general prosperity of the Branch under his supervision. Mr. Morgan is a Fellow of the Faculty of Actuaries in Scotland, having passed the three examinations prescribed by the Faculty, and is the author of several papers on Insurance and other subjects, amongst others, "Investments: How money may be made and invested" and "Life Branch Work." One of his papers has been reprinted in the Austrian Insurance press by special request.

Murray, James, is the Resident Manager of the Caledonian Insurance Company at its Manchester, Liverpool, and Leeds Branches. Mr. Murray was formerly Resident Secretary of the East of Scotland Branch of the Scottish Commercial Assurance Company, and when that Company was amalgamated with the Lancashire he became Secretary of the Scottish Metropolitan Fire Insurance Company, with which he remained until its absorption by the Caledonian. On that event taking place he was appointed Assistant Secretary of the Caledonian at their Head Office in Edinburgh, in which capacity he won the confidence of his Directors to such an extent that in May 1888 he was promoted to his present important position, the district under his charge embracing the whole of Lancashire, Yorkshire, North Wales, and Derbyshire. Mr. Murray is universally acknowledged to be a Fire Insurance expert of more than ordinary ability. He also takes a keen interest in Accident Insurance : so much so, that in 1877, recognising the fact that an Accident Insurance Company was required in Scotland, he projected and took a prominent part in the formation of the Scottish Accident Insurance Company, and acted as its appointed Auditor for the first seven years of its existence. Mr. Murray is an energetic Volunteer, and formerly held a commission as Captain and Honorary Major in the 5th V.B., The Royal Scots. He now holds the rank of Honorary Major and Quartermaster in the 4th V.B. (The King's), Liverpool Regiment.

W. W. Naismith, C.A.

Charles Naismith.

Naismith, William Wilson, is the Manager for the West of Scotland of the County Fire Office and Provident Life Office.

Mr. Naismith is the only son of the late Dr. W. Naismith, J.P. He was educated at Gilbertfield House School and Glasgow University. Trained in the office of the well-known Chartered Accountants, McClelland, Mackinnon, and Blyth, in 1879, after passing the necessary examinations, he was admitted a Member of the Institute of Accountants and Actuaries in Glasgow.

In 1881 he was appointed Branch Secretary of the Alliance. In 1883, when that Company took over the Fire business of the Scottish Imperial, the Directors of the latter office appointed him Secretary at their Head Office; which post he held till 1887, when he received his present appointment to the Glasgow Office of the County and Provident. In Mr. Naismith's hands the revenue of these old-established Offices is steadily advancing.

Naismith, Charles, District Manager to the Norwich Union Life Insurance Society at its Branch Office at Manchester, commenced his Insurance career in 1874 by joining the Glasgow Branch of the Life Association of Scotland. He left that Office in 1876 to take the post of Agency Inspector under the Manager for Scotland of the Norwich Union Life Assurance Society, which Office had taken steps to acquire a position north of the Tweed which it had not previously held. In December, 1877, he was transferred to Edinburgh, where a Branch Office of the Norwich Union was opened, and in connection with it he was, as District Inspector, so successful that, in November, 1879, the directors promoted him to the management of the Manchester Branch, which position he now holds. At the time of this promotion he was in his twenty-third year. Since Mr. Naismith assumed control of this district it has been enlarged by the addition of Westmoreland. The business of the Branch has been increasing steadily, and every successive year shows a considerable advance in new assurances.

H. B. MEADOWS.

JOHN MUNRO.

Meadows, H. B., is the Manager to the Sun Fire Office at its Charing Cross Branch. Mr. Meadows has passed the whole of his Insurance career in the service of the Sun Fire Office, having entered the Head Office in 1860 when nearly sixteen years of age; and, after having passed through the various departments of the business, he was, in 1872, appointed Surveyor to the South-Western District, in connection with his present Branch. In this capacity he remained till 1890, when, after eighteen years of outdoor work, he was promoted to his present Managership.

Munro, John, is the Secretary at the City Branch of the English and Scottish Law Life Association at 11, Ludgate Hill, E.C. He began his Insurance career as Agent of the Imperial Fire and Life Offices in 1873 while cashier in a provincial Bank. In 1884 he was appointed Superintendent of Agents in Yorkshire of the Imperial Life Company, and subsequently transferred to Lancashire and London. He received his present appointment in 1889.

FRANCIS MIZON.

THOMAS NICHOLSON.

Mizon, Francis, London Manager of the Leeds and North of England Boiler and Accident Insurance Company, is a native of the Eastern Counties, where he was born in 1854, and received his first business training in the telegraph office of the Great Eastern Railway, where at the age of twelve he was employed in receiving, taking down and delivering messages. When fourteen he was appointed by the Railway Clearing House Committee to take charge of a Junction to check the foreign traffic, and in the following year sent to London in a similar capacity; subsequently being transferred to Cambridge, an important station, where he stayed for three years. Being desirous of entering the Head Office of the Clearing House, he studied for the necessary examination, which he succeeded in passing, and was called to the Chief Office, where he remained for ten years. During that time he worked up a good Insurance connection, and in February, 1886, he was asked by the Manager of the Sickness and Accident Assurance Association to take charge of their London Branch, which appointment he accepted. After three years' service with the Sickness and Accident, he resigned his position to take charge of the London Branch of the General Accident of Perth, which post, however, he also resigned at the end of twelve months to open up the London Branch for his present Company, of which he is still Manager. Mr. Mizon enjoys a good reputation for business capacity and ability, and has nearly doubled the business of his Company since his connection with it.

Nicholson, Thomas, F.S.A., the Agency Superintendent of the Scottish Imperial Insurance Company for the South-Eastern District, with head-quarters at Surbiton, is a Scotchman by birth. He has been connected with his present Company since 1884, and does a very large business; previous to that year he was partner in the firm of Nicholson and Co., bankers and brokers in the City of London, with a good connection. Mr. Nicholson has always devoted all his energy and business ability to carrying on his Assurance work, and has earned himself a reputation for working conscientiously not only as a matter of profit but as conferring the benefits of Assurance on his fellow-creatures. He has written several pamphlets on the subject of Assurance, which have had a very extensive circulation. He is the proud possessor of three decorations, one of which is from the Royal Humane Society, he having saved no less than five lives from drowning, fire and accident, and he has received several valuable testimonials from agents, policy-holders, and friends, and in addition to being esteemed in his business capacity, he is held in very high regard in private life. One of his generous gifts to his poorer brethren has been the erection of a church for a congregation too needy to meet the cost themselves.

EDWARD NEILD.

THOMAS NIVEN.

Neild, Edward, is District Manager of the Manchester Branch of the Mutual Life Insurance Company of New York. He is a partner in the firm of Isaac Neild and Son, Estate Brokers, 19, Chapel Walks, Manchester, and has, previously to his present appointment, had a long and varied experience as Agent and Broker for the best British Life Offices.

He was appointed in May, 1887, to his present position, carrying on the business of the company at 19, Chapel Walks. These premises proving inadequate for the growing needs of the Company, he was in September, 1890, associated with A. B. Scholfield, as Resident Secretary, in new and larger premises situated on the ground floor of the building of 28, Brown Street, Manchester, nearly opposite the General Post Office.

Mr. Neild was educated at a private school and at Owens College, Manchester, and has been for some years Honorary Secretary of the Manchester and Salford District Temperance Union. He is a member of the executives of the British Temperance League and Central Sunday Closing Association, whose Head Office is in Manchester. He has been most successful in the Life Insurance field, and is at present securing a very large amount of business for the Mutual of New York.

Niven, Thomas, is the Resident Secretary of the Equitable Life Assurance Society of the United States at their Liverpool Branch, to which post he was appointed in 1889, on the Branch being first established. Mr. Niven had, previous to taking up his present duties, acted as Secretary to the County Fire and Provident Life, and is well known and respected in Liverpool Insurance circles.

THOMAS M. A. NOLAN.

G. H. NICHOLS.

Nolan, Thomas M. A., the Secretary in Ireland for the Equitable Fire and Accident Office at the Dublin Office, was born in Manchester in 1862, and at the age of twenty-four was appointed to the management of the Birmingham Branch of the South British and National Companies. He relinquished that post, however, a year later, to take up the more important position of Manager in Ireland for the same Offices, and when the home business of those Companies was purchased by the Equitable in 1890 he was retained by the latter Office to manage their Irish business. Mr. Nolan's earlier years of business life were spent in the headquarters of the Palatine (then Mutual) Fire Office.

———

Nichols, George Henry, is the District Manager of the Eastern Counties Branch of the Ocean Accident and Guarantee Corporation, Limited, which is situated at 45, New Square, Cambridge. Mr. Nichols was previously for six years in the employ of the Corporation at their Office at Bristol, as Cashier, and after that, Inspector, from which position he was promoted to his present appointment, with satisfactory results to the Corporation.

Noverre, Charles E., the London Manager of the Norwich Union Fire Insurance Society, was born at Norwich in 1845, and was educated at King Edward the Sixth's Grammar School in that city. At the early age of sixteen—in 1861—he entered the Head Office of the Norwich Union Life Insurance Society, of which his father, Frank Noverre, Esq., was then a Director. His grandfather, Francis Noverre, Esq., was also a Director, having indeed been one of the original Board of Direction, and had given material assistance in its foundation in 1808. After spending seven years here, Mr. Noverre in 1868 transferred his services to the sister Society—the Norwich Union Fire, and in 1882 was called upon to assume the management of the Policy and Tariff Department. In 1887, after an open competition, he was selected to fill his present important position of the Society's Manager at 50, Fleet Street, London. Upon leaving his native city, his fellow-clerks presented him with a handsome silver claret jug, and the Committee of Management of the Jenny Lind Infirmary for Sick Children, for which he had several years acted as Honorary Secretary, presented him with a magnificent silver inkstand. The Lady Superintendent and nurses also added to these testimonials of respect and esteem with an album, containing photographs of the medical and nursing staff and members of the Committee of the Institution. All of these were accompanied with very flattering encomiums on his past career, with bright hopes for his future, and were each suitably inscribed in similar terms. He had also acted since its foundation as Honorary Secretary of the Children's Convalescent Home at Great Yarmouth, during which period it was visited on separate occasions by the Prince of Wales and Prince Albert Victor, and the Committee of Management here received his resignation with great regret, and emphasised their expressions with the present of a splendid silver and ivory-fitted travelling bag, in grateful

C. E. NOVERRE.

remembrance of his untiring and successful efforts. Nor does this complete the list of testimonials his work and character had won. The Vicar and parishioners of St. Stephen's Church, where he had acted for twenty-one years as organist and choirmaster, presented him with a magnificent silver salver and chiming-clock, as a token of sincere esteem, and the members of the choir added an elegantly-fitted inkstand, while the Vestry ordered a record of his services to be entered on its minutes. For eleven years he had been a Churchwarden of St. Martin-at-Palace Church, and on leaving, the Vicar, the Rev. Dr. Cunningham Geikie, gave him a complete set of his well-known works " in gratitude to him for his kind services as my churchwarden, and as a small expression of my sincere respect and esteem for him as a man"; to this the parishioners of the Church added a handsome drawing-room cabinet and mirror. He had been Joint Honorary Secretary of the movement for presenting the Corporation of the City of Norwich with a public organ for St. Andrew's Hall at a cost of £2,000. For sixteen years previous to leaving Norwich he had been a member of the literary staff of the *Eastern Daily Press* and *Norfolk News*, and the proprietors and his colleagues of these papers presented him with a minute of congratulation on his appointment inscribed on vellum, with a splendid album of Norfolk views, specially prepared. Among other literary work, Mr. Noverre is the author of "The Life and Works of the Chevalier Noverre," and "Life Insurance for the benefit of Charitable Institutions," in addition to several musical compositions, and he has been honoured by dedications of works by Monsieur Alexandre Guilmant, Dr. Gladstone, &c. In London he is a Vestryman of the Parish of St. Dunstan-in-the-West, and a Member of the Charities Committee, in addition to which he is Honorary Secretary of St. Agnes' National Schools, Kennington Park, S.E.

JOHN OLIVER.

WILLIAM OATES.

Oliver, John, the Resident Secretary in London of the Lancashire Insurance Company, with the exception of three years' spent in the London office of the Scottish Provincial Insurance Company, has spent his whole business career in the service of the company he is now with. He has been with them altogether now nineteen years, of which the first four were spent at the Head Office in Manchester, and the remainder in London, and five years since he was appointed to his present position.

Oates, John Francis, District Manager to the Economic Fire Office at its Yorkshire Branch at Bradford, has seen a great deal of service in the Insurance profession, having been long connected with the Northern Assurance Company and the Liverpool and London and Globe Insurance Company in various capacities in each of these offices calculated to ensure him a most profitable experience in all departments of the business; and, immediately previous to his undertaking the duties of his present position, being employed in the Bradford Branch of the Scottish Union and National, under the able supervision of Mr. Macmillan. In 1887, on the formation of the Economic Fire Office, Mr. Oates was selected as the Manager of this important Branch, which is under the control of a Local Board of Directors.

Oates, William, the City Manager of the Norwich Union Life Insurance Society, was born at Worksop, Notts., on the 30th of August, 1844. His Insurance career commenced early in 1881 when he was appointed Agency Superintendent for the Scottish Imperial Insurance Company, in the Birmingham and Midland District, in which position Mr. Oates was most successful, considerably increasing the business and Agency connections of that Company, which, at that time, was little known, having but a very small connection in the Midlands. Early in the year 1884, J. Heron Duncan, Esq., resigned his position as London Manager of the Scottish Imperial, having accepted an important position in connection with the Royal Insurance Company, and Mr. Oates was appointed Mr. Duncan's successor, which position he held, with considerable success, until September, 1891.

In August, 1891, Mr. Oates submitted to the Directors of the Scottish Imperial certain important recommendations, tendering the usual notice to terminate his engagement should they not see their way to carry those recommendations into effect. The Directors not approving thereof, accepted his resignation, and he retired from the London Managership early in September. Immediately upon his retirement he received the appointment of City Manager to his present Office, the Norwich Union Life Insurance Society.

M. S. O CALLAGHAN.

THOMAS O'BRIEN.

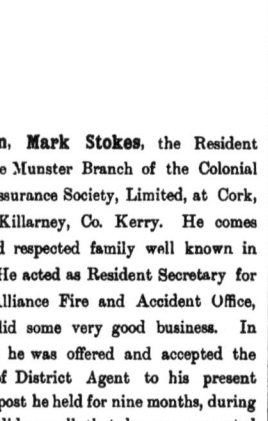

O'Callaghan, Mark Stokes, the Resident Secretary of the Munster Branch of the Colonial Mutual Life Assurance Society, Limited, at Cork, is a native of Killarney, Co. Kerry. He comes from an old and respected family well known in that county. He acted as Resident Secretary for the Scottish Alliance Fire and Accident Office, for which he did some very good business. In January, 1890, he was offered and accepted the appointment of District Agent to his present Society, which post he held for nine months, during which time he did so well that he was promoted in September, 1890, to his present post of Resident Secretary for Munster. Since his promotion he has been continuing his successful career, and has opened up very nearly all the towns in Munster for the Society.

O'Brien, Thomas, District Agent at Cork to the Marine and General Mutual Life Assurance Society, first started in Insurance work about ten years ago, when he undertook an agency for the London and Provincial Horse and Carriage Insurance Company, for which he is still acting. About the same time he became also a representative of the English and Scottish Law Life and the Phœnix Fire Offices, the latter of which Agency he still holds, though he discontinued the former in 1888, when he was appointed District Agent for the South of Ireland for the Marine and General. He holds a similar office for the Boiler Insurance and Steam Power Company, Limited, Manchester, having for several years previously represented the Northern Accident Insurance Company, and has recently taken up a like post for the Economic Fire and Guarantee Insurance Offices.

WILLIAM PERRING O'KEEF.

HERBERT O'LEARY.

O'Keef, William Perring, Resident Secretary for Yorkshire to the Colonial Mutual Life Assurance Society at Bradford, has been engaged in Insurance work for the whole period of his business life, having been for seventeen years in connection with the United Kingdom Temperance and General Provident Institution, first acting in the capacity of assistant to his father, the late Mr. T. D. O'Keef, the District Manager to the Institution for South-West Lancashire, etc., at the Liverpool Branch, later on being taken into partnership with him, and finally on his death succeeding him in the sole District Managership. In 1889 Mr. O'Keef resigned his position with the United Kingdon Temperance and General Provident Institution, to take up a similar appoinment which had been offered him at Manchester, to control the South-East Lancashire District of the Mutual Reserve Fund Life Association of New York, which post he held for nearly twelve months, resigning it in its turn to undertake his present duties for the Colonial Mutual Life Assurance Society. The post which he holds is a most important one, this Society's branch being regarded as one of the most important Insurance Branches in Bradford, and the policies issued by it showing an abnormally large average, mostly being on the Tontine system, which has proved to be very popular in the District. Mr. O'Keef's unbroken record of success has fully justified the Directors in putting him into his present place; and the result of the appointment has been quite equal to their expectations, for he has most ably carried on the work which was left to him by his predecessors in office, and, not content with that, has himself done much to add to the business of his office in this district.

O'Leary, Herbert, is the Secretary at Birmingham of the Life Association of Scotland, which appointment he has held for several years, and previous to which he had been engaged in the business of Life Insurance for a long period.

ROBERT OLIPHANT.

SAMUEL OLDFIELD.

Oliphant, Robert, is the Manager for Scotland of the Law Union and Crown Insurance Company, with Head Offices in Glasgow. Mr. Oliphant's first experience was acquired in the office of a Writer and Banker at Auchtermuchty, in Fifeshire, where he received a sound practical training which has been of great use to him in his after career. In 1872 he left Auchtermuchty, having applied for and obtained an appointment in the Head Office of the Scottish Commercial Insurance Company in Glasgow, where he advanced by rapid stages through the various grades of the profession, and in the short period of two and a half years had attained to no less a responsible position than that of Head of the Fire Department. In 1877 he resigned that position to take up the duties of Chief Surveyor and Inspector of Agents to the General Life and Fire Assurance Company for the West and North of Scotland, working from the Head Offices in Glasgow, in which capacity he proved eminently successful in building up and increasing both branches of the business of the Company. In 1882 he was selected by the Queen Insurance Company, which was at that time taking steps to increase its Life business and connections in Scotland, for the post of Life Superintendent for Scotland, and fully justified his appointment by carrying out both items of his Director's programme in their entirety. Three years later, however, he resigned his post with the Queen Insurance Company, to accept that of Secretary for Scotland to the Glasgow and London, which he retained until the close of 1890, when he was appointed Manager of the Midland Branch of the Norwich Union Life Insurance Society at Birmingham. He relinquished that post at the end of April, 1892, and accepted his present appointment with the Law Union and Crown Fire and Life Insurance Company.

Oldfield, Samuel, is the Resident Secretary at Sheffield of the Queen Insurance Company. He received this appointment in 1867, and under his management the business of this Company in this district has been very materially increased, and under the amalgamation arrangement of the Queen and Royal Mr. Oldfield continues in the service of the latter Company.

JAMES OSTLER.

J. LLOYD OWEN.

Ostler, James, is the Secretary of the Northern Assurance Company at Manchester. Mr. Ostler received his early business training in a London office, preliminary to entering the Bristol Branch of the Royal. There he remained thirteen years, latterly having the practical management. He relinquished that position in 1877 to found, at Bristol, the West of England and South Wales Branch of his present Company. In 1882 the Directors promoted him to the more important sphere in Manchester, in succession to Mr. James Robb. The Branch in that city controls the Company's business in Lancashire (Liverpool excepted), the West Riding of Yorkshire, Cheshire, and Derbyshire.

Owen, J. Lloyd, is Secretary of the Alliance Assurance Company at their Branch Office at Newcastle-on-Tyne. Mr. Owen acquired his previous Insurance experience at the Manchester and Dublin Branches and at the Head Office of the Alliance. He was appointed to his present post in 1889.

A. OWEN.

GEORGE A. PANTON.

Owen, A., District Superintendent of the Rock Life Assurance Company at Birmingham, was, previous to the year 1884, employed as Station Master at the Great Western Railway Station at Leamington, and while engaged in that capacity also worked an Insurance Agency, in which, during his twenty years' service with the railway, he achieved a considerable success. In 1884 he left his railway work to accept the offer of an Agency Inspectorship offered him by the Scottish Imperial, but only remained in the service of that company for a short period, leaving it to take up his present appointment with the Rock Life Assurance Company, for which he has since worked up a handsome business. Mr. Owen takes a leading part in the local affairs of Leamington, where he resides, being a member of the Town Council, as well as of the Town Improvement Association, the Church Council, etc., etc.

———

Panton, George A., is the Resident Secretary of the Scottish Provident Institution at their Birmingham Branch. Mr. Panton was educated at the High School and the University of Edinburgh, of which city he is a native, and received his subsequent training in the Insurance profession in the English and Scottish Law Life Office, Edinburgh, under Mr. W. Smith, LL.D., Actuary, the able Manager of that Association. Mr. Panton was appointed to his present post in November, 1875.

J. HAMER OWENS.

C. H. PARKER.

Owens, J. Hamer, is the Manager of the Law Courts Branch of the Royal Insurance Company, Chancery Lane, W.C. Mr. Owens has been engaged in the Insurance business for many years, and is a valued member of the staff of the great Company he represents.

Porter, Christopher W., Secretary to the Bristol and West of England Local Board of Directors of the North British and Mercantile Insurance Company, is the son of the late Rev. Thomas Porter, of Bristol. He has passed the whole period of his Insurance career in the service of the North British and Mercantile, having entered the Bristol Office of the Company more than a quarter of a century ago. He was appointed to his present post in 1871.

Parker, Charles H., the London Secretary of the Northern Accident Insurance Company, Limited, is a Novocastrian by birth, and has had upwards of twelve years' Insurance experience. He commenced his career in the Newcastle Office of the Commercial Union Assurance Company under Mr. Thomas West, afterwards joining the City of London Fire Insurance Company as Chief Clerk and Surveyor in the same town. Six years ago he was appointed Resident Secretary to the Northern Accident Company, and in July of 1890 he was promoted to the London Office. We understand that Mr. Parker's career has been a very successful one, and his Directors and Manager have every confidence in him. He has always displayed an exceptional amount of interest in his Company's affairs, and we have every reason to believe he will make his Branch a great success.

HUGH PANTON.

W. PARKINSON.

Panton, Hugh, is the District Manager at Newcastle-on-Tyne of the Norwich Union Fire Office. Mr. Panton comes of an old Insurance family, his grandfather having been appointed Agent at Sunderland of the Norwich Union in 1808, since which time the agency has been conducted by him, his son, and the present District Manager, Hugh Panton, who was appointed to his present position in August, 1889, at which time the Directors resolved opening a Branch at Newcastle to include Northumberland, Durham, Cumberland, and Westmoreland. Mr. Panton is well known and highly respected throughout this district.

———

Pocklington, Henry, the Leeds Manager of the Commercial Union Assurance Company, entered upon his career of a District Manager in the year 1869, in the service of the Britannia Fire Association, whom he represented first at Exeter and Hull, and subsequently at Leeds, having supervision of the counties of Yorkshire, Durham, Northumberland, and Lincolnshire. He at the same time acted for other offices, in the capacity of Surveyor and Assessor of Losses. He entered upon his present duties as District Manager for the Commercial Union Assurance Company in January of 1878, when that Company opened their Yorkshire Branch, and being in want of a good Insurance man to supervise its business, were fortunate enough to obtain Mr. Pocklington's services. Mr. Pocklington was at one time a frequent contributor to the scientific press. He is very strongly in favour of the thorough practical education in their business of young Insurance men, and devotes much of his spare time to the furtherance of this object. He is a Fellow of the Royal Microscopical Society of many years' standing, a Member of the Yorkshire Geological and Polytechnical Society, of the Society of Chemical Industries, and of several other scientific and literary societies.

———

Parkinson, William, is the Resident Secretary in charge of the Branch Office of the Sun Life Assurance Society at Liverpool. Mr. Parkinson first came to Liverpool nearly twenty-four years ago, and commenced his career as an Insurance man by entering the Head Office situate in that town of the London and Lancashire Fire Insurance Company. He remained in the service of that Company for a period of no less than seventeen-and-a-half consecutive years, during that period passing through several of the various departments of the Office, until the year 1884, when being desirous of doing something more to improve his position, he made an application for a post to the Sun Life Assurance Society, and having as the result, received the appointment to be the active representative of that Company in the same Liverpool District, he quitted his former Fire Insurance work to take up the kindred duties of the Life Insurance business. The Sun Life Assurance Society had had an Agency for a great number of years previously in Liverpool, one of the Agents, Mr. N. S. Bold, having been then Agent for no less than forty years, and Messrs. Pickford Brothers, having held the post since the year 1870, that firm still continuing to act for the Society under the title of District Managers, but Mr. Parkinson was their first Resident Secretary under the new *régime*, when their Branch Office was opened in accordance with the progressive policy which the Office has adopted in recent years. Mr. Parkinson has worked hard since his appointment and given much satisfaction to his Chief Office.

T. G. Parkinson.

R. Dolphin Paull.

Parkinson, Thomas Gray, the Local Secretary of the Westminster Fire Office at their Birmingham Branch, was born in 1859, was privately educated, and at the age of 17 entered the service of the Manchester Fire Office, twelve months later receiving a junior clerkship in the Imperial Fire Insurance Company, Birmingham, where he was soon promoted to the head of the Fire Department. In 1882, he left them to become Head Clerk of the Scottish Union and National. In 1885, Mr. Parkinson was offered, and accepted, the control of the Midland Branch of the Reliance Life Office, whose business rapidly increased under his management. In 1886, he was appointed to the post he now fills so ably. Mr. Parkinson is one of the founders of the Birmingham Insurance Institute.

Phillips, E. St. John, is the Yorkshire District Manager of the London Assurance Corporation at Leeds. Previously to becoming connected with his present Company he was for eighteen years in the service of the Alliance, four years of which period he spent at the Ipswich Branch of that Company, and the rest at the Head Office in London, being some years in charge of

the Guarantee Department. He joined the London Assurance Corporation in 1882, first as Manager of their London West End Office, whence, in 1886, he proceeded to his present charge.

Paull, R. Dolphin, Resident Secretary to the Ocean Accident and Guarantee Corporation at its Branch Office for the Midlands at Birmingham, is the brother of the Secretary to the Corporation at their Head Office, which Office he entered as a Clerk in 1874. In that capacity he displayed so much energy and talent for the business that he was appointed to the more responsible post of Inspector of Agents for London and the provinces, which position he was still occupying when, in 1882, on the Corporation establishing their Midland Branch, he was promoted to take charge of it as Resident Secretary. The Midland Branch was the first experiment on the part of the Directors in the direction of opening Branch Offices, and though others have since been established in all the important towns in the Kingdom, the Birmingham Branch still maintains a leading position. Mr. Paull holds the post of Honorary Treasurer to the Birmingham Insurance Institute, of which he was one of the original promoters.

JOHN S. PATTERSON.

GEORGE PEARSON.

Patterson, John S., is Agency Inspector of the Rock Life Office at its Leeds Branch. Mr. Patterson, who is a young man of energy and ability, received this appointment in 1890, having previously been Resident Secretary at Newcastle-on-Tyne of the Sickness and Accident Assurance Association.

———

Pears, E. A., is the Secretary of the Australian and New Zealand Underwriters' Association, and has also acted for many years as the Settler of Claims of the New Zealand Insurance Company in London. He has held his position as Secretary to the Association since the first formation of that institution, and has consequently identified himself with all its proceedings from the beginning. The assiduity with which he has applied himself to the furtherance of its interests and objects affords ample proof of his heartfelt devotion to the cause for which he is worthily respected by all its Members. As representative of the Association, he is a Member of the Average Adjusters' Association.

———

Pearson, George, is the Resident Secretary at Liverpool of the Manchester Fire Office, which post he has held since 1874. Mr. Pearson had previously held a similar position in the Provincial Insurance Company, and has had a long and successful experience in the Insurance business.

JAMES E. PERKINS.

JOHN PETRIE.

Perkins, James E., is the District Manager at Liverpool, of the Royal Exchange Assurance Corporation, which appointment he has held since July, 1887, when the Branch was opened. Mr. Perkins received his training in the Head Office of the London and Lancashire Fire and Life Companies, when the two worked in conjunction, and was, in 1879, appointed Resident Secretary to the Life Company upon their separation. This post he held until the Royal Exchange selected him for his present appointment.

———

Petrie, John, is the Assistant-Secretary at Dublin, of the Life Association of Scotland. Mr. Petrie is a Life Insurance official of experience, in which field he has met with much success.

W. G. PIDDUCK.

J. H. PIPER.

Pidduck, William Gilbert, Resident Manager to the County Fire and Provident Life Offices, and captain of the County Fire Brigade at Canterbury, was born in 1825, the eldest son of a farmer and the descendant of a long line of yeoman freeholders in Kent. Captain Pidduck was educated at Wye College, on leaving which he became a Railway Surveyor, which profession he continued in until the inevitable collapse that followed on Hudson, the Railway King's, colossal speculations. Finding little promise of a livelihood left from his first essay, Pidduck then determined to go to sea, and accordingly became a sailor before the mast, in which sphere of life he met with a good many ups and downs. He then returned to Canterbury, where he became an Agent to the County Fire and Provident Life Offices in 1863. Shortly after his appointment, a disastrous conflagration in the High Street having shown how ill-equipped Canterbury was at that time against outbreaks of fire, Captain Pidduck set to work and formed a Volunteer Fire Brigade, and the directors of the County having found the plant, he was chosen to command the Brigade. The usefulness of this step was proved in 1872, when, on the Cathedral taking fire, it was only saved from destruction by the prompt and gallant action of Captain Pidduck and the firemen of Canterbury, who thus won for themselves a name which resounded throughout the world. Captain Pidduck was not long before he raised his Agency to the dignity of a Branch office, of which he was made Manager, which post he still occupies. He holds several public appointments in his City, notably that of Clerk to the Commissioner of Taxes for the City of Canterbury and the borough of Fordwich, and notwithstanding the thanklessness of his office, his invariable readiness to explain to and assist all who seek his advice has gained for him universal esteem. He was one of the founders of the St. Laurence Amateur Musical Society, which has taken the place of the Old Canterbury Catch Club. He built and started the Canterbury Club, now numbering over 400 members, and was the introducer of the telephone into the City, in spite of strenuous opposition. He is likewise an author, his " Babs Oak Will 'o the wisp," having been written to help the fund towards the organ of his parish church.

———

Piper, John H., is the Resident Secretary of the Scottish Accident Insurance Company at Birminghan. He commenced his Insurance career in 1883, as Agency Superintendent in the west of England for his present company. In 1885 he removed to Birmingham to take up the appointment of District Manager there for the New York Life, which appointment he resigned in 1886 to return to the Scottish Accident as Agency Superintendent at the Birmingham Branch, in connection with Mr. Weldon Underwood. In 1888 the Northern Accident Company decided to open a Branch Office in Birmingham, and Mr. Piper was offered and accepted the appointment of Resident Secretary. In December, 1890, he again returned to the Scottish Accident, the Directors having offered him the post of Resident Secretary at Birmingham, in succession to Mr. Underwood, who had resigned on account of continued ill-health. This appointment was entirely acceptable to the leading agents in the district, several of whom had in fact specially expressed a desire for Mr. Piper's return.

T. A. POLSON.

WILLIAM POOLE.

Polson, Thomas A., is the Resident Secretary of the Employers' Insurance Company of Great Britain at their London office. Mr. Polson, who is an Irishman, having been born at Tuam, county Galway, and educated at Dublin, started his business career in the Banking profession, and passed the best part of ten years in the service of a London bank. His introduction to Insurance occurred in 1886, and his success as an ordinary agent, while yet a bank cashier, resulted in an offer from the Scottish Accident Company of the superintendency of their London Agents, whereupon he abandoned the counter for the, to him, far more congenial profession he now follows. While with the Scottish Accident, Mr. Polson most effectually made his mark as a successful Insurance man, and his diligence was rewarded by his selection to fill the post he at present holds.

Poole, William, is Senior Partner in the firm of William Poole and Co., Insurance Brokers and Agents, Manchester. Mr. Poole entered the Insurance business in 1864. He has held several Insurance appointments, and was District Manager at Manchester of the Belfast Fire Insurance Company some time prior to its amalgamation with the late Standard Fire Office. In addition to being Agents of several good Companies, the firm of William Poole and Co. is well-known as popular and reliable Insurance Brokers, and has the placement of a large number of home and foreign risks.

P. F. PORTWAY.

EDWIN POSTON.

Portway, P. F., Branch Manager to the Atlas Assurance Company at Birmingham, was originally brought up as a farmer and architect, but not finding either of these professions so congenial to his tastes as he would have liked he went into the Insurance business, and after having acquired some experience in Fire Insurance, was in 1878 appointed to the post of Inspector of Agents to the Edinburgh Life Office, the district under his supervision including the twenty southern counties of England and Ireland. He remained with the Edinburgh Life Office till 1881, when he transferred his services to the Atlas Assurance Company, and received the appointment of Inspector for that Company for the whole of the United Kingdom, and retained that post until the time of taking up his residence at Birmingham to establish the Branch in that city.

———

Poston, Edwin, the Resident Secretary of the Sickness and Accident Assurance Association, Limited, at the Liverpool Branch, is a native of Liverpool, where in 1875 he commenced his Insurance career in the service of the Liverpool Clerks' Association. After remaining with this Association for a period of ten years he entered the service of the Sickness and Accident Assurance Association, at that time just newly-formed, in his present capacity, and since then has done much to increase the prosperity and popularity of the Association in his district.

R. J. POSNETT.

JOSEPH POWELL.

Posnett, R. J., Resident Secretary of the Life Association of Scotland at its Dublin Branch Office, has held that post since 1878, during which period he has done a large business for his Office.

———

Powell, Joseph, is the Resident Secretary at Liverpool, of the Scottish Union and National Insurance Company, which appointment he has held since the opening of the Branch in 1883. Mr. Powell was formerly on the staff at the Liverpool Office of the Imperial Fire and Life Companies, and, prior to his appointment to his present position, was Local District Manager of the London and Provincial Fire Insurance Company, Limited. He is recognised in Liverpool as a very successful Insurance official, and has largely developed the business of his present Company in both departments.

FRANK E. PRESTON.

WILLIAM PRINGLE.

Preston, Frank E., the Resident Secretary to the Edinburgh Life Office at Liverpool, commenced his Insurance career in the service of the Scottish Provident Institution at their Birmingham Branch, where he received a sound training in the details of the profession from Mr. G. A. Panton, F.R.S.E., the Resident Secretary, who has turned out more than one successful Insurance man. In 1888, after six years with the Scottish Provident, Mr. Preston was appointed to take charge of the newly-formed West of England District Office of the Edinburgh Life Office at Bristol, that district having till then been worked from the London Office, and during his sojourn in the West he was most successful in increasing the Company's returns from that district. He was promoted to his present post in 1891. On leaving Bristol, Mr. Preston was presented with a handsome testimonial in the form of a complete *edition de luxe* of Sir Walter Scott's novels, which was the more appropriate as Sir Walter was one of the first Policy Holders in the Edinburgh Life Office.

———

Pringle, William, is the Resident Secretary of the Northern Assurance Company at their Branch Office at Dundee. Mr. Pringle has passed the whole of his Insurance career in the service of the Northern Assurance Company, and also at the Dundee Branch, having entered it in 1867, the Branch being at that time under the management of Mr. Alexander Duncan, the present Manager of the Scottish Union and National Insurance Company. In 1871 Mr. Duncan resigned his post, and was succeeded by Mr. Thomas Kyd, who in 1885 was appointed Resident Manager of the Northern at Aberdeen, and Mr. Pringle who had by that time served for eleven years as Chief Clerk to the Branch under Mr. Kyd, was appointed Resident Secretary in his stead.

WILLIAM PURSER, B.A.

JOSEPH E. PURSER, J.P.

Purser, William, B.A., the Resident Secretary of the Scottish Widows' Fund Life Assurance Society at their Branch Office at Birmingham, has been associated with that Society for the whole of his business career, with the trifling exception of one short period. He entered the service of the Scottish Widows' Fund in 1875 in the Dublin Branch, of which his father was and still is Resident Secretary. He subsequently served in connection with the Head Office, and with the Branches in Bristol, London, Newcastle, and Manchester. In 1887 he accepted the appointment of Resident Secretary to the Birmingham Branch of the Scottish Equitable, which post he held for just twelve months, that being the period of his absence from the service of his original Society above referred to. In May, 1888, on the transference of Mr. G. A. Woodward, the late Resident Secretary of the Scottish Widows' Fund at Birmingham, to Manchester, Mr. Purser was chosen to fill the vacancy. Mr. Purser was admitted to the degree of Bachelor of Arts at Trinity College, Dublin, in 1876, while serving in his father's office.

Purser, Joseph E., is the Resident Secretary at Dublin of the Scottish Widows' Fund Life Assurance Society. Mr. Purser has been in this Society's service many years and is one of its most esteemed officials; his son, Mr. William Purser, is the Resident Secretary at Birmingham of this Society.

S. W. PULLEN.

J. PYKE.

Pullen, S. W., is the District Manager of the Palatine Insurance Company at its West of England Branch at Bristol. Mr. Pullen has had a long Insurance experience, which commenced in the Bristol Office of the Liverpool and London and Globe, where he was employed for more than eight years. He was appointed to his present post with the Palatine in 1879. The Palatine enjoys a prominent position among the Insurance Companies doing business in Bristol, and during Mr. Pullen's management the Office has obtained a large and valuable connection throughout the district.

Pyke, Joseph, District Manager of the Patriotic Assurance Company at Belfast, commenced in the Insurance profession some twelve years ago in the office of the only Agent the Norwich Union had in Belfast, which Office being subsequently advanced to the rank of a Branch Office, he was also promoted to the position of Inspector of Agencies for the district of Ulster. When the Patriotic Assurance Company decided to open a Branch in Ulster, Mr. Pyke was offered the Managership, which he accepted, and has held now for over three years with credit to himself and advantage to his Company, whose income he has largely increased in his district.

W. C. RANKIN.

FRANCIS RANKINE.

Rankin, W. C., is the District Manager of the Economic Fire Office, at their Branch Office for Scotland, situated at Glasgow. He commenced his career in the Insurance profession in the Local Branch of the Liverpool and London and Globe Insurance Company, at Glasgow, which he left to take up the appointment of Chief Clerk and Surveyor in the Scottish branch of the Queen Insurance Company. After holding this appointment for a period of seven years, Mr. Rankin, in 1887, was selected for his present post of District Manager to the Economic Fire Office, on that Office establishing their Scottish Branch ; since which time he has been very successful in securing for his Office a substantial and constantly increasing share of public support in the northern portion of the United Kingdom.

Rankine, Francis, the Local Secretary of the Gresham Life Assurance Society at their Edinburgh Branch, has been in the service of the Society since 1884 as Inspector of Agents, his work in that capacity lying principally in the Eastern District of Scotland. During part of 1887 he left Scotland for a time to take up a similar post in the Dublin and Cork Districts of Ireland. He was recalled thence to Scotland to take up his present duties in the December of that year, and since then has succeeded in building up a very considerable business for the Society in the District under his supervision.

H. C. RAWLINS.

W. W. W. REID.

Rawlins, H. C., is the Resident Secretary of the Legal and General Life Assurance Society at its Liverpool Branch. Mr. Rawlins, who is well-known in Liverpool, where he has an influential connection, formerly acted in the same capacity for the Lancashire and Yorkshire Accident, and more recently for the London Guarantee and Accident, combining with the latter the District Managership of the London and Provincial Fire. These positions he resigned to take up the representation of the Legal and General Life together with that of the Law Guarantee and Trust Society, and The Insurance Company of North America of Philadelphia.

———

Reid, W. W. W., is the Manager of the Glasgow Branch of the Alliance Assurance Company, which appointment he accepted in 1883, previous to which time he had for nearly 13 years held the position of Manager of the Scottish Imperial Insurance Company. Previous to his connection with the Scottish Imperial, Mr. Reid had been engaged in business as a calico printer. He is a gentleman of large local influence and is held in high esteem in Glasgow.

WILLIAM RICHARDSON.

G. W. REYNOLDS.

Richardson, William, the Local Manager of the Liverpool Branch of the North British and Mercantile Insurance Company, entered the service of that Branch in 1866 as Junior Clerk, and by dint of steady hard work, combined with sterling business qualities and an excellent disposition, worked his way through every department of the Office until he arrived at the position of Chief Clerk and Surveyor. This post he held for five years, when, on the removal of the then Manager to Manchester, Mr. Richardson was appointed Acting Manager, ultimately receiving his formal appointment from his Local Board to his present important and responsible position in September, 1891. Mr. Richardson's universal geniality and courtesy towards all who know him make his appointment most popular, while the thorough knowledge of his business, which he has acquired during his patient and devoted service, ensures that it is a most profitable one to his Company.

———

Reynolds, George William, Resident Secretary of the Guardian Assurance Company at Dublin, commenced his business life in the Office of an Insurance Broker in London, leaving that Office to join the legitimate ranks of the profession by becoming a member of the staff of the Northern Assurance Company at Dublin, in which Branch he rose to be Inspector of Agents. He was then successively transferred to Liverpool as Chief Clerk, to the Head Office as Inspector of Agents, and to Nottingham as Resident Secretary for the same Office, resigning the last post in September, 1889, to take up his present duties for the Guardian Assurance Company in Ireland.

J. WARD RHODES.

W. HEWAT RIDDEL.

Rhodes, J. Ward, the Local Secretary of the Scottish Provident Institution at their Nottingham Branch, was originally connected for nine years with the legal profession, subsequently holding an appointment in the offices of Messrs. Henry S. King and Company, East India Agents, Bankers, &c., of London, but finding that the Metropolis was not suited to his health he accepted an appointment at Nottingham as District Superintendent of the Sceptre Life Office. This post he held for nine years, eventually resigning it to assume his present duties in 1889. His District comprises the counties of Nottingham, Derby, Lincoln, Leicester, and Northampton, thus embracing a large and important field for business, of which Mr. Rhodes has effectually availed himself, both in his original service of the Sceptre and subsequently in connection with the Scottish Provident Institution.

———

Riddel, W. Hewat, is the Branch Manager of the Atlas Assurance Company at their Office at Bristol. He received his early Insurance training in the Branch Office of the Northern Assurance Company at Edinburgh, and on leaving that, entered the service of the Commercial Union, with which Company he remained for a period of over 12 years at different Branches, the last of which was Bristol. On the Atlas, which had up to 1885 been represented in the Bristol District by Agents only, opening a Branch Office, Mr. Riddel was appointed Branch Manager.

HENRY L. RISELEY.

WILLIAM RICKMAN.

Riseley, Henry L., the Branch Manager of the West of England Insurance Company at Bristol, is a native of Clifton, where he was born in 1842. He began his Insurance career at the early age of fourteen in the Bristol Branch of the Norwich Union Insurance Society. There he gradually worked his way up, acquiring a sound knowledge of all the details of his business, till, in 1868, the West of England requiring a Manager for their Branch at Bristol, Mr. Riseley was selected for the post. He is also Resident Secretary of the Employers' Liability Assurance Corporation, with which Office he has been associated since its establishment in 1880, and Secretary of the British and Irish Plate-Glass Insurance Company of which he is the original founder.

Rickman, William, is the District Manager at Nottingham of the Commercial Union Assurance Company, Limited, which position he has occupied since the Branch was opened in 1880, with the exception of a short time, during which he was the Manager of a local institution called the Nottinghamshire and Midland Fire Insurance Company, Limited. That Company was transferred to the Commercial Union in March, 1889, when Mr. Rickman returned to his old position as District Manager to the Commercial Union.

J. B. ROBERTS.

WILLIAM ROBERTS.

Roberts, J. B., the District Manager at the Leeds Branch of the Sun Fire Office, commenced his Insurance career with a non-tariff Company, occupying a junior post for a short time at the Chief Office in Manchester and the Yorkshire Branch, Leeds. In 1881 he obtained an appointment from the West of England Fire and Life Insurance Company in connection with their Leeds Branch. After a few months' service he was transferred to Bradford to manage a large Agency for the Company in that town. This post he relinquished in 1883, on his appointment as Surveyor to the Yorkshire Branch of the County Fire Office. In January, 1887, he accepted an offer from the Fire Insurance Association to open a Branch in Leeds, and having successfully developed that Company's business in Yorkshire, he obtained, in October, 1888, his present appointment.

During the three years he has held the position the business and connections of the Office in Yorkshire have been considerably extended.

Mr. Roberts took an active part in the formation of the Insurance Institute of Yorkshire; he is a member of the Council of that body, and holds the post of Honorary Librarian.

Roberts, William, is the Secretary of the Liverpool Branch of the Alliance Assurance Company, which appointment he has held for upwards of 23 years. He is a gentleman of large experience in Fire Insurance matters, and is highly respected throughout his district.

JOHN ROBERTSON.

JAMES ROBERTSON.

Robertson, John, is the Secretary at the Dublin Branch of the Northern Assurance Company. Mr. Robertson entered the service of the Northern in 1877 as a junior clerk under Mr. Bremner in Glasgow; and after some years' experience in that branch office he was promoted to Chief Clerk at the Bristol and South Wales Branch, where he remained less than two years, when he was transferred, in a similar capacity, to the Dundee Branch. In Glasgow, Bristol, Dundee, &c., Mr. Robertson gained such experience as warranted his third promotion: hence, after being in Dundee two and a half years he received the appointment of Secretary for Ireland of the Northern, and in 1888 came to Dublin, where he has since managed the Company's interests.

Robertson, James, Manager for Scotland at the Glasgow Office of the United Kingdom Temperance and General Provident Institution, became connected with that Association in 1848, when he entered the Edinburgh Office, at that time the headquarters of the Association for Scotland. After a few years' service he was appointed Superintendent of Agencies, which post he filled for some time, subsequently removing to Glasgow as Agent for the Association, and also in charge of that District. Here his work brought the Glasgow District into such predominatory importance that, on the death of the then Secretary for Scotland, the Head Office quarters were transferred from Edinburgh to Glasgow, and Mr. Robertson was placed in charge of it; a post which he has now held for upwards of twenty years.

T. G. ROBINSON.

S. G. ROBINSON.

Robinson, T. G., District Manager of the British Empire Mutual Life Assurance Company at their Manchester Branch, has passed his entire Insurance career in the service of that Company, having been associated with it for a period of over twelve years. Commencing as Clerk at the Manchester Branch, he was subsequently appointed a Special Agent in connection with that Branch, in which position he remained until the January of 1890, when his services in that capacity pointed him out for promotion to his present post on its becoming vacant.

We believe it is Mr. T. G. Robinson's intention to shortly commence business as a General Insurance Broker.

———

Robinson, S. G., is Resident Secretary at the important Dublin Branch of the Standard Life Assurance Company. Mr. Robinson succeeded to this position in 1889 on the promotion of the former Secretary, Mr. Bentham, to the London Secretaryship of this Company. Mr. Robinson was especially qualified for this responsible position by many years' experience in the Company's service in Ireland, where he is greatly esteemed.

Ro. ROBISON.

R. E. ROBSON. .

Robison, Ro., is the popular Birmingham Manager of the Royal Insurance Company. Mr. Robison has held this appointment several years, and was previously in the service of the Royal for a very long time, and prior to his removal to Birmingham held appointments for the Company at Newcastle and afterwards at Bristol.

Robson, R. E., is the District Inspector of the Scottish Equitable Life Assurance Society at Newcastle-on-Tyne, which appointment he received in 1887, having previously served for 13 years in the Head Office of the Society, where he was for three years Inspector of Agents in the North, and South East of Scotland. Mr. Robson is a very energetic and able member of this popular Society's agency staff.

W. D. ROE.

THOMAS SALTER ROBJENT.

Roe, William Davin, is the Local Manager at Newcastle-on-Tyne of the Union Assurance Society. Mr. Roe received his Insurance training at the Head Office of the Liverpool and London and Globe Insurance Company, from which he was sent to the Newcastle Branch of that Company to take the position of Chief Clerk. He subsequently left the Liverpool and London and Globe to represent the Scottish Provincial Assurance Company in Newcastle, and on the amalgamation of that Office with the North British and Mercantile received his present appointment.

Riley, T. S., is the Resident Manager of the Law Union and Crown Fire and Life Insurance Company at Leeds, his district comprising the whole of the County of York. Mr. Riley received his early business training under his father, who was a wool merchant in Leeds. Circumstances, however, led him to turn his thoughts to the Insurance profession as his future career, and in 1879 he became the District Agent of the Law Union Fire and Life Insurance Company, a post he continued to hold until August, 1890, when he accepted the position of Resident Manager, it being the opinion of Mr. Grant Watson, the late General Manager, that the office ought to be represented by an official of the Company. Mr. Riley's policy has always been to seek to make his district pay, and he has the satisfaction of

knowing that he has not failed to attain this object. He is on the best of terms with his contemporaries in Leeds, and in 1888 joined with some of them in founding the Insurance Institute of Yorkshire. A circular letter was issued to the members of the Insurance profession in Yorkshire, calling a meeting to discuss the question, which was most heartily and generally responded to, the result being the formation of the Institute. He has, for three years, been one of the Vice-Presidents, taking an active part in its affairs, and has specially urged upon the junior members and associates the importance of a scientific knowledge of their profession. As a means of assisting them in this course, Mr. Riley has always endeavoured to secure high-class lectures and papers which will point out the course of study necessary to be pursued. At the general meeting in May, the members and associates showed the estimation in which his services were held by electing him to the distinguished position of President of the Institute.

Robjent, Thomas Salter, is the Resident Secretary at Bristol of the Midland Counties Insurance Company, which appointment he has held for some years. Mr. Robjent is also a well-known Stockbroker, through which connection he has been able to get together a very valuable business for his Company in this District.

G. F. ROONEY.

HON. HERCULES ROWLEY

Rooney, George F., is the Manager for the East Midland Counties District of the Mutual Reserve Fund Life Association of New York. Mr. Rooney commenced work in the Insurance profession in 1876 as District Agent for the Walsall District of the Prudential Assurance Company at Walsall, in which capacity he acted for thirteen years, meeting with considerable success. At the end of that period, in 1889, he received an appointment from the New York Life Insurance Company as District Agent for the County of Stafford; and after holding that post for over three years, he was in March, 1891, appointed Inspector of Agents for the same Company in the Birmingham District. From that position he was again promoted to the District Managership for the South Staffordshire District again at Walsall, where he continued till April, 1892, when he accepted his present appointment with the Mutual Reserve Fund of New York, removing his head-quarters to Leicester.

Rowley, The Hon. Hercules, the District Manager of the West of England Insurance Company's Irish Branch in Dame Street, Dublin, has held that post since 1885. He was educated at Eton and Sandhurst, and served in the Army; he is at present Honorary Colonel of the 5th Battalion Leinster Regiment, besides being a Justice of the Peace for the Counties of Dublin and Meath, and a Deputy-Lieutenant of the latter.

C. K. RUTHERGLEN.

F. A. RUFF.

Rutherglen, C. K., is the Resident Secretary at Glasgow of the National Assurance Company of Ireland. Mr. Rutherglen is a native of the Second City in the Empire, and is there a well-known man in circles beyond the actual limits of his profession. He joined the staff of the National Assurance Company of Ireland as Secretary for Scotland in May, 1879, and has been successful in gathering together a large and good business; and as an indication of progress it may be stated that he has now under his charge sub-branches at Edinburgh and Dundee. Mr. Rutherglen has at various times been a contributor to the literature of the profession, and his paper on "Corn Mills," read some years ago before the Glasgow Insurance and Actuarial Society, received most favourable notice from the press of both this country and America. A later paper on "Woollen Mills," read before the same Society, was also well received and may yet, if leisure permits, be somewhat extended and given a wider circulation than the limits of the local Society. Mr. Rutherglen is a gentleman of long-tried experience and practical knowledge of risks; and his judgment, exercised in a cautious and conservative spirit, has been of great service to the Company he represents.

———

Ruff, F. A., Agency Superintendent for Scotland of the National Provident Institution at Glasgow, was for two years at the commencement of his career Cashier to the Queen Insurance Company at the Glasgow Branch of that Company, from the Resident Secretary of which Branch, Mr. J. Carswell, he received a sound training in Insurance work. He was then, for three years, in the service of the Scottish Imperial, in the London Office, as Accountant in the Foreign Department, and subsequently as Fire Surveyor. He next accepted a very pressing offer of the District Inspectorship of the Norwich Union Life Assurance Company for the Edinburgh and East Coast District, which post he held for three years, eventually resigning it, in 1883, to undertake his present duties.

ALEXANDER C. RUTHERFORD.

JOHN RUSHTON.

Rutherford, Alexander C., Resident Secretary of the Scottish Metropolitan Life Assurance Company at their Glasgow Branch, has been established in Glasgow as an Accountant for a number of years, and has had the advantage of an Insurance training in the Head Office of the Queen Insurance Company in Liverpool. In 1887 he accepted the appointment of Resident Secretary for the West of Scotland for the Scottish Economic Life Office ; and upon the amalgamation of that Company with the Scottish Metropolitan, he was selected for the same post in connection with the united Company. Mr. Rutherford, who is an energetic and successful man of business, is a Commissioner of Supply of the County of Dumbarton, and a Magistrate of the Burgh of Kirkintilloch, in which he resides. He has been very successful in developing the Company's business, in both Life and Accident Departments ; and the Branch has largely benefited by the fusion of the two Companies.

Rushton, John, the Agent of the Boiler Insurance and Steam Power Company at Birmingham, is a Lancashire man, and began his connection with Boiler Insurance with the English and Scottish Company of Manchester soon after its formation. After working the whole of England amongst its Agencies he settled as District Manager in Birmingham, where he was very successful in Boiler, Life, and other branches of Insurance. Near the close of that Company's career he formed a local Company, the Staffordshire. This Company was very successful, but owing to severe competition and being undesirous of taking ruinous rates, he advised his Directors to transfer to the oldest and largest Company, viz., The Boiler Insurance and Steam Power Company, Limited, of Manchester. For this Company he now acts as Agent at Birmingham.

M. J. REGAN.

R SAMBROOK.

Regan, M. J., the Resident Secretary of the Gresham Life Assurance Society at its Manchester Branch, was born in Sligo, and commenced life as an Insurance Broker, in which capacity he sojourned first in Canada, then in New York, and then in London, for one, four, and three years respectively, but in none of these places did he achieve any extraordinary success. At the end of his third year in London he was offered the post of Agency Inspector to the New York Life Insurance Company, which he accepted, and whose duties he fulfilled with so much *eclat* that, on the District Managership for the North of Ireland falling vacant, he was selected to fill it from among many other competitors. Here he remained for a year, prosecuting his duties with the utmost vigour and assiduity, at the end of which time, the Secretaryship of the Ulster Branch of the Gresham Life Assurance Society becoming vacant, he accepted it. Here, in spite of many difficulties at the outset, he succeeded in placing

the business of the Society in a most flourishing condition, and increased it to the most satisfactory proportions. His diligence was rewarded by being appointed to the Secretaryship in Manchester, which post he still retains.

Sambrook, Richard, is a leading Insurance Broker in Liverpool, and is the principal representative in the North of England of the Security Company Limited. He was for many years in one of the largest shipping houses in Liverpool. He also represents the Scottish Accident Insurance Company, the Royal Insurance Company, and the Liverpool and London and Globe Insurance Company, also the British Natural-Premium Provident Association. He is a great advocate of the Security Company, and the principles on which it has been established, and hopes to soon make it one of the most prolific Companies in the North of England in the field of Burglary Insurance.

WILLIAM P. REID.

JEFFERSON SUGGIT.

Reid, William P., is the London Manager of the General Accident Assurance Corporation, Limited, which appointment he has held several years. Previous to taking charge of this Branch, Mr. Reid was Sub-Manager of the Company at its Head Office in Perth. He has had a large experience in Accident Insurance and is well-known in the Insurance profession

Suggit, Jefferson, is a partner of the firm of Messrs. Gray and Suggit, Secretaries of the Whitby Mutual Marine Iron Steamship Insurance Company, which was founded in 1873, and has since enjoyed an uninterrupted career of prosperity.

J. R. SANDILAND.

C. W. SARGEANT.

Sandiland, James Ramsay, the Manager of the Glasgow Branch of the General Fire and Life Assurance Company of London, is a Scotchman by birth, having been born in the County of Lanark in 1854. His first experience in the Insurance business was obtained in the Glasgow Office of the Equitable Fire Insurance Company. In the year 1881 the North British and Mercantile Insurance Company appointed him Superintendent of their Agents in the Glasgow District. On the death of Major A. C. Scott, who for many years represented the General Assurance Company in Glasgow, Mr. Sandiland was selected to fill the position. His management proved so successful that his district has been from time to time increased, until at the present time he has charge of the whole of the Company's business in Scotland with the exception of the City and County of Edinburgh.

Sargeant, Christy W., District Inspector of the Mutual Life Assurance Society at Exeter, is a native of Windsor, where he was born in 1863, but his parents removing to Exeter in 1874, he was educated at Hele's School, at Exeter, where he received a sound commercial education. He then entered an old-established business firm, with a view to an ultimate partnership, and it was while there that he first became connected with the Mutual Life, acting as principal Agent for that Office in conjunction with his other business. In 1887, on the Directors resolving to appoint District Inspectors, to increase their business, Mr. Sargeant was promoted to his present position, being the first ever appointed to a particular district, and having a large and influential connection in the West of England, was enabled to appoint a useful staff of Agents and secure a very considerable business for the Society.

CHARLES C. SAVILE.

H. C. SAUNDERS.

Savile, Charles C., is the District Manager at Bristol of the Royal Insurance Company. Mr Savile has had a long experience in the service of this Company ; and, being a gentleman of high attainments and undoubted ability, has largely increased its business in the West of England.

Spiller, William Hutchinson, was born in London in 1838, and was educated first at Highgate School and afterwards on the Continent. His early Insurance experience was gained in the Sun Fire Office, where he remained over twelve years. His next engagement was with the Scottish Imperial Insurance Company, in whose London Office he spent just over twelve months, leaving it to take the position of Secretary and Manager of the London Office of the Azienda Assurance Company of Trieste. Mr. Spiller is a Barrister-at-Law, having been called to the Bar, in 1874, by the Honourable Society of the Middle Temple He is at present the Manager in London of the Insurance Company of America (of Philadelphia, Pa., U.S.A.), and also of the Svea Assurance Company of Gothenburg, Sweden.

Saunders, H. C., is the Resident Secretary at Newcastle-upon-Tyne of the Scottish Widows' Fund Life Assurance Society. Mr. Saunders commenced his Insurance career in the Head Office of this Society at Edinburgh, in November, 1876, and after passing through the various departments, he was, in 1885, appointed Inspector of Agents in connection with the Liverpool Branch, which position he occupied until March, 1889, when he received his present appointment to succeed the late Mr. John Anderson. Mr. Saunders is a native of Edinburgh, having been born in that city in the year 1859.

Stewart-Brown, Egerton, is the District Manager of the London Assurance Corporation at Liverpool.

Mr. E. Stewart-Brown was educated at Harrow and Trinity College, Cambridge, where he obtained numerous distinctions and scholarships of great value, concluding his career at Cambridge with a first-class in classics and the degrees of B.A. and M.A. For many years previous to his present appointment he occupied the position of Manager in the Liverpool Office of the well-known firm of bankers, &c., Messrs. Brown, Shipley and Company.

A. E. SCEALES.

GEORGE W. SHARP.

Sceales, Adolphus Edward, Resident Secretary of the Scottish Widows' Fund Life Assurance Society in Liverpool, began his Insurance career in 1869, as an indentured apprentice to the Standard Life Assurance Company, in Edinburgh, for five years. After serving his time he remained with the same Company. He passed as a Fellow of the Faculty of Actuaries in Scotland in 1878, and in 1881 he was sent to the London Office of the Standard on a matter of special correspondence. After his return to Edinburgh he acted as interim Inspector of Agents in 1883, which post he held till May, 1884, when he was appointed to the position of Inspector at the Newcastle Branch of the Scottish Widows' Fund. After three years' stay in that town, he was transferred to Manchester, from which place, in 1888, he was promoted to the Resident Secretaryship of the Society in Belfast. Having spent three years in the busy commercial capital of Ireland, he was, in May, 1891, promoted to the Secretaryship of the same Society in Liverpool, which position he now holds.

Sharp, George W., is the District Manager at Liverpool of the Mutual Life Insurance Company of New York, which appointment he has held since the early part of 1889, prior to which he was connected with the Equitable Life Assurance of the United States for upwards of eight years. Mr. Sharp has met with a large measure of success in the Life Insurance field, and is now largely increasing the membership of the Mutual Life in his district.

ARTHUR B. SCHOLFIELD.

SAMUEL SHAW.

Scholfield, Arthur B., is the Resident Secretary at Manchester of the Mutual Life Insurance Company of New York and of the General Accident Assurance Association. He was educated at Allesley Park College, near Coventry, and commenced his career as an Insurance man in the Surveyors' Department of the Mutual Fire Office, at Manchester, in the December of 1871, at the age of seventeen. In the course of a very few years he had risen to be the Chief Surveyor, and in the December of 1878, on the nomination of Mr. J. N. Lane, he accepted the appointment of Manchester District Manager to the Standard Fire Off.ce, for which Company he continued to act until the transference of its business to the Fire Association in the year 1883. About this time there was a great difficulty experienced in the placing of large Insurances, and Mr. Scholfield, seeing his opportunity, determined on setting to work to revive the old Insurance Agency which had been started by his late father about the year 1838, and carried on after the death of the latter by his widow, Mr. Scholfield's mother. This Agency he has continued to the present time under the style of S. J. Scholfield and Son. In the year 1886 he was appointed District Manager to the Manchester Branch of the Pelican Life

Office, which post he vacated in 1890 to accept his present appointment with the Mutual of New York in connection with Mr. E. Neild. His appointment to the General Accident of Perth took place later; in that office he has the assistance of Mr. R. G. Jenkinson, as Resident Secretary.

Shaw, Samuel, is the Local Manager of the General Assurance Company at their Yorkshire Branch at Leeds. Mr. Shaw first determined to devote himself to Insurance work early in the year 1864, and accordingly entered the service of the British Equitable, with whom he remained for ten years, ultimately resigning his position with that Company to transfer his services to the General Life and Fire in 1874. In 1881 he was requested by the late Secretary to accept his present appointment, to which request he acceded, and has managed the Yorkshire Branch ever since. Mr. Shaw has seen many changes in Insurance work, not the least in Yorkshire itself, the competition being much greater, the business larger, and the work much harder than when he first entered upon his duties. He is, however, of opinion that there is still room for the extension of Insurance, and is a great advocate for the profession as a career for young men.

W. S. SHIELD.

T. B. SHERWOOD.

Shield, W. S., is the District Manager of the Norwich Union Life Insurance Society at their Northern Counties Branch at Newcastle-on-Tyne. He is a native of Newcastle, and very popular and well-known in the district. His Insurance career, though not a very lengthy one, has nevertheless been very successful throughout. Previous to his present appointment he acted as Inspector of Agents for his present Office, the North of England business being then worked from Glasgow, where the Head Office for Scotland is situated; but the phenomenal progress made by the Society and the growth of its popularity under Mr. Shield's auspices influenced the Directors to establish a separate Northern Counties Branch, of which he was put in charge. The success of the Branch under Mr. Shield's management was a foregone conclusion, and so it has proved. He has some of the most influential men in the District as his Agents, and being accorded the most liberal support of his Directors he has worked this excellent Society's business up to a pitch of prosperity and continuous increase which cannot but excite admiration and inspire public confidence.

———

Sherwood, Thomas B., is the District Manager of the Patriotic Assurance Company at their Branch Office in Manchester. He commenced his Insurance career in the Royal Insurance Company and was for many years associated with the Manchester Fire Office, where he held an important appointment. He opened the Branch for the Patriotic some five years ago, and has practically opened up the North of England for that Office. Mr. Sherwood is a member of the Manchester Insurance Institute and has contributed to its papers.

W. J. SHORE.

JOHN SIBERRY.

Shore, W. J., District Manager of the Positive Government Security Life Assurance Company at their Branch at Liverpool, was born in 1853. Prior to his entry into the service of the Positive Life Office, which took place in 1889, he was for eight years engaged in business as a Shipowner and Shipbroker at Runcorn, Cheshire, and it was owing to the reputation which he had made for himself in the District in this capacity that, on the Positive Life Office requiring an efficient representative to open a Branch Office for them at Liverpool, he was selected to undertake the work. He has since his appointment fully justified that selection, having established a valuable connection for his Company in the City and surrounding District, and formed an influential Local Board of Reference. Mr. Shore has always taken a leading part in social and philanthropic institutions, and during his residence at Runcorn acted as a Member of the Public Free Library Committee, of the Local Board Parliamentary Committee, and as Savings Bank Manager.

Siberry, John, is the Resident Secretary of the Gresham Life Assurance Society at their Branch Office at Dublin. Mr. Siberry, who has held his present position since 1884, is an earnest and indefatigable worker, and since his appointment has succeeded in increasing the business of his Society to a very profitable degree, thereby winning the most substantial expressions of approval from the Board of Directors.

" JOHN SIME

J. B. SLUMAN.

Sime, John, is the Resident Manager of the Patriotic Fire and Life Assurance Company, at its Chief Office for Scotland, in Glasgow. Mr. Sime commenced his apprenticeship in 1874, at the Dundee Branch of the Edinburgh Life and Scottish Fire Offices. In 1877 he became Chief Clerk at the Dundee Office of the Caledonian Insurance Company. In 1880 he was appointed Surveyor and Chief Clerk at the Scotch Branch (in Glasgow) of The Fire Insurance Association and London and Lancashire Life Office. A year later he opened a Branch in Aberdeen for the Scottish Metropolitan Life and Fire Offices. In 1883 he returned to the Caledonian as Secretary in Aberdeen; in 1886 he was appointed to the Birmingham Secretaryship of the same Office. In December, 1888, on the appointment of Mr. Robert Muir as General Manager of the Scottish Alliance, Mr. Sime joined the Patriotic as Manager for Scotland.

————

Sluman, J. B., is the District Representative at Norwich of the British Empire Mutual Life Assurance Company, to which post he was appointed in 1884. He had previously had an extended experience in Life Insurance, and among other appointments had been in the service of the Western Counties and London Life Office for upwards of five years.

WILLIAM SIMPSON.

GEORGE SIMPSON.

Simpson, William, the District Secretary of the Scottish Equitable Life Assurance Society at Dundee, began his Insurance career in May, 1869, when he was appointed Cashier and Accountant to the Briton Life and Britannia Fire Offices. In 1871 he was appointed Inspector of Agents at Dundee by the Life Association of Scotland, and in 1873, having made his name in that District, was selected by the Directors of the Scottish Equitable to be their District Inspector to break ground for them there. At that time the District was limited, but it has from time to time been extended, until it now embraces the whole of the counties north of the Firth of Forth. When about eight or nine years ago, the Scottish Equitable opened a Branch at Dundee, Mr. Simpson was selected to fill the post of Secretary there.

Simpson, George, is Secretary for the Caledonian Insurance Company, at the Company's Branch Offices at Dundee and Aberdeen. Mr. Simpson commenced his business experience in 1876, in the Dundee Offices of the Edinburgh Life Assurance Company and the Scottish Fire Insurance Company; removing to the Caledonian when that Office acquired the business of the Scottish Fire. About six years ago he was promoted from the Chief Clerkship at Dundee to take charge of the Aberdeen Branch, and in May (1891) Mr. Simpson was appointed by the Directors of this old-established office to act as Secretary at their Dundee and Aberdeen Branches. Mr. Simpson's Insurance career has been most successful owing to his business ability and energy.

CHARLES SMITH

A. SCARISBRICK.

Smith, Charles, is the Resident Secretary of the National Assurance Company of Ireland at its London Branch in Nicholas Lane, E.C. Mr. Charles Smith is brother of Mr. Cozens Smith, Manager of the Imperial Fire Insurance Company, and coming from the same stock as a gentleman of such well-known ability as the latter, it is not surprising that Mr. Charles Smith's Insurance career has been one of uninterrupted success.

Scarisbrick, Anthony, the Manager of the West End Branch (London) of the Atlas Assurance Company, was born in 1855. In 1870 he entered the London Office of the Scottish Commercial Insurance Company, where he remained until receiving an appointment (in 1871) in the Head Office of the Commercial Union. By the Board of this Company he was appointed to the Management of their Southern Branch in 1882, and this position he held until the year 1885, when he resigned it to take up the appointment he holds at present.

JOHN SMITH.

R. MARTIN SMITH.

Smith, John, Resident Manager to the Sun Fire Office at Manchester, commenced his Insurance career in 1867 in the service of the West of England Insurance Company, with whom he remained for several years, subsequently going to the Caledonian Office for three years. Upon the London Assurance Office establishing a Branch in Manchester, Mr. Smith was appointed Chief Clerk and Surveyor, subsequently being promoted to the position of Branch Manager. That appointment he relinquished to take up the District Managership of the newly-established Economic Fire Office, with supervision over Lancashire, Westmoreland, Cumberland, Derbyshire and Cheshire, which he held till March, 1891, when he was appointed to his present post. Mr. Smith is highly esteemed in the Insurance profession.

Smith, R. Martin, Resident Secretary of the Northern Assurance Company at their Branch office in Tithebarn Street, Liverpool, first commenced his Insurance career in the service of the Royal Assurance Company at their Head Office at Liverpool, subsequently quitting that Office to take up the management of the Liverpool Branch of the Scottish Commercial Insurance Company, now the Lancashire, with whom he remained nine years. He succeeded to his present post with the Northern Assurance Company in 1879 on the resignation of Mr. J. B. Moffat, now of the Manchester Fire Office.

TREVOR N. SMITH.

EMIL SCHÖTT.

Smith, Trevor N., is the District Manager of the City of London Fire Insurance Company, the Insurance Company of North America, and the Employers' Liability Assurance Corporation, and Resident Secretary for Ireland of the Imperial Life Insurance Company. He has been con-nected with the Insurance business in Dublin since boyhood, with the exception of three or four years which he spent in the Natal Civil Service. He received his training in the Dublin Branches of the Scottish Imperial, London and Lancashire, West of England, and Sun Fire Office, which latter Company he left in 1886 to assume the District Managership of the Employers' Liability Assurance Corporation, which he represents for the provinces of Munster, Leinster, and Connaught. In September, 1887, he was appointed to a similar position by the City of London Fire Office, first to supervise the same Districts as for the Employers'

Liability Assurance, and on that Company deciding to consolidate its Irish business, he obtained the management for the whole of Ireland. He became District Manager of the Insurance Company of North America in the latter part of 1889, and the Resident Secretary of the Imperial Life in the early part of 1891. He has been Honorary Secretary and Treasurer of the Insurance Institute of Ireland. He has recently become a member of the Dublin Stock Exchange.

Schött, Emil, is one of the Managers and Underwriters in London of the United Swiss Marine Insurance Companies, which post he has held since 1885. Previous to that he was for some time in the service of this Company in another capacity, and before joining these Companies he was with Messrs. Corneville, David and Co., merchants and foreign bankers.

G. J. SOUSTER.

C. W. SOUTHWELL.

Souster, George James, the Resident Secretary at Bristol of the Colonial Mutual Life Assurance Society, Limited, was born in the month of November, 1850. His first connection with the Insurance world was made when he was appointed an Agent of the Rock Life Insurance Company. This he resigned to take up an Agency for the United Kingdom Temperance and General Insurance Office. While he held this he was appointed District Manager at Hereford of one of the large American Life Offices. This position he resigned to take up the appointment of District Superintendent of the London and Lancashire Life Assurance Company at the Bristol Branch Office of that Company. In the year 1888 he was appointed Life Inspector for the West of England and South Wales District of the Caledonian Insurance Company, and this position he held until receiving an offer of his present position, which he accepted.

Southwell, Charles William, the Local Secretary at the Manchester Branch of the Westminster Fire Office, commenced his Insurance career and his connection with his present Office at the same time, being appointed Junior Clerk at the Head Office in January, 1871. During the twenty years that he has been connected with the Westminster Fire Office he has acted successively as Inspector of Agents and as Local Secretary at the Leeds Branch, and in October, 1885, he was selected to open the Branch in Manchester, which having been successfully effected he was placed in charge.

C. W. SOUTER.

W. H. STARKEY.

Souter, C. W., is the Local Secretary at Sheffield of the Gresham Life Assurance Society Mr. Souter became connected with the Gresham Life Office in 1878 at the age of twenty-one years ; in the following year he was appointed Assistant Local Secretary of the Sunderland and Newcastle Branches, and in 1883 he became Local Secretary of the Stockton and Sheffield Districts. In 1887 the North Eastern Amalgamated District was placed under his charge, which included the Branches at Bradford, Hull, and Stockton, with headquarters at Sheffield, and he now holds that appointment.

Mr. Souter has met with great success in the Life Insurance business, and that he is held in high esteem by the Head Office officials of the Gresham is shown by his promotions. The Sheffield Office of the Society is in Parade Chambers, High Street.

Starkey, W. H., the Liverpool District Secretary of the English and Scottish and Law Life Assurance Association, commenced his Insurance life with the Sickness and Accident Insurance Company, for which he opened out part of the Midland Counties, being afterwards transferred to the Glasgow Branch of the same Company as Resident Secretary. While there he applied for and obtained the position of Resident Secretary, in Liverpool, to the Scottish Economic Life Assurance Society, and remained in the service of that Society until it became amalgamated with the Scottish Metropolitan, when he took up his present appointment. In June, 1891, he was further appointed to the District Secretaryship of the British Law Fire Office, and has now the charge of the two Companies.

CHARLES STEVENSON.

W. F. STRATFORD.

Stevenson, Charles, the Local Secretary of the Standard Life Assurance Company at their Manchester Branch, commenced his Insurance career a quarter of a century ago in the Head Office of his present Company in Edinburgh, where he remained for seven years ; subsequently transferring his services to the City of Glasgow Life Office, with whom he remained for four years in the capacity of Agency Superintendent. He then took charge of the Insurance Department in the Office of Messrs. Thomas Wade, Guthrie, and Company, the large firm of Chartered Accountants in Manchester, for a period of two years, and then joined the English and Scottish Boiler Insurance Company, first as Secretary, and afterwards as Manager and Secretary, for about nine years. He was appointed to his present position with his first Company in 1888, on the resignation of the late Local Secretary, Mr. W. H. Taylor. Mr. Stevenson is an Associate of the Institute of Actuaries. He was in conjunction with Mr. W. G. Walton, now of the Scottish Provident Institution, the founder of the *Policy Holder*, which was established in 1883, but of which he disposed of his share soon after his appointment to the Standard Life Assurance Company.

Stratford, W. F., Local Secretary of the Gresham Life Assurance Society at its Branch Office at Norwich, is the oldest Local Secretary in the service of that Society. He was appointed to the charge of the Norwich Branch in 1875, at which time the business done in the district was very small ; but through Mr. Stratford's indefatigable industry and persevering efforts in spite of the ever increasing competition from other offices, the business has so steadily and largely increased year by year that at the present time it ranks as one of the most prosperous of the Gresham Society's Branches.

CHARLES STEWART.

DAVID STEWART.

Stewart, Charles, is the Manager for Scotland of the Lancashire Insurance Company, which position he has now occupied for many years. He is a brother of Mr. George Stewart, the General Manager of the Company, and it is needless to say that coming from such a stock he is a most zealous and successful controller of the extensive business now done by the Company in Scotland. Much of his success is no doubt due to the legal training which he received before entering the Insurance profession, which has given him powers of perception and exactness which have been of invaluable service to him in his later career. He is a member of the Glasgow Insurance and Actuarial Society, and has contributed some papers to its transactions of very great importance to those engaged in Fire Insurance, the chief being:—" Fire Insurance : a historical sketch " and "The Contract of Fire Insurance," the latter forming Mr. Stewart's inaugural address when President of the Society during the session of 1885-86.

———

Stewart, David, is the Resident Secretary at Glasgow of the Liverpool and London and Globe Insurance Company, which appointment he has held for a long series of years. He is one of the most experienced and able Insurance officials in Scotland, and no member of the Insurance profession in Glasgow is more universally respected and esteemed.

R. STRICKLAND.

G. B. STRIDE.

Strickland, R., the Superintendent of the Inverness Branch of the Lancashire Insurance Company, acquired his earlier Insurance experience in the Office of the Northern Assurance Company at Glasgow, where he entered as Junior Clerk in 1869, and remained until 1877, gradually working his way up through the higher grades; leaving the Northern in the latter year to join the Lancashire Insurance Company as Chief Clerk at his present Branch. Besides the immediate duties of that Office, he also assisted in the Inspection of Agents in the Inverness district. On the promotion of the late Resident Secretary in the September of 1890, Mr. Strickland was, in his turn, promoted to take charge of the Branch in his present capacity.

———

Stride, G. B., the Local Manager for Ireland of the Royal Insurance Company, received his early education at the College, Liverpool. He has passed the whole of his Insurance career in the service of the Royal Insurance Company, having entered the Head Office at Liverpool in 1853, and after working his way up through the various departments of the office, exhibiting great ability and energy in mastering the details of the business, he was ultimately appointed to his present post.

JOHN SUGDEN.

BENJAMIN SUGDEN.

Sugden, John, is the Branch Manager for over 33 years of the United Kingdom Temperance and General Provident Institution at Manchester. In 1859, when in the employ of Messrs. Rylands and Sons, of Manchester, he was solicited by his present company to become their principal Agent for that city and district, having received a warm recommendation from a friend of the Manager of the Institution, who had known Mr. Sugden for some time as a successful local Insurance Agent. Mr. Sugden's then employers, Messrs. Rylands, expressed great regret at his leaving them to take up this new appointment, but finally acquiesced when they learnt that the preliminary steps having been taken, it was too late to go back, and Mr. John Ryland's was indeed the first policy which he obtained. After he had done very well for a short time in Manchester and the suburbs, Mr. Sugden's charge was next extended to include the whole of Lancashire, to which were subsequently added Cheshire and part of Derbyshire. The business he worked up becoming very large, he afterwards handed over, first Liverpool and district, and then Cheshire, to other hands, taking up in their place, at the request of the Head Office, Cumberland and Westmoreland, which had up to that time proved very unproductive to the Company, in addition to the section of Lancashire which he still retained. For some years the business which he had worked, though very considerable, now remained at about the same average, but in 1887, his son, Mr. Frank H. Sugden, joining him as Agency Inspector, the business began to increase, and has since continued to do so. Mr. Sugden is well known also in Manchester for his management for twenty-seven years of the Pendleton Mission and Ragged School.

Sugden, Benjamin, of Manchester and Bowdon, Cheshire, is the District Manager for the Cheshire District of the United Kingdom Temperance and General Provident Institution. His connection with the Temperance Provident dates back for nearly 30 years, and has continued without a break to the present time. As a broker he has also had a very large Fire Insurance business, with an extensive connection amongst the cotton spinners and manufacturers, and, for nearly twenty years, has personally been closely associated with the staple trade of the district as a cotton doubler, producing yarns both for the home and export trade.

PHILIP SWANWICK.

THOMAS SWANSTON.

Swanwick, Philip, the District Superintendent of. the Eagle Insurance Company at Manchester, began his Insurance career in 1875 as Agent for the Scottish Widows' Fund in Manchester, which post he held until 1878, in which year he floated the Lancashire and Yorkshire Company for the original promoters, who appointed him Secretary to the Company. He remained in this post for two years, at the end of which period he was appointed to his present post of District Superintendent, which is practically that of General Superintendent, supervising as he does the whole of the country between Carlisle in the north and Birmingham in the south, besides making special journeys anywhere north of London. Mr. Swanwick is also Agent to the Sun Fire Office, Manchester Agent to the Railway Passengers' Assurance Company, and District Agent to the National Guarantee and Suretyship Association, in all of which capacities he does a considerable. business.

Swanston, Thomas, is the Resident Secretary at Manchester of the Edinburgh Life Assurance Company, which appointment he has held since 1868. Mr. Swanston received his training in the Head Office of the Life Association of Scotland, in Edinburgh, where he remained for nearly eight years. At the end of that time, he accepted an appointment as Inspector of Agents to the City of Glasgow Life Office, performing the arduous duties of that post for about two years. He was then appointed to his present position. Mr. Swanston's success as the representative of the Edinburgh has been very great, and must have more than realised the anticipations formed on his appointment. As an Assurance official, Mr. Swanston commands much respect in the district for his shrewdness and conscientiousness. He is an indefatigable worker; and, besides being thoroughly master of his business as a Life Assurance Officer, has had considerable experience in the working of Fire business. He has also, from the first, been a valued Director of the Lancashire and Yorkshire Accident Insurance Company.

A. A. TAVENER.

JAMES TEMPLETON.

Tavener, Alfred A., Bristol Secretary of the Northern Assurance Company, entered that Company's service as a junior in Bristol, and, passing through the various classes of indoor and outdoor branch work there, was appointed to his present post in 1890. His more immediate and personal training was received at the hands of Mr. James Ostler, Northern Secretary in Manchester; Mr. Richard Walton, London Secretary of the Manchester ; and Mr. John Robertson, Secretary to the Northern in Dublin.

Tate, Charles M., is the Resident Secretary to the Ocean Accident and Guarantee Corporation at its Branch Office at Leeds. Previous to entering upon that appointment in 1886, Mr. Tate was for a short time employed on the Head Office staff of the Corporation in London. He has since been very successful in building up steadily a large premium income and placing his Branch on a very

prosperous footing. This result may be attributed greatly to his personal popularity with his Agents: indeed, no Accident Officer stands higher with his men than he does. Mr. Tate was one of the original promoters of the Yorkshire Insurance Institute, and there is sufficient proof of the general confidence and respect in which he is held in the profession outside his own Office in the fact that whereas the constitution of that Institute provides that only one Accident man shall be eligible to serve on the Council, Mr. Tate has been, at each general meeting of the members, unanimously elected to that honour.

Templeton, James, is the District Secretary at Exeter of the Sun Life Office. Mr. Templeton is also engaged in the Banking business in connection with the firm of Fox, Fowler and Co., at Exeter and Crediton.

W. PERCIVAL TAYLOR.

WILLIAM TAYLOR.

Taylor, W. Percival, is the Resident Secretary of the British Empire Mutual Life Assurance Company at their Yorkshire Branch Office at Leeds. He is an Accountant by profession, and a Member of the Incorporated Society of Accountants. He began his connection with the British Empire Mutual Life in 1887, when he was appointed an ordinary Agent to that Company; but three years later, on the Company opening a Branch Office at Oxford, he was promoted to the position of Local Secretary in charge of the District, which comprised the Counties of Oxfordshire, Berkshire, and Buckinghamshire. He proved most successful in the working of this District, and in recognition of his services he was in 1891 again promoted to the more important position which he now occupies.

Taylor, William, the Local Secretary at Ipswich of the Essex and Suffolk Equitable Fire Office, commenced his business life in 1867.

In that year he received an appointment in the Branch Office of the Alliance Assurance Company at Ipswich. His aptitude for Insurance business was quickly manifested and his abilities quickly recognised, for in a very short time he was appointed to the position of Chief Clerk. While occupying this post he gained a great and varied experience of both the Life and Fire Branches of Insurance business, and was very successful in the local development of the Company's business in the latter branch.

With the Alliance he remained until 1888, when he resigned his position with them to take up the one he at present holds, and in which he has also been very successful.

LATIMER THOMAS

WILLIAM THOMAS.

Thomas, Latimer, is the District Secretary at Bristol for the English and Scottish Law Life Assurance Association, which position he has occupied since 1889. His first experience of Insurance business was gained as an Insurance broker in Bristol, where he worked with much success until 1886, when the Norwich Union Life offered him the Inspectorship at Leeds. After a period of successful work in Yorkshire, the Norwich Union promoted him to Newcastle-on-Tyne, where he laboured till the English and Scottish Law Life Office offered a more tempting appointment in his native city, where he now remains. Besides the life appointment which Mr. Thomas makes the chief feature of his business he also holds the Resident Secretaryship of the Scottish Alliance (with which is now incorporated the Mercantile), for Fire, Accident, Fidelity, Guarantee and Burglary Insurance, and the Employers' Liability and Workpeople's Provident and Accident Company.

Mr. Thomas is a very active friend of the Temperance cause, and takes a very prominent part in several temperance organisations in Bristol.

Thomas, William, is the genial and popular Superintendent of Agents for the Home Counties District of the British Equitable Assurance Company. He was born in 1834, and at 21 years of age began his Life Assurance work as Inspector of Agents for that Company. In 1864 he went to the Atlas Assurance Office to occupy the post of Superintendent of Agents, returning to the British Equitable in 1868, where he has since remained, and since 1880 has held the position which he now so ably fills. In the course of his professional career, Mr. Thomas has been very successful in training and placing a large number of men who have turned out excellent agents, and many of whom are now holding good posts in connection with leading offices. Mr. Thomas has, by his unchanging courtesy, his conspicuous ability, and his well-known integrity, made firm friends wherever his business avocations have called him.

W. A. TIPPING.

C. ROSS TODD.

Tipping, Walter Abbott, Resident Secretary of the Manchester Branch of the Guardian Assurance Company, commenced in the service of the Royal Assurance Company, in their London Office, subsequently leaving that Company to take up the duties of Surveyor and Agency Inspector to his present Company at their Dublin Branch. He then became Assistant Secretary at the Dublin Office of the Caledonian Insurance Company, which post he held until, at the age of twenty-seven, he was appointed to take charge of the extensive Irish business of the Sun Fire and Sun Life Offices, at their Branch Office, also in the Irish capital. Thence he was promoted to be Superintendent of Branches at the Head Offices of those Societies, in which capacity he lent material assistance to the organization and extension of their business throughout the United Kingdom. More recently he acted as Superintendent of Branches and Resident Manager for the Sun Fire Office alone at their Manchester Branch, leaving that post to return to his old Company, the Guardian, early in 1891. His Branch is one of the largest and most important in the North of England, comprising as it does portions of the Counties of Lancashire, Yorkshire, Cheshire, Derbyshire and Lincolnshire.

As we go to press with these pages, Mr. Tipping has received the appointment of General Manager of the Scottish Alliance Insurance Company, Limited.

Todd, C. Ross, is the Resident Secretary at Dublin of the Scottish Equitable Life Assurance Society, which post he has held since the death of his father (the former Resident Secretary) in 1874. Mr. Todd is now the senior Resident Secretary of this Society, having held this appointment for nearly 16 years, which is a longer period than any other Resident Secretary has been in its service.

CHARLES H. TORR

W. T. TOMLINSON

Torr, Charles Hawley, of Nottingham, is now the oldest Insurance Broker in the Midland Counties. He began life with an old-established local Lace firm, but left them very soon to start on his own account, and on the Queen Insurance Company finding it necessary, shortly after their foundation, to have someone to represent them who understood the staple trade, Mr. Torr was recommended to their notice, and, though rather against his will at the time, was persuaded to accept the post of Resident Agent to that Company. This step, however, he never afterwards regretted : he threw himself keenly into the business, and having observed the dangers attendant on the bad gas lighting, and the structural defects of some of the warehouses and factories in his district, made the acquaintance of that eminent Fire Surveyor, the late Mr. Hancock, who instructed him as to the causes of many fires, and the remedies against them, also in salvage work, which has been of the greatest service to him in his business since. Mr. Torr is now not so actively engaged in business, and though representing many of the leading Insurance Offices is resting in the confidence he is held in by several of the leading firms with, which he is connected, without canvassing or seeking for new business, but always ready to place risks or to advise on lighting and heating. Mr. Torr is a rigid temperance man, to which he attributes much of his success and reputation ; he is also closely associated with many of the leading philanthrophic societies, but particularly with the Society for the Prevention of Cruelty to Animals, in which connection he has taken a prominent part

in the opposition to vivisection, having been one of the speakers of the Deputation to the Home Secretary in 1876 on the subject, the outcome of which was the Vivisection Commission. He was also one of the founders of the International Society for the Suppression of Vivisection, and contributed several papers to the literature of the Society, which had an extensive circulation. He was also a member of the General Committee of the British Association at their meeting at Leeds in 1889. In 1890, on the nomination of the Right Reverend Dr. Trollope, Bishop of Nottingham, the well-known archæologist, he was appointed the Honorary Acting Secretary for Nottinghamshire of the Architectural and Archæological Societies of the Counties of Lincoln and Nottingham, and in 1891 contributed a paper to the Transactions of the Society on "The Discovery of an Ancient Cave Dwelling in Nottingham."

Tomlinson, W. T., is the Secretary at the Leeds Branch of the Life Association of Scotland. Mr. Tomlinson is the oldest-established Life Insurance Agent in Leeds, he having been in the Life business here for thirty years—twenty in connection with the Briton Life Office, and ten in connection with the Life Association of Scotland. This Branch has been established seventeen years, and has a very large number of policy-holders paying premiums through its medium. There is no Life Insurance Manager in Leeds possessing in a greater degree the confidence of the public.

T. TOWNSEND.

LEWIS E TRANT.

Townsend, Tom, is the Local Manager of the London and Lancashire Assurance Company for Yorkshire at their Branch Office at Leeds. He has had a large and successful experience of Insurance business, and holds a recognised and respected position among the ablest workers in the kingdom. When Mr. Townsend first took up an agency with the British Equitable he for two years combined with it his own private business, but afterwards received the appointment of District Agent for Shipley, and devoted himself solely to the work and did a large business. He then took up the position of Inspector of Agents for the Blue Ribbon Life Company, and, being a life-long abstainer, threw himself into the service of the Company with characteristic enthusiasm. He was first connected with the Head Office at Birmingham, and subsequently opened up the Company's business in Scotland and the North of Ireland, where his success was phenomenal. On resigning the appointment, after four years' service, he was presented by the Agents with a silver tea and coffee service and a travelling bag, as an evidence of their respect for him as a man, and their appreciation of his work on behalf of

Insurance. In November, 1889, he was appointed to his present position, and has raised the Company in his native county to a height never previously attained. He has associated himself with a number of public movements, and has held honourable positions on the School Board and Local Board of the district where he resides (and in November, 1891, was again elected as a member of the Local Board at Shipley.) He is highly respected by those who know him, and his vigour of mind and body, knowledge of men, enthusiasm and ability, give him special fitness for the position he holds. His activities cannot be encompassed by his business engagements, and he serves the Primitive Methodist Church with which from his boyhood he has been connected in a variety of important offices.

Trant, Lewis E., is the Agency Inspector at the Birmingham Branch of the Scottish Amicable Life Assurance Society. Mr. Trant, who has been engaged in the Insurance business for many years, previously held a similar position at the Exeter Branch of the Sun Life Office.

CHARLES H. TRENAM.

H. B. TURNBULL.

Trenam, Charles H., the Resident Secretary of the Northern Accident Insurance Company at Leeds, is a native of that town, and after receiving his education at the Grammar School there took an appointment in the Civil Service, where he remained for ten years. His Insurance career commenced by taking up an Agency, and meeting with so much success and becoming so devoted to his work he determined on obtaining, if possible, a permanent appointment. He was appointed to his present post in 1890, and since that time has very considerably developed the district under his charge. Mr. Trenam is warmly attached to the Northern Accident, and although he has had more than one offer of appointments from other Companies has consistently declined.

Turnbull, H. B., is the Resident Secretary at Newcastle-on-Tyne of the Travellers' Accident Insurance Company, which appointment he received after the Company's formation in 1891. Mr. Turnbull had previously been the Resident Secretary at Newcastle of the Ocean Accident and Guarantee Corporation, occupying the position for upwards of five years.

ALEXANDER D. M. TUCKER.

Tucker, A. D. M., the genial and courteous Secretary of the West End Branch in London of the Scottish Imperial, was born at Wimbledon in 1859, and is consequently now in his 33rd year. He is the son of the late Mr. E. Tucker, who was Private Secretary to Earl Cairns when Lord Chancellor; and was also First Gentleman of the Chamber to the House of Lords. His attention was first directed to Life Assurance some six years ago, and he has been remarkably successful in introducing new business, his social position bringing him in contact with a high grade of business, both as regards status and amounts of policies. Previous to his advent into Life Assurance matters, Mr. Tucker studied for the Bar; but found that it would prove uncongenial, and consequently abandoned the profession for the more attractive, to him, field of dealing in Life contingencies. He has been connected with the Scottish Imperial for the greater part of his Insurance career, and before attaining to his present position was their London Superintendent of Agents, in which capacity he was very successful. As Secretary of the West End Branch, now opened at 16, Cockspur Street, S.W., a selection has been made that will no doubt be of great value to the office.

Turner, Joseph, is the District Manager at Hull of the Star Life Assurance Society, which appointment he has held since September, 1891, having previously represented the same Society with much success in the southern part of the county of Lincoln.

R. T. THOMSON.

W. W. WAINWRIGHT.

Thomson, R. T., is the London Secretary of the Scottish Employers' Liability and Accident Assurance Company, Limited, which appointment he has held for a series of years. Mr. Thomson has made a very successful record as an Accident Insurance Official in connection with this and other Accident Companies.

Wainwright, William Walter, is the London Manager of the Patriotic Assurance Company. Mr. Wainwright commenced his Insurance career in 1866 in the London Office of the Midland Counties Insurance Company, and left the service of that Company in 1869 to accept an appointment with the London and Lancashire Fire Company.

With this Company he remained until 1880, when, having attained to the position of Chief Clerk, he was offered, and accepted, a similar appointment in the Fire Insurance Association. This he relinquished in 1885 to become Fire Superintendent of the Employers' Liability Assurance Corporation, and left that Company in 1888 to assume the duties of his present position. He is a gentleman of much ability and experience, and is universally esteemed in the Insurance profession. Under his management the business of his Company has considerably increased, and since his appointment the Office has rapidly taken that position in London to which its age and funds entitle it.

E. A. WALFORD.

RICHARD WALTON.

Walford, Edward Arthur, is the London Manager of the Midland Counties Insurance Company. Mr. Walford may be regarded as essentially a City man, having been born in the very heart of the City in 1853, and educated at Christ's Hospital. Immediately on leaving school he entered the London Office of the Scottish Provincial, and in 1874 he was selected to take the management of the Fire Department of that newly-established Branch Office of that Company in Nottingham. It is perhaps worthy of note that the reason of opening this Branch was owing to the retirement of a first-rate agent, who had been appointed about 1859 by the late Mr. Cornelius Walford, a relation of the subject of our present notice, when acting as Inspector of Agents to the Scottish Provincial. After spending five years in Nottingham, picking up a good deal of valuable knowledge of the lace and hosiery trades, and of the trades carried on in Leicester, Birmingham, and other Midland towns, Mr. Walford returned to London, and since 1879 most of his time has been spent in the Caledonian Office, being as equally ready to deal with one department of Insurance business as with another. For some time Mr. Walford undertook the settlement of Fire Losses, and was invariably able to give satisfaction to all concerned—at times a by no means easy task. Mr. Walford also spent some time extending the Agency connection of the

Caledonian in London and the provinces. In May, 1888, he received his present appointment with the Midland Counties Insurance Company.

Walton, Richard, the recently-appointed Secretary in London to the Manchester Fire Office, is a thoroughly competent man, of sound judgment, and very varied experiences, having in 1870 entered the service of the North British and Mercantile Insurance Company at their Glasgow Branch, and two years later joined the Northern Assurance Company (both admirable training schools), whence he was transferred to Newcastle-upon-Tyne as Chief Clerk in 1876.

In 1878 he was appointed Resident Secretary to the Scottish Commercial Company at Newcastle, where he gained much experience in the chemical and other staples of that district, and on the amalgamation of that Office with the Lancashire Company, he still continued at his post as Secretary.

In 1883 he was appointed Secretary to the Northern Assurance Company at Bristol, where he resided until 1890, when he was transferred, in the interests of the same Company, to Birmingham, gaining thereby considerable experience in the hardware and pottery industries; such a career being fully appreciated by the Manchester Fire Office, as, in 1891, he was selected for the important post which he now holds.

HUBERT WHITE.

AUGUSTUS WALLIS.

White, Hubert, Resident Secretary in London of the Palatine Insurance Company, Limited, of Manchester, and also of the Mutual Accident Association of that city in London, received his earliest training in the Insurance business in the Head Office of the West of England Insurance Company at Exeter, where he remained for eight years. From there he came to London to enter the service of the Globe Insurance Office, and was with them for two years, when the amalgamation of that Company with the Liverpool and London took place. Mr. White's experience was then utilised by the Commercial Union Assurance Company, and with that Office he remained eleven years, filling the onerous position of Chief Surveyor. In 1877 the Mutual Fire Insurance Company of Manchester (which is now merged into the Palatine) appointed him Resident Secretary in London, and when the amalgamation of the two offices took place he was confirmed in his appointment.

———

Wallis, Augustus, is the London Manager of the Kent Fire and Life Offices, which position he has held since 1889, having succeeded Mr. Edgar Rice in that position. Mr. Wallis formerly occupied a responsible position at the Head Office of the Guardian Assurance Company, and is well-known to the Insurance fraternity as a gentleman of ability and energy.

HENRY VALENTINE.

GEORGE A. WAGSTAFF.

Valentine, Henry, of Belfast, only commenced his Insurance life in 1890, on his return from India, where he had spent a large part of his life, but the short space of time that he has been engaged in it, may be considered to have had very great success. He is the representative for Ireland of the Commercial Fire Insurance Company of Scotland, the Northern Assurance Company, and the Employers' Liability Assurance Company of Great Britain, acting as Resident Manager or Secretary for all these Companies. The Northern Assurance Company was the first Company whose business he took up, adding the Irish Managership of the Commercial Fire Insurance Company of Scotland to his business, with the consent of the Directors of the former Company, in February, 1891. He has held the Resident Secretaryship of the Employers' Liability Assurance Company since the latter part of 1890.

Mr. Valentine is also occupied in the tea trade, his Indian knowledge being of great service to him in this respect, and has also met with great success in this line, being now the second largest retailer in Belfast, besides doing a very large wholesale business. He is at present also concerned in the opening of a very large tea establishment in Dublin.

———

Wagstaff, George A., is the District Superintendent at Sheffield of the Scottish Temperance Life Assurance Company. Mr. Wagstaff, who is also an Insurance broker with a considerable business, commenced his Insurance life in 1887; he is very energetic and has built up a good business for the Companies in whose interests he acts.

———

Venables, W. H., is the Superintendent of Agents at the Birmingham Branch of the Scottish Boiler Insurance Company. He has taken an active part in the rapid advance of the Company's business in that district, which business has been considerably increased by the acquisition of the English and Scottish Boiler Insurance Company, as well as of the local office known as the Midland.

FRANCIS M. WALFORD.

CHARLES S. WALKER.

Walford, Francis Montagu, is Local Secretary of the Liverpool Branch of the Scottish Provident Institution. Educated at King Edward the Sixth Royal Grammar School, Guildford, Surrey, under the late Dr. Merriman, Mr. Walford commenced his business life in the office of a well-known firm of Cotton Brokers in Liverpool, in whose service he remained eleven years. In 1878 Mr. Walford joined his late father's firm, and in 1881 succeeded his brother as Local Secretary to the Scottish Provident Institution. The family has now represented this favourite Institution in Liverpool for over twenty years.

Walker, C. S., the Resident Secretary of the General Life and Fire Assurance Company at their Branch Office in Brunswick Street, Liverpool, is the son of the late Resident Secretary, who had held the post for fifteen years. Mr. Walker succeeded his father on his death in 1888, and under his management the Company's business in the District has made very satisfactory progress.

JOHN A. WALKER

W. WALKER

Walker, J. A., is the Manager for Ireland of the Palatine Fire Insurance Company at Dublin.   Mr. Walker's first connection with the Mutual Fire was in 1879, when, in company with his partner, Mr. Mills, as Joint District Managers, he opened the Dublin Branch for the Company, and met from the outset with great success.   In the following year it was found necessary to elevate the Belfast Branch into a District Agency, and Mr. Mills was accordingly appointed to take charge of it, and seven years later, in 1887, on that gentleman's removal to Huddersfield as Resident Secretary, the whole business of the Company in Ireland was consolidated and placed under Mr.

Walker's management.   Subsequently the Mutual was merged into the Palatine as has also been the City of London Company, so that the Palatine is now one of the largest of our Fire Companies. Mr. Walker is a J.P. for Dublin, a member of its Corporation, and of several public bodies.

———

Walker, W., is the District Manager at Nottingham of the General Assurance Company. Mr. Walker has represented this Company as Agent in this district for upwards of twenty-five years, and has succeeded in building up a large and prosperous business for it.

G. F. WALLERS

J. M. WALLACE.

Wallers, George F., is now Superintendent of Agencies for the Star Life Assurance Society, under Mr. Chambers, J.P., the Secretary for Ireland, of that Society. When our portrait was taken Mr. Wallers was acting as District Manager for the New York Life Insurance Company for Dublin and South of Ireland, a position which he held for five years with very great success, and which he recently resigned. He was born in London about thirty years ago, and trained at first-class colleges in Staffordshire and Ireland, entering business life in Liverpool first as a junior in the New York Life Office there, then receiving an appointment as Assistant Secretary to the Mersey Tunnel Railway during the construction of that great feat of engineering and financial enterprise, then returning to his "life" work. Mr. Wallers has obtained an extended knowledge of men and of financial affairs, which is now most valuable to him.

Mr. Wallers is an active member of the Insurance Institute of Ireland, and a frequent contributor to its literature and discussions.

Wallace, Joseph Macknight, the Secretary at Belfast of the Northern Accident Insurance Company, the Economic Fire Office, and the Marine and General Life Office, is the son of a Presbyterian clergyman of Coleraine, where he was educated at the Academical Institution. He commenced life in the service of the Provincial Bank of Ireland, being employed at different times at several of its Branch offices, but owing to the remote prospects of promotion, he resigned his post in that concern, and having obtained an appointment in the Union Bank of Australia he went out to Melbourne to take it up. His health, however, only allowed him to remain in that country for about two years, at the end of which time he returned to Ireland, and in 1884, on the Northern Accident Insurance Company opening an Irish Branch at Belfast, he applied for and obtained the post of Resident Secretary. He obtained his kindred appointments to the Economic Fire and the Marine and General Life Offices in 1887. He has since been very successful in securing a very fair business for each of the Companies for which he acts.

G. F. WALTER.

A. W. WAMSLEY

Walter, George F., District Manager for the Stoke-upon-Trent District of the Colonial Mutual Life Assurance Society, Limited, is a native of Birmingham, where he was born in 1853. He commenced work in his native town as a Special Agent for various branches of Insurance, and carried on a very successful business for many years. In 1880 he was admitted an Associate of the Chartered Accountants. He next acted as Birmingham Local Secretary for the Gresham Life Assurance Society, which position he resigned to take up the supervision of the Potteries District for the Colonial Mutual Life Assurance Society when they first opened their business there, being one of the first District Managers appointed by that Company. Here he commenced, not knowing a single person, but he has been most successful in the staff of Agents which he has got together, and he takes such pride in the business which he has built up that though he has had more than one offer from different Companies to represent them, he has declined all such proposals.

Wamsley, A. W., is the Resident Secretary of the Sickness and Accident Assurance Association at their Branch Office at Newcastle-on-Tyne. Mr. Wamsley received his education at Kingswood School, Bath, and at the age of seventeen commenced his Insurance experience in the Office of the Prudential Assurance Company at Newcastle-on-Tyne. He was not long before he received promotion to the post of Head Clerk, whence, on the opening of a new District Office at Middlesbrough, he was sent to take charge of that Office. On the Newcastle Resident Secretaryship of the Sickness and Accident becoming vacant, he applied for it, and having been chosen returned to the scene of his former operations. Since then he has applied all his energies to bring his Branch into a first-class position.

HERBERT H. WALTON

J. HERBERT WALTON.

Walton, Herbert H., is District Manager at Newcastle-on Tyne of the Law Union and Crown Fire and Life Insurance Company. Mr. Walton, previous to his present appointment, was for eleven years Chief Clerk of the Northern Branch of the Royal Insurance Company, and is a gentleman of much ability and excellent judgment.

Walton, J. Herbert, is the District Manager of the Marine and General Life Assurance Society at Leeds and Nottingham. Mr. Walton formerly practised as an accountant at Leeds, at which time he held an Agency for the Marine and General, which he prosecuted with so much success that the Directors offered him his present appointment. Since that time the business of the Society in this district has been very rapidly developed.

H. F. WARDEN.

J. WARDLE

Warden, Henry Forrester, Resident Secretary at the Manchester Branch of the Yorkshire Insurance Company, has been associated with the Office (as Surveyor or Resident Secretary) for upwards of twenty-five years.

Commencing his Insurance training at Manchester in 1860 under Mr. James Robb, he afterwards joined the Alliance in that city, as Fire Clerk and Surveyor, under the management of Mr. Robert Lewis. On the retirement of Mr. James Robb from the Surveyorship to several Companies to manage the Northern's Manchester Branch in 1866, Mr. Warden was appointed by the Alliance Yorkshire and other Companies as Surveyor in the Manchester District—extending also to the North and Midlands—a position which he held in conjunction with Mr. Benjamin Miller, up to the year 1883, when he received from the Yorkshire the appointment to open the important Branch of which he has the management. Mr. Warden is one of the promoters of the Manchester Insurance Institute, the first Society of the kind established.

Wardle, J., is the Manager of the Leeds Branch of the Liverpool and London and Globe Insurance Company. Mr. Wardle entered the service of the Liverpool and London and Globe in 1874, and served at the Manchester Branch of that Company till 1883, when he was appointed Surveyor to the Country Department at the Head Office of the Sun Fire, leaving that in June, 1886, for the District Managership for Yorkshire, in conjunction with a similar appointment to the Sun Life Office, from which position he received his present post. Mr. Wardle's Branch of the Liverpool and London and Globe transacts the largest business of any Company in the Yorkshire District, and it is therefore one of the most important Branches carried on by any Insurance Company in the United Kingdom. Mr. Wardle is Vice-President of the Insurance Institute of Yorkshire, and he holds a commission in the 2nd W. Y. V. Royal Engineers.

SAMUEL WATERS.

J. CHARLES WARDROP.

Waters, Samuel, is the Manager of the Eastern Counties Branch of the Employers' Liability Assurance Corporation at Ipswich, for which he, at an early date, took up an Agency in the same town, subsequently becoming District Agent for the County of Suffolk. In 1889 he was appointed to the position which he now holds. He has also been Agent to the Provident Life and County Fire Offices since 1859, and does business besides in Hail Storm, Plate Glass, Horse and Carriage, Burglary, and every other kind of Insurance. He takes a prominent part in many County philanthropic institutions, being Secretary to the Suffolk Provident Society, the Suffolk Discharged Prisoners' Aid Society, the Suffolk County Medical Club, the Suffolk Village Club and Reading Room Association, the Suffolk Branch of the Royal Society for Prevention of Cruelty to Animals, the Ipswich and Suffolk Coffee Public House Company, Limited, and is Agent for Stubbs Mercantile Offices.

Wardrop, J. Charles, is the Secretary in London of the Life Association of Scotland. Mr. Wardrop, who has had a very long and valuable experience in Life Insurance matters, was for some years the Joint Secretary at the Head Office of this Company in Edinburgh, and under his able management the business of this important Branch is in a highly flourishing condition.

ALFRED P. WATKINS.

THOMAS WATSON.

Watkins, Alfred P., the District Manager of the Norwich Union Fire Insurance Society at its Branch in Worcester, began as an Agent for the Society in 1852, in which capacity he acted till 1883, during which time he increased the business to such an extent that he purchased his present premises in Foregate Street. In 1883 he was appointed District Manager, with complete supervision over the large and important business which he has succeeded in building up in the counties of Worcester, Hereford and Monmouth. He is the Chief Officer of the Norwich Union's Fire Engine Establishment at Worcester, the only one in the city, having a Steam and a Manual Fire Engine and all appliances under his control. Mr. Watkins also acts as an Insurance Broker, doing business with most of the leading offices. He has held the Agency of the Norwich and London Accident Assurance Association since 1856, and has been Sole Agent in the District for the Equitable Life Insurance Society of the United States since 1883, for both of which Companies he does a good and steadily-increasing business.

Watson, Thomas, Resident Secretary of the Scottish Widows' Fund Life Assurance Society at the Branch Office of that Society in West George Street, Glasgow, received a great part of his early training in the details of the Insurance profession on the staff of the Local Branch in Glasgow of the North British and Mercantile Insurance Company, subsequently leaving the service of that Company to undertake the duties of the Resident Secretaryship of the Life Association of Scotland, also at their Glasgow Branch. He again transferred his services in 1882, this time to his present Company, taking up the Glasgow Resident Secretaryship on its becoming vacant by the removal of Mr. J. G. C. Cheyne, his predecessor in the office, to the position of Head Office Inspector to the Society at Edinburgh. Since his appointment to his present post Mr. Watson has been eminently and exceptionally successful in developing the business of the Scottish Widows' Fund Life Assurance Society in the district under his supervision, which comprises the whole of the West of Scotland. Mr. Watson is deservedly popular both within and without the Insurance profession. He has filled the office of Honorary Treasurer of the Glasgow Insurance and Actuarial Society since 1882.

JOHN WATSON.

WILLIAM WATSON.

Watson, John, is the Resident Secretary in London of the Lancashire and Yorkshire Accident Insurance Company at its newly-established Branch in King William Street, E.C. Previous to receiving this appointment, Mr. Watson was for several years Superintendent of Agents for this Company in the West of England, with head-quarters at Bristol, where he met with much success, as is indicated by his present promotion.

———

Waugh, Alexander Lees, the District Manager of the New York Life Insurance Company at their Branch Office in Liverpool, commenced his work in the Insurance profession in 1879 at the Manchester Branch of the Royal Insurance Company as Cashier. There he remained till 1882, when he was appointed Resident Secretary for the Manchester Branch of the Northern Accident Insurance Company, which office in its turn he held till 1885. He was then promoted to the London Secretaryship of the same Company, which he held till 1890, when he resigned that post to take up that which he at present holds.

Watson, William, Local Secretary to the Westminster Fire Office at its Branch Office at Leeds, with supervision over the whole of Yorkshire, is one of the oldest Insurance men in that town. A descendant of old county families, he entered early upon a business career in commercial houses, and his first step in the Insurance profession was taken under the Leeds and Yorkshire Insurance Company, which was amalgamated in 1864 with the Liverpool, London, and Globe Insurance Company. Having served some years with the latter Office, and subsequently acted as District Manager for one or two minor Offices now extinct, he received his present appointment, which he has held for about fourteen years. His career as an Insurance man therefore covers a period of nearly thirty years, and he is now all but one the senior Branch Manager of the town. Mr. Watson has a reputation more than local as a conscientious and astute Insurance manager and skilful Surveyor. Outside the profession he has more particularly distinguished himself in the Masonic Craft, having filled many important offices, and acquired a world-wide reputation as a writer on the subject, and as a distinguished authority on the Archæology and Bibliography of the Fraternity. He fills with conspicuous ability the position of Honorary Librarian to the Provincial Grand Lodge of West Yorkshire.

A. L. WEBB.

EDWARD WHALLEY,

Webb, Arthur Lionel, the Resident Secretary at Bristol of the Scottish Life Assurance Company, Limited, received his Insurance training at the Western Branch of the Royal Insurance Company. After being with that Office several years, during which period he acquired a thoroughly practical knowledge of the Fire and Life business, Mr. Webb, in the early part of 1891, undertook a Special Agency for the Scottish Life in Bristol, and thenceforward had so successful a record that on the resignation of the Bristol Secretary in June, 1891, he was offered the vacant appointment, which he accepted.

Whalley, Edward, is the Local Manager to the Union Assurance Society at its Liverpool Branch. Prior to his appointment to his present post, Mr. Whalley had the advantage of a long and valuable local experience, having originally been for eight years on the Head Office staff of the Liverpool and London and Globe, and, more recently, for twelve years in an important position on that of the London and Lancashire Fire, which he left on the establishment of the Union's Liverpool Branch in 1878, when he was appointed to his present post in charge of it. The Branch has prospered greatly under Mr. Whalley's management, and it is needless to say that he holds a prominent position in local Insurance circles.

A. W. WHITE.

J. HOLMES WHITE.

White, Albert W., the District Manager of the Marine and General Mutual Life Assurance Society, at Newcastle-on-Tyne, commenced his business career in 1876 with a firm of Shipowners and Export Merchants of extensive connection in the North of England, in which place he received a good sound business training. After travelling abroad for four years, he elected to enter the Insurance profession, and with this in view connected himself with various offices locally established at Newcastle-on-Tyne, and thus gained a sound knowledge of Insurance matters generally. In 1886 he made successful application for the position of District Manager to the Marine and General, whose directors at that time had decided to establish a Branch in the North of England. Since then, by steady and systematic work, he has formed a most valuable connection for a Society which, prior to his appointment, was practically unknown in the northern counties, and has worked up the Branch to be one of the leading and most lucrative possessed by the Society in the provinces.

White, J. Holmes, the Resident Secretary to the Scottish Accident Assurance Company at their Branch Office at Newcastle-on-Tyne, is a member of an old and distinguished North Country family. He received his education at Gosberton School, in Lincolnshire, and commenced his Insurance career in the Newcastle Office of the Fire Insurance Association in 1884. He had not been long there before he was appointed Local Manager to the English and Scottish Boiler Insurance Company. After being some months in the service of that Company, since amalgamated with the Scottish Boiler, he was offered and accepted his present appointment, in which he has remained ever since, though his services have frequently been sought by Life and other Accident Companies. Mr. Holmes White has worked hard and successfully for his Company, and has given satisfaction to directors and agents alike.

W. J. WHITE.

ALLAN G. WHITTAKER.

White, W. J., Resident Secretary of the British Empire Mutual Life Office at their Branch Office at Plymouth, commenced and passed the whole of his previous career in the service of the Western Counties and London Life Assurance Company at Plymouth, where the Head Office of that Company was situated. He gradually worked his way up until he was eventually appointed in 1883 to the post of Secretary and Principal Officer, which post he held at the time of the amalgamation of the Western Counties and London Life Office with his present Company, when he was appointed to the post which he now occupies in the service of the absorbing Company.

Whittaker, Allan G., late Secretary of the General Accident Guarantee and Indemnity Insurance Company of Dublin, now holds an important appointment in connection with the Dublin Branch of the English and Scottish Law Life Office. Mr. Whittaker received his Insurance training in the Dublin Branch of the Scottish Equitable Life Assurance Society, and his Insurance career has been a very successful one.

G. T. LOCKYER WILLIAMS.

GEORGE WILL, JUN.

Williams, G. T. Lockyer, is the District Inspector at Bristol of the Scottish Equitable Life Assurance Society. Mr. Williams is the eldest son of the Rev. T. Lockyer Williams, late Vicar of Porthleven, Cornwall, and was born in the year 1850. He entered the Insurance profession at the age of eighteen, as Junior Clerk in the Office of the Clerical, Medical and General Life Office, and after acting as Clerk for six years, he travelled as Inspector of Agencies in the Midland Counties and West of England for that Society for eighteen months, with considerable success. In 1876 the representation of the Scottish Equitable Office for the West of England and South Wales became vacant, and Mr. Williams was selected for the post from a large number of applicants, and has held it since that date, a period of sixteen years, during which he has considerably more than doubled the Society's business in his district.

Will, George, jun., is the Agency Superintendent of the National Provident Institution for the Northern Counties, with headquarters at Newcastle-on-Tyne. Mr. Will has been connected with the Insurance business for a long time, having occupied a similar capacity for several years with an Accident Insurance Company, and subsequently for a Scottish Life Office in Scotland.

J. W. WILLIAMSON.

GRAHAME H. WILLS.

Williamson, J. W., is the present Resident Secretary of the Yorkshire Fire and Life Insurance Society at their Branch Office at 16, Tithebarn Street, Liverpool. Mr. Williamson has now been engaged for twenty-seven years in the Insurance profession, having originally entered it as a Clerk in the Glasgow Branch of the North British and Mercantile Insurance Company in the year 1867, in which Office he continued for seven years until 1874, when he left it in order that he might take up the appointment of Fire Superintendent to the Northern Assurance Company at their Branch Office in Edinburgh. Mr. Williamson's first appearance at Liverpool, the present scene of his labours, was in the capacity of Local Manager to the South British and National Insurance Companies, in the year 1883, when he was entrusted with the opening of the Branch which they had then newly-established in that city. He continued to occupy this last-named post until the year 1887, when he severed his connection with the South British and National and undertook the office which he still holds. Mr. Williamson took over the Resident Secretaryship of the York-shire Assurance Company at Liverpool at a very early stage of the Branch's existence, it having been instituted barely two years previous to his accession to office, the Company having for thirty years been only represented in that District by Agents, but his experience, which, as may be gathered, has been very long and varied, has been of great use to his employers, and has contributed in no slight degree to the success of his Branch, which has undoubtedly been making steady progress ever since its first formation.

Wills, Grahame H., is the District Manager of the Straits Fire Insurance Company Limited, at their West of England Branch at Bristol. Mr Wills, who is a well-known Bristol Insurance man, was appointed to that post in August, 1891, since which time he has opened up a very good business for his Company. Besides the above, he also holds the District Managership of the Bristol Branch of the Boiler Insurance and Steam Power Company, Limited, to which he was appointed in 1890.

F. H. WINDER.

ARTHUR R. WINN.

Winder, F. H., is the Resident Secretary at Birmingham of the Midland Counties Insurance Company, which appointment he has held since the establishment of this Branch in 1882. Mr. Winder had previously had considerable experience in Insurance matters, and is a young man of much ability.

Winn, Arthur R., is the District Manager of the Economic Fire Office at its Branch at Birming-ham. He commenced his professional career, in 1876, in the Head Office of the Millers' Fire, a local Company, which went into liquidation in 1884. He subsequently held the post of Chief Clerk at the Birmingham Branch of the Fire Insurance Association, which he left to become Surveyor to the Birmingham Branch of the Equit-able Fire Office, a position which he held for four years, when he received his present appointment from the Directors of the Economic.

WM. M. WISELY.

RICHARD A. WOOD

Wisely, William M., the Resident Secretary in charge of the Glasgow Branch of the Scottish Provident Institution, is the second son of the well-known Presbyterian Chaplain to the Forces in Malta, and before his appointment to his present post was the Manager of the Glasgow Branch Office of the International Marine Insurance Company and a Member of the Glasgow Association of Underwriters. He entered upon the duties of his present post in 1887 and since then his efforts to maintain and develop the business of the Institution have been very successful.

Wood, Richard A., is the Local Manager at Newcastle-on-Tyne of the Liverpool and London and Globe Insurance Company, and has been connected with this Company since 1863, when he joined it in Newcastle as District Agent and Inspector, and has continued in its service since that time. He is one of the most respected, as well as one of the oldest, Insurance officials in the North of England.

ALFRED WOODBURN.

G. A. WOODWARD.

Woodburn, Alfred, the District Manager of the Church of England Life and Fire Assurance Institution at their Branch at Manchester, commenced his business career in the Head Office of the Liverpool and London and Globe Insurance Company in Liverpool, where he remained for thirteen years, at the end of which period he removed to Manchester to take up his residence there as Agency Inspector to the Rock Life Assurance Company. In the September of 1889, on the Church of England Assurance Institution establishing their first Branch Office in Manchester, Mr. Woodburn was selected for the post of District Manager, the extensive experience which he had acquired in his former position in Agency work chiefly influencing the Directors in their choice; which choice has already been amply justified by the results.

Woodward, George Arthur, is the Resident Secretary in Manchester of the Scottish Widows' Fund Life Assurance Society. He is a native of Worcestershire, being born at Ryall in that county in December, 1841. He was educated at Cheltenham. His first entry into the Insurance world was made in the service of the office he at present represents in so important a city. He joined the staff of the Liverpool Office in the year 1870. Here he remained some three years, resigning then on being appointed to open a Branch Office for the Edinburgh Life Insurance Company in the same city, which he did successfully, returning, however, to the service of the Scottish Widows' Fund in December, 1873, and by that Office was appointed Resident Secretary in Birmingham. For fourteen years and a half he held this position, when he received the offer of his present appointment, and accepted it on the 1st of May, 1888.

E. G. WOOTTON.

J. W. WOOTTON.

Wootton, Edward Gower, Secretary of the Imperial Fire and Life Offices for the Midland District, commenced his Insurance career with the Royal Insurance Company, and assisted in building up the very substantial business the Royal have acquired in the Midland district. After twelve years' service with the same Company he left them to open a branch in Birmingham for the Imperial, and on the occasion of his leaving he received the most flattering testimonials from the Manager and other officials of the Royal. The local business of the Imperial was at that time very small, and Mr. Wootton has had the satisfaction of obtaining not only a considerable, but probably the largest, business of natural growth in the town. His long connection with Birmingham has rendered him peculiarly fitted to deal with the rather complicated risks of the district, for to a wide general knowledge of Insurance matters he adds an extensive and intimate acquaintance with the special features of the multifarious trades of the hardware and other industries, and justly is looked upon as a leading authority on the risks and rates of the district. A readiness to assist his younger brethren, combined with his genial and kindly temperament, have made him a general favourite with the Insurance fraternity of the city, and, although still a comparatively young man, he is now one of the "fathers of the profession" in the Midlands.

———

Wootton, John William, the Resident Secretary of the Sun Life Office at its Yorkshire Branch at Leeds, commenced his career in the Insurance profession in the Consolidated Fire Office in Bucklersbury, E.C. Leaving that Office, however, after only a few months' service, he entered the London Office of the Edinburgh Life Assurance Company, where he remained for a period of seven years, his duties in that Office being, in the first instance, in connection with the correspondence and the general office routine, and the last two or three years being spent in the outside work of the office in connection with the extension of the business in London, Bristol, Somersetshire, Wiltshire, Dorsetshire, and the Channel Islands. He left the Edinburgh Life Assurance Company in November, 1885, and removed to Yorkshire in the capacity of District Inspector to the Sun Life Office, which post he held for two years, when he was promoted to the position of Resident Secretary, which he continues to hold. His efforts in behalf of his Company have from the beginning been attended with thorough success.

RICHARD WRIGHT.

HERBERT E. C. YARROW.

Wright, Richard, is the Local Manager of the Royal Insurance Company at their Branch Office at Manchester. Mr. Wright had, previous to entering upon his present duties, been for many years in the service of the Royal, first as Chief Fire Clerk at their Head Office at Liverpool, and subsequently as their Local Manager at Birmingham. He was promoted from the latter post to that which he now holds in 1879. The business under his supervision is very large and important, embracing as it does that of the whole of the cotton manufacturing districts, and it has greatly profited by Mr. Wright's practical experience and sagacity, having been considerably increased and consolidated since his appointment to the charge of it.

———

Yarrow, Herbert Edward Colebrook, is the Manager of the London Office of the State Fire Insurance Company, Limited. He was born in 1860, and entered the London Office of the Royal Insurance Company at an early age. All his experience has been gained in that Company, in whose service he remained for fifteen years, filling various positions, the last being that of Superintendent of Agents to the London Office, which post he resigned on receiving his present appointment in September, 1891.

JOHN YOUNG.

HENRY W. YOUNG.

Young, John, the Resident Secretary of the G eneral Assurance Company at their Branch Office at Newcastle-on-Tyne, received his first training in the Insurance business from the Scottish Union and National, at their Glasgow office. He subsequently acted as Chief Clerk and Surveyor at the Glasgow Branch of the Fire Insurance Association, leaving that office to work in a similar capacity for the General Assurance Company in Glasgow. He remained in the last mentioned position for about five years, until the November of 1888, when he was promoted to his present position.

———

Young, H. W., is the Resident Secretary at Dublin of the General Assurance Company, which appointment he has held since early in 1889. Mr. Young was for many years Inspector of Agents at Dublin for the Scottish Provincial Assurance Company, and is consequently well-known throughout Ireland where he is regarded as a successful and capable insurance official.

THE INDEX,

A Leading Insurance Journal.

LIVE, INDEPENDENT AND ENTERPRISING.

Illustrated with PORTRAITS, VIEWS OF INSURANCE BUILDINGS, CARTOONS, etc.

NO INSURANCE AGENT SHOULD FAIL TO SUBSCRIBE FOR THIS JOURNAL !

Terms : SEVEN SHILLINGS per Annum, post free.

PUBLISHED MONTHLY BY

The Index Publishing Company, Limited,

6, KING STREET, CHEAPSIDE, E.C., LONDON.

INDUSTRIAL BRANCH OFFICIALS.

HENRY ADAMS.

WILLIAM ADAMS.

Adams, Henry, Director and Sheffield Branch Manager of the Refuge Assurance Company, is a well-known and respected citizen of that city. The district covered by this Branch embraces portions of the West and East Ridings of Yorkshire, taking in the Yorkshire towns of Sheffield, Barnsley, Pontefract, Doncaster, Hull, and up to Driffield ; it covers also the whole of Lincolnshire, Nottinghamshire, and Derbyshire, with fringes of one or two other counties. There are about three hundred superintendents, assistant-superintendents, and agents under the management of Mr. Adams. There was not a policy-holder of the Refuge in the town when Mr. Adams came here to start the business, twenty-eight years ago, and he personally introduced the business of this Company into many of the towns embraced in his Branch. At present there are twenty-seven sub-districts under the control of the Sheffield Branch.

Mr. Adams owes his position entirely to his own efforts. He was born at Hollinsend, near Sheffield, in 1836, the son of working folk, and at the early age of nine had to begin to earn his own livelihood in a coal pit, thus getting very little time for education. This defect, however, he to a great extent remedied by a scrupulous attendance at the Primitive Methodist Sunday School and at a night school, and being in good health and full of hope he did not let any early disadvantage deter him from his resolution to eventually succeed. His parents subsequently removed to Intake and Barnsley, at which latter place he married ; and it was shortly after this, when he was twenty-five years of age, that he felt himself impelled by conscience to give up his life to preach for the welfare of others. The local authorities objecting to his using his house for this purpose, he removed to Sheffield, and since then he has continued the good work as a preacher and helper of his weaker brethren, to which he was called nearly thirty years ago. It was after his removal to Sheffield that his connection with the Refuge Assurance Company began ; but though by his own hand and brain he has worked himself up to his present position, he has never ceased labouring for his Church.

Adams, William, is the Manager of the Birmingham Branch of the Refuge Assurance Company, Limited. Mr. Adams has had a long experience in connection with Industrial Insurance, he having been for upwards of ten years Assistant Manager to the Company in the Sheffield District, and so great was his success in connection with it that eight years ago he was elected a Member of its Board of Directors, and seven years ago he transferred his services from Sheffield to Birmingham, since which time the business of the Refuge in this District has been enormously developed.

A. ARKINSTALL.

A. E. ALDERSLEY

Arkinstall, A., is the District Superintendent of the Prudential Assurance Company, Limited, at King's Lynn. He has been in the service of that Company during the whole of his Insurance career, having commenced as an Agent at Whitby, Yorkshire ; and, proving very successful in that capacity, he was after nine months promoted to be Assistant-Superintendent. Continuing his former success in his new rank, first at Ripon and afterwards at Sheffield, he was eventually rewarded by being promoted to his present position at King's Lynn, which appointment took place in 1889, and since that time he has obtained a very considerable amount of business for his Company.

Aldersley, A. E., District Superintendent of the British Workman's Assurance Company at Middlesbro', is a native of Nelson, Lancashire, where he commenced as an Agent for his present Company in 1887, and for two years worked very successfully, gaining the respect and esteem of his fellow Insurance men in that town. In 1889 he was appointed District Manager of the Building Societies' Trust, which appointment he relinquished in March, 1890, to take up the duties of his present position at Middlesbro' with supervision over the towns of Stockton and East and West Hartlepool. Mr. Aldersley has been successful in both consolidating and increasing the business of the Company in his District, and we should predict a prosperous future for the Middlesbro' district of the British Workman under his superintendency.

E. ARNOLD.

JAMES E. AUSTIN.

Arnold, E., Superintendent of the Prudential Assurance Company for the Mile End, London District, commenced to work for the Prudential in 1874, when he was appointed Agent in Birmingham. Since then he has represented the Company in Leicestershire and Hampshire as Assistant and District Superintendent, and in his present District in East London since 1880.

Ashley, T., is the District Superintendent of the Wesleyan and General Assurance Society at Leeds. Mr. Ashley, who was appointed to his present post in 1881, is a gentleman of large experience in Industrial Insurance, having been an Assistant-Superintendent for the Prudential Assurance Company for upwards of ten years previous to his connection with the Wesleyan and General. He has done much since his appointment to work up the business of his Society in Leeds, which, though commenced in 1841, had made but little progress before his accession to

office. His District is a large and important one, including Leeds, Wakefield, Doncaster, Skipton, Harrogate, etc., and the intermediate towns and villages.

Austin, James E., is the Superintendent at Newcastle-on-Tyne of the Pearl Life Assurance Company, Limited. Previous to receiving this appointment Mr. Austin had successfully managed operations for this Company in the South, Midland and Eastern Counties, where the results of his work warranted his promotion to this important District. Mr. Austin is an active Temperance worker, and has also contributed some important articles to the press; he is very popular with the Insurance fraternity here, and is at the present time Chairman of the Newcastle Superintendents' Association, which is composed of the Local Managers of all the Industrial Offices doing business in this town

JOSEPH BAKER.

W. BAKER.

Baker, Joseph, District Superintendent of the Wesleyan and General Assurance Society at Wolverhampton, commenced as an Agent with the Society in July, 1873, with a very small business transferred to him, but which he worked so hard and so successfully to increase that two years later he received the appointment which he still holds. Mr. Baker prides himself on being the first Superintendent appointed by the Wesleyan and General Assurance Society in any District, a well-deserved mark of esteem from the Directors of the Society.

Baker, W., the Superintendent of the Prudential Assurance Company at Brockley, was born at Horncastle, in Lincolnshire, in 1842. He entered the service of the Prudential in 1865, and was appointed to his present position in 1871. Mr. Baker has trained many of the present agents of the Company, to which he is enthusiastically devoted.

FREDERICK BARNES.

J. BAMFORD.

Barnes, Frederick, the District Superintendent of the Pearl Life Assurance Company at Nottingham, was born on March 13th, 1863. He commenced his Assurance career in October, 1880, as District Agent in Tunstall, Staffordshire, where he speedily built up a very considerable connection. In the January of 1886 he was promoted to be Assistant-Superintendent in the same district, being subsequently drafted to Crewe. Here he remained for ten months, still working his best, at the end of which period he was appointed to the Superintendency of the Northampton District, reciving a handsome testimonial from his colleagues at Crewe on the occasion. In two years he had done so much to increase the influence of the Company there that he was transferred to the more important district of Nottingham, again receiving handsome testimonials from the staff which he was leaving. He has since then continued all his former success. Mr. Barnes enjoys the proud satisfaction of having trained more than one of the present Superintendents of the Company.

Bamford, J., the Superintendent of the East Birmingham or Aston District of the Prudential Assurance Company, commenced his Insurance career as Sub-agent at Dewsbury, Yorkshire, in 1876. In 1877 he was appointed Agent at Birmingham, in which capacity he was so successful that in the next year he was promoted to the Assistant-Superintendency of the Edgbaston Section of Birmingham. Here he still continued his successful progress, and in 1883 was rewarded by further promotion to his present position. Since then Mr. Bamford's practical knowledge of his business, together with his activity as a Superintendent, has enabled him to raise his district to the condition of one of the most prosperous under the Company's control.

J. M. BARNES.

G. BATE.

Barnes, John Meredith, District Superintendent of the British Workman's Assurance Company at Walthamstow, was born at Stourbridge, in Worcestershire, in 1860, the son of the late Mr. H. J. Barnes, for many years of the Birmingham Gas-Light and Coke Company. He received his education at the Birmingham Grammar School, afterwards going to London, where he was employed in several of the large drapery houses in the City. He devoted his leisure time, however, to the study of Insurance business, and in 1889 turned the knowledge thus acquired to account on obtaining his present appointment, since which time he has done much to extend the business of his Company in his District, in every department.

Bate, G., the District Superintendent of the British Workman's Assurance Company at Burslem, Staffordshire, commenced work as an Agent for the British Nation Office and the Sceptre Life Association, gaining great credit for himself by his success in that capacity. On the foundation of the British Workman's Assurance Company, Mr. Bate was chosen to be their first Superintendent, since when he has represented the Company in the Dudley, Wolverhampton, Leeds, London, Glasgow, Sunderland, Barrow-in-Furness and his present District successively. Mr. Bate is the author of "The Life Assurance Agent's Pocket Hand-book," a little work of great value to the Agents' branch of the profession.

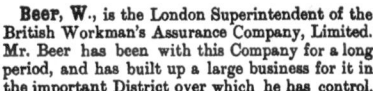

W. BEER.   A. BELLAMY.

Beer, W., is the London Superintendent of the British Workman's Assurance Company, Limited. Mr. Beer has been with this Company for a long period, and has built up a large business for it in the important District over which he has control.

Barker, J. H., the Superintendent of the Newcastle-on-Tyne District of the Wesleyan and General Assurance Society, was born at Heworth, not far from Newcastle, in 1850. In 1877 he commenced Insurance work as an Agent to the Prudential at Newcastle, and a few months later was, in reward for his services, promoted to be Assistant-Superintendent of the Newcastle District for that Company. This position he filled satisfactorily for some time, showing substantial increases each year. In December, 1882, he transferred his services to the Wesleyan and General Assurance Society as Assistant-Superintendent of the Newcastle District, with Gateshead under his supervision, which post he held till 1890, building up a good business for the Society out of what had been nothing. In the September of that year he was appointed to his present post.

Bellamy, A., the District Manager of the Liverpool Victoria Friendly Society at Sheffield, has been associated with that Society for the whole period of his Insurance career, having acted in the capacity of District Manager for upwards of thirty years. He enjoys the highest esteem, both of his Directors and Agents, and has on more than one occasion received testimonials to that effect from the latter.

Bray, John W., the District Superintendent of the Pearl Life Assurance Company at Ipswich, was born in Kent, but commenced his Insurance business at Plymouth, where he worked hard, and as a result was appointed Assistant in charge of the Launceston Sub-district. Here he remained for twelve months, and was then transferred to the Dover Sub-district, being subsequently promoted to his present post at Ipswich. On leaving Dover he was presented by his staff with a handsome address and testimonial. He has completely reorganized his District and raised it from the position of one of the worst to one of the best under the Company's influence, his record being the highest in the Eastern Counties Division.

ROBERT P. BEATTIE.

Beattie, Robert P., is the London Manager of the Scottish Legal Life Assurance Society of Glasgow. Mr. Beattie commenced his Insurance career in the service of the Pearl Life Assurance Company at Edinburgh, his native place, where he became Assistant Superintendent of that Company subsequent to his appointment as Superintendent to the same Office at Dundee, which district included Perthshire and Forfarshire. He retained this appointment until May, 1885, when he was offered and accepted the management of the London, Edinburgh and Glasgow Company's business in the same district, remaining in that position until the end of 1886, when he returned to the Pearl Company as Superintendent at Glasgow. In May, 1889, he accepted his present position as London Manager of the Scottish Legal, and the result of his work in this district has been most satisfactory to the Directors of his Society.

Brasier, Alfred, the Bristol Superintendent of the Royal London Friendly Society, was born at Guildford in 1844, and has been associated with the above Society for over twenty-six years, having started as Agent in the Deptford and Greenwich District. In 1875, on his Superintendent being removed to Birmingham, Mr. Brasier also migrated there in the capacity of Assistant-Superintendent, being subsequently transferred to Bristol, with full power to appoint agents and develop the district independently of the then Superintendent. So successful was he that on the removal of the Superintendent to another district, the whole of the business was placed under Mr. Brasier's superintendence. He has now over forty Agents under him, and his own popularity and perseverance have done much to further the progress of his Society in the Bristol district.

W. H. BENSON.

J. W. BERRY.

Benson, W. H., is the Superintendent to the Prudential Assurance Company for the Stoke-on Trent District. He has passed the whole of his Insurance career in the service of that Company, having commenced as Agent in May, 1876, at Liversedge, Yorkshire, and so successful was he in increasing the business of the Company that less than six months afterwards he was promoted to be Assistant-Superintendent at Dewsbury. Here there had been little or no increase in the business during the two years preceding his arrival, but so energetically did Mr. Benson work that, at the end of three years, he had fully retrieved the character of the District, and at the same time had qualified himself for his further promotion to the Superintendency of Kidderminster. He remained there for five years, subsequently removing to North Manchester, where he stayed for three years, leaving behind him at both places a worthy record of his diligence. He was appointed to his present District in 1890, where he has since increased the Company's business by a very large amount.

Berry, J. W., District Manager of the Liverpool Victoria Legal Friendly Society at Lancaster, commenced his career as an Insurance man in 1877, from that time until 1883 doing a very fair general business, in addition to his other occupations. At the end of that year he was appointed Travelling Auditor to the Liverpool Victoria Society, in connection with the Leeds Branch covering the North and East and a portion of the West Ridings of Yorkshire, and six months later was promoted to be Travelling Agent or Inspector, and transferred to the Chief Office Staff. This position he held until September, 1887, when, on the various Superintendencies in North Lancashire, Westmoreland, and Cumberland being amalgamated, Mr. Berry was put in charge of those counties as District Manager, since which time the Society's business in the district has been largely increased. Mr. Berry is a strong advocate of mutual good feeling between Manager and Agents, and as an acknowledgment of his practical support of this principle he was in October, 1890, on completing the third year of his management, presented with an elaborate illuminated address by the members of his staff.

T. W. BODEN.

J. L. BESWICK.

Boden, T. W., District Superintendent of the British Workman's Assurance Company at Bournemouth, is a native of Lancashire, born in 1860, and, being one of twelve children, commenced life at the early age of ten in a calico-printing works in North East Lancashire. He remained there till 1879, in the December of which year he took up a small Agency for the Prudential at Tunstall, in the Staffordshire Potteries, and after working there with considerable success for eleven months removed to Burnley as Agent for the same Company for nearly two years. He then left Insurance work for a time to take a place as book-keeper at Northwich, Cheshire, after a year of which he obtained another situation as traveller and book-keeper to a firm just outside Manchester, with whom he stayed for two years. His inclination, however, was still in the direction of Insurance work, and so in 1884 he removed to Hanley, in the Pottery District, to take up an Assistant-Superintendency for the Refuge; subsequently after a period of three and a-half years removing to Bournemouth, of which the Directors of the Company had offered him the Superintendency. At the end of six months' residence at Bournemouth he left the service of the Refuge to take up the District Superintendency of the British Workman's Assurance Company, which he has held ever since to good purpose for the Company, having entirely opened out the District which he found in charge of only one spare-time Agent, but which now boasts a large business.

Beswick, J. L., District Manager of the London, Edinburgh and Glasgow Assurance Company at their Branch Office at Hull, is the son of a cotton manufacturer at Darwen, under whom he worked for some time, afterwards taking up a coal agency at Stockport. It was while engaged in this latter business that, in 1880, he commenced Insurance work as well, continuing this dual occupation until 1884, when he decided to try his fortune in America. Eleven months of that country, however, sufficed for his tasks, and on his return he took up a full-time Agency of the Prudential at Manchester, during his tenure of which post he acted as Secretary of the Miles Platting Branch of the National Union of Life Assurance Agents. He received the appointment of District Superintendent to his present Company in 1888, first being put in charge of Oldham, where he remained for a year, and subsequently of Rossendale Valley for another year, and of Manchester, temporarily, for five months. He was next transferred to the Wells and Weston-super-Mare District, where he was also for twelve months, working very successfully, and eventually was promoted to his present appointment at Hull. Mr. Beswick has been the fortunate recipient of congratulatory letters on his work and successive promotions from the Offices under whom he has worked, also of testimonials from the various staffs over which he has in his time had supervision.

S. BOYD.

A. BRUNT.

Boyd, S., District Superintendent of the Prudential Assurance Company at its Branch Office at Hull, has passed the whole of his Insurance career in the service of that Company, having commenced work for it as an Agent in the Bradford District. His success in that capacity was rewarded by his promotion to an Assistant-Superintendency in the same district, where he remained until December, 1883. He was in that year again promoted, this time to the position of Superintendent of the Shrewsbury District, and after three years of further success he was in March, 1887, placed in his present post in Hull. Since then the increase of business has been steady and satisfactory.

Brunt, A., the Gloucester and Worcester District Superintendent of the Wesleyan and General Assurance Society, was appointed Agent to the Society at Bircheshead in Staffordshire in 1880, where he met with so marked a success that on the opening of the London District he was invited to go up there as a Special Agent with a view to his promotion to an Assistant-Superintendency. Here he still continued his success, and the promised promotion having soon taken place, he remained in that post till July, 1888, when he was deputed to open up his present District. On his leaving London, he was presented by the Branch Manager, Fellow Assistants, and Agents and Clerks of the District with handsome testimonials of their esteem and friendship.

W. BURNS.

J. W. BURDEN.

Burns, W., District Superintendent of the Prudential Assurance Company at Stornoway, joined the service of that Company in 1870 as Agent at Plymouth. There he continued till 1879, when he was appointed Assistant-Superintendent at Tavistock, but he had not been long there before he was transferred in the same capacity to Torquay. He was again removed in 1881 to Central London till 1886, when he was promoted to the post of Superintendent of the Stratford District. In 1889 he removed to his present post at the special request of the Directors, in order to develop the Company's operations in the Western Highlands and the Islands of Scotland, which programme he has faithfully carried out.

Previous to embarking on an Insurance career, Mr. Burns was engaged in scholastic work with a view to joining the Ministry, and although he eventually decided on adopting a commercial life, he frequently preaches and lectures in the Chapels and Churches of the District in which he may happen to be residing.

————

Burden, John Walton, is District Superintendent of the Prudential Assurance Company in South-West London, having worked himself up to that position from that of an Agent, in which latter capacity he joined the Prudential in 1868.

H. A. BURTON.

JOHN BUSHELL.

Burton, Henry A., District Superintendent of the Prudential Assurance Company at Tunbridge Wells, was born in 1850 in London, where his father carried on the business of a grocer. He started canvassing as a part-time Agent for the Prudential in 1867, but was not long before he obtained an appointment as full-time Agent in London East, he then being only 17½ years old. In July, 1869, his services had pointed him out as fitted for the duties of Travelling Agent, which post he held till 1873, journeying from town to town and residing in each for about three months, opening them up and starting agencies in them. In this connection he visited over 70 towns, receiving the first proposals for his Company and appointing the first agents in each, a record, perhaps, unique in the annals of the Prudential. At that latter date he became Assistant Superintendent at Croydon, whence, after a lapse of a year, he was removed to a country District in Ireland, of which two years subsequently he was made full Superintendent. In 1879, having worked up his District from almost nothing to a very considerable status in the books of the Company, he was promoted to the Dublin District, eventually leaving Ireland in 1881, having worked most efficiently in practically

introducing the business of the Company into that country. He was then placed in charge of the South East District of London, which post he held for nine years, leaving it in 1890, at his own request, owing to failing health, to take up his present duties at Tunbridge Wells.

Bushell, J., the Sheffield District Superintendent of the Wesleyan and General Assurance Society, was born at Burton, in Wiltshire in 1850, and commenced in the Insurance profession as an Agent to the Wesleyan and General in 1879 at Bolton, in Lancashire. Here, in three and a-half years, out of nothing, he built up so profitable a business that in 1880 he was appointed by his Superintendent to open out the business of the Society at Burnley and other important localities, all of which missions he fulfilled with marked success. In 1882 he was, in recognition of his talents, appointed by the General Manager to the District Agency at Sheffield, and subsequently in 1883 to the District Superintendency, with supervision over Lincolnshire, North Notts, and part of Derbyshire and Yorkshire, in all of which Districts he has established the Society's business on a firm and substantial footing.

JOSEPH CHADDERTON.

B. CHALLENGER.

Chadderton, Joseph, District Superintendent of the Wesleyan and General Assurance Society, was born at Failsworth, Lancashire, in 1842. When seven years old he was apprenticed to a silk weaver, in which trade he continued until the age of twenty-two, leaving it to better himself by becoming a labourer for a Railway Company. In this latter occupation he remained about three years, and at the end of that time settled at Earlstown, and married. Considering the disadvantages both of the age and condition in which he was living, it is highly to Mr. Chadderton's credit that he at that time obtained a Teacher's Certificate of the Science and Art Department, South Kensington, as self-taught, qualifying him to instruct Science Classes at Warrington, Earlstown, Golborne, and Newton-le-Willows, and very soon he held no less than eight teacher's certificates, all self-taught. His next step was to be draughtsman to the L.N.W.R. Company, at their wagon works, Earlstown, which position he retained for four years, only resigning it for health's sake. He then, in January, 1872, opened an Agency for the Wesleyan and General Assurance Society, being then nearly the only agent who devoted his undivided exertions to the Society. His services in this post pointed him out as deserving his present post at the head of the Manchester District, with control over more than 100 agents. Mr. Chadderton resides at Eccles, where he is a Member of the Local Board of Health. He has been the recipient of several testimonials to his worth and ability from all with whom he has been associated.

Challenger, B., District Superintendent of the Prudential Assurance Company at Worthing, was born near Bristol in 1860, and at the age of ten went to work in a coal mine, receiving no educa-tion but that which he found time to acquire at his own expense of time and money. When seven teen, however, with a view to improving his very unpromising prospects, he accepted an agency for the Prudential in the Frome District, which, with several other commissions, he worked with considerable success for five years, and at the end of that time he was appointed Assistant Superintendent at Southampton, which post he held till 1889, and his success still increasing he was rewarded with his present Superintendency. Since then he has largely increased the business of his District, and on going to press we learn he has been removed to Stroud, a district twice the size.

Cane, Reginald, the District Superintendent of the British Workman's Assurance Company at Newport, was born in 1865, and has been in the service of the Company since 1874, when he commenced as Collector in Windsor, under the London General Superintendent. His energy in this capacity was rewarded by his promotion to the Assistant-Superintendentship of Gloucester under his father, where he particularly distinguished himself by the successful unearthing and defeat of a considerable amount of fraud on the part of many of the Collectors in that District. He was then successively removed to Hereford, where he opened out the district, and to Newport, Monmouthshire, as Assistant-Superintendent, where he was working at the time of the Abersychan explosion, in which no fewer than 173 lives were lost, many of them having claims on the Company. He then was removed to Cardiff as Assistant Superintendent, and eventually to his present post as Superintendent of the British Workman's at Newport.

W. H. CHICK.

E. O. CLARKE.

Chick, William H., District Manager of the Liverpool Victoria Legal Friendly Society for Sunderland and District, was born at Bristol in 1846, and went to sea at the age of sixteen, where he remained till 1873. He then started as canvasser for the Liverpool Victoria Legal Friendly Society at Liverpool in 1874, where he built up a large book and became Tester for Liverpool District. In November, 1878, he removed to Cardiff to open out that district, which was at the time doing a very small business, but, thanks to Mr. Chick's exertions, before he left it for Oxford, Cardiff was the largest collecting district in Wales or West of England, excepting Bristol. In November, 1887, at the request of the head of the Agency Department, Mr. Chick moved to Oxford to open up the counties of Oxfordshire and Buckinghamshire, and during his first year of work there effected a large increase in the business of his new district. In August, 1890, he was appointed by the Committee of Management Manager for Sunderland and District, where he has now put everything into thorough working order; indeed, under his auspices the Sunderland employés are very sanguine of restoring their District to the position which it formerly held of the leading district of the North.

— — —

Clarke, E. O., is the Superintendent at Brixton of the Prudential Assurance Company, Limited. He has been in the service of this Company for some years, and has a very important district under his charge, which he works with great success.

R. S. CLOSE.

E. P. COGAN

Close, Richard Shepherd, the District Super-intendent of the British Workman's Assurance Company at Rochdale, was born at Claughton, in Lancashire, in 1848, and spent his early years at work on a farm, but not finding farming congenial work he migrated at the age of eighteen to Accrington, where he was engaged in various employments till 1872. He then made the acquaintance of an agent of the British Workman's Assurance Company, who, after having given him some business under himself for a little while, in which Mr. Close acquitted himself with credit, introduced him to his Superintendent, who in his turn appointed him the Company's Agent for Rochdale. Mr. Close was then a complete stranger to the district, and the Company itself was very young and comparatively unknown, but Mr. Close succeeded in opening the district, and after a few years' single-handed work was made District Agent with the supervision of two small Agencies, and the responsibility of preparing the accounts for the Superintendent's inspection. In November, 1880, having worked up a very considerable business, he was appointed Assistant Superintendent with two collectors under him, his former business being split up among various Agents, and his duties now being to assist these Agents and introduce new men. In 1886, the District was taken away from Manchester, to which it had hitherto been subordinate, and made a District of itself, Mr. Close being put in charge of it as Superintendent. Mr. Close can boast of having introduced all the Agents under him, seventeen in number, except one, to the Company, besides seven of the present Superintendents of the Company, while the flourishing state of his district is entirely due to his own personal efforts, he having worked it up from absolutely nothing at all.

Cogan, E. P., District Superintendent for the British Workman's Assurance Company for Cork and Munster, was born in the suburbs of Cork, a farmer's son, and at an early age removed into that city with his father, who set up in business as a flour merchant. In 1882 Mr. Cogan became agent for a Dublin Society, and was only engaged in that capacity for twelve months when he was appointed District Manager, a proof of the great interest which he took in Insurance business from the first. On the British Workman's Assurance Company opening a Branch Office in Cork, Mr. Cogan was so impressed by the wisdom and prudence of their programme that he resigned his District Managership to take up an Agency for the newly-arrived Company, a distinct sacrifice on his part, but one which he has never had cause to regret. After serving as Agent for only two years he was promoted to be District Agent, which was followed in another two years by the further promotion to his present District Superintendency, which took place on the 1st of January, 1890. The Office for this District is at 70, South Mall, Cork.

J. J. COWPER.

G. COLLINS.

Cowper, J. J., District Superintendent for the British Workman's Assurance Company at Edinburgh, was born in 1866 in the mining village of Dunaskin, Ayrshire, and, after receiving his education at the village school, commenced work at the age of twelve in the ironworks of the locality. Seeing no prospects for himself, however, in this employment, he removed with his parent's consent to Glasgow, where he found work in a furniture warehouse, at the same time attending evening classes with a view to improving his education ; and taking up amongst other things elocution, he received a certificate in that subject, and gave some very successful recitals in the principal halls of Glasgow. At the age of eighteen he had already insured his life in the Prudential, and his attention being thus turned towards Insurance he thought of applying to the British Workman's for an Agency, which post he obtained and worked with considerable success ; and in a very short time he was promoted to be Superintendent to the Company at Glasgow. Here he remained for three years, and in spite of the obstacles put in his way by the various strikes, both at the ironworks and on the railways, he succeeded in doing an excellent business. He was at the end of the above period removed to his present post at Edinburgh, where, in spite of the new difficulties occasioned by the different ground on which he has to work, of more leisured in lieu of working classes, he looks forward to a success equal to that obtained at Glasgow.

Collins, George, the District Superintendent at Penzance for the Wesleyan and General Assurance Society, was born in Birmingham in 1852, and entered the service of the Society before he was eleven years of age as office boy in the Head Office. Here he passed through the whole routine of the office, acquiring a thorough experience in every branch of the work, and eventually rose to the position of Chief Clerk of the financial and issuing department of the Society. Unfortunately, his assiduous attention to his duties caused a breakdown in his health, and his doctor having advised his removal to a more southern district, the General Manager and Board, recognising his value, very generously sent him down to Penzance, first as Agent on his full former salary, and when it proved advisable for him to remain in Cornwall, created the Superintendency of the same District on purpose for him. Mr. Collins has always been most popular amongst his colleagues, and on his leaving the Head Office was presented with a handsome album containing the photographs of the staff, together with a fine collection of books.

W. DASH.

F. E. R. DAVEY.

Dash, W., Superintendent of the Somerset District to the British Workman's Assurance Company, is a native of Penzance, born in 1854. At the age of seventeen he went into business with his father, and continued in the same till 1880, when he entered into the Insurance business, in which he had already acquired a slight experience by introducing new clients to other Agents, taking his first Agency with the Prudential Assurance Company at Taunton. This he held for nine months, during which time he met with a very fair success: he then removed to the Penzance District and took up another Agency there for the same Company. While there he heard that the British Workman's Assurance Company required a Superintendent for their Somerset District, and having applied for the post, received the appointment in 1881. The District was an entirely new one, and Mr. Dash had hard work in opening it, meeting with much opposition in laying the benefits offered by the Company before the people, and establishing it in the County, but nevertheless, he has made a great success of it, and although his District is a very scattered one, he has business in every town into which he has taken the Prospectus. Indeed his District now stands amongst the highest in order of results of the whole of those now worked by the Company.

Davey, F. E. R., Superintendent of the Bristol District of the Wesleyan and General Assurance Society, commenced his career at an early age in the office of a well-known Bristol Solicitor, where he remained for four years, during which time he acquired a good deal of knowledge that has been very useful to him in his subsequent career. He then took to journalism, and was for nearly twenty years engaged on the staff of the *Western Daily Press*. In 1880, the Directors of the Wesleyan and General being desirous of filling up the vacancy caused by the retirement of the Society's representative at Bristol, Mr. Davey was selected to be their Agent, and did much in that capacity to work up the Industrial business of the Society, before that time scarcely attempted, the principal transactions having been in the Ordinary and Sickness Departments. In 1882 Mr. Davey's success had been so marked that the Society determined to still further open out the Bristol District, and he was accordingly appointed Superintendent, with supervision over Bath, Wells, Radstock, Frome, Weston-super-Mare, Bridgwater, and surrounding places. Since then the progress of the Society has been very marked, the business in all departments steadily increasing year by year under Mr. Davey's fostering care.

RICHARD DAVIS

E. DAVIES

Davis, Richard, is the Superintendent of the Stoke District of the British Workman's Assurance Society. He commenced work for the Company in a small way in the autumn of 1881 at Chorley, Lancashire, and on migrating thence to Liverpool, made application for a regular agency in the latter town, getting fairly to work as a recognised Agent in the early part of 1882, and with such success that two years later he had achieved a weekly debit of £7 10s., which, in the following year, he had increased to £9, while the arrears represented twice that debit. At this point in his career he received his appointment to the post of Assistant-Superintendent to the Company at Liverpool, which he held until the August of 1887, when he was promoted to the Stoke District Superintendency to work up that District. At that time there was not a single Agent stationed there, and Mr. Davis, though quite a stranger in the town, had to make all appointments and obtain all the first business through his own personal industry. However, after three years' hard work he had met with such success that he found himself in charge of a flourishing District, with an Assistant-Superintendent and Clerk and twenty-five Agents

under his personal supervision. Here he has since remained to the present date, the work under his charge meanwhile progressing steadily and satisfactorily.

———

Davies, E., is the District Superintendent for the British Workman's Assurance Company at Pontypridd. Prior to the commencement of his Insurance career Mr. Davies was employed in a colliery in that district. He commenced Insurance business in 1882 in the capacity of Agent to the City Life Assurance Company, since defunct, but foreseeing the approaching end of that Company, he resigned his post at the close of the same year, and transferred his services to the British Workman's Assurance Company. After working as Agent for four and a half years, Mr. Davies was appointed Assistant Superintendent in the Swansea District to open up his own locality, commencing with only one Agent and practically no business, but after plodding steadily on for two years, he had raised his sub-district to a pitch of sufficient importance to justify its being formed into a separate District, of which he was given charge as Superintendent.

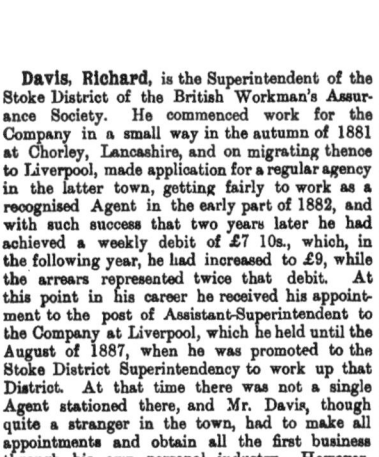

I. S. DE LA CAMP.

E. DEFTY.

De la Camp, Isidor S., is the District Superintendent of the Prudential Assurance Company for the South Marylebone District of London, Oxford Circus being its centre. He first became connected with the Prudential in 1873, since which time he has steadily worked his way up to his present position.

Datson, W. C., Assistant-Superintendent of the Provident Association of London for the Camborne District, was born at Bissoe, Cornwall, in 1864. He commenced as a Collector to the Pearl Assurance Company, and was soon afterwards promoted to be Assistant-Superintendent to the Truro District. After working some time in this capacity, he left the Pearl to take up the Cornwall District Agency for the National Life Assurance Society, which he held until May, 1891, when on the Provident Association requiring a represen-

tative to take charge of their Cornwall District, Mr. Datson was eventually selected for the post.

Defty, Emanuel, District Superintendent of the British Workman's Assurance Company for the Lancaster and Kendal Districts, commenced in the Industrial Assurance business, after a few years' experience as a Mining Engineer Student under his father, as Agent to the Prudential Assurance Company at Radcliffe, in 1877, where he remained till 1883. In the March of that year he was appointed to an Assistant Superintendency to the Refuge Assurance Company at Carlisle, which post he held till the following September, when he was appointed District Superintendent for the British Workman's Assurance Company at the same place. He was transferred to his present Superintendency in September, 1887. Mr. Defty is locally very popular with all classes.

W. J. DEAVIN.

A. I. DIXON.

Deavin, Walter J., District Superintendent of the British Workman's Assurance Company at Swindon, is the son of the Rev. C. Deavin, a Baptist minister, and was born at Winchester in 1846. He received his education at Southsea, whither his father had removed at the time, and in 1858, his family having again moved to Minchinhampton, in Gloucestershire, he there served his time as apprentice to the wool-sorting trade, which trade, together with that of a grocer, he followed till 1877. He then undertook the post of Agent to the British Workman's Assurance Company at Stroud, and proving very successful in working up a hitherto very small business to one of considerable profit to his Company, he was in 1890 promoted to be Assistant Superintendent of the Stroud Sub-district. On Stroud being made a separate district, Mr. Deavin was again promoted to be its Superintendent, which post he held till 1891, when he was given charge of the Swindon District in conjunction with Stroud, his son, Mr. C. H. Deavin, being appointed his Assistant-Superintendent.

Deakin, W., the Superintendent of the Hull District of the Pearl Life Assurance Company, commenced work for the Company as a Collector at Normanton in 1886, in which capacity he did so well that it was not long before he was appointed to an Assistant-Superintendency with the same District under his charge. He was sub-sequently removed to Wakefield as Superintendent of that Sub-district under Leeds, and there, in spite of the lugubrious prophecies of his colleagues as to the impossibility of any good business ever being done at Wakefield, his energy and perseverance told to the extent of doubling the Society's income from the Sub-district. As a consequence he was, at the beginning of 1890, promoted to his present important position. Here he again had a poor prospect before him, but he has not quailed from the task, and already the District stands amongst the most profitable of those under the influence of the Company, with much promise for the future. Mr. Deakin was on leaving Wakefield presented with a handsome clock as a testimonial from his staff there.

Dixon, A. I., is the District Manager to the Liverpool Victoria Legal Friendly Society for Bristol, Somerset, and Wiltshire. Mr. Dixon has during the whole of his Insurance career been in the service of the Liverpool Victoria, having received his first training in the details of the profession in the Chief Offices of the Society in Liverpool. Thence he was promoted to the District Managership at Warrington, and eventually transferred to his present post at Bristol. He is a gentleman of untiring energy, broad views, and sound judgment, and a valuable officer to his Society.

G. G. DODD.

T. DOBINSON.

Dodd, G. G., Superintendent of the Brighton District of the Wesleyan and General Assurance Society, was born at Portsmouth, where his father was in business for over 33 years, in 1850. Mr. Dodd himself began life as a compositor, and first became connected with the Society in 1878 as a half-time Agent, and succeeded so well that he was persuaded by his Superintendent to throw up his profession and take to the Insurance business entirely. In 1879 he was sent to open Southampton single-handed as District Agent, and though he had to contend with the difficulties of the Society being unknown and there being many rivals already in the field, he worked to such purpose, still alone, that he eventually established the Society on a firm basis in the district after nine months' work, at last obtaining the assistance of two sub-Agents. Seven months later he was recalled to Portsmouth, and for two years was employed as Travelling Auditor between Dorset and Dover, visiting every Agent once a month and inspecting his books. In 1882 he was appointed Assistant Superintendent in charge of the Portsmouth District, and in 1883 further promoted to his present post at Brighton.

———

Dobinson, T., District Superintendent of the Prudential Assurance Company at Middlesbrough, was first appointed Agent to that Company near Newcastle-on-Tyne in 1876, after serving in which capacity for twelve months he was promoted to an Assistant Superintendency at North Shields. This post he held till towards the end of 1881, when he received a fresh proof of confidence from his Directors in an unsolicited appointment to the Superintendency of the Stockton-on-Tees District, which was subsequently enlarged by the inclusion of the neighbouring town of Darlington. He superintended this District till the end of 1889, when he was transferred to his present post at Middlesbrough, the great iron-producing centre of the North Country. Mr. Dobinson has therefore passed the whole of his Insurance career in the service of the Prudential, to which Company he is heartily devoted.

J. W. DRAKE.

H. ELLISON.

Drake, J. W., District Superintendent of the British Workman's Assurance Company at Sheffield, is a native of Leeds, where he began life as a shoemaker, but having taken up a spare-time agency for the British Workman's Assurance Company, he found the work so comparatively profitable that he determined to abandon his former trade, and having sold his tools, so as to avoid any risk of temptation to return to it, devoted himself to Agency work in its entirety. This was in the September of 1875, and though he met with some rebuffs at first from the people amongst whom he canvassed, he persevered, and it was not long before he began to find his efforts crowned with success; his book growing both in size and quality, the bad payers dropping out and the good being left, till he ultimately had the satisfaction of gaining more from his agency than he had ever gained from his workshop. In 1878, the Manager of the Company having decided on making Sheffield a District, after two other Superintendents had been tried there and failed, Mr. Drake was offered, and accepted, the post. When he took up his new duties there was only one spare-time agent in the district, but so energetically has Mr. Drake worked that he now has a very large staff of Agents under him with a constantly-increasing weekly Industrial debit, and a fair amount of general business as well. He has also opened up for his district the neighbouring towns of Barnsley, Chesterfield, Claycross, Glossop, Gainsborough, Retford, Worksop, &c. Mr. Drake is a Primitive Methodist, and has done much towards promoting the spread of that connexion in Sheffield, being Circuit-Steward for that district. He is an active member of the Ecclesfield School Board, to which he was elected without even the intervention of a Committee.

Ellison, H., the Superintendent of the Liverpool District of the British Workman's Assurance Company, has had a very varied career, and is a thorough example of what perseverance and a dogged determination to get on can effect in spite of almost every disadvantage. He was born at Lancaster, the son of a working engineer, in 1852, and had very little education during his boyhood, being taken away from school when only nine years old to gain his livelihood in various capacities, as office boy at the Royal Insurance Company's Branch Office, as a printer's devil, and as apprentice to a silk dresser. He then served in a paint shop for some years, eventually rising to be warehouseman. During this last period he set himself diligently to fit himself for the position of a clerk, and attended evening classes at the Mechanics' and other Institutes, receiving at the same time much assistance from his father in his mathematical studies, and likewise teaching himself shorthand. At the age of twenty-one, Mr. Ellison obtained a clerkship in Messrs. Copestake's warehouse in London, where he remained four years, leaving it for another clerkship in an Engineering establishment, but he not long afterwards was thrown adrift again by the failure of the firm. He then obtained a situation as Correspondent and Shorthand Writer in an Iron Merchant's Office, being the selected candidate out of 250 applicants, but the hours were so long that, in 1878, having obtained an introduction to the Manager of the British Workman's Assurance Company, through the Chairman, he was put in sole charge of the correspondence department of the Company. Here he remained till the latter end of 1887, when a vacancy of his present post occurring, he was appointed to fill it.

HENRY EMMERSON.

D. L. EVANS.

Emmerson, Henry, Superintendent of the Prudential Assurance Company for the South District of Liverpool, was born at Misterton, Nottinghamshire, in 1852, and spent the first twenty-four years of his life, first as a farmer and then as a coal miner, till in 1876, desiring to enter the Wesleyan Ministry, he accepted a lay preachership near Hastings, in which capacity he was very successful. Here he met with an Agent for the Star Life Office, who persuaded him to try for an Agency with that Company, in which attempt he failed. In the following year, however, he was offered an Agency at Burley-in-Wharfedale by the Prudential Superintendent at Harrogate, which having accepted he succeeded so well that his Superintendent on his removal to Leeds nominated him to be his Assistant, giving him charge of the Beeston Hill Section. In 1883 his efforts in his new sphere were rewarded by his further promotion to the Superintendency of the newly-formed Attercliffe District, which District was subsequently increased by the addition of the Rotherham District. Here he had serious difficulties to contend

with, owing to continued strikes on the part of the mining district, but Mr. Emmerson weathered them all, and in March, 1886, was transferred to his present still more responsible District.

Evans, D. Illtydd, the District Superintendent of the British Workman's Assurance Company at Newport, Monmouthshire, is a native of Glamorganshire, and started in 1884 as an Assurance Agent in the Carmarthenshire District, being chiefly induced to reside and work in that District by his failing health. On his thorough recovery he returned to his native county to undertake the more serious work of the large towns of Wales, and at this time he began to work for the British Workman's Assurance Company, first at Neath and then at Swansea, and having by this time acquired a considerable experience in the business, and working with the utmost confidence in his Company and himself, was so successful that in 1888 he was appointed to the Superintendency of his present District.

J. C. EVANS.

W. EVANS.

Evans, J. Cymry, is General Superintendent to the South Wales District of the British Workman's Assurance Company. He began Insurance business in 1875 as Agent to the Mutual Provident Alliance Assurance Company, which he successfully represented for eighteen months, when he was promoted to the rank of District Agent or Superintendent for South Wales. During his tenure of this post some unfortunate disagreement arose between himself and one of the home officers of the Company, which forced Mr. Evans to the decision that it would be better to send in his resignation, which accordingly he did, after four years' faithful service; but the Directors having duly discussed the matter, they offered him promotion to the rank of Inspector if he would remain with them. This offer he accepted, and held his new office for twelve months, at the close of which he became District Manager for the City Life Assurance Company; and this post he again held for two years, when the unsatisfactory progress of the Company, which has since ceased to exist, determined him to sever his connection with it. He now applied to the British Workman's Assurance Company for an appointment as District Superintendent, and having obtained it, set to work to build up a large and progressive business. When Mr. Evans first began work, the Company was unknown in South Wales, and he had a hard uphill task to establish a connection for it, but his indefatigability proved irresistible, and by the end of the first year his weekly debit was £30. His subsequent success has been correspondingly great, and indeed is considered by his brother officers to be unprecedented, the whole of it being of course attributable to his personal energy and persistency. In 1889 his faithful service was rewarded by his promotion to the General Superintendency of the South Wales District, and the promotion has already borne worthy fruit.

Evans, W., the District Superintendent at Derby of the Wesleyan and General Assurance Society, began life as Clerk in a Chartered Accountant's office, subsequently removing to the same position in a Mining Engineer's firm. He commenced his connection with the Wesleyan and General Assurance Society in 1883, as part-time Agent at Sheffield, the experience which he had acquired in his former situations proving of great service to him in his new career, and met with such success that in March, 1885, he was appointed Assistant Superintendent. Here he remained till the end of the year, when he was removed into the Nottingham District, being eventually promoted to his present post in January, 1891.

T. E. EVANS.

R. M. FEATHERSTONE.

Evans, T. E., the District Superintendent to the Wesleyan and General Assurance Society at Exeter, commenced as an Industrial Assurance Agent in that city in 1879, but shortly afterwards removed to London, where he worked for the same Office, in whose service he originally started, for more than five years. After building up a fairly good business in behalf of that same Office, he in 1884 undertook an Agency for his present Society in the Clapham Junction District, where he met with such success that at the end of fourteen months he was promoted to be Assistant Superintendent for the same District, comprising nearly the whole of the South-West of London and the immediate suburbs. Here he remained, still continuing his career of success, till 1889, when he was promoted to be Travelling Assistant for the whole of London, which important post he occupied to the utmost advantage of his Society till the end of 1890, when, as a reward for his services, he was further promoted to his present post at the original scene of his Insurance labours, his District comprising East Devonshire, West Somersetshire, and North and West Dorsetshire. Mr. Evans has already done much to increase both the business, and, as a consequence, the Agency Staff of the Society in his District, and has proved himself thoroughly worthy of his selection for the post by his Board of Directors.

Featherstone, R. M., is the Superintendent in one of the Northern Districts of London of the British Workman's Assurance Company, Limited. Mr. Featherstone is an old and tried servant of this Company, and his district is an important and growing one.

J W FEATHERSTONE.

A. FIDOE.

Featherstone, J. W., the District Superintendent of the British Workman's Assurance Company at Hull, has been connected with that Company for over fifteen years, first as part-time and then as full-time Agent, during which time he built up a good substantial business at Hull, and was promoted first to the position of Accountant, and, after seven years' service in that capacity, to that of Superintendent of the District. Mr. Featherstone is the oldest representative of the British Workman's Assurance Company in Hull, and it is mainly through the energy and intelligence that he has displayed, and which has won him the confidence and esteem both of his Directors and all who have been brought in contact with him during the time that he has been passing through each grade of his career and qualifying himself for the position that he now holds, that the Company's business is in a vigorous position in the Hull District, the annual premium income being over £8,000, and still steadily progressing.

————

Fidoe, A., District Superintendent to the British Workman's Assurance Company at Worcester, began his Insurance work as Agent to the United Family Life Insurance Society, subsequently becoming a Director and Trustee of that Society. In 1876, the business of the Society was transferred to the British Workman's Assurance Company, and the staff went over likewise in a body to that Company, Mr. Fidoe being made Superintendent for his old District. He started business with a few men under him and a weekly debit of £4 ; but so effectual have his labours in his Company's cause proved that the agents whom he now has under him number thirty-five, and the weekly debit of the district is over £112, beside a large amount of monthly and general business.

B. FIELDEN.

'H. E. FISHER.

Fielden, B., District Superintendent of the British Workman's Assurance Company, Limited, at Preston, commenced at the age of twenty as Agent for that Company in Todmorden in 1878, in which capacity he proved very successful. He left the British Workman's for a time, however, to take up an Agency for the Prudential Assurance Company in Rochdale; but though his success was still continued he returned to the service of his original Company, leaving Rochdale for Heywood, Lancashire. Here he remained for five and a half years, working up a good and profitable connection for his Company, till, in 1886, he was promoted to his present post at Preston, where he has succeeded in working up a large and substantial business.

———

Fisher, H. E., is the Superintendent of the British Workman's Assurance Company, Limited, at Grimsby. Mr. Fisher has had an extended experience in industrial Insurance, and his connection with the British Workman's Company has been long, pleasant, and prosperous.

C. E. FOSTER.

JOHN FLETCHER.

Foster, Charles E., District Superintendent of the British Workman's Assurance Company at Dudley, was born in 1865, and, after leaving school at the early age of ten, served for some years in a lawyer's and in an accountant's office successively, where he acquired a very considerable experience in the details of both professions. He commenced in the Insurance business in October, 1889, when he undertook the duties of an Agency to his present Company, and after serving seven months in that capacity was promoted to the Assistant Superintendency at Warrington, where he remained for another period of ten months. He was then offered and accepted the position of Superintendent to the St. Austell District in Cornwall, which appointment he held till 1891, when he was again removed to be promoted to the Superintendency of his present large and important District. Mr. Foster's rapid promotion is sufficient criterion of the marked success which has attended him through his career from a simple Agency to his present post of distinction.

Fletcher, John, the District Superintendent to the British Workman's Assurance Company at Workington, first commenced his Assurance career as Agent for the Pearl Assurance Company at Newcastle-on-Tyne in 1876, afterwards serving the same Company as District Superintendent at Carlisle, which District included the counties of Cumberland, Westmoreland, and Dumfriesshire. He subsequently held the same office at Birmingham, where his District, besides the town itself, included a radius of some forty miles round about it ; at Shrewsbury, having under his charge the whole of Shropshire and a considerable portion of North Wales; and at Sheffield, where he had control over the surrounding country for a radius of about thirty miles. In May, 1887, he applied for and obtained the appointment of District Superintendent for the British Workman's Assurance Company, and returned to the North of England to his present post, where his District includes a great part of that which he first supervised for the Pearl, viz., the counties of Cumberland and Dumfriesshire.

W. T. GARTLAND.

Gartland, William Thomas, is the only son of Mr. Thomas Gartland, a respected Member of the Committee of Management of the Royal Liver Friendly Society. Mr. W. T. Gartland is one of the Travelling Inspectors of the Royal Liver, the position being to some extent equivalent to that of a Superintendent of Agents to an Industrial Assurance Company. He was born in Liverpool in the year 1868, and after receiving a liberal education at the Institute, Hope Street, and Maryland Street, in that city, commenced his business career as a Mechanical Engineer. This pursuit, however, not proving congenial to his taste, he applied for, and succeeded in obtaining, an Inspectorship in the Royal Liver. His appointment as such being of longer standing than that of any other Inspector in the Society, he may fairly be considered the premier Inspector. By the exercise of a considerable amount of discretion in the unravelment of intricate details Mr. Gartland has gained the esteem of his employers and the respect of those with whom in his official capacity he has come in contact, and it is generally conceded that he has been eminently successful in preserving the interests of the Management in matters where an exercise of inferior business tact would have endangered them.

German, Lewis, is the highly-respected Superintendent of the Wesleyan and General Assurance Society in the Neath (South Wales) District. He was born in Devonshire in 1840, and his career as an Assurance Agent and Superintendent has been very successful. He is one of those men who thoroughly win and retain the respect, confidence, and admiration of the best class of their fellow men. His strength of character, nobleness of mind, kind ness of heart, faithfulness to duties and great energy have engrafted a growing respect for him in the minds of his superiors, and have created a great and lasting admiration for him in the minds of his subordinates. His experience as a Canvasser for the Wesleyan and General, and his experience as a Sunday School teacher and Superintendent for many years, have unfolded the powers of his mind. He is a vigorous and eloquent speaker, and an earnest and successful representative of his Society.

W. GASKELL.

JAMES GERMAN

Gaskell, W., District Superintendent at Nottingham of the Prudential Assurance Company, commenced his Insurance career in 1871 as an Agent to his present Company at St. Helens, where he remained for the next eight years. His success in this comparatively restricted field of operations being somewhat remarkable, Mr. Gaskell's energy was rewarded by his promotion to the position of Assistant Superintendent to the Company for East Lancashire, in which district he had for a period of three and a-half years, the organisation and control of a body of over two hundred Agents, which task he performed to the utmost satisfaction of his employers. In 1882 he was further promoted to the post of Superintendent in the North-West District of London, the duties of which important office he discharged with assiduity and still with the same remarkable success for nearly six years. He was transferred to his present post in 1888, since which time, having found very little on his first taking over the district to work upon, he has laid down the foundations of and built up a very large business. Mr. Gaskell is a gentleman of exceptional energy and activity, qualities which can hardly fail to make themselves felt to good purpose.

German, James, the Cardiff Superintendent of the Wesleyan and General Assurance Society, was born in Devonshire in 1848, and after serving under his brother as Agent in the Neath District for eight years, entered on his present duties in 1882. Here his career has been one of the most uninterrupted success; beginning with a district which produced absolutely nothing for his Society, he now counts the income which he collects for it by thousands, all of which happy result is entirely due to his power for work, his sound business principles, and the amiability and tact with which he treats his agents and clients. He is thoroughly devoted to the service of his Society, and loses no opportunity of impressing its benefits on all with whom he comes in contact, both rich and poor, throughout his district, which is a very extensive one, including Newport and the Monmouth Valleys, as well as the Rhymney, the Taff, and the Rhondda Valleys. Two years ago, as a token of the great respect in which they held him both as a friend and a Superintendent, the Agents working under his supervision invited him to a public dinner, and presented him with a valuable gold chronometer watch.

JAMES GIBSON.

R. GLENTON.

Gibson, James, General Superintendent of the British Workman's Assurance Company for the Midland Counties, is a native of Manchester, and commenced work in 1875 as Agent to the Refuge Assurance Company at Oldham. He was in a very short time selected to take charge of the Huddersfield District, which he worked so satisfactorily that in 1878 his District was considerably enlarged by the addition of Dewsbury, Batley, Heckmondwike, and Morley so as to march with the Leeds District. In 1880 he was promoted to Birmingham as District Manager, where he remained till 1885, being then transferred to Plymouth with charge of the Devonshire District. Soon afterwards he left the Refuge to take up the Resident Secretaryship of the Whittington Life Assurance Company at Birmingham, which post he held till October, 1891, when he again transferred his services, this time to the British Workman's Assurance Company, for which he holds his present post.

Mr. Gibson is the author of several Insurance leaflets, amongst them being: " Every-day Stimulants," " The Difference between Two Forms and One Signature," &c., &c.

Glenton, R., the Barnsley District Superintendent of the Pearl Life Assurance Company, has been but a very short time in the Insurance business, having till within about three years ago been engaged in business on his own account in Filey, near Scarborough. He then commenced as a spare-time Agent at Filey, under the Scarborough Superintendent, and though meeting with poor encouragement at first, persevered so as to justify his appointment as Assistant Superintendent, with his duties lying in the Filey, Bridlington and Driffield portion of the Scarborough District. Thence he was removed to Hull for special work, under the new Superintendent there, returning after six weeks' profitable work to his Assistancy at Scarborough. In 1890 he was transferred to Barnsley Sub-district, and on its being made into a District of itself he was put in charge of it. Here he has done already such good work that his District stood first in its Division for increase during the first six months of 1891.

W. GRAY.

Gray, William, District Superintendent to the Prudential Assurance Company in Edinburgh, commenced his career as Agent in Leith in 1874. The Company's business in Leith was then so small as to be entrusted to one Agent; but so successful was Mr. Gray's natural ability and resoluteness of purpose in building it up, that Leith now ranks as one of the most important independent branches in the Company's system. In March, 1876, Mr. Gray's progress was already so conspicuous that the Company promoted him to the post of Assistant Superintendent at Leith, under Mr. R. T. Armstrong, Superintendent of the Edinburgh and Leith Districts, and in 1880 his continued perseverance in his Company's behalf was further rewarded by his appointment to the Superintendency of the Falkirk District, comprising, besides Falkirk itself, a large surrounding circle of towns. Mr. Gray's sojourn as Falkirk Superintendent lasted over eight years, during which period he raised his District from the semi-dormant state in which he found it to its present high standard of proficiency and greatness, and this, too, in spite of the then existing depression in the coal and iron trades (the principal industries of that locality) with their constant strikes. In 1888 Mr. Gray was deservedly promoted again to his present important position—the Management of the Company's principal District in Scotland. On leaving Falkirk Mr. Gray was presented with a beautiful illuminated address by his Assistants and Agents, a fact which conclusively proves the respect and esteem in which he was held by his staff, and shows the concord and good feeling existing between them, to which fact more than any other is, perhaps, attributable his great success.

Baldwin, C. W., Superintendent of the Lambeth District of the Prudential Assurance Company, was born at Harrow-on-the-Hill in 1852. In 1869, while assisting his father in his business, at Chertsey, the latter first became connected with the Prudential, first as a policy-holder, and afterwards as its agent at Chertsey. Mr. C. W. Baldwin having thus gained an insight into the work, in 1871 started an Agency at Farnborough, Hants., where he was the Company's first representative. In 1873 he migrated to London, where he acted till 1881 as Agent for the Company in South London; in the October of the latter year being appointed Assistant-Superintendent in his present District. He was promoted to the Superintendency in April, 1884.

HUGH HALL.

JOHN GREEN.

Hall, Hugh, a well-known Industrial Superintendent, now engaged in the Glasgow field, is a native of Sheffield, where he entered the service of the Refuge in 1875 as Canvasser under Mr. Henry Adams, Manager in Sheffield for this Company; he remained in this position about seven months, and in the meantime gave such evidence of his ability to influence business that he was appointed Superintendent of the Nottingham District, where he remained till 1891, when he accepted an appointment with another Company at Glasgow.

Green, John, District Superintendent of the Prudential Assurance Company at Wakefield, commenced life as a Commercial Traveller, but having in the course of his rounds fallen in with a Superintendent of the Prudential, he was persuaded, against the advice of his friends and employer, to undertake an Agency for that Company at Harrogate in 1876. Here, in spite of his friends' warnings, he proved so successful that he was after a short time as Agent promoted to be Assistant Superintendent at Leeds, a post which he held for four years, eventually becoming District Superintendent at Harrogate, the former scene of his labours. He was transferred to his present post in 1888. Mr. Green is the eldest of six brothers, all of whom he has persuaded to enter the service of the Prudential, three of them being at present Superintendents, one an Assistant Superintendent, and two Agents.

B. GREEN.

THOMAS GREEN.

Green, B., Superintendent of the Prudential Assurance Company for the Castleford District, commenced as an Agent in 1877 at Wetherby, Yorkshire, under the Harrogate Superintendent, and having proved himself capable of doing a substantial Assurance business was transferred to Wakefield in 1878, where he shortly produced the largest increase of any Agent in the District. After remaining at Wakefield until September, 1879, he was promoted to the sub-section of Morley as Assistant Superintendent, and at the end of another four years again promoted to the Superintendency of the City of Lincoln District. Here in six years he succeeded in almost doubling the Company's return from the District, and in 1890 he was transferred to his present post to take charge of Castleford, an important District

as being a rising coal, pottery, and glass-bottle making centre.

——

Green, Thomas, District Superintendent of the Prudential Assurance Company at Halifax was, prior to embarking in Assurance work, Manager in a grocery and drapery business at Garforth, near Leeds, which he left to start as an Agent to that Company at Harrogate in 1877. Here by steady perseverance he progressed to such an extent that in 1885 he was eventually promoted to be Superintendent of the Gainsborough District in Lincolnshire, where during the three years that he held that post he enjoyed an almost unprecedented success. He left Gainsborough in 1888, greatly regretted by all who had known him there to take up his present duties.

W. GREENHALGH.

W. GRIGG.

Greenhalgh, W., the Superintendent of the Bolton District of the British Workman's Assurance Company, is a native of New Mills, Derbyshire, whence he came into Lancashire at the age of eight years to earn his livelihood. At fourteen he was apprenticed to a block printer, but by the time he had served his apprenticeship the trade had depreciated so much that he determined to make a fresh start in something else. Having shortly afterwards obtained an introduction to the British Workman's Assurance Company's Manchester Superintendents, he now commenced his Insurance career as Agent for the Company in Bolton, in June, 1877. He began work at a great disadvantage, being a complete stranger in the town, and his success was so poor that he was more than half inclined to give up the business, an inclination which all but became conviction when, a short time after his arrival, a strike was begun in the town which lasted for several weeks, and ruined even the little business that he had yet got together. However, he lingered on till the end of the strike, and then at last his prospects gradually improved. Finding things not so hopeless as he had first thought, he set to work in real earnest, and by September, 1881, had obtained a membership of nearly 3,000. By this time Mr. Greenhalgh had several sub-agents under him, and he was

accordingly promoted to the position of Assistant Superintendent, his sub-agents becoming Agents of the Company, Bolton being constituted a Sub-district under Manchester ; but business now became so prosperous that, in 1886, on the death of the senior Manchester Superintendent, it was raised to a District, with Mr. Greenhalgh in sole charge of it. Since then the business has increased fourfold in every department, the Industrial members numbering at present between 30,000 and 40,000. Mr. Greenhalgh is a thorough example of his own belief that single-heartedness in one's profession is the only key to success in Insurance work.

———

Grigg, W., is the Superintendent to the Prudential Assurance Company for the Bermondsey District. He commenced work in April, 1878, as an Agent to his present Company at Walworth, and, though at that time an entire stranger in London, succeeded in building up a large and prosperous business. At the end of six years, in 1884, his diligence was rewarded by his appointment to an Assistant Superintendency in the Vauxhall District, where he remained for nearly another six years, till January, 1890, when he was further promoted to his present Superintendency of the Tanneries District.

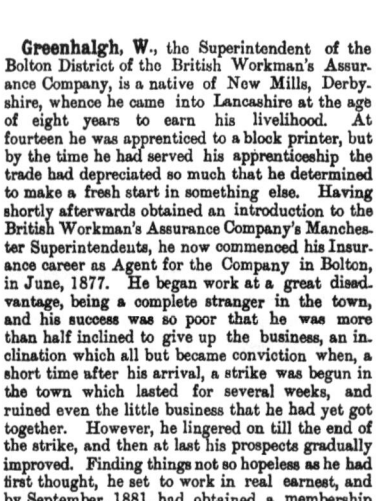

CHARLES STEPHEN GUEST.

W. HAINES.

Guest, Charles Stephen, the District Superintendent of the British Workman's Assurance Company at Penzance, after receiving a good education, commenced his business career with the Trade Protection Society of London at their Branch Office in Bristol. He remained two years with this firm, and then obtained an appointment with Messrs. John Lysaght, of Bristol and Wolverhampton, which appointment he relinquished to enter the Chief Offices of the British Workman's Assurance Company at Birmingham. After gaining valuable experience in several Departments of the Office, he was entrusted with the charge of the West Cornwall District, where the Company have a large connection. Mr. Guest has since been actively engaged in promoting the interests of his Company in Cornwall. He has had many difficulties to surmount, but is fortunate in having secured the goodwill of all who know him, both inside and outside his profession.

Haines, W., is the District Agent of the Liverpool Victoria Legal Friendly Society at Leytonstone, E. He commenced his Insurance career at the end of 1882, when he entered the service of the Integrity Assurance Society, since defunct. After two and a-half year's experience in the business, however, he resolved to make a change, and his choice of an office having fallen on the Liverpool Victoria Legal, he commenced as a Collector for that Society in 1885. His work in that capacity proved so satisfactory that two years later, in 1887, he was promoted to his present post, since which time the district has made very considerable progress. Mr. Haines now works the whole of South Essex as far as Shoeburyness and Burnham with a large staff of Collectors and Canvassers, of whom he is extremely proud, having personally introduced them into the business and educated them. He attributes his success first to his thorough confidence in his Society, secondly to his own untiring perseverance, thirdly to his judgment in the selection of his Agents, with all of whom he works in the greatest harmony and unison.

T. W. HARDWICK.

N. HARRISON.

Hardwick, T. W., District Superintendent to the British Workman's Assurance Company at Northampton, is a native of that town, where he has resided all his life. He decided to become an Insurance Agent in 1885, and having selected and applied to the British Workman's Assurance Company, was duly appointed. After four years of successful labour, and uninterrupted by any disputes with rival Companies, he was appointed to his present Superintendency, in which capacity he has not been long in doubling the business of the Company in his district.

Hughes, Laurence, District Superintendent of the Pearl Life Assurance Company, is the son of Mr. L. Hughes, the District Manager to the Royal Liver Friendly Society at Belfast, and was born in 1864. He commenced Insurance work at Salford in 1879, as a Collector to the Royal Liver, also assisting in the District Office as Clerk. Later on he was entrusted with the testing of the genuineness of new business returned, and in 1885 he was appointed District Agent to the Royal Liver at Burnley. This post he resigned in September, 1887, on account of ill health, but in the January of the following year, having recruited himself by the rest, he obtained an appointment to his present Company as Assistant Superintendent at Manchester. In the July of the same year he was promoted to the charge of the Halifax Sub-district, subsequently removing to York, with which is included Selby and Harrogate. In May, 1889, he was sent to Sheffield on a special mission to protect the business of the Pearl against the rivalry of other Companies, and in January, 1890, to Hull for the same purpose. He was promoted to the District Superintendency of Chesterfield in July, 1890, where he remained, more than doubling the ordinary business of the district and making an increase of 50 per cent. in the industrial and middle class, till his removal to his present District, in November, 1890.

Harrison, N., Superintendent of the Carmarthen District of the British Workman Assurance Company, has been with that Company since its commencement, working for it first as a part-time and afterwards as a whole-time Agent, in which capacity he so won the confidence of the Managing Director that in 1874 he was promoted to be Superintendent, his District comprising part of Birmingham, with Wolverhampton, Walsall, Redditch, Lichfield, Worcester, Kidderminster, Shrewsbury, and Cannock Chase, now divided into many districts. In 1887 he was transferred to Gloucester, and after successfully working up that District, to Bristol, where he remained till last year, when he removed to his present District, having under his charge Carmarthenshire, Cardiganshire, and Pembrokeshire.

J. HARVEY.

J. T. HARWOOD.

Harvey, Joseph, who is at present Superintendent of the Leicester District of the British Workman's Assurance Company, commenced his Insurance career in the year 1874 as Agent for the Royal Albert Friendly Society in Birmingham, which post he retained until the year 1879, when a meeting having been held to consider the advisability of transferring the Society's business to the British Workman's Assurance Company, and the question having been decided in the affirmative, Mr. Harvey likewise transferred his allegiance to the latter Company, and remained as their Agent at Birmingham for a period of twelve months, until the 8th of September, 1880. At the end of that time his services had marked him for promotion, and he was accordingly removed to Leicester to take up his present post, a post of considerable importance, including, as it does, the management of the Company's business for the whole of Leicestershire and a large part of the adjacent county of Warwickshire.

Harwood, John Thomas, is District Superintendent of the Prudential Assurance Company, in charge of the District Office of that Company at Southampton. Having commenced business for them as an Agent in 1874 at Wednesbury, working a year and a-half in that position, he was appointed as an Assistant Superintendent, being transferred to West Bromwich, and subsequently to Walsall. After six years of successful working at the latter place, he was appointed District Superintendent at Winchester, whence he was transferred to the Dover District and from that place to his present post at Southampton. His career has been one of unbroken success, and he occupies a worthy position among those workers that have assisted in building up the business of the Prudential Assurance Company.

T. HAWORTH.

SAMUEL HENDERSON.

Haworth, Thomas, the Bolton District Superintendent of the Wesleyan and General Assurance Society, was born in Blackburn, and commencing work for the Society as an Agent in his native District, succeeded so well that in 1875 he was promoted to the Superintendency, having Bolton as his Headquarters, with all the surrounding towns under his supervision. Naturally, in such a busy District, he has had much to compete with in the way of rivalry from other Companies, but in spite of all disadvantages he has laboured so well as to have increased his members' list sixtyfold that which he found it. He is an energetic worker, too, for his Denomination, and by his street preaching and other good works has done much to elevate the people of his District. He has recently been the proud recipient of a handsome testimonial to his excellent qualities both as an officer and a friend from the Agents of his District.

Henderson, Samuel, the District Superintendent of the Prudential Assurance Company for the Channel Islands District, was born in 1859, and started as an Agent for the Prudential in London in 1880. He went to Scotland in the following year in the same capacity, and was promoted to be Assistant Superintendent in 1884 in Dundee, which post he held during one of the great strikes, in which he took an active part on the side of the workers. In 1889 he was appointed Superintendent for the District of Jersey, which was increased in 1891 to include the whole of the Channel Islands. Mr. Henderson is best known to Insurance men as a versatile contributor to the Insurance Press both of the United Kingdom and America. He is the author of numerous Insurance tracts and leaflets in English, French, and the Scotch dialect; the best known of these being the widely-known series of " Assurance Arrows."

WILLIAM HILL.

W. J. HEWETT.

Hill, William, is the Superintendent in charge of the Bradford Branch of the Prudential Assurance Company, which is one of the most prosperous Branches of this great Life Office. Mr. Hill commenced his Assurance career in 1872, in the service of the Prudential, in the town of Wishaw, Lanarkshire, Scotland ; in 1875 he was promoted to the position of Assistant-Superintendent at Motherwell in the same County. In the next year the Company removed him to the more important town of Coatbridge. Early in 1880 he was promoted to the position of District Superintendent, and placed in charge of the Kilmarnock District. After one successful year there he was placed in charge of the Paisley District, where he laboured with marked success for the next eight years, during which he increased the annual premium income of the Company in that District over £13,000. During the first week in 1889 the Company removed, and placed him in charge of one of their most important districts at Bradford, Yorkshire ; and in proof of the wisdom of this appointment it is only necessary to state that during the three years he has laboured there he has succeeded in increasing the annual premium income of the Company in his District by £10,000. One of the secrets of Mr. Hill's success is his knowledge of human nature, and his consequent power to get the best possible results out of the men with whom he works, by whom he is very highly esteemed.

Hewett, William J., has been connected with the Refuge Assurance Company, as their London Manager, for a period of nearly 20 years, their offices being situated at 29, New Bridge Street, Blackfriars.

When he commenced work for the Company in London it was practically unrepresented, there not being any policy-holders in the district.

There is now an income of £40,000 per year in the London district, which is rapidly increasing, and under his supervision a large staff of Agents are actively engaged in all directions in advocating the advantages of this popular Company.

R. P. HILL.

W. HILLIER.

Hill, Ralph P., District Manager to the Bolton Branch of the Liverpool Victoria Legal Friendly Society, is a native of Bolton, and commenced life as a filecutter, becoming first connected with the above Society in 1877 as a Canvasser and Collector. Starting with a blank book he worked for two years, at the same time carrying on his own trade, but at the end of that time, seeing, by the success he had already achieved, that a good business was to be done in his District, he abandoned file-cutting altogether, and devoted his attention solely to Insurance. This materially increased his success, and in 1881 he was appointed Sub-agent with power to appoint canvassers under him, receiving a small salary for inspecting their work, while at the same time he continued to increase his own business. In 1884, on the removal of the former District Mana. ger from Bolton, Mr Hill was promoted to fill the vacancy, since which time, though he has ceased collecting himself, he has through his judicious supervision increased the business of his District to a very great extent.

Hillier, W., District Superintendent of the Prudential Assurance Company at their Notting Hill Branch, began as a part-time Agent, and becoming satisfied that there was a great future for the Company and those connected with it, he gave up his other business, although a very flourishing one, to devote the whole of his energies to Insurance work. He has now been Superintendent for nearly twenty years, during which time he has never had occasion to repent of his resolution.

Hooper, W. G., the District Superintendent of the Wesleyan and General Assurance Society at Nottingham, was, previous to his connection with that Society, engaged eleven years as an Assistant Schoolmaster. He commenced his Insurance work in 1889 as an Assistant Superintendent to the Society in the Liverpool District, whence he was transferred to Nottingham at the beginning of 1891, to take charge of that District on its being separated from Derby and Leicester, with which it had formerly been jointly worked. Mr. Hooper's District now includes the town and county of Nottingham, and he has already by his personal influence done much to increase the success of the Society in this district.

HENRY HIRST.

C. HOLLAND.

Hirst, Henry, the District Superintendent of the Wesleyan and General Assurance Society at their Stockport Branch, began his work for the Society in the September of 1880 as an Agent, in which capacity he acted so successfully that at the end of two years he was promoted to be Assistant Superintendent to his present District, which was then under Mr. W. Syers, of Liverpool. Mr. Hirst's labours, however, raised the Sub-district to sufficient importance to justify its being made into a separate district, and he was accordingly put in charge of it. Mr. Hirst is a kind man to his Agents, but a strict disciplinarian, and has that great essential for a good Agent—a firm belief in his Society.

Howell, E., Superintendent of the British Workman's Assurance Company for the Coventry District, commenced work for that Company at Wolverhampton under Mr. N. Harrison as a part-time Agent in 1881, in which capacity he remained for three years, eventually, in August, 1884, abandoning his other pursuits and giving up his whole time to the Insurance business. He was appointed to his present post in May, 1889.

Holland, C., the District Superintendent of the Wesleyan and General Assurance Society at Hanley, began at Crewe in 1881, when, as an agent, in twenty months he introduced some sixteen hundred members, which brought him prominently before the Directors and General Manager, who in 1883 promoted him to the Hanley District. Here also he has been eminently successful, gathering around him a very fine staff of Assistants and Agents, and reporting splendid increases from year to year, raising the quarterly income from £204 to £2,800 in nine years. Being considered a good speaker, he is frequently called upon to occupy some of the leading pulpits and platforms of the district, and has often been pressed to stand for the Town Council, School Board, and other prominent positions, but lack of time forbids. He is, however, one of the principal delegates for the Tunstall district to the forthcoming Primitive Methodist Conference. He has certainly laid the foundation of a bright and prosperous future.

JOHN HUNT.

W. H. JENKIN.

Hunt, John, is the District Superintendent to the British Workman's Assurance Company at Aston. Mr. Hunt's connection with the Company dates back twenty-four years, he having commenced business as Agent in 1867. He worked in that capacity for eight years, when in 1875 he was made Superintendent, and at once proceeded to open up a number of districts and large towns for the Company; amongst these being Burton, Derby, Leicester, Nottingham, Banbury, Leamington, Coventry, Walsall, Hednesford, and many others, from some of which towns the Company now receives a splendid debit. From Burton alone, where Mr. Hunt canvassed the first £1 worth of business, the debit now being £60 weekly; and in most of these towns the Company now has Resident Superintendents, so that it will be easily seen that Mr. Hunt had no small share in the early struggles of the Company. Nor is Mr. Hunt's career of usefulness by any means finished, for even now in his present post he heads the list of British Workman's Assurance Company Superintendents in result of work both as regards premiums and number of members, the first being over £3,000 in excess of, and the second more than twice as much as, that achieved by any other officer of the Company. Mr. Hunt now devotes the whole of his time to the Ordinary Branch of the Company's business.

Jenkin, W. H., is the Superintendent of the Prudential Assurance Company, Limited, at Gloucester. Mr. Jenkin, who is a native of Redruth, Cornwall, commenced his career as an Agent of the Prudential. In 1873 he was promoted by his Company to the post of Assistant-Superintendent, and removed to Newton Abbot, Devonshire; the counties of Devon and Cornwall being, at that time, under the supervision of one Superintendent and three Assistant-Superintendents. Mr. Jenkin was so successful in performing the duties of his new post that, in December, 1875, he was promoted to the responsible position of District Superintendent, and removed to a district in the Western Counties; subsequently returning to the Southern Counties division, where, in September, 1880, the Exeter District was placed under his control, which position he held for nearly ten years. In 1890 he removed to the South Midland Division as Chief Superintendent in the Gloucester District. His career has been marked by continuous ability and success; and, it is needless to say, that the Prudential has a very large business in his district. Mr. Jenkin, who is an enthusiastic adherent of the Temperance cause, and a local preacher in one of the Methodist bodies, is universally recognised as a man of remarkable zeal, energy and self-reliance. He has nominated a large number of agents, in many of whom he has succeeded in implanting a share of his own good qualities.

S. W. JENKIN.

G. E. JOBLING.

Jenkin, Samuel Williams, Superintendent of the Camborne (Cornwall) District of the Prudential Assurance Company, was born at Redruth in 1839, and commenced life in his father's business, that of a master tradesman. In 1867, having removed to Camborne, he became Agent to the Ordinary Branch of the Prudential, not being willing to undertake the Industrial Branch, but in the following year, on the inducement of his Superintendent, he undertook business for that Branch also. Though starting under some disadvantage owing to the small earnings of the population of his District, he succeeded so well that in 1869 he was offered the post of Assistant Superintendent for Cornwall, which, however, he declined, not wishing to desert his Agency, and it was not till January, 1873, that he was actually promoted to an Assistant Superintendency at Richmond, Surrey. Here he continued his successful progress till December, 1874, when he was further promoted to the post of Superintendent at Trowbridge, only quitting that to take up a similar position in Bath in 1877. Here he remained for over six years,

when, at his own request, desiring a more working-class district, he was removed to Swindon, and in 1888 a vacancy occurring at Camborne, with which place his early life had been associated, was offered to him, and he accepted it, where he has continued to do good service to his Company.

Jobling, George Edward, Superintendent of the British Workman's Assurance Company for the Gloucester District, was educated at a private college and at Oxford University, and commenced his Insurance career in 1886 as an Agent for the Prudential Assurance Company. In the December of the following year he accepted an offer from the Directors of the British Workman's Assurance Company to open out the Fen country round Peterborough, with that city for headquarters, which work he carried out to their utmost satisfaction; and in 1890, after handing over the connection which he had worked to a Superintendent, he was himself rewarded by being promoted to his present post.

R. H. JOHNSON.

J. T. JOHNSON.

Johnson, Robert H., is the Superintendent of the Southwark District of the Prudential Assurance Company, Limited. He began life in the Tea trade, and was for ten years with the Civil Service Stores, Haymarket, but in 1872 he abandoned that calling to take up that of Assurance, entering the service of his present Company. He has now held his present position since April, 1885.

———

Johnson, J. T., District Superintendent to the Prudential Assurance Company for North London, was born in London in 1843, and entered the Civil Service as Clerk in the Post Office. While in that position he was attracted to the Prudential, and applied for an Agency to the Company, which he held till 1873, when he was appointed Superintendent of one of the South London Districts. He subsequently removed to the Balham or South Suburban London District, and the Hammersmith or North Suburban London District in 1874 and 1875 respectively, in charge of which latter District he remained till 1879. His success there induced the Directors of the Company to transfer him to the more important City District, including the N., N.W., and W.C. Districts. Owing to the enormous growth of business, he ultimately relinquished the central portion of the District, retaining the portion of it in the North of London which he now supervises. It will thus be seen that the whole of Mr. Johnson's Insurance career has been passed in the Metropolitan area, in which he has done his share in the development of the Company business.

Mr. Johnson takes an active part in local and parochial affairs. He has been a Member of the Islington Vestry since 1887, and is Chairman of the Commissioners for Public Baths and Workhouses, Overseer of his Parish, and Member of the Executive Council for the North London Technical Institute.

J. N. JOHNSON.

E. JONES.

Johnson, J. N., is the District Superintendent of the Prudential Assurance Company for North London. He commenced active service for that Company in 1868, under the Superintendency of his father, in the district of Nottinghamshire and Derbyshire.

He was next appointed District Superintendent by the Company at Derby, early in 1876, so that he has passed by far the greater portion of his career in that capacity.

At the latter end of 1882 he removed to Nottingham, and early in 1888 took charge of the district in North London, where he is at present.

Jones, E., District Superintendent of the Prudential Assurance Company for Central London, has been in the service of that Company since 1875, commencing as an Agent at Hammersmith. After being promoted to the position of Assistant Superintendent, Mr. Jones worked in the Kilburn and North London district successively, and became Superintendent in 1883, taking charge of the Hampstead District. In the following year he removed to his present District, since which his record has been one of steady and continuous increase of the Company's business

THOMAS KIRK.

THOMAS LAMB.

Kirk, Thomas, the District Superintendent to the British Workman's Assurance Company at its Bradford Branch, has passed the whole of his Insurance career in the service of this Company. He commenced as an Agent at Leeds in 1870, and in 1876 was transferred to the Bradford district. Bradford was at that time worked through the Leeds Branch, and continued to be so till 1883, but at that latter date· was promoted to be an independent Branch, with Mr. Kirk in the position he now holds, in charge of it. Mr. Kirk is a faithful officer, and untiring in his zeal for his Company, and his supervision has been productive of good results, the business done in Bradford by the British Workman's Assurance Company being very large.

Lamb, Thomas, the District Superintendent for the British Workman's Assurance Company at Selby, served in the Royal Artillery, joining in May, 1853, and after serving his country with honour in the Crimean war, also in India and Aden, Arabia, was invalided from the Abyssinian Expedition in 1868, and discharged as corporal with a small pension, with medal and clasp for Sebastopol, also Turkish War medal. Mr. Lamb was amongst those who were shipwrecked in the *Old Bombay* on her way out to India in 1858, afterwards sailing in the *Cospatrick*. He commenced his Insurance career in 1870 as a canvasser and collector under Agents in Hull. In 1872 he was invited by the Manchester Superintendent for the Prudential Company, Mr. J. Moon, who then had charge of the Hull district, to accept an Agency and open out the Selby and Howden district, and in this he achieved so great a success that in March, 1876, he was appointed Assistant Superintendent to work the district more authoritatively. In 1880 he resigned this post to take up the District Superintendency for the British Workman's Assurance Company, which up to that time had not been represented in that district, but since Mr. Lamb has been working for it, it has prospered and increased from year to year under his fostering care. Mr. Lamb is still a thorough soldier at heart, and regrets greatly not having been able to put in his full time of twenty-one years' service; and he has brought all his old soldier's energy into his present work.

T. L. LEAK.

WILLIAM LESLIE.

Leak, Tom Lawson, the District Superintendent of the Prudential Assurance Company at Greenwich, was born at Birmingham in 1852, and having left school at the age of fifteen became junior clerk to a firm of brokers at Lloyds. Here he acquired so intimate a knowledge with the details of the work that he was made head book-keeper at the age of eighteeen. Three years later, having come into possession of a legacy, he left London to set up in business in Cardiff on his own account, but though he at first succeeded fairly well, a long strike and bad trade eventually compelled him to give his business up, and return to London in search of a situation. After one or two minor attempts he at last took service with the Prudential, and as soon as he had mastered the details of Industrial business, began to make good headway, and was appointed Assistant-Superintendent. In 1884 he resigned his post temporarily to assist the candidature of Mr. Harben, the Vice-Chairman of the Company, for Cardiff, the former scene of of his labours, as Registration Agent, and greatly distinguished himself by his activity and accuracy of work. On his return to Assurance work he was re-appointed Assistant-Superintendent, this time at Dunstable, but not finding sufficient scope for his activity, he returned to London, and there put in so good a year's work that he was appointed to his present post.

Leslie, William, District Manager of the Scottish Legal Life Assurance Society at Stirling, was born in Dunfermline in 1859, and his parents shortly afterwards removed to Glasgow. He was at an early age apprenticed to the joinery trade. He subsequently entered a shipbuilding firm, where he soon attained to the highest rate of wages, while at the same time he so gained the esteem of his fellow workmen that he was elected Branch Treasurer of the Amalgamated Society of Carpenters and Joiners. He also at this time took an active part in more than one scheme for the betterment of the condition of his fellow workers. In 1886, having had for some time a great desire to take up Insurance work, he started in Glasgow with a very small business and a great many arrears to make up, and in a very short time succeeded not only in reducing the latter but in increasing the former to such an extent that he received the congratulations from the Treasurer of the Society. In May, 1889, he received a still more substantial reward in his promotion to his present post in the centre of the most agricultural district of Scotland, where he has continued his career with all his former success.

G. LEIGH.

W. J. LEIGH.

Leigh, G., District Superintendent of the Wesleyan and General Assurance Society at Hull, commenced his first experience with a well-known Insurance Company as an Agent in the year 1874. By tact and perseverance he rose to the position of Assistant-Superintendent, and not long after this promotion he received an offer from a first-class Insurance Company in America, which he accepted. On returning to England he still continued to carry on the Insurance business, and had not been long at work before he was promoted to his present position, which he has held since the year 1883, in Hull District. He has done good service during the period, and is highly respected by all who know him.

Leigh, W. J., the District Superintendent of the Prudential Assurance Company at Stockport, comes of an old Cheshire family, and was born in Macclesfield, where his grandfather and father were in the silk trade. His own tastes not lying in the same direction, he entered the goods department of the Manchester, Sheffield, and Lincolnshire Railway, but this not suiting him either, he went to America, where he remained for five years, farming and running a saw mill in Wyoming County. He returned to England in 1874, and taking up an Agency for the Prudential at Wilmslow was so successful that he was in a very short time appointed to an Assistant Superintendency at Ashton-under-Lyne. This was soon followed by his promotion to the Superintendency of his native town, and in 1882 he was selected to work up the Company's business in the North of Scotland, at Aberdeen. Here he still continued his success, and in 1888 was appointed to the Dundee District, with supervision of Forfarshire and East Fife, where his ability has had ample opportunity of evidencing itself, opportunity which has by no means been neglected. Mr. Leigh has recently been transferred to the important District of Stockport.

ALBERT A. LORD.

JAMES LETHBY.

Lord, Albert Alexander, is the Superintendent at Newcastle-on-Tyne of the Prudential Assurance Company, Limited.

Mr. Lord was brought up in the business, his father being the well-known Mr. Riley Lord. After receiving his education at Mill Hill school, he was appointed an agent of the Prudential in 1878, and was so successful that he was made Assistant-Superintendent in 1880; his success continued, with the result that he was appointed Superintendent at Newcastle in 1882.

During his Superintendency the Industrial debit has been nearly doubled; the Ordinary Branch has also been specially pushed here, the Newcastle district having had the honour of being second of all the districts of the Company three years in succession.

Lethby, James, is the District Superintendent of the British Workman's Assurance Company, Limited, at Reading. Mr. Lethby's experience in Assurance business dates from the year 1878, when he commenced as a Collector for an Agent of the Prudential Assurance Company, at Caer-

philly, South Wales, being then only twenty years of age. Such was his success, that in a few weeks he was offered, and accepted an Agency at Risca (Monmouthshire), for the same Company. This position he retained for eight years, which he then relinquished for political work, being given the appointment of Secretary and Registration Agent to the South Monmouthshire Liberal Association, out of one hundred applications. Two years later Mr. Lethby again accepted an offer of a small Agency under the same Company, and this he retained for a year, during which time he was elected unopposed as a member of the Risca Local Board. Mr. Lethby now felt anxious to give up political strife, and in September, 1889, accepted the appointment which he holds at the present time. The District then only possessed seven Agents, but after two years' work there are now covering the same area one Assistant-Superintendent and twenty Agents, with a proportionate increase of business. Mr. Lethby has been the recipient of many complimentary letters from his Managing Director, which are evidences of his ability and success.

A. M. MACKAY.

C. E. MAJOR.

Mackay, A. M., General Superintendent of the Pearl Life Assurance Company at Glasgow, is a native of Caithnesshire, N.B., where he was born in 1856, and after being educated at the local school, put to his father's calling as a farmer. At sixteen years of age, however, he went to South Wales and worked for two years as a draper, but disliking the business, started as a Canvasser to the Pearl. Thence he was sent to Bristol as a Collector for five years, at the end of which time he accepted the Superintendency of the Gloucester District, being subsequently promoted to the more important District of Glasgow. After two years in that capacity, he was further promoted to his present post with supervision over Scotland and the North of Ireland.

May, Henry W., the District Superintendent of the Pearl Life Assurance Company at Norwich, commenced work as an Agent for the Company in a small way at Exeter in 1888, where, after working for a short time, he was promoted to the Assistant-Superintendency. Here he worked to good purpose for another nine months, at the end of which period he accepted the offer of the supervision of the Torquay District as Assistant in charge. On the District being formed into an independent Superintendency in May, 1891, he was appointed Superintendent, and in December, 1891, Mr. May was again promoted to his present position.

Major, C. E., the District Superintendent of the British Workman's Assurance Company at Aberdeen, commenced his Insurance work ten years ago as an Agent for the Prudential Assurance Company at Manchester, where he remained until April, 1886, meeting with great success in building up a large and profitable Agency, and achieving the largest increase of any Agent in the section in which he worked for three years in succession. At that latter date he was promoted to an Assistant-Superintendency at Burnley. In November, 1887, some small misunderstanding having arisen between himself and his Superintendent, he resigned, and was at once appointed District Superintendent by the British Workman's Assurance Company, migrating to Oxford to open the district there; but after about seventeen months' hard work, finding his success was only very partial, and that the district afforded no promise of satisfaction in any class of business either to the Company or himself, he decided on removing to some other more profitable district, and having laid his views before the General Manager of the Company, he was appointed to his present post at Aberdeen. Here he found a large field for work, his district extending over a hundred miles in length, whilst his predecessor had started an opposition scheme called the Scottish Workman's Assurance Company, predicting that it would drive the English out of the country in two months; but a sharp and decisive struggle soon showed that the result was to be otherwise: the Scottish Workman's Assurance Company no longer exists, and Mr. Major has raised his Company's business to a most flourishing position in both branches, and is rapidly extending it over the whole of the north of Scotland.

S. MALLINSON.

T. J. MALLET.

Mallinson, S., District Superintendent of the Prudential Assurance Company at Blackburn, was born in Manchester in 1851, and after completing his education, commenced as an Agent to the Prudential Assurance Company in 1876, at the age of twenty-five. Starting with no business at all, he gradually built up so substantial a connection that at the end of five years he was appointed Assistant-Superintendent in Bury, Lancashire. Here he continued his former success for another three years, at the end of which time his services had pointed him out for further promotion to the District Superintendency of Leigh, at first with one Assistant-Superintendent under him, but he had not been long in that position before his District was first enlarged so as to give him two more Assistants under him, and again so as to bring up his total of Assistants to four. He remained altogether five and a-half years at Leigh, during which time he distinguished himself very materially in behalf of his Company, and he eventually was promoted to his present post, in the largest cotton manufacturing district in England, where he has had ample opportunity for the exercise of his abilities, opportunities of which he has fully availed himself.

Mallet, T. J., District Superintendent to the Pearl Assurance Company at Chatham, was born in 1862, in Guernsey, and commenced business there as an Agent for his present Company in 1882. In 1883, he was made Assistant-Superintendent for Jersey, being subsequently re-transferred to Guernsey as Assistant in charge. Here he worked hard for three years, and with such good effect that he was removed to England, where, after having opened out Winchester for the Company he was promoted to be Superintendent of the newly-formed district of Salisbury. Another year found him at Brighton, which was but a step to the still more important district of Chatham, where he took up his present duties in October, 1889. Mr. Mallet is deservedly popular with his Agents, and has received more than one testimonial from them in the various districts over which he has had supervision, among them being a silver teapot presented to his wife on their leaving Brighton, and his portrait from the Agents of his present district.

W. MANNING.

W. H. MASON.

Manning, W., is the District Superintendent at the Liverpool Branch of the Wesleyan and General Assurance Society. Mr. Manning commenced his Insurance work in the year 1878, when having some leisure time from the other work on his hands, and having a constitutional dislike of being idle, he applied for and was appointed to the post of agent to the Society in Crewe. Having made a good commencement, and finding the work to his taste, and his further progress tolerably well assured, at the end of only six months from his first appointment to his Agency, he determined to devote his entire energy to the Insurance business alone, and so successful was he in his efforts, that during the next three years he had built up a most valuable Agency for his Society. At the end of that time he was offered and accepted the position of Assistant-Superintendent to the Liverpool District Manager, after holding which position for a period of twelve months, he was, in 1883, appointed to take the full charge of the Liverpool district. It has been since Mr. Manning's appointment to its headship that the Liverpool branch of the Society has attained to its present prominence in the locality, and his Directors have no reason to repent their choice of him for the post. Without quoting figures, it will suffice to show the extent of Mr. Manning's ability by the statement, founded on the best authority, that in the course of his seven years of office the premium income of his branch has increased to an extent of nearly nine times that which he found when he first took it over from his predecessor.

————

Mason, W. H., District Superintendent to the British Workman's Assurance Company at Gloucester and Cheltenham, commenced as a clerk in the Issue Department of the Wesleyan and General Assurance Society's Head Office, in Birmingham, in 1883, when he was transferred to the Accounts Department, first taking charge of one of the smaller and afterwards being promoted to the charge of one of the largest of the Society's Districts. Towards the end of 1890, he applied for an Assistant Superintendentship, but having failed in his application, which was a somewhat exceptional one in the ordinary course of the Society's affairs, he offered his services to various other companies, and at length, in February, 1891, succeeded in obtaining an appointment as Superintendent for the British Workman's Assurance Company, at Gravesend. In December of the same year he was offered the more important District of Gloucester and Cheltenham, which position he now holds.

D. MATTHEWS.

JOHN McCULLOCH.

Matthews, D., District Superintendent to the Prudential Assurance Company at Gloucester, started as an Agent for that Company at Pontypool, in 1872, with a clean book, but his success there resulted in a request from his Superintendent to remove to Abergavenny to work up an Agency there, subsequently removing to Abercarne, Neath, Monmouth, and Bristol, successively, at all of which places, though the business of the Company had till then been languishing, he succeeded in establishing it on a firm footing. He then returned to Abercarne, but had not been long there before he was offered and accepted an Assistant-Superintendency at Llanelly, Carmarthenshire, where he met with very considerable success. Thence he went to Tredegar, and after a few years as Assistant-Superintendent, was again promoted to be Superintendent at Ludlow, where his results were so satisfactory that his District was very soon enlarged. Soon afterwards, however, he was transferred to the Weston-super-Mare District, a very difficult one to take, owing to the opposition from the Swansea Royal Society, but Mr. Matthews triumphed over all obstacles, and ultimately saw the opposing Society come to an end altogether. His next appointment was to the Nuneaton District, whence, after three years of further success he was transferred to his present District. Mr. Matthews is devoted to the Prudential's cause, so much so that he has trained up three sons and a son-in-law to follow in his footsteps. One of them is a Superintendent, and the others Assistants to the Company.

McCulloch, John, Resident Manager to the Royal Liver Friendly Society at its Branch Office at Bradford, commenced his career in the Insurance profession in the service of the Scottish Legal Assurance Society, at the small town of Ballymena, in Ireland, in 1872. There he remained for two years, at the end of which period he had given so much satisfaction to his Directors by the energy and ability which he had displayed in the exercise of the duties hitherto allotted to him, that they transferred him to England to put him in charge of their Widnes District. He did not, however, remain very long, after his removal from Ireland, in the employment of the Scottish Legal Assurance Society, being soon offered the appointment of District Manager in the same town to the Royal Liver Friendly Society, which post he held with the most satisfactory results to his Society for a period of twelve years. At the end of that time he was transferred to his present post in charge of the more important manufacturing district of Bradford in 1886, on that District, which had, since its opening in 1851, been worked under the supervision of the Leeds Branch, being made independent with a Branch of its own. Since Mr. McCulloch's appointment the business in the Bradford District has been largely increased as a result of his efforts, and the Branch is now taking high rank among the most important Districts in the occupation of the Royal Liver Friendly Society.

G. MILLS.

DONALD McGREGOR.

Mills, G., Superintendent of the Prudential Assurance Company, at Westminster, though still in the prime of life, bears the proud distinction of being the oldest in service amongst the Superintendents on the staff of that Company. His first appointment to that rank was in March, 1866, when he was given supervision over the Peterborough District of the Company, from which centre he opened out the counties of Northampton, Rutland, Cambridge, Norfolk and Suffolk, for the Prudential, so that he is well experienced in provincial work. He remained in charge of the Peterborough District for no less than eighteen years, at the end of which period, in August, 1884, he was removed to his present District. Mr. Mills bears a high character with his Board for his ability, energy, and the practical results of his work, and commands the respect of his fellow-workers.

McGregor, Donald, District Agent of the Scottish Legal Life Assurance Society at Dundee, is a very old supporter of that Society, and in 1882 took an active part with other influential persons in his present District to endeavour to reform the management, which was at that time showing symptoms of weakness. With the help of other Districts, Mr. McGregor and his friends succeeded in their object ; and having been elected a Delegate at the first meeting held under the new rules, he was at the first meeting of Delegates at Glasgow, in 1883, elected a Member of the Finance Committee, which position he held till 1885. In the July of that latter year Mr. McGregor was requested by the Board of Management to undertake the charge of the Agency of his present District, which request he complied with, and has remained in the same post ever since. The business of the District has progressed under Mr. McGregor's superintendence to a very great extent, that gentleman enjoying the full confidence of the Board of Management and the Head Officials of his Society.

JOHN MOON.

JAMES MOON.

Moon, John, Agency Inspector to the Head Office of the Prudential Assurance Company, is the son of one of the most successful Industrial Assurance Agents in this country, Mr. John Moon, who afterwards continued his success as Superintendent over Lancashire, the West Riding of Yorkshire, Hull and Sheffield, and Lincolnshire, so that Mr. Moon himself enjoyed an unique early training and experience. He assisted his father with his books when a mere schoolboy, and in the winter of 1859, his father falling ill, he was entrusted with some of his collecting work. This he did so well that he was entrusted with regular collecting work at a very early age. At one time he was apprenticed to a leading Lancashire Doctor with a view to taking a medical degree and so ensuring a good stand in the business, but his father's health becoming weak, he had to abandon this idea to devote the whole of his time to a co-partnership in the business, which soon led to his formal appointment to the Superintendency of half of the District, but still in conjunction with his father. In 1871 the joint business had grown so large that Mr. Moon removed to Preston as his centre, where he remained nearly twelve years, at the end of which time he was appointed to his present post, and relieved of the wear and tear which he had undergone so long of working so hard a District. Mr. Moon's success has been chiefly in the fact of his having always worked on high commercial principles. He has always been a great favourite with his Agents and other subordinates, and is devotedly attached to his Company.

Moon, James, District Inspector to the Prudential Assurance Company at Liverpool, began his connection with the Insurance business at a very early period of his life, his late father, Mr. John Moon, having been intimately connected with the Prudential Assurance from the beginning in 1848, and having opened out most of the districts in Lancashire, Yorkshire, and the bordering districts, so that he may be said to have been bred in the atmosphere of Insurance. Mr. Moon has only served in one Insurance Office, namely, the Prudential, during the whole of his time, having entered its service in 1874 in the Preston (Lancashire) Office. Not long after this he was admitted as an associate of the Institute of Actuaries, and leaving business for a time he betook himself to London, in order that he might study for the examinations of that Institute. He soon returned to Preston to take a more active part than he had hitherto taken in the office there. He subsequently removed to the position of Assistant-Superintendent at Manchester, until the year 1880, when he was promoted to be Superintendent of the Manchester District. The years following this appointment proved very gratifying to Mr. Moon and his Company, the premium income of the latter increasing by rapid strides. On the occasion of Mr. Moon's marriage in 1882 the agents of his district presented him with a gratifying address of congratulation. Subsequently the Manchester District, owing to its rapid growth both in extent and business, was divided into five superintendencies, and Mr. Moon received the appointment of Inspector, taking charge of the new District Office opened at Liverpool, which is now his headquarters.

S. G. MOXEY.

JOHN MOORFIELD.

Moxey, S. G., is the Superintendent at Bristol of the Prudential Assurance Company, Limited, which position he has occupied for upwards of twelve years. Mr. Moxey has been in the service of the Prudential for twenty-six years, having represented it in Devonshire and Kent before taking the Bristol district ; in fact, he is one of the oldest of the Company's Superintendents, and in consequence is valued and trusted as all old officials are sure to be if they do their duty. In Bristol the Prudential has over one hundred agents and a good staff of assistants, and the many promotions from their ranks to various parts of the country show their efficiency and ability.

Moorfield, John, the District Superintendent of the British Workman's Assurance Company at Warrington, spent the early years of his life in hard work, commencing when he was only eight years old. He thus had to get what education he could in the few hours that he could snatch between his long periods of work, but nevertheless, his perseverance and industry were so far successful, that for fourteen years previous to his entering the Insurance profession, he was carrying on a very profitable business as a Contractor. His Insurance career commenced in 1888, with an Agency for the British Workman's Assurance Society at Runcorn and Widnes, with a small salary and a most chaotic state of affairs in the Sub-District. So great, however, was the energy with which he approached his work, that in two years he had reduced the state of chaos to one of order and progress, and he was rewarded by his Directors with the appointment to his present post.

WILLIAM MUSGROVE.

J. T. NELSON.

Musgrove, William, District Superintendent to the British Workman's Assurance Company at Oldham, is a native of Oldham, whence he went to America, in 1866, remaining there for nearly ten years. On his return to England he was persuaded to undertake an Agency for the Refuge Assurance Company, and after encountering many difficulties at the outset, he succeeded in getting together a certain amount of business, and was eventually appointed District Superintendent at Derby. Here he remained for nearly four years, at the end of which time he returned to Oldham, where he set up as a Commission Agent on his own account. After eighteen months in this capacity he accepted an offer in 1883 from the British Workman Assurance Company to act as Agent for them under Manchester, and having built up a very considerable business for the Company, he was promoted first to be Assistant-Superintendent under Manchester, and, on the establishment of Oldham as a separate District, to his present post as Superintendent.

Nelson. John T., District Superintendent of the British Workman's Assurance Company at Cardiff, was born at Burnley, in Lancashire, in 1860. His first connection with this Company was in 1879, when he was introduced to the Manchester District Superintendents as a candidate for the junior clerkship in their office, which post he obtained. After three years service, during which he received rapid promotion in the office, he was removed to Accrington as additional Assistant, where he so distinguished himself by the energy which he displayed in his work, though he was considerably handicapped by a strike of cotton operatives which took place in 1883, that after another three years, on the promotion of the chief Assistant, he was appointed to fill the vacancy. In this capacity he still continued to win the golden opinions of his Superintendent, with the result that in 1889, on his applying for a District Superintendency he was again promoted to his present post at Cardiff. Here he has already considerably increased the Company's business, having now under him a staff of an Assistant-Superintendent, two Clerks, and about fifteen Agents. Mr. Nelson having thus in his twelve years service worked himself up from the post of Junior Clerk to that of District Superintendent, has in spite of his comparative youth, a thorough grasp of all the details of the business that is of the utmost service to his Company. He has always enjoyed the confidence and friendship of his Agents, and on leaving Accrington, after his seven years service, parted with those under his charge in that District with the utmost mutual good-will.

H. PARKER.

J. A. PATRICK.

Parker, H., is the Superintendent at Sheffield of the Prudential Assurance Company, Limited. Mr. Parker's whole career as an Insurance man has been occupied in the service of the Prudential. Entering the Company's service as Agent at Ely, in 1869, he sufficiently evidenced his usefulness there to justify his promotion to the post of Assistant-Superintendent at Northampton, in 1873. Since then he has acted in the superior capacity of Superintendent in the districts of Boston, Nottingham, and London respectively, and in 1888 was removed to his present position at Sheffield, since which time the rate of increase has been doubled. Mr. Parker's success is undoubtedly in a great measure due to his happy faculty of ingratiating himself with all those who have the pleasure of serving under him.

Patrick, J. A., the General Superintendent for the City of Birmingham and District for the British Workman's Assurance Company, was born in Leeds in 1847, and for the first twenty-six years of his life worked as an engineer, being elected in his twenty-sixth year President of the Leeds Branch of the Amalgamated Society of Engineers. However, just at that time he took up his first Agency for the British Workman's Assurance Company, and since then he has never earned a sovereign outside Insurance work. Starting in Leeds as Agent at the very bottom of the profession without any business, in three and a-half years he had worked up a business in which there were 1,300 policy-holders, and which at that time was the largest book that had ever been made in Yorkshire. This success pointed him out to his Directors as a fitting man for a Superintendentship, and accordingly, in 1877, he was appointed to the Hull District. Hull up to that date had been one of the Company's failures: so much so

that two Superintendents had already given it up in despair, and Mr. Patrick's appointment might almost be regarded as a forlorn hope. When he first took up the District it had only 132 members, paying an annual premium of £54 9s. 10d., but Mr. Patrick brought with him an energy and a thorough confidence in his mission that had never been put into the work before ; and by his judicious choice of agents, his untiring perseverance, his honest convictions, with power of imparting them to others, of the worth of the Company, and his firmness, tempered with judicious kindness towards all, opponents or subordinates, with whom he was brought into contact, succeeded in restoring animation to the almost inanimate District, to the extent that in May, 1889, when he resigned his Superintendency to transfer his services elsewhere, the number of members had increased to 19,311, and the annual premium income to £10,591 15s. 8¼d. In 1887 he was presented by the Agents of his District with an oil-painting of himself, as a mark of their esteem and appreciation of his merits. In May, 1889, he was transferred to the South Birmingham Superintendency, and since then his success has even exceeded that which he had previously enjoyed, making the largest increase in the annual premium of the weekly department of any of the Birmingham Offices, besides very considerable ones in the month'y and yearly departments as well. He has got a fine staff together to work under him, and has, as in his former District, won their thorough confidence. Mr. Patrick attributes all his success to a careful study of the principles of Life Assurance, and makes a rule of reading all the current literature on the subject, especially the Insurance Magazines; his experience being that the majority of failures as Agents and Superintendents is owing to a neglect of such literature.

J. Phillips.

J. W. Peel.

Phillips, J., is the Superintendent for the British Workman's Assurance Company, Limited, at Hereford. Mr. Phillips has been very successful in the Insurance business, and the district under his charge is in a very prosperous condition.

Peel, J. W., District Manager of the Liverpool Victoria Legal Friendly Society at Gloucester, began as a Canvasser for an Insurance Agent in 1873, and as soon as he became of age took up an Agency on his own account for the Prudential in his native town of Halifax. He removed thence to Dewsbury, and was subsequently, in 1879, appointed Assistant Superintendent at York. Leaving the service of the Prudential, he became Travelling Agent to his present Society, afterwards being promoted to be District Agent for West Cumberland in 1882, Superintendent at Salford in 1884, and District Manager at Blackburn in 1885 successively. On leaving Salford for Blackburn he was presented with a handsome testimonial by his staff of the former District. In 1887 the Committee of Management of the Society decided to open out the Midland Counties, and Mr. Peel was selected to be Manager for the County of Gloucester, South Worcestershire and South Herefordshire being added to his District in 1889. He was again the recipient of a testimonial from his staff at Blackburn on leaving that District, and since taking up his duties in the Gloucester District he has been presented with his portrait by his staff.

J. PILKINGTON.

RICHARD PINCHES.

Pilkington, J., the District Superintendent for the British Workman's Assurance Company at Nottingham, was born, in 1844, at Rising Bridge, near Haslingden, Lancashire, and commenced life at the early age of seven as a half-timer in a mill at Rawenstall, whither his parents had removed, continuing the same life at Accrington, where they again moved to in 1854. He commenced Insurance work in 1872, at the instance of a friend, for a Society which has since ceased to exist, and afterwards at Bolton for the Refuge, whence he removed to Burnley, still as a Canvasser, till 1876. He had long wished to become a full Agent, and now he obtained a post as such to the British Workman's Assurance Company, under the Accrington Superintendent, in which capacity he continued for four years, and, at the end of that time, had built up such a large business that he was made Assistant-Superintendent and divided his work amongst several Agents. In 1886, on the death of his former Superintendent, Mr. Pilkington was appointed to succeed him.

Pinches, Richard, the Superintendent of the Chester District of the Wesleyan and General Assurance Society, was born at Asterton, Salop, in 1844. For many years he resided at Middle-

wich, Cheshire, and there introduced the Wesleyan and General Assurance Society, becoming their Agent for that neighbourhood, and, being a man of perseverance, soon brought the office into great popularity amongst the inhabitants, in a very few years building up a very considerable amount of both industrial and ordinary business. He was then appointed Assistant Superintendent of the Crewe District, and after about twelve months in that capacity, on the removal of the District headquarters to Chester, he was also removed and promoted to the post of Superintendent. Since his appointment the business of the District has increased to such an extent that it is now more than twelve times what it was eight years ago when he took up his appointment. As a man of business Mr. Pinches is energetic, and persevering, never allowing himself beaten. As a gentleman he is kind and agreeable, always ready to sympathize with and help those who are down, as all who know him can testify. For over twenty years he has been a Member and Local Preacher of the Primitive Methodist Church ; in his present circuit he is held in high esteem, and in the circuits where he has formerly lived and laboured he has left memories and impressions that will not easily be effaced.

J. REYNOLDS

C. H. RAY.

Reynolds, J., Superintendent of the Newry District for the Prudential Assurance Company, was born in 1846 at Greenwich, and spent the greater part of his early youth on the Continent, whither he was sent to study for the medical profession. After the Franco-German war, he returned to his parents, who had now removed to Dublin, but owing to family misfortunes he found himself not in a position to resume the career for which he had been originally intended. In 1873 he married and removed to the South of Ireland, and it was while there that in 1874 his connection with the Prudential commenced by his taking up an Agency in the town of Wexford. The following year he crossed over again into England, having been appointed to an unattached Assistant Superintendency at Plymouth, subsequently becoming an attached Assistant Superintendent at Newton Abbot in the same District. He returned to Ireland in 1875 to take up an Assistant Superintendency at Dublin, and during the succeeding three years took charge of Sub-districts in Dublin, Portarlington, and Naas successively. In 1878 he was promoted to be Superintendent at Waterford, which District then included counties Waterford, Tipperary, Kilkenny, Carlow and Kildare, and finally in April of the following year he was transferred to his present District—Newry, which being a great centre of the linen industry is generally considered one of the most important Districts in Ireland. Mr. Reynolds has thus had a very wide and varied experience, and is devoted to his Company and profession. He is a very strong opponent of the theory advocated by some people that Infantile Insurance is conducive to crime.

Ray, C. H., the Plymouth District Superintendent of the Prudential Assurance Company, was born in 1855, and began as Agent to the Prudential in May, 1881. After two and a-half years' Agency work he was appointed Assistant Superintendent in the January of 1884, and promoted to the post of Superintendent in April, 1888. He took charge of his present District in March, 1891.

J. P. RICHARDSON.

HENRY RHODES.

Richardson, J. P., the District Superintendent of the British Workman's Assurance Company at Norwich, commenced his Insurance work as an Agent to the Pearl Life Assurance Company in 1881, since which time he has served that same Company as Assistant-Superintendent and Superintendent, in Norwich, King's Lynn, Burton-on-Trent, and Leicester. Mr. Richardson transferred his services to the British Workman's Assurance Company in order that he might reside in his native city, Norwich, as the post of Superintendent to that district, which was offered him, enabled him to do. He was born in 1860.

Rhodes, Henry, is the Superintendent at Birmingham of the Royal London Friendly Society, which position he has held for a number of years. Mr. Rhodes is a most capable official, and is held in high esteem by the Directors of his Society and the Agents in his district.

J. RILEY.

A. J. ROBERTS.

Riley, Joseph, District Inspector of the Prudential Assurance Company at Birmingham, was born at Stockport, and comes from a good old Cheshire family, more than once celebrated in the annals of that county. Mr. Riley's Insurance career commenced in 1863 in connection with the Prudential, first as an Agent, but in a very short time being promoted to a Superintendency in London. Here he remained for several years, winning golden opinions from his Directors by his fidelity and energy, so much so that on their resolving to open out Ireland as a field of operations, they selected him as the most fitting officer to undertake the management of the scheme. He again distinguished himself in this capacity, even beyond the expectations of his Directors; and so conspicuous did he make himself in the Insurance world that he received an offer from America in 1871 to come over and establish an Industrial Company there, which highly complimentary offer, however, he declined. He was next appointed to the Superintendency of the Worcestershire District, comprising that and several of the neighbouring counties, whence, after again making a record for himself, he was removed to Glasgow. There he met with some difficulties owing to the recent failure of the City Bank and the consequent scarcity of money, but, nothing daunted, he continued on his progress with unflagging energy, and in time not only reduced the affairs of the Company to proper order again, but put them on a firmer and more profitable basis than they had ever been before. In 1891 he was promoted to the highest position on the outside staff possible,

namely, that which he at present holds, Birmingham, for family reasons, being chosen as his District. Mr. Riley is well known as a connoiseur in art and as an amateur photographer. He has been Secretary in the Science and Art Department, South Kensington, of one of the Glasgow Colleges, is Member of the Glasgow Insurance Institute, the Natural History Society, and other Institutions. He has been repeatedly requested to stand for more honours, but has always refused. He is looked upon as a reliable authority on Insurance matters.

Roberts, A. J., the District Superintendent for the British Workman's Assurance Company at Halifax, was born in 1832, and from the age of ten to that of forty-three followed the business of a mechanic both in England and America. In 1874 he undertook a part-time Agency at Leeds for the British Workman's Assurance Company, and about a month after this first essay adopted the Insurance business as his real profession. At that time the Company was still young, and he had to make a start quite from the bottom of the ladder without even having any business given him, but so implicit a faith did he put in the ultimate success of the Company, that although only three months after beginning work for it, he received an offer from another office that would at the time have doubled his income, he determined to decline it. He continued at Leeds for six years, at the end of which time he was appointed Assistant Superintendent to the Company at Halifax, and after another three years was promoted to his present post.

E. ROBERTS.

GEORGE ROYLE.

Roberts, Edward, Superintendent of the Truro District of the Prudential Assurance Company, commenced work in 1869 as Agent to the Prudential for Cornwall, being nearly the first Agent appointed by the Company in Cornwall. So successful was he in building up a business out of what had been nothing that at the end of 1870 he was put in charge of the Cornwall District as Assistant Superintendent, and on the post being changed into a Superintendency in 1874 he was naturally chosen to fill it. Commencing with a staff of one Assistant and five Agents, the District had developed in 1883 to such an extent that the staff had been increased to seven Assistants and 140 Agents, while the premium income showed an increase of sixteen fold, and it became necessary to divide the District into four Superintendencies, all of which redounds to Mr. Roberts's sole credit. He has had several offers of advantageous changes to other districts, but has always refused them, remaining loyal to his native county and his original sphere of action, in which perhaps he is unique amongst the members of the Insurance profession. He is a Member and has been returned constantly unopposed to the Town Council of Truro, and is Chairman of the Committee for the establishment of a new Cemetery. He is a little over fifty years of age.

———

Royle, George, F.R.G.S., the District Manager of the Liverpool Victoria Friendly Society for Bedfordshire, Cambridgeshire, and Hertfordshire, is a native of Lancashire, where he was born in 1860. Before entering upon the duties of his present position he had for many years been in the service of the Society, and, having worked his way up gradually from being a Clerk in a District Office, had only just been appointed Manager to the West Middlesex District when, on the Committee requiring a good man to work up the almost hopeless District of Bedfordshire and Cambridgeshire, their choice fell on him as being the most likely to effect an almost impossible task. He left his position as Travelling Agent and Organiser, determined to make the District go in spite of all difficulties and former failures, and he has most effectively succeeded in carrying out his determination, with the satisfactory result that his District is now one amongst the flourishing centres of the Liverpool Victoria Friendly Society.

J. T. ROSCOE.

J. W. B. ROSCOE.

Roscoe, J. T., is the District Superintendent for the British Workman's Assurance Company at Leeds, to which post he was appointed in December, 1874. At that time the Company was not doing a very large business in the District, but so energetically did Mr. Roscoe work that by the end of 1882 it had quadrupled, and at Mr. Roscoe's suggestion the Directors saw fit to make Bradford and Halifax into separate Districts, Wakefield following suit a few years later, owing to the still continuing increase of business. Mr. Roscoe, who is still in the forties, can be said without doubt to have achieved his great success through his personal courtesy and power of hard work: he respects his Agents and they respect him. He also enjoys the personal esteem of his Manager. He is a firm believer in Life Assurance and particularly in the British Workman's Assurance Company.

Roscoe, J. W. B., District Superintendent for the British Workman's Assurance Company at York, was, previous to commencing his Insurance career, engaged in an accountant's office at Leeds, the experience he gained there afterwards proving of great service to him in the Audit Department of the Leeds Branch of the British Workman's Assurance Company, which he first entered in 1882. He remained for seven years in that district, dealing during that time with nearly every change in the agencies, besides introducing a large amount of business himself, till, in 1889, having asked for a removal, he was appointed Agency Inspector at Manchester. This post he held for twelve months, at the end of which time he was promoted to the District Superintendency at Scarborough, being subsequently transferred to his present district in October, 1891.

R. SATTERFORD, SEN.

N. SHAW.

Satterford, R., the District Superintendent of the British Workman's Assurance Company at Plymouth, was born in 1845, and commenced his connection with the Company as Agent in Devonshire, his native county. In August, 1878, he was appointed Agency Inspector, which office he held for nearly six years, during that time exhibiting unflagging energy in the performance of his work, travelling all over the United Kingdom, as he was then the only Inspector, and earning the full confidence of his Board of Directors. In the month of February, 1884, Mr. Satterford resigned his post of Inspector, and was at his own request appointed Superintendent of Agents for the Stockton-on-Tees District, where he remained for two years, doing good work in the appointment of new good men and cleaning or clearing the weed out of the district. In the December of 1885 he received an invitation from the Managing Director to take charge of the Plymouth District, the reason given being that he was a Devonshire man, and was likely to be of great service there, the district having hitherto never been a success. Mr. Satterford met with very disheartening forebodings from the people whom he found in his new District, but so well did he labour that though on his arrival, in 1886, the industrial weekly debit amounted to only £36, in 1890 it had increased to £109, and a fairly good standard has been attained as well in the ordinary yearly business. Mr. Satterford has been the recipient of a testimonial and address from his present staff.

Shaw, Nelson, the Jersey District Superintendent to the British Workman's Assurance Company, began his Insurance work in 1876 as Agent to a Company doing a local business in the Channel Islands. Most of the larger Assurance Companies were then well established there, and in December, 1881, he opened the District for the British Workman's Assurance Company, commencing his duties as part-time Agent, but three months later changing them to those of full-time Agent, and in the July of 1882 his efforts were rewarded by his appointment to the District Agency of the Channel Islands, with the duties of a Superintendent. This inspired him with even additional energy, and he plodded on with a firm determination to succeed, never losing heart, although he had at times some uphill work and leviathan Companies to contend against, till the January of 1883, when he was put on probation for six months, and in the following July received his official appointment as District Superintendent. Since then, notwithstanding the limited field of operations, and the keen competitions Mr. Shaw's district has advanced steadily and surely, the members of the Industrial Branch of the Company alone numbering over 5,000 with a weekly premium of nearly £100, while the General Department is showing a like satisfactory increase. Mr. Shaw may congratulate himself on having fixed the British Workman's Assurance Company very firmly in the Channel Islands.

W. J. SHIMMELL.

JAMES SLEE.

Shimmell, W. J., is the Superintendent for the British Workman's Assurance Company, Limited, at Newcastle-on-Tyne. Mr. Shimmell commenced his Insurance life as Agent for the following Companies in Burton-on-Trent :—British Workman, The United Kingdom Temperance and General Life Office, Westminster and Commercial Fire Offices. He was presented by the Good Templars and Temperance Societies of Burton with an illuminated address on his promotion to be Superintendent at Huddersfield in February, 1889 ; and in February, 1890, he was again promoted to the District Superintendency of Newcastle-on-Tyne.

Shaw, George, District Manager for the West of Scotland for the Liverpool Victoria Friendly Society, is a native of Liverpool, where he was born in 1856. He commenced his career in the Insurance profession as an office boy in the Economic Assurance Society, from which position he rose to that of Clerk, and five years afterwards left the Economic to enter the service of his present Company. It was not long, however, before he rose to be Collector, being sent in that capacity to Glasgow, and there he proved so successful that at the end of 1889 he was again promoted to be Assistant-Superintendent, returning to Liverpool. After three years there he was sent to Bedford as Assistant, but had scarcely arrived there when he was sent on to Maidstone as District Superintendent for Kent. Here he worked hard and to good purpose for his Society, and made himself at the same time so popular that he was presented by the Officers and Agents of the Society with a handsome testimonial as a

mark of their esteem and friendship. He was removed to his present post in April, 1891.

Slee, James, District Manager for Norfolk of the London, Edinburgh and Glasgow Assurance Company, was born in 1850 at Combe Martin, and commenced his Insurance career in 1875 at Swansea, as a Canvasser for the Swansea Royal Society. Leaving this position he removed to South Molton, Devonshire, and took up a spare-time Agency for the Pearl, which he held till 1880, though in the meantime offered an Assistant Superintendency at Barnstaple. In 1880 he returned to Swansea, and after working some time under his brother, who was an Agent to his first Company, the Swansea Royal, on the latter being promoted to be Superintendent, he took over his Agency and retained it till 1884. In June of that latter year Mr. Slee was appointed Superintendent to the Royal, and was employed almost immediately in taking over the business of the City Life Assurance Company, which had been merged into the Swansea Royal, both at Reading and Newbury and in Ireland, in all of which districts he succeeded in his object without losing a fraction of the City Life connection. In 1886, on its being found advisable to transfer the business of the Swansea Royal to the London, Edinburgh and Glasgow, Mr. Slee entered into his connection with the latter company in his old capacity, being subsequently, in January, 1891, made District Manager over four districts, and in June of the same year removed to his present district in Norfolk. Mr. Slee has been the fortunate recipient of more than one testimonial from his staff and admirers in his various districts.

W. SMITH.

J. C. STREDDER.

Smith, William, District Superintendent for the Prudential Assurance Company at Bath, was born at Coniston Cold, Skipton-in-Craven, Yorkshire, in 1855, subsequently residing for some years at Bramley, near Leeds, and at Bradford. After six years' service in the mercantile office of Gilson Homan and Co., he became engaged as Cashier and afterwards as Manager in the Commercial Department of the *Bradford Daily Telegraph,* where he remained for more than five and a-half years. Acting under the advice of the present District Superintendent to the Prudential in West London, Mr. William Hillier, he decided to sever his connection with that paper, and became an Agent for the Prudential in Bradford, in June, 1883. In July, 1884, he was made an Assistant Superintendent in the same town, and remained in that capacity until March, 1889, when he was appointed as Superintendent to his present district, in which city he has since met with marked success.

———

Stredder, J. C., District Superintendent to the Prudential Assurance Company at Bolton, comes of an old Lincolnshire family, but was himself born near Dublin in the year 1851, where his father held an appointment, and lived there during his early boyhood. His parents, however, returning to England, he was placed at Liverpool College, where he remained till he was seventeen, receiving a sound commercial and classical education, which has been of great use to him in after life. He started in the Insurance profession soon after leaving school in connection with the Prudential,

and, working his way up through all grades, was in 1874 appointed Assistant Superintendent at Bolton, then a Sub-district to Manchester, to work up the business, which he did to such good purpose that in 1878 his industry was rewarded by his promotion to the Chief Superintendentship for the Barrow-in-Furness and Lancaster District, he being the first Superintendent ever stationed there. There he again proved a great success, and his name is still remembered as an incentive to emulation to all Insurance men in that district. He afterwards acted as Superintendent of the North Liverpool and the Crewe and Northwich Districts successively, still continuing his former triumphant progress; and in 1883, on his old Sub-district Bolton being promoted to the rank of a District, he returned to take charge of the business whose seeds he had sown, and which had in the meantime increased to a gigantic extent. Since that time he has for two years running had the honour of standing first on the Company's list of Superintendents for increase in his District of Industrial Premiums. Mr. Stredder is energetic, with plenty of tact, a good organiser, and a firm though always kind officer to his subordinates, and is deservedly respected by them, while at the same time they know that when in difficulty they can always go to him for help. In these virtues lies the secret of his success. He is now one of the oldest Superintendents in the Prudential's service. He takes a leading part in local affairs, and in 1889 was elected a Councillor for the West Ward of the County Borough of Bolton, the metropolitan ward of the Borough, in which capacity he has more than once distinguished himself on behalf of his fellow-townsmen.

WILLIAM SYERS.

Syers, William, is Manager of the London Branch of the Wesleyan and General Assurance Society. Mr. Syers commenced his Insurance life when a mere youth, and has been connected with the Wesleyan and General Assurance Society for over fifteen years, his first appointment with the Society being that of Superintendent of the Cheshire District, after which he took charge of the Liverpool Office, still retaining his former District. He remained at that latter post until ten years ago, when he was appointed to his present post, and has done much since to extensively develop the Society's London business.

Sproul, A., the District Superintendent of the Pearl Life Assurance Company at Greenock, is a native of Renfrewshire, and entered the service of the Pearl in 1885. He received the whole of his Insurance training under the able tuition of Mr. Mackay, the General Superintendent to the Pearl for Scotland and the North of Ireland, to whom he acted as District Superintendent at Glasgow for some time before his appointment to his present post.

Stagg, A. A., the District Superintendent of the Wesleyan and General Assurance Society at Chatham and Rochester, began his Insurance career and his service with the Wesleyan and General simultaneously, commencing as Agent at Southampton in 1881. So soon as in 1882 he was selected to open out the City of Salisbury for the Society, and his success there marked him as fit to undertake the Assistant Superintendency of the Chatham District in February of 1883, his further promotion to the District Superintendency following in the May of the same year. The Society had up to that time not been prosperous in the District; many of the old agents were practically of no use whatever, and the mismanagement of a former Assistant had put the Society into somewhat bad odour. Mr. Stagg, however, has spared no pains in the thorough organisation and reformation of the District. He has now more than sixty Agents working under him, and nearly every town and village in Kent is opened to the Society. Mr. Stagg is devoted to the service of his Society, and though he has repeatedly received invitations of an alluring character to desert it for other Companies he has steadily resisted them.

WILLIAM TAIT.

H. W. TAYLOR.

Tait, William, District Superintendent to the Pearl Life Assurance Company at Glasgow, was born in Caithnessshire in 1863, and received his early education in the Stemster Public School and completed it at the Free Church School, Thurso. In May. 1882, he went to South Wales and soon after joined the Pearl Assurance Company at Cardiff, where he remained till 1887, when he was appointed Assistant-Superintendent in charge of the Company's business in Merthyr. Three months later he was appointed Superintendent of that District, which included Brynnmawr, Tredegar, and Ebbw Vale, and after a successful career of three years was transferred to Manchester, where he remained until November, 1891, leaving it to take up his present post. Mr. Tait is one of the most successful of the Pearl Superintendents and very popular amongst his subordinates, having received more than one testimonial of appreciation from his various staffs when summoned to leave them for higher posts.

———

Thompson, J., the Bournemouth Superintendent of the Pearl Life Assurance Company, and whose District Office is at Longfleet, Poole, Dorset, commenced his work for the Company at Plymouth, and threw himself with so much fervour into his business, that in a very short time he was promoted to the sub-charge of the Plymouth District. On the Superintendency of Torquay becoming vacant, he was promoted to that post under Exeter, and he there remained until towards the end of 1890, when the newly-opened Bournemouth District, extending over a large part of Dorsetshire and Hampshire, requiring a Superintendent, he was selected to fill the post. He has already done much to promote the welfare of the Company in his District. He is quite at one with all his staff, as indeed he always has been in all the positions which he has held, having received testimonials from his Agents, both at Plymouth and Torquay.

———

Taylor, Harry Walter, is the Superintendent of the Prudential Assurance Company for the North West District of London. He was appointed agent for that Company in July, 1871, at Portsmouth, whence in 1875 he was appointed Assistant-Superintendent at Guildford, being promoted in the following year to the Superintendency of the same district. In 1879 he was transferred to take charge of the East London District, whence, in 1888, he was removed to his present charge.

A. TOWERS.

W. H. TUCKER.

Towers, A., the District Manager of the Royal Liver Friendly Society at Burnley, Lancashire, was, previous to entering the Insurance profession, engaged in the engineering and weighing machine trade at Heaton Norris, near Stockport, in which he held an important position. He commenced his Insurance career in Preston, where he had previously taken part in many of the chief philanthropic movements of the District, as representative of his present Office. He soon succeeded in opening up a large business for the Royal Liver in Preston and the surrounding District, at the same time winning the respect of all his contemporaries and the confidence of his Directors, the latter to such an extent that he was next promoted to be Claim-paying Agent of the Society for the Preston District. In this new capacity he continued his successful career, binding together by his infinite tact Officers and Members of the Royal Liver, with the result that during the trying episode of the Commission of Enquiry into the Royal Liver's affairs his business remained intact throughout, he thereby again receiving the highest commendation from his Directors. He next volunteered to open up his native District, Burnley, which offer the Directors accepted, and, though he found it very uphill work, he soon made headway, and very shortly had raised Burnley to the position of one of the leading Districts of the Society. He was rewarded by his promotion to his present rank, while at the same time he was publicly thanked by his Directors and presented with a handsome testimonial from his Staff. Mr. Towers takes an active part in all the philanthropic movements of his District, which has in a great way assisted towards his success.

Tucker, W. H., the Superintendent of the North London District of the British Workman's Assurance Company, is a native of Devonport. In 1881, when working for Messrs. Henry S. King and Co., Cornhill, he was induced by Mr. Bates, then Branch Manager for the British Workman's Assurance Company in London, to start as an Agent for the Company. When Mr. Tucker first commenced, his business was very much scattered, embracing the districts of Tottenham, Holloway, Islington, Kilburn, Fulham, and Putney, and he recalls with some pride the fact of his sometimes having had, after canvassing and collecting diligently throughout the day, to walk seven miles to regain his home in the Old Kent Road; but he nevertheless persevered, and at the end of two-and-a-half years his list had attained to the very creditable size of over 1,000 members, with an annual premium of over £500. At the end of 1883 he was appointed District Agent for the North of London, and from then to the August of 1887 his membership roll increased to over 3,000, with an annual premium of over £1,500. At that latter date he became Superintendent of the district. His list of members now numbers nearly 7,000 names, with annual premium of nearly £4,000. He has an Assistant Superintendent and more than thirty Agents working under him. Mr. Tucker's great difficulty when he first started lay in the comparative obscurity of his Company in London, and it is in no slight degree owing to his exertions that it has emerged from that obscurity and is now so widely known, as the above results abundantly testify, while there is still every reason to suppose that Mr. Tucker's future exertions will be as successful as his past ones have been.

A. H. VERNALL.

S. J. VINCENT.

Vernall, A. H., is the Superintendent of the Rotherhithe District for the Prudential Assurance Company. He commenced work for the Company in 1876 as Agent in the South-East of London, and after three years of successful work was promoted to an Assistant Superintendency at Rotherhithe. In 1884 he was further promoted to the post of Superintendent, being transferred in his new capacity to Dorchester. There he remained till 1887, when he was again removed to Tunbridge Wells, eventually returning to his former scene of operations at Rotherhithe in 1890.

———

Vincent, S. J., the District Superintendent of the Pearl Assurance Company in Cornwall, commenced as Assistant Superintendent in the Plymouth District, whence he was successively and rapidly promoted to the Newton Abbot and

Torquay, the Poole, and the Bournemouth Districts. In September, 1887, the Directors of the Pearl wishing to develop the Truro District, embracing nearly the whole of Cornwall, Mr. Vincent was removed thither to succeed Mr Cock, who had been Superintendent of the district for 10 years, and since then the result has been even beyond their expectations. Cornwall being a county of small population and low wages, it could hardly be expected to be worked at any great profit, but so unflagging has been the energy with which Mr. Vincent has worked himself, and so judicious has been his selection of agents, that his District for the quarter ending June, 1891, was second on the Company's books for increase in premium income. Mr. Vincent is held in the highest respect and esteem of all his Agents, who in 1890 presented him with a handsome marble clock as a testimonial.

T. WANN.

J. WARDLE.

Wann, Tom, the District Superintendent of the Prudential Assurance Company at Stirling, commenced his Insurance career in the service of that Company in 1874 in the town of Leicester, and in a very short time was made Assistant Superintendent. Soon afterwards he was transferred to Nottingham, and having in both places given good evidence of his working powers he was again transferred to London, in which more important position he continued all his former success. He was then sent to Northampton as Assistant Superintendent, a District which was at that time a source of considerable trouble to the Company by reason of the desertion of the former Assistant Superintendent and five of his Agents who left for America, but Mr. Wann soon settled the difficulty, and succeeded in placing the district on a better footing than it had ever been on before. In the following year he accepted the Superintendency of the Boston District, and though he found absolutely no business worth speaking of on his arrival there he succeeded in making it a most profitable one. He was appointed to his present District in 1889, and since then has done much to improve it for his Company in spite of its small extent. Mr. Wann is an energetic and business-like man in all his habits, and, though of retiring habits, is in great request for many public posts. In 1891, he was, much against his will, pressed to stand for the Stirling School Board, and, though a stranger, was elected with the greatest ease. In the November of the same year he was, also against his wish, nominated for the Town Council. He is a great advocate of the Temperance Movement, and has lectured on the subject all over his district.

Wardle, Joseph, is the District Superintendent for the Prudential Assurance Company at their Branch Office at Birmingham. He was born near Buxton, in Derbyshire, of farmer parents, and himself worked on the farm from the age of thirteen until he was twenty. He had thus little opportunity for education, but at the latter age, having developed a decided interest in Christian work, he became a Wesleyan Preacher, and diligently set himself to qualify for the work by making up the deficiencies in his education. When twenty-five years of age he became a City Missionary in Manchester, where he laboured with much good effect. His health compelled him to resign his post in Manchester after many years of not unprofitable toil, much to the regret of the Superintendent of the Mission. In 1869 he became Agent for the Prudential Assurance Company at Buxton, and consequently has served that Company for twenty-three years. His success at Buxton marked him for promotion to the post of Assistant Superintendent to the Derby District under Nottingham, where he continued to make satisfactory progress in behalf of his Company, and two years later he was selected by his Directors for a District Superintendency. In that capacity he served in Coventry, Leicester, and Bradford (Yorkshire), and has in his twenty-three years' service contributed over £60,000 per annum increase of income to the largely-increased business of the Company. He was removed to the important centre of the Midlands (Birmingham) in 1889, and the three years in that City has shown that he wields in influence over his men for good as they have in the three years increased the Company's returns by over £13,000 per annum.

J. R. WEST.

JAMES WARREN.

West, J. R., is the District Manager at Sheffield of the London, Edinburgh and Glasgow Assurance Company, Limited, which appointment he has held for several years. Mr. West is a gentleman of considerable business experience, and is well known throughout his district.

Warren, James, District Manager of the London, Edinburgh and Glasgow Assurance Company at Croydon, commenced at the age of nineteen as an Agent to the Prudential Assurance Company at Pimlico in 1875. Here he did not meet with any great success in the first six months of his work, but receiving encouragement from another Agent he took heart and persevered till he had overcome all difficulties. The next year he left London to take up another Agency for the same Company in Yeovil, where he worked successfully for twelve months, subsequently removing to the Isle of Wight, where he remained for the same period of time. He was then promoted to an Assistant Superintendency at Dublin, where he worked for another year, in that time increasing the business in his District threefold, but was unfortunately compelled to resign his post owing to an attack of ophthalmia, which necessitated his leaving Dublin. He then successively worked as Agent at Boston, Special Canvasser at Nottingham, and Agent at Kettering, which latter place he left, owing to a misunderstanding with some of his colleagues in 1881, severing his connection at the same time with the Prudential, and transferring his services to the United Kingdom Assurance Corporation. Ten months later he accepted the Superintendency of the Portsmouth District, where he was very successful, removing in 1883 to Croydon in the same capacity, in which he remained till 1889, when, on the United Kingdom's business being taken over by his present Company, he was, in view of his past services, appointed District Manager.

R. WHEELOCK.

T. B. WETHERILL.

Wheelock, R., the Resident Secretary for Yorkshire, at the Leeds Branch of the London, Edinburgh and Glasgow Assurance Company, began his connection with that Company in the November of the year 1882, at which time he became their Agent at Bromsgrove, in Worcestershire. His efforts in that capacity proving fairly successful, in April, 1883, he was promoted to a salaried position, and six months later, in the November of the same year, when himself only twenty-eight years of age, he was removed to Birmingham to take up the duties of District Manager in that locality, the Company having just at that period commenced carrying on industrial business. From that time down to May, 1889, nearly six years, Mr. Wheelock remained at the same post, and from first to last met with very considerable success, having had the good fortune to have secured several very energetic Superintendents to work under him, and with their assistance, and the help and confidence which he deservedly received from the officials of the Company, his success was continuous, while his relations with the outside staff, as well as with the Chief Office, were always of the most satisfactory character. When Mr. Wheelock left the office at Birmingham the condition of the Branch was most flourishing. The final departure from the Birmingham District on Mr. Wheelock's part, in the May of 1889, was only brought about by his acceptance of the position which he now holds at Leeds. Mr. Wheelock has gained the whole of his Insurance experience in connection with the London, Edinburgh and Glasgow, he having only been besides in the employment of the British Workman's Assurance Society for a very brief period.

Wetherill, T. B., Superintendent of the Bradford Branch of the Liverpool Victoria Legal Friendly Society, has been in charge of that Branch ever since its establishment in 1870, previous to which date he had been in the service of the Society at its Leeds Branch, for a period of ten years. Mr. Wetherill is a most successful Insurance man, he being able to secure and retain the services of good men as Agents and Assistants, as well as excelling in field work himself. He is highly esteemed in Bradford, and his Society has in every way benefited from his management. He comes of an old North of England family, of which he is now the only living representative.

J. WILCOCK.

JOHN WILSON.

Wilcock, James, the Superintendent of the Blackburn District of the Refuge Assurance Company, is a man who has good reason to look back upon his past career with pride. He was born at Accrington in 1846, the son of a basket maker, and after his parents removal to Blackburn, was, at the early age of eight, apprenticed to his father. This naturally put a stop to school for him, but, determined not to let his education suffer from that circumstance, he spent his evenings either in home study or in attendance at night classes, and speedily acquired that knowledge that had been denied to him through the more customary sources; gaining especially a mastery over figures, which has been of the utmost service to him in his after career. At the age of 22, finding that the basket trade afforded him no scope for his self-conscious talents, he entered the service of the Refuge Assurance Company, and set himself with all his heart and soul to open out the District. He was then, as now, District Superintendent, but his work then was very different from what it is at present; then his Superintendency covered a very modest area, the number of the members scarcely amounted to two figures, and his weekly returns were hardly more than *nil*. But it was not very long before his perseverance began to tell: his business increased, his Agents multiplied, and he was soon obliged to form a large staff of clerks to assist him in his office. Then his Directors, seeing what sort of a man he was, gradually handed over to him other Districts, which had not previously been conducted with any very great success, till his District is now one of the largest under the control of the Company, comprising North West Lancashire and the West Riding of Yorkshire, and he has under him nearly forty clerks, besides a large number of Assistant Superintendents and Agents. His office itself is typical of his continuous progress;

beginning as it did in quiet unpretentious premises in King Street, it has since been twice removed to two houses in Montague Street in ascending order of size and accommodation, and in May, 1890, to a spacious building specially erected for the purpose in Ainsworth Street. Mr. Wilcock, besides his particular post, is also a large shareholder and a Director of the Company. In spite, however, of his great professional activity, he is of a very retiring disposition, and has always held aloof from public life, steadily declining to stand for any municipal or other public honours, with the exception of a share in the management of the Nonconformist Higher Grade School. He is generous in giving to the deserving, and in a true Christian spirit, without any parade; a true and agreeable friend, and a pattern employer, considerate to, and esteemed by, all who have the good fortune to be under him.

Wilson, John, the Dublin District Superintendent of the Refuge Assurance Company, was born at Whitburn, Linlithgowshire, in 1858, commencing life in his father's business, that of a Railway Contractor. He commenced in the Insurance profession in 1880, at Edinburgh, in the service of the Refuge Assurance Company, whence he was shortly transferred to Dumbarton. Here he showed so evidently the sort of stuff that he was made of, that he was considered by his Directors fit for promotion to the post of Assistant Superintendent at Glasgow, and subsequently still further to that of Superintendent at Dublin. He found his present District in a very unsatisfactory state, but he has worked hard, and by his steady perseverance, his tact in choosing his Agents, and his power of communicating his own spirit to them, he has worked it up till now it embraces the whole of the centre of Ireland.

WALTER WILSON.

THOMAS WISE.

Wilson, Walter, the Scottish Border District Superintendent of the Refuge Assurance Company at Galashiels, is one of the youngest Superintendents of the Company, but has, nevertheless, one of the best records. Previous to his appointment to that post he acted as Assistant in the Dublin District, where he did much for the Company, opening out every town and village in the south of Ireland, placing Agents therein and putting them all in good business order. His promotion to his present post took place in September, 1890. The Scottish Border District had hitherto brought in no income to the Company, and it was owing to Mr. Wilson's success in his Irish work that he was chosen to fill the difficult post. He met with considerable opposition from all quarters on commencing his work, but he was not disheartened, and, by his business-like habits and courteous manner to all brought in contact with him, has raised the reputation of his Company to quite an exalted pitch in the neighbourhood. In September, 1891, he was presented by his Assistants and Agents with a gold hunting lever watch as a token of their appreciation of his merits.

Wise, Thomas, is the District Manager of the Scottish Legal Life Assurance Society at its Manchester Branch. He commenced life in commercial pursuits, and eventually worked himself up to an important position in one of the largest commercial establishments in Glasgow. This, however, he left, in order that he might set up in business for himself as an Insurance Agent and Accountant, and having obtained an appointment from the Scottish Legal Life Assurance Society he effected some very advantageous operations in its behalf at Glasgow. So successful was he, indeed, that towards the close of 1886 the Board invited him to go to Manchester to take charge of the business there, since which time he has held his present position. During the period of his residence at Manchester he has continued to do good work for the Society, of which the Board has more than once afforded him the gratification of expressing their approval.

ALEXANDER WISELY.

CHARLES WILLIS.

Wisely, Alexander, is the District Manager for the Scottish Legal Life Assurance Society at Newcastle-on-Tyne. He began his Insurance career for the same Office at Aberdeen in 1878. The satisfactory record of his work there warranted his promotion to this important District, to which he was appointed in 1883. Mr. Wisely is an active, energetic man, and transacts a large and profitable business in his District, and is universally esteemed by all who know him, both for his business abilities and personal worth.

Wilkins, C., the Lincoln District Superintendent of the Pearl Life Assurance Company, has served in the Royal Navy, the Mexican Navy, and the merchant services for over fourteen years, having visited nearly every quarter of the globe, and been present through the Abyssinian Campaign and the Mexican Revolution, and it was only five years ago that he commenced as an Assurance Collector in Lincoln. Business was very bad then, and his friends prophesied that his new venture would be a failure, but so well did he work that in four months he became Assistant Superintendent, and after another five months was promoted to be Assistant in charge at Grantham. Here in sixteen months he increased the business to such an extent that he was removed to Grimsby to work up that business, and thence, after eleven months, he was again promoted to be Superintendent of his old field at Lincoln, where, since his appointment, he has most effectually succeeded in making business go where two other Superintendents had already failed before him. Mr. Wilkins is a most popular man

amongst his clients, and his lectures on his travels and adventures have often been useful in breaking ground which would have been difficult to get at in any other way.

Willis, Charles, is the Local Superintendent for Rochester and the surrounding district to the Prudential Assurance Company, and also holds the appointment of District Superintendent for the Ordinary Department of the Company's business for the County of Kent. His brother having taken an Agency in 1853 with the British Industry Life Office, Mr. Willis followed his example, and joined the staff of that Company a few months later. Having shortly afterwards become a shareholder in that office, he, a few years later assisted in the transfer of their business to the Prudential, and taking service with them, has remained with them ever since. Mr. Willis therefore enjoys the proud distinction of being one of the oldest servants of the Prudential, and, what is more important, his career has been throughout a very successful one.

Whitehead, W., the Belfast District Superintendent of the Refuge Assurance Company, was born in Manchester in 1843, and has passed the whole of his Insurance career in the service of that Company. He took up his present post in 1885 at a time when the affairs of the Company in Ireland were in a very bad state owing to speculation and dishonesty on the part of its Agents, all of which, however, he suppressed by his firm and judicious management, restoring the business to the proper standard of order.

T. Woods.

J. T. Wratten.

Woods, T., District Superintendent of the Leeds Branch of the Prudential Assurance Company, commenced his Insurance career as an Agent for the Prudential in 1875. By his inexhaustible enthusiasm and quick energetic business-like qualities, he soon qualified himself for a position of trust, and having passed through the preliminary stages of Agent and Assistant Superintendent, was promoted to the Superintendency of the Norwich District. The Halifax District was next offered to him, and accepting it, he met with such remarkable success, that he was again promoted to the more important Leeds District, where he has since done yeoman service, not only for his own Company but for Insurance principles in general, by making them exceedingly popular amongst all classes of the community.

As an organizer of men and districts, Mr. Woods stands high amongst the Officers of his Company.

Young, J. H., District Manager of the Pearl Life Assurance Company, was born in 1868, and commenced his Insurance career by taking up a spare time Agency for that Company in the East End of London. His progress was rapid, and he soon won the attention of the Superintendent of the district in which he was engaged, who offered him a regular Agency in the district. This he accepted, and in his new capacity continued the steady increase of his business to such a degree that in July, 1890, he was appointed to his present important post in charge of the Company's business in the Northern capital. He met with considerable difficulties when he first took up his new duties, the Edinburgh business having been allowed to lapse into a state of almost complete chaos, but he persevered in his determination to make everything a success which he undertook, with the happy result that in less than a year he had raised Edinburgh to the rank of first among the Scottish divisions for increase of business.

Wratten, J. T., District Superintendent to the British Workman's Assurance Company at Blackburn, first became connected with the Insurance profession by insuring his own life when twenty-one years of age in the Briton Life and Medical Office, the Local Manager for which at Southampton, being a friend of the Secretary of the Imperial Union Assurance Company, persuaded Mr. Wratten to apply for the Superintendency of the South of England to the latter Company. This he did in 1866, but not having any practical experience in the work did not retain the appointment long. However, he next became connected with the Prudential, and was one of the first Agents whom they sent to the Channel Islands. He then served as Assistant-Superintendent at Portsmouth and Birmingham successively, and though at that time Insurance had not gained the hold on the public mind that it has now, he was very successful in his labours to propagate its principles. Mr. Wratten became connected with the British Workman's Assurance Company in 1880, first as probationary Agent at Birmingham, and the result being satisfactory, he was sent as Assistant Inspector to Stockton-on-Tees, where he had much to do to oppose the attacks made on his Company by rival offices. Thence he removed, first to Sunderland and then to Leeds, and then on his promotion to the position of Superintendent to Dundee. From Dundee he went to Glasgow, and in 1889 took up his present appointment at Blackburn, where he found much underhand speculation, calculated to lower the reputation of his Company, but has already almost entirely stamped it out.

BRITISH EQUITABLE

ASSURANCE COMPANY,

QUEEN STREET PLACE, E.C.

CAPITAL—A QUARTER OF A MILLION.

THIRTY-SEVENTH ANNUAL REPORT, MAY, 1892.

New Business.

1,123 Policies issued for ...	...	£206,853
New Premium Income ...		6,623

Revenue of the Year.

Premiums ...	£138,318	
Interest, &c.	55,387	
		193,705

Accumulated Fund.

Laid by in the Year	...	40,302
Accumulated Fund on 31st Jan., 1892	...	1,368,532

Claims and Bonuses paid under Company's Policies...	...	1,526,342

ACTIVE AND INFLUENTIAL AGENTS WANTED.

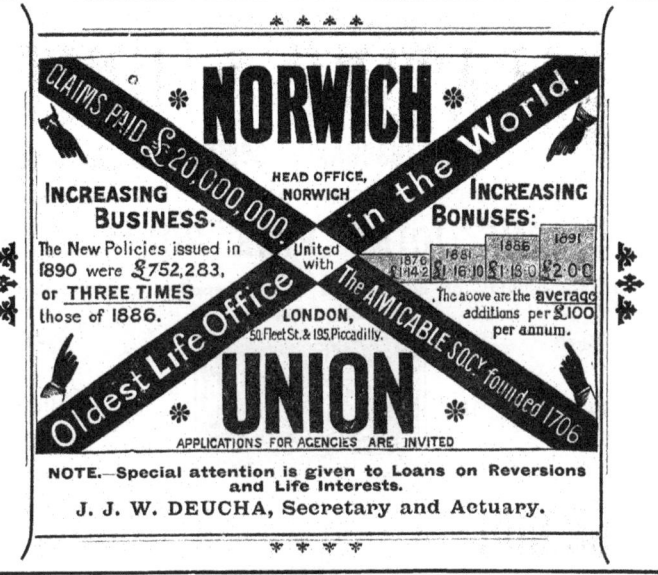

SUN

(Founded 1710.)

INSURANCE

(FIRE.) # OFFICE.

Sum Insured, 1890, £361,500,000.

Chief Office:
63, Threadneedle Street, London.

E. H. MANNERING, *Secretary.*

Branch Offices:

LONDON.—
{ 60, Charing Cross, S.W.
332, Oxford St. (Corner of Vere St.), W.
40, Chancery Lane (Law Courts Branch).

BIRMINGHAM.—10, Bennett's Hill.
BRISTOL.—Corn Street.
LEEDS.—1, East Parade.
LIVERPOOL.—Exchange Buildings, North.

MANCHESTER.—71, King Street.
NEWCASTLE.—21, Collingwood Street.
EDINBURGH.—41, Princes Street.
GLASGOW.—159, Hope Street.

DUBLIN.—10, Trinity Street.

THE SECURITY COMPANY, LTD.,

CHIEF OFFICES AND SAFE DEPOSIT:

63, ST. JAMES' STREET, LONDON, S.W.

Subscribed
Capital,

£120,000

Paid-up
Capital,

£65,000

By merely enclosing the Prospectus of the Security Company with their Fire and Life Renewal Notices many Agents obtain Burglary Proposals. Try it ! !

References are dispensed with in dealing with **Applications for Agencies** from Agents of first-class Fire, Life, and Accident Companies in any part of the United Kingdom.

Branch Managers, Resident Secretaries and Agency Inspectors are invited to introduce Agents to the Company. A liberal over-riding commission will be paid on the business of such Agents.

C. WILLIAMSON MILNE,
GENERAL MANAGER.

The Straits Insurance Companies,

SINGAPORE.

London Office:—25 and 26, CORNHILL, E.C.

BOARD OF REFERENCE:

A. VON ANDRÉ, of Messrs. André, Mendel & Co. | A. M. MACKAY, of Messrs. Laughland, Mackay
E. H. FORWOOD, of Messrs. Forwood Bros. | and Baker.
& Co.

CRAWFORD D. KERR, *Manager.*

Marine.	Fire.
THE STRAITS INSURANCE COMPANY LIMITED.	**THE STRAITS FIRE INSURANCE COMPANY, LIMITED.**

<table>
<tr><td colspan="2">Established 1886.</td><td colspan="2">Established 1886.</td></tr>
<tr><td>Capital Fully Subscribed ...</td><td>£450,000</td><td>Capital Fully Subscribed ...</td><td>£300,000</td></tr>
<tr><td>Reserve Liability of Shareholders</td><td>£350,000</td><td>Reserve Liability of Shareholders</td><td>£250,000</td></tr>
<tr><td>Capital paid up ... ...</td><td>100,000</td><td>Capital paid up ... ...</td><td>60,000</td></tr>
<tr><td>Reserve Fund, 31st December, 1891</td><td>10,000</td><td>Reserve Fund, 31st December, 1891</td><td>10,000</td></tr>
<tr><td>Balance of Working Account, at 31st December, 1891 ... ...</td><td>80,000</td><td>Fire Fund, 31st December, 1891</td><td>23,000</td></tr>
<tr><td>Total Security for Policy-holders</td><td>£540,000</td><td>Total Security for Policy-holders</td><td>£343,000</td></tr>
</table>

W. CASTLETON LOCKHART, *Underwriter.*

ALFRED FORD, *Fire Superintendent.*

BANKERS:
CHARTERED BANK OF INDIA, AUSTRALIA AND CHINA.

BANKERS:

HONG KONG AND SHANGHAI BANKING COMPANY.

BRANCHES:

BRISTOL: Foster's Chambers, Small Street
    GRAHAME H. WILLS, *District Agent.*

DUBLIN: 1, St. Andrew Street.
    J. W. MARTELLI, *Local Secretary.*

GLASGOW: 12, St. Vincent Place.
    CHARLES CHRISTIE, *Local Secretary.*
    J. GRANT MACLEOD, *Agent.*
    R. S. MURRAY (Rutherglen), *Agent.*

BRANCHES:

GLASGOW: 7, Royal Bank Place.
    W. EWING & CO.

LIVERPOOL: Queen Insurance Buildings.
    MACVICAR, MARSHALL & CO.

MANCHESTER: 25, Booth Street.
    JOHN WILLIAMSON.

LIVERPOOL: 13a, Batavia Buildings.
    HAROLD C. STUART, *Local Secretary.*

MANCHESTER: 4, Chapel Walks.
    JOHN D. SUGDEN, *Local Secretary.*

SPECIAL ATTENTION IS DIRECTED TO THE FOLLOWING—
A Discount will be allowed on Insurance Premiums for
two or more years paid in advance, viz.:—

For 2 years, 5 % on the ordinary one year's premium.
  ,, 3   ,, 15 ,,   ,,   ,,   ,,   ,,
  ,, 4   ,, 30 ,,   ,,   ,,   ,,   ,,
  ,, 5   ,, 50 ,,   ,,   ,,   ,,   ,,
  ,, 6   ,, 75 ,,   ,,   ,,   ,,   ,,
  ,, 7   ,, the whole of ordinary ,,   ,,
Claims for loss or damage by Lightning will be recognised.

All classes of Marine Insurance business effected at low rates.

All losses under Companies' Policies will be settled promptly and liberally at their Offices in London or elsewhere, as may be desired, full powers being vested in the local management for this purpose.
The substantial amount of Companies' Invested Funds affords ample security to policy-holders.

INSURANCE REPRINTS
FROM
"FINANCE CHRONICLE."

FIRE CHART OF 50 BRITISH FIRE OFFICES, ten years' business, 1880-1890. Price 3d.

FIRE CHART OF 55 BRITISH FIRE OFFICES, for year 1890-91, with Index of their Financial Position. Price 2d.

FIRE CHART—21 FOREIGN AND COLONIAL OFFICES IN GREAT BRITAIN with Index of their Financial Position. Price 2d.

THE A B C OF ELECTRIC LIGHTING, in relation to Fire Risks, with Index. 32 pp. demy 8vo. 1s.

THE LEVEL PREMIUM SYSTEM. Second Edition. Demy 8vo. price 6d.

FACTS.—RE MUTUAL RESERVE FUND LIFE ASSOCIATION: a Ten Years' Retrospect. Fcp. 4to. 6d.

SURRENDER VALUES, with Tables. 24 pp. demy 8vo. 1s.

HOW TO POPULARISE LIFE ASSURANCE. 24 pp. demy 8vo. 1s.

BONUSES: an Aid to the Selection of a Life Office, with Tables. Royal 8vo. 2s. 6d.

LIABILITY OF MUTUAL LIFE POLICY HOLDERS. 6d.

FINANCE CHRONICLE (Established 1869 as the *Insurance Circular*).

Subscription, post-free 9s. per annum, home or abroad.

London : RUSSELL & CO., 8, John Street, Adelphi, W.C.

Published Annually in June.

THE INSURANCE BLUE-BOOK AND GUIDE.

A handy Book of Reference, containing a large amount of information useful to Insurance Officials, Brokers, Agents, Bankers, Financiers, and a

Public Guide to Safe and Profitable Insurance.
Limp Cloth, 2/-; Handsomely Bound and Gilt, 3/6; Postage, 4½d.

The Insurance Agent and Insurance Review.
ESTABLISHED 1866.
THE OLDEST INSURANCE MONTHLY IN THE UNITED KINGDOM.

It is addressed particularly to Agents and stimulates and educates them in their work.

Price 2d.   *Annual Subscription, post free, 2/6.*

THE INSURANCE AGENT PAMPHLETS.
1/6 to 10/- per 100.

Addressed to Agents and to the Public on the subjects of Life, Fire, and Accident Assurance. They save a deal of talking, and have had a great run of success for twenty-five years.

THE WORK AND PROFITS OF AN INSURANCE AGENCY.
By the Late W. S. CHAMPNESS.
A valuable Instructor in Agency Work. Cloth **1s.**

FIFTY WAYS OF OBTAINING INSURANCE BUSINESS.
Price Twopence.

Published by CHAMPNESS & CO.,
33, IMPERIAL BUILDINGS, LUDGATE CIRCUS, LONDON, E.C.